P9-DOA-822

JN
201
.W47
1972

Monarchy and Revolution

The English State in the 1680s

J. R. WESTERN

Professor of Modern History,
University of Manchester

ROWMAN AND LITTLEFIELD

TOTOWA, N. J.

 Tennessee Tech. Library
Cookeville, Tenn.

289217

FIRST PUBLISHED IN THE UNITED STATES 1972
by Rowman and Littlefield, Totowa, New Jersey
© 1972 Blandford Press Ltd

ISBN 0–87471–066–9

All rights reserved. No part of this book may
be reproduced in any form or by any means, electronic
or mechanical, including photocopying, recording or any
information storage and retrieval system, without
permission in writing from the publisher.

*Set in 11pt Times, Printed in Great Britain by
Richard Clay (The Chaucer Press), Ltd.,
Bungay, Suffolk*

CONTENTS

List of Illustrations

ACKNOWLEDGMENTS

Acknowledgment is due to the following for their kind permission to reproduce photographs:

Ashmolean Museum, Oxford, Nos. 6, 9, 11, 12, 13, 15
Bodleian Library, No. 1
National Portrait Gallery, Nos. 10, 14
Public Record Office, No. 3
Trustees of the British Museum, Nos. 2, 4, 5, 7, 8

Prefatory Note

John Western had just finished the main draft of this book when he fell ill last summer; it was still in proof when he died, aged only forty-three, on 26 November. The proofs have been read for him, with devoted care, by his wife, who has prepared the names index; with some technical help from colleagues, including one or two minor adjustments to the text. The book remains essentially its author's work, as he left it; he might have amended it further in detail, had he lived. He might also have wished to add acknowledgments to other people who had helped him, who will have to remain without formal thanks.

It was his third book; his many friends will mourn that he can never write another.

Department of History
Manchester University

7 December, 1971

Author's Note

Spelling and punctuation have been modernized in the quotations.

Dates are mostly given in the 'old style' still current in England. In the seventeenth century this was ten days behind the 'new style' Gregorian calendar already current on the continent. When discussing continental affairs, I have sometimes given a date in both styles to facilitate comparison with books concerned with the continent and using continental dating. The year is taken to begin on 1 January.

ABBREVIATIONS

CJ.   Journals of the House of Commons.
CSPD.   Calendar of State Papers, Domestic.
CTB.   Calendar of Treasury Books.
LJ.   Journals of the House of Lords.
HMC.   Historical Manuscripts Commission, reports (followed by short title of report).

Books and articles referred to in the footnotes are cited in full on the first occasion and thereafter normally by the name of the author or editor. A short version of the title is used, however, when this is more intelligible.

1

Introduction

'REVOLUTION' is a word that has almost reversed its political meaning since the seventeenth century. Originally it had been an astronomical term, used in reference to the revolving of the heavenly bodies. Then it was applied to historical developments which seemed to follow a similar cyclical pattern. 'All things run round,' wrote William Camden in 1605, 'and as the seasons of the year, so men's manners have their revolutions.' The word was especially applicable to events which seemed to bring the situation back to what it had been before—to complete the historical cycle. Sir William Temple called the restoration of Charles II a 'revolution', as also the restoration of the Prince of Orange in 1672 to the offices which his ancestors had held in the Netherlands. In so far as 'revolution' simply meant 'change', it meant change of a natural and moderate kind.[1] Thus the Jacobite Earl of Ailesbury wrote that he hoped to restore the fugitive James II to his throne 'by a revolution, and not by fire and sword'.[2]

The 'glorious revolution' of 1688 was so called precisely because so much of it was not in the modern sense revolutionary. It was carried through with a minimum of violence and very largely by men at the top of the existing social and political structure, who naturally wished to avoid radical change. Their aim was to restore certain established rights and institutions threatened with encroachment. They appealed to the widespread belief in the existence of an ancient free constitution which was the nation's birthright and which had from time to

---

[1] This paragraph is based on V. F. Snow's article 'The Concept of Revolution in Seventeenth-Century England', *Historical Journal*, vol. v (1962), pp. 167–74.

[2] *Memoirs of Thomas, Earl of Ailesbury* (Roxburghe Club, 1890), vol. i, p. 247; cf. pp. 334, 526.

time to be defended against inroads by the king. 'Nolumus leges Angliae mutari' was the fine old slogan on the banner behind which the rebel lords of the north marched into Oxford on their way to join the Prince of Orange.[1]

To those who have accepted this 'whig' view of English historical development, the Revolution has naturally seemed a great event because it was the last time that the traditional institutions of the country needed to be defended by force. Macaulay, for whom 'our Revolution was a vindication of ancient rights', thought that it 'finally decided the great question whether the popular element, which had, ever since the age of Fitzwalter and De Montfort, been found in the English polity, should be destroyed by the monarchical element, or should be suffered to develop itself freely and to become dominant'. That question having been decided, 'in all honest and reflecting minds there is a conviction, daily strengthened by experience, that the means of effecting every improvement which the constitution requires may be found within the constitution itself'. And 'it is because we had a preserving revolution in the seventeenth century that we have not had a destroying revolution in the nineteenth'.[2]

Since Macaulay's day the sense of difference between historical periods has grown much sharper and the idea of an ancient English constitution surviving through the ages by mere piecemeal adaptation has come increasingly to seem unhistorical. There have been deep, radical changes as well as continuity. In the seventeenth century, the defeat and execution of Charles I was a breach with the past after which nothing was ever the same again. Though the monarchy was restored, the innovations of the Interregnum had a dominant and lasting effect on national institutions and attitudes that will be apparent throughout this book. Taxation, the armed forces, municipal government and the religious situation were all transformed. Beliefs about the position of the king and of parliament in the state also changed, though here the pull of tradition was very strong.

It is therefore tempting to dismiss the Revolution of 1688 as a mere tailpiece to the Interregnum, confirming the earlier victory of parlia-

---

[1] E. Carpenter, *The Protestant Bishop . . . Henry Compton, Bishop of London* (Longmans, 1956), p. 138.

[2] T. B. Macaulay, *History of England* (ed. C. H. Firth, Macmillan, 1913–15), vol. ii, pp. 1310–12.

ment over the crown. This is misguided. The strivings of the Inter-regnum determined that England would never be the same again—they failed to fix the future shape of the English state, however, and certainly did not mean that it was bound to become a fairly liberal parliamentary monarchy. Great revolutionary upheavals, though at first destructive of authority, often end with the emergence of a highly authoritarian government. They destroy old institutions and customs hitherto acting as a brake on the ruler, they generate intense party hatreds, so that each group tries to exercise a dictatorship in order to suppress its opponents, and the chaos resulting from them makes a strong-arm restoration of order widely acceptable. Napoleon and Stalin represent the final outcome of two great revolutions and similarly the English civil wars were followed by the dictatorship of Cromwell. The quarrels among those who had fought for parliament and the almost total suppression of the more radical among them led to the recall of the Stuarts and it was they who inherited Cromwell's mission. After 1680 England seemed to be moving inexorably towards absolutism and only the events of 1688 led to a change of direction, perhaps at the last possible moment.

The little revolution of 1688 is therefore worthy of attention, but no more than the civil wars did it 'finally decide' England's political future, as Macaulay would have us believe. Opposition to the monarchy had been so completely crushed by 1688 that the English and Scots were no longer able, as they had been forty years before, to overthrow the king without foreign aid. A foreign prince with an army had to be called in; that prince had no wish to see the monarchy weakened and most of those with political influence agreed that it ought to remain strong. This meant that there was little danger from radical extremism, but it also meant that only modest progress was made in securing parliamentary supremacy and individual freedom after 1688. It is only in retrospect that it is apparent that no further revolutions were needed to achieve them. The great positive develop-ment that did immediately result from the Revolution was the trans-formation by King William of England's place in Europe. It was the wars which this involved that led to a crucial loss of royal power and the establishment of parliamentary supremacy. But the process was so paradoxical, so far from being a natural development, that only the passage of time could ensure that it would work. Constitutional government has endured because it became a habit in the eighteenth century, not because it was established by revolution (great or small) in the seventeenth.

This book is by no means a complete history of the Revolution of 1688 but concentrates on two aspects of the crucial years after 1680: the development and working of the machinery of government and the opinions current in influential (*i.e.* mainly upper-class) quarters about how it ought to work. These two subjects are very closely linked. The king was able to rule in the way that he did largely—perhaps mainly—because so many people thought that he ought to rule in that way. Both subjects have a religious as well as a secular aspect for religion and politics were then intimately linked. A great deal of source material in this field has long been available in print and so it is fairly easy for anyone to study much of the evidence at first hand. The output of illuminating scholarly work on particular questions has in recent times been considerable. I have tried in the text to indicate by reference and quotation the richness of what is available. The footnotes do not aspire to list in full the sources and authorities for each topic. They indicate rather whom I am following at each point. In some cases I have worked directly from the primary sources but in others I have relied more on the past labours of other writers: in those cases I have not usually repeated their references for the quotations which they have culled and I have used.[1] The indications in the footnotes will be sufficient, I hope, to allow and encourage the reader to probe further into the subjects discussed, rejecting perhaps the conclusions of the present writer. A concluding bibliographical note gives some guidance for further browsing in monographs and printed sources and also mentions some general histories of the period. This book assumes that the reader is familiar with its outlines and does not attempt a narrative treatment except in patches, where the explanation of particular points requires it. A fair amount of narrative respecting James's reign and the relations between Louis XIV and his neighbours is indispensable for the understanding of the Revolution. But what is attempted here is only an indication of the general character of these events. A full discussion of why they happened as they did must be sought elsewhere.

[1] I have also used their translations of foreign documents, translating myself only some passages hitherto available only in French.

2

King or Parliament?

THE English civil wars ended in the death of the King and the triumph of parliament. But they did not mean the end of monarchy or even of its power. The victorious parliamentarians were unable to establish a workable and durable system of government. Eventually Charles II was restored without conditions, inheriting all his father's powers save those few abolished by the prewar legislation of the Long Parliament. The civil wars moreover had created a new monarchy of sorts—the ascendancy of Cromwell, deriving from the new military force which parliament had allowed him to create. To some extent Charles II was the heir of Cromwell as well as of his father: in particular, he always had some regular troops at his disposal and he was able to draw on sources of revenue created to pay for the wars (notably the excise). The building up of royal power could continue, partly on traditional and partly on new foundations.

But it would be wrong to picture the civil wars as a triumph in disguise for the defeated Stuarts. Rather they were indecisive, failing to determine whether supreme power should go to parliament or to the king. This is not surprising because most thinking men did not yet accept that such a decision had to be made. The prevailing belief before the wars, shared with differing emphases by partisans of parliament and of the king, was simply that both the one and the other had very great powers. It was still possible to believe that harmony rather than conflict might result from this situation: as in medieval times, it was supposed that there was a lawful order in the state, ultimately of divine institution, and that men could resolve their disputes by conforming to it. *Doctor and Student*, a law manual published in 1523 and still influential in the next century, said that 'when anything is grounded upon the law of nature' lawyers 'say that reason will that such a thing be done, and if it be prohibited by the law of nature, they say it is against reason'. There was a law deducible by reason

> And it is written in the heart of every man, teaching him what is to be done and what is to be fled. And because it is written in the heart, therefore it may not be put away ... and therefore against this law, prescription, statute nor custom may not prevail.[1]

A manual for *The Countrey Justice* published in 1661 began by speaking of

> The common laws of this realm of England, receiving principally their grounds from the laws of God and nature (which law of nature, as it pertaineth to man, is also called the law of reason) and being for their antiquity those whereby this realm was governed many hundred years before the Conquest.[2]

Whatever the merits of these ideas, the political framework which they provided was inadequate to prevent the disruption of 1642. Nevertheless, the attempts at a constitutional settlement during the Interregnum were mostly based on the premise that king and parliament (or Cromwell and parliament) could share power amicably without either becoming dependent upon the other. The Restoration, which involved a free parliament as well as the return of the king, was based on the same premise.

But governments were stronger and parliaments more independent than they once had been. If the constitutional settlements of the Interregnum broke down, so did that of the Restoration. Charles II increasingly went his own way and much of what he did was unpopular even when it was wise. In foreign policy, in religious affairs, in building up his forces and revenues he offended parliament and he was not financially strong enough to dispense completely with it. By 1680 king and parliament were again completely at loggerheads. If anarchy was to be avoided, one or other must be allowed to have the last word. The opening chapter of this book concerns a great debate on this subject: a debate which the King and his friends won.

The anarchy of the civil war period had made more acceptable the

---

[1] Christopher St. Germain, *Dialogues in English between a Doctor of Divinity and a Student in the Laws of England*, ff. 4, 8 *recto*: quoted in J. W. Gough, *Fundamental Law in English Constitutional History* (Oxford University Press, 1955), p. 18.
[2] Quoted in Gough, pp. 140–1. The author was Michael Dalton.

idea that there must be some person or persons in the state invested with supreme authority, from whose decisions there could be no appeal. But the defenders of this idea did not necessarily agree about anything else. They were all conservatives in the sense that their object was to preserve the subject's property and his liberties—usually thought of as customary, old-established liberties—from the threat of disorder. Political movements whose aims were radical, in the sense of challenging the political or economic power of the wealthier classes, existed only during the Interregnum and did not thrive even then. In the choice of means, however, some of the 'conservatives' were radical while others clung more closely to tradition. The most radical viewpoint was that of supporters of the Commonwealth such as Anthony Ascham who tried to reconcile the nation at large to the Oliverian dictatorship with the argument that might is right. Conquest, it was said, was the normal means by which governments were originally established. When a conqueror set up a government, the conquered ought to obey him because he protected them—he maintained law and order. Thomas Hobbes, though supposedly a royalist, was close to these views and influenced some of those who held them. He believed that men were not naturally sociable but rather inclined to 'perpetual fear and diffidence one of another'. But for the existence of governments there would be a 'perpetual state of war of all against all'. Hobbes too believed that a conqueror should be obeyed if he gave protection. He also envisaged men setting up a government by contracting with one another to obey a particular man or group. In either case the subject had to obey the government even when he thought himself oppressed, for oppression was better than returning to a state of war.

These views repelled most educated people because they made force and egoism the basis of government—if not of human life in general—in place of a divine law founded on right and reason. They had also the drawback of providing only a flimsy support to any government: Hobbes, for instance, specifically says that if a government is overthrown, it is the new conqueror to whom obedience is now due. They were useful to a usurper with strong military backing who had subdued all challengers. They were no use to Charles II whose physical power was less, whose claim was to be the 'rightful' ruler and whose problem was that there was another authority in being, parliament, also claiming 'rights'. But we shall meet the ideas of the

Interregnum again after 1688 because this too (in some people's eyes) was a triumphant usurpation.[1]

In 1680, when the names 'whig' and 'tory' were first bestowed on the respective partisans of parliament and king, it was the writings of Sir Robert Filmer that provided the most spectacular defence of royal power. A cultivated Kentish squire, who died in 1653, Filmer too was primarily a writer of the Interregnum, though his best known work, *Patriarcha*, was written before the civil wars. In 1679 the pamphlets that he had published in the years immediately before his death were reprinted. *Patriarcha* was published for the first time in 1680. There were several editions at this time and his works were again reprinted in 1684–5 and 1695–6.[2] Filmer thus aroused considerable interest in his own century, but his ideas have become so outmoded that it has been almost impossible for anyone since to take him seriously. He believed that God had given the sovereignty of the world to Adam and that it had passed by hereditary descent, through the sons of Noah and the heads of the nations into which mankind was divided at the Confusion of Tongues, to all the modern rulers of the world. Adam was the father of all mankind and so all other men were bound to obey him: this plenary power has passed to his successors.

Filmer's great merit was that he saw government as conforming to the generally accepted pattern of social organization in his time. The basic social unit was the household, in which the father expected to be obeyed by wife, children, servants and workers alike. Nobody doubted that this pattern was in accordance with God's will and if the king was truly a father, the moral case for obeying him in all things would be very strong. Filmer seems virtually to have invented this argument, which is present only in embryo in earlier upholders of the divine right of kings.[3] Its historical aspect would not have seemed as absurd then as it does to us. It was generally supposed that the world was only a few thousand years old and perfectly serious attempts were made to trace the genealogies of royal families back to biblical—and

---

[1] Q. R. D. Skinner, 'History and ideology in the English Revolution', *Historical Jol.*, vol. viii (1965), pp. 151–78; 'The ideological context of Hobbes' political thought', *ibid.*, vol. ix (1966), pp. 286–317. The latter argues against the view that Hobbes's ideas do not really conflict with the traditional religious approach.

[2] P. Laslett, ed.: *Patriarcha and other Political Works of Sir Robert Filmer* (Blackwell's Political Texts, 1949), pp. 3, 7–9, 34, 47–8.

[3] J. N. Figgis, *The Divine Right of Kings* (Cambridge University Press, 1914), pp. 148–52.

Homeric—times. Scholars were still not sure whether to take these seriously or not.[1] Filmer's whig opponents showed at great length that he had drawn false inferences from history and that the power of a father was not the same as that of a king. But Filmer's disciple Leslie was not being unfair when he argued that whig principles logically applied would bring disorder in families and that political liberals were tyrants at home. It is interesting that Locke, who maintained against Filmer that parental power is 'a temporary government which terminates with the minority of the child' and 'rather the privilege of children and duty of parents than any prerogative of paternal power',[2] was also an early intellectual ancestor of 'permissive' education. The argument about forms of government was linked to wider arguments about human behaviour and Filmer did a service to his cause by making this more apparent.

Filmer, however, did more than appeal to scripture and prejudice. He put forward a view of human society that can be defended without reference to either and is by no means absurd. He held 'that the people are not born free by nature' and that 'there never was any such thing as an independent multitude, who at first had a natural right to a community' (*i.e.* to share equally all the fruits of the earth). 'This conceit of original freedom', as he said, was 'the only ground' on which thinkers from 'the heathen philosophers' down to Hobbes had built the idea that governments were created by the deliberate choice of free men.[3] He believed on the contrary, as an early opponent put it, that 'the rise and right of government' was '*natural* and *native*, not *voluntary* and *conventional*'.[4] Subjects therefore could not have a right to overturn a government because the original bargain had not been kept. There were absurdities and dangers in the opposing view. 'Was a general meeting of a whole kingdom ever known for the election of a Prince? Was there any example of it ever found in the world?' Some sort of majority decision, or the assumption that a few men are allowed to decide for the rest, are in fact the only ways in which

---

[1] W. H. Greenleaf, 'Filmer's patriarchal history', *Historical Jol.*, vol. ix (1966), pp. 157–71.

[2] J. Locke, *Second Treatise of Government*, para. 67. But others thought this too, cf. P. Laslett's notes to para. 58 in his edition of the *Two Treaties of Government* (revised edition, Mentor Books 1965), pp. 348–9.

[3] Laslett: Filmer, *Works*, pp. 229 and 188. For the ensuing quotations from Filmer, the page reference for this edition is given.

[4] Edward Gee, *ibid.*, p. 38.

government by the people can be supposed to have been either initiated or carried on. But both are as inconsistent as monarchy with the idea that men are naturally free.

> If it be true that men are by nature free-born and not to be governed without their own consents and that self-preservation is to be regarded in the first place, it is not lawful for any government but self-government to be in the world. . . . To pretend that a major part, or the silent consent of any part, may be interpreted to bind the whole people, is both unreasonable and unnatural; it is against all reason for men to bind others, where it is against nature for men to bind themselves. Men that boast so much of natural freedom are not willing to consider how contradictory and destructive the power of a major part is to the natural liberty of the whole people.[1]

The claims of representative assemblies to embody the will of the people are attacked on these lines, in a manner recalling Rousseau. Filmer also points out that large assemblies cannot really do business and so assemblies have to delegate power to a few of their number: 'hereby it comes to pass, that public debates which are imagined to be referred to a general assembly of a kingdom, are contracted into a particular or private assembly'.[2] In short 'Those governments that seem to be popular are kinds of petty monarchies'[3] and

> It is a false and improper speech to say that a whole multitude, senate, council, or any multitude whatsoever doth govern where the major part only rules; because many of the multitude that are so assembled . . . are governed against and contrary to their wills.[4]

It is noteworthy that Filmer closely links the cause of monarchy with that of property. The idea that men were naturally free was dangerous to both.

> Certainly it was a rare felicity that all the men in the world at one instant of time should agree together in one mind to change the natural community of all things into private dominion: for without such a unanimous consent it was not possible for community to be altered: for if but one man in the world had dissented, the alteration had been unjust, because that man by the law of nature had a right to the common use of all things in the world.

Therefore

> if there hath been a time when all things were common and all men equal and that it be otherwise now; we must needs conclude that the law by which things

---

[1] pp. 81–3, 225.   [2] p. 223.
[3] p. 227.   [4] p. 205.

were common, and men equal, was contrary to the law by which now things are proper [*i.e.* privately owned] and men subject.

If we will allow Adam to have been lord of the world and of his children, there will need no such distinctions of the law of nature and of nations.[1]

Adam had been sole proprietor as well as sole ruler. All property as well as all thrones was inherited ultimately from him.

Filmer argued that a monarchy was the only form of government that could work properly. 'The supreme power, being an indivisible beam of majesty, cannot be divided among, or settled upon, a multitude.'[2] An assembly attempting to govern

are constrained to epitomize and sub-epitomize themselves so long [*i.e.* by delegation of their powers], till at last they crumble away into the atoms of monarchy, which is the next degree to anarchy, for anarchy is nothing else but a broken monarchy, where every man is his own monarch, or governor.[3]

Nor was it any use allowing subjects to resist a king who was thought to have transgressed:

It is impossible for a monarch to make his defence and answer and produce his witnesses, in every man's conscience, in each man's cause, who will but question the legality of the monarch's government. Certainly the sentence cannot but be unjust when but one man's tale is heard. For all this, the conclusion is, every man must oppose or not oppose the monarch according to his own conscience.

The result could only be 'utter confusion and anarchy'.[4] As for 'the freedom and liberty that they say is to be found in popular commonweals', the truth is 'there are more laws in popular estates than anywhere else; and so consequently less liberty'.[5] Monarchs might be oppressive but Filmer thought that there had been 'no tyrants in England since the conquest',[6] whereas 'there is no tyranny to be compared to the tyranny of a multitude'.[7] In Roman history 'the cruelty of all the tyrannical emperors' did not 'spill a quarter of that blood that was poured out in the last hundred years of her glorious commonwealth'.[8] Even a bad king needed to conserve the resources of his kingdom because they were the source of his power: 'the cruelty of such tyrants extends ordinarily no further than to some

---

[1] pp. 262, 273. [2] p. 189.
[3] p. 224. [4] p. 297.
[5] p. 224. [6] p. 94.
[7] p. 93. [8] pp. 90–1.

particular men that offend him and not to the whole kingdom.' In a 'popular state' nobody 'takes the public to be his own business' and nobody was personally responsible for acts of oppression: a tyrant on the other hand always lived in fear of assassins.[1]

Filmer tried to make a synthesis between his religious beliefs and worldly wisdom and in this he was typical of the tories and at one with many on the other side. There were some, especially among the clergy, for whom obedience to the king was due simply because God commanded it. For most men this did not exhaust the matter. Filmer drew much of his inspiration from Jean Bodin, who had lived through a similar time of troubles (the French wars of religion) and drawn the conclusion that there must be a single sovereign authority in the state, supreme above all others and possessing the power to make laws.[2] It is interesting to see how much in tune he was with the more radical Hobbes and Ascham writing at the same time. He read Hobbes 'with no small content', agreeing with him 'about the rights of sovereignty', though not about the 'means of acquiring it'.[3] He too believed that usurpers ought to be obeyed in order to maintain the state in being, which was God's intention. When the usurpation had taken place long ago and the true heir was known, it was right to obey the usurper in order to reserve the people for the future service of their lawful sovereign—'when time shall serve'.[4] God moreover might 'for the correction of the Prince or punishment of the people' allow a ruler to be dispossessed: the usurping authority, even if republican in character, should be obeyed.[5] (The Cromwellian-sounding idea that a conqueror should be obeyed because God gave him victory had a certain vogue both during the Interregnum and after 1688.) Filmer himself seems to have taken no active part on the King's side during the civil wars, though this may have been due only to ill health.[6] His views on usurpation meant that, like a Hobbist, he was open to the objection that he did not give unambiguous guidance as to what constituted the lawful government. More important to us, they indicate that realism, not just romantic sentiment, lay at the bottom of tory thinking.[7]

It was tory belief that kings were not subject to the control of the

[1] p. 92.
[2] He published a selection of Bodin's ideas, pp. 315–26.
[3] p. 239.   [4] pp. 23–5.
[5] p. 62.   [6] pp. 4–8.
[7] Cf. the views of Nalson in 1678, cited by Figgis, pp. 163–4.

laws and yet the tories perhaps as much as anybody believed in the rule of law. It is worth considering whether this was a contradictory point of view. Filmer said

> There can be no laws without a supreme power to command or make them. In all aristocracies the nobles are above the laws, and in all democracies the people. By the like reason in a monarchy the king must of necessity be above the laws.

Since

> a legislative power cannot be without being absolved from humane laws, it cannot be showed how a king can have any power at all but an arbitrary power.

But

> he is accountable to God, and therefore not guiltless if he violate divine laws: humane laws must not be shuffled in with divine, they are not of the same authority.

The king is 'always tied by the same law of nature to keep this general ground, that the safety of his kingdom be his chief law'.[1] Even 'humane' laws were accounted worthy of respect by supporters of monarchy. At the trial of the regicides in 1660, Sir Orlando Bridgeman who presided said

> Though this is an Absolute Monarchy, yet this is so far from infringing the people's rights that the people, as to their properties, liberties and lives, have as great a privilege as the king. It is not the sharing of government that is for the liberty and benefit of the people; but it is how they may have their lives and liberties and estates safely secured under government.[2]

At about the same time George Morley, Bishop of Winchester, explained that 'despotical government is that of the Turks and Muscovites; but political is, and ought to be, the government of all Christian kings; I am sure it is of ours'.[3] Even James I thought that his coronation oath bound him 'to the observation of the fundamental laws of his kingdom'.[4]

Of course these differing emphases should remind us that the tories

[1] pp. 96, 105, 254–5.
[2] Gough, p. 140.
[3] K. G. Feiling, *History of the Tory Party, 1640–1714* (Oxford University Press, 1924), p. 32.
[4] Gough, p. 53.

and their precursors were not a monolithic body. But at the same time, they can be reconciled. The new idea that a sovereign authority was needed in the state overlaid but did not supersede the older idea of a 'natural law' which reason would lead men to acknowledge. The king's power might not have formal limits, but its purpose was limited to the protection of certain recognized interests. As Bacon once put it, 'the law favoureth three things, life, liberty and dower' because 'our law is grounded upon the law of nature, and these three things do flow from the law of nature'.[1] The king needed absolute power in order to be able to take unprecedented measures in response to an emergency. That he would use it to alter the whole fabric of the laws was not just obviously wrong to a tory (as to a whig) but virtually inconceivable. How little a tory expected absolute power to be used is well brought out in a paper of advice that Lord Keeper Guilford wrote for the second Earl of Clarendon when he was appointed (1685) to govern Ireland. Pointing out that Ireland was 'subordinate to England in so absolute a manner that the king in his parliament of England' could legislate for it, he waved aside the complaint that there were no Irish representatives in that parliament: 'they are the king's subjects, and the king will have that care of them that is fitting. And it is not unreasonable that a conquered nation should receive laws at the pleasure of the king alone.' But after this formidable beginning he goes on to say that 'their not having representatives in the parliament of England, makes it unreasonable the parliament of England should give away their money, or make any laws to change property'. Even other laws should not 'be made without great occasion'. Of course this was no academic question: it was feared that the Irish catholics would induce James II to give them back the land in protestant hands.[2] But Guilford would not have argued as he did if the argument had not seemed plausible to him.

The king's powers and the subject's rights were seen as standing together, the king having an indefeasible right to his powers because they enabled him to defend the subject. In 1660 Fabian Philipps essayed the hopeless task of proving that the obsolete system of landholding by knight service ought not to be abolished: he believed it to be necessary for national defence. Because

[1] Gough, p. 45.
[2] S. W. Singer (ed.), *The Correspondence of Henry Hyde, Earl of Clarendon and of his brother Laurence Hyde, Earl of Rochester* (1828), vol. i, pp. 183–7.

God's law and the law of nature and nations have taken care not only to preserve the rights of sovereignty and the means and order of government but the rights and property of every particular subject and do prohibit all injustice

it followed among other things that an act of parliament would be void if it enacted that the king 'should not defend the kingdom, or that he should have no aids from his subjects to defend the realm'.[1] The king was still thought of—and not only by tories—almost as the proprietor of his powers, able to use them as he thought fit but only so far as they did not conflict with the rights of the other proprietors, his subjects. This is particularly apparent in the workings of the dispensing and suspending power, opposition to which was such a marked feature of political struggles between the Restoration and the Revolution.

The crown had always been held to have the power of ordering that a particular law should not apply in certain cases. This seems to have been regarded as an aspect of his supreme power and duty to see that justice was done to all. But it also enabled him to nullify a statute which trenched on his 'inseparable' powers in the way discussed by Philipps—the power, for instance, to require service from his subjects. No less a person than Sir Edward Coke had upheld the dispensing power in such a case.[2] This was of great importance when parliament tried to deprive the king of the services of his catholic subjects. In 1674 Sir John Vaughan, chief justice of the common pleas (whose opinions tended to be 'whiggish'),[3] compared the king's freedom of action to that of a father of a family whose estate

may be said to be *pro bono communi* of his family, which yet is but at his discretion and management of it; and they have no interest in it but have benefit by it.[4]

But the dispensing power was limited by the doctrine that the king might only act for the common good. It could not be used to permit things that were *mala in se*, that is morally wrong in themselves, like killing and stealing. It related only to offences artificially created by statute (*mala prohibita*). The offences created by the Navigation Acts

[1] Gough, pp. 145–6.
[2] 'The case of non obstante'. See *e.g.* Gough, p. 46.
[3] Below, p. 55.
[4] The case of Thomas *v.* Sorell. See J. A. W. Gunn, *Politics and the Public Interest in the Seventeenth Century* (Routledge and Kegan Paul, 1969), pp. 295–6.

for the regulation of English trade after the Restoration are an example of this. Charles II used his power to dispense with them quite widely, for purposes varying from the procurement of naval stores to the provision of fruit from the Levant for the royal kitchen.[1] The dispensing power might not be used in such a way as to infringe the rights of the subject. Vaughan in 1674 had before him a statute relating to the sale of wine and he ruled that a dispensation could alter opening and closing time but not permit adulteration or higher prices.[2] Finally, the arbitrary power was thought of as an emergency one: royal attempts to extend the dispensing power into a suspending power which could nullify a whole statute were resisted. References were made to this at the famous trial in 1688 of the seven bishops who had protested against the King's use of the suspending power to introduce religious toleration. One of the (supposedly subservient) judges (Powell) said

> if this be once allowed of, there will need no Parliament; all the legislature will be in the king, which is a thing worth considering.[3]

Not only did the tories usually expect the King to use his unlimited power in a relatively restricted way but they seem also to have expected him to govern by invoking the aid of his more influential subjects and relying on the deference of the populace to the upper classes rather than on brute force under royal control. Filmer perhaps recalled that Bodin had wanted 'sovereignty' to be monarchical but 'government' democratic: the final authority in every matter was to be the king, but he was to consult the estates of the realm and recruit his advisers and servants from the middle as well as the upper class. 'Great are the advantages,' said Filmer,

> which both the king and people may receive by a well ordered parliament. There is nothing more expressing the majesty and supreme power of a king than such an assembly, wherein all his people acknowledge him for sovereign lord, and make all their addresses to him by humble petition and supplication, and by their consent and approbation do strengthen all the laws which the king at their request, and by their advice and ministry, shall ordain. Thus they facilitate the government of the king by making the laws

[1] See E. F. Churchill, 'The dispensing power and the defence of the realm', *Law Quarterly Review*, vol. xxxvii (1921), esp. pp. 422–5.

[2] W. S. Holdsworth, *A History of English Law*, vol. vi (1924) p. 223 n. 3.

[3] *ibid.*, p. 223. See further pp. 217–25 and D. Ogg, *England under Charles II* (Oxford University Press, 2nd ed., 1955), vol. i, pp. 353–4.

unquestionable, either to the subordinate magistrates or refractory multi-tude.[1]

This of course was the Tudor version of parliamentary government. Where Filmer differed from any sort of parliamentarian was in believing that parliament was a purely consultative body, that the law made there and all other laws were made by the authority of the king alone. The ultimate issue in the debate between whigs and tories was whether king or parliament was to be regarded as the higher source of authority. They differed far less over the amount of power that the king ought in practice to have and we shall see whigs eager for a strong king and tories sometimes content for him to be quite weak.

The debate had an important historical dimension. The whigs and their precursors believed that the law was superior to the king and that parliament was at any rate not his inferior. It was tacitly assumed on all sides that this could not be true if the monarchy had existed longer than had law and parliament. Opponents of absolute monarchy went to ridiculous lengths in maintaining that this was not so. Coke believed that the common law was of truly immemorial antiquity—anterior to the coming of the Saxons or indeed of any other inhabitants of whom record survived. The 'cynical' theory that states were founded by conquest was far more damaging to the parliamentarian than to the royalist case. The well-authenticated record of the Norman Conquest and the great changes that the Conqueror had introduced were something that had endlessly to be explained away. The explanation did not convince everyone, and Peter Heylyn wrote in 1658 that 'the power of making laws' because of the Conquest 'is properly and legally in the king alone'.[2] The biographer of Laud here spoke the language of Hobbes.

Filmer did not do this, but he did try to show that law and parliament alike had been created by the crown. His historical work and that of intelligent tories later was quite damaging to the parliamentary case. Filmer was able to show that there had been no popular representatives in parliament until Henry III's time, that both precedent and the form of election writs still used suggested that the commons were meant to be markedly inferior to the lords, that the role even of the lords had been to give counsel and not to overrule the king: his use of current historical learning was far sounder than his

[1] Laslett: Filmer, *Works*, pp. 113–14.
[2] Skinner, 'History and ideology', esp. pp. 168–9.

use of the Bible.[1] The further advance of historical learning clinched the case by providing a new and spectacularly apposite interpretation of the Conquest. The Restoration, we have seen, was followed by the final abolition of an institution which the Conqueror had diffused through the land—the tenure of estates in return for the performance of military service. The system had so decayed that its original character had been forgotten: Coke had been able to write of a knight's fee as though it was the same as a freehold. It was Sir Henry Spelman, partly through his study of continental feudalism, who first realized that this was wrong. The article on parliament in his archaeological glossary laid down that the Conqueror had divided the conquered kingdom among his barons in return for military service and that parliament had started as the court of his vassals. Sir William Dugdale was responsible for publishing this part of Spelman's work (1664) and in his *Baronage* pointed to Montfort's rebellion as the moment when parliament ceased to consist solely of tenants-in-chief. For the whigs, William Petyt answered both Dugdale and Filmer in *The Ancient Rights of the Commons of England Asserted*, published in the crisis year, 1680. At the suggestion of Archbishop Sancroft, Dugdale left his defence to Robert Brady, Master of Caius College, Cambridge. A physician by profession, Brady had lost a brother in the civil wars and had been an active royalist agent. Believing that brave and useful servants of the crown had been brought to their death 'by fragments and partial story (picked out of mouldy parchments and obscure authors . . .)', he had for some years been working on a History of England that would 'begett a cheerful submission and obedience'. His reply to Petyt appeared in 1681 and the first volume of the History in 1685. He had a much clearer sense of the importance of the new knowledge than Dugdale, who merely argued from it that the Conqueror had been free from control by the law. Brady argued that since the Conqueror introduced feudal tenures, he was responsible for introducing the customs and laws by which they were regulated. The crown was the sole source of property and privilege: by the reasoning then in vogue, this meant that the people had no rights against it. Moreover, the barons' assertion of rights against the king during the middle ages were merely concerned with their rights under the feudal system and provided no basis for the current claims of the commons against the king, though the language was sometimes the

[1] Laslett: Filmer, *Works*, esp. pp. 113–84.

same. Here was the beginning of a really genuine historical backing to the patriarchal view of the state: in 1686 James II appointed Brady acting keeper of the records to continue the good work.[1] Thus the tories could appeal not only to sentiment and religious belief but also to a Hobbes-like reason of state, and they could readily meet their enemies on their chosen ground of 'precedent'.

(II)

The whigs meanwhile were in the embarrassing position of holding views that were 'traditional' and very popular but at the same time obsolescent—as intelligent members of the party showed signs of realizing. Their natural sympathy was with the old views that the law was supreme, that not even the king was superior to it, that the highest authority in the state lay with the king and the two houses of parliament jointly and that agreement between them should be the basis of government. Their position differed little from that of the 'trimmer', Lord Halifax, who was their most impressive opponent in the house of lords in 1680. Indeed the term 'trimmer' was brought into political debate in the ensuing years by the tories as an abusive epithet for moderate whigs: men who professed to be loyal to the king but did not stand by him as the tories did. The *Character of a Trimmer* which Halifax wrote in defence of the species in 1684 is in fact a protest against the excesses of the victorious tories:[2] significantly it was not published until 1688.

But though whigs might continue to say in traditional style that 'sovereign power is no parliamentary word' and 'magna charta is such a fellow that he will have no sovereign' and 'no prerogative is infinite in England nor any power omnipotent (except that of God alone)',[3] this view was being subverted from the whig side as well as by tories and Hobbists. 'There must be a supreme, uncontrollable power lodged somewhere', said one pamphleteer: being a whig, he sited it not

[1] J. G. A. Pocock, 'Robert Brady, 1627–1700', *Cambridge Historical Journal*, vol. x (1951), pp. 186–204. For the historical argument in general see the same author's *The Ancient Constitution and the Feudal Law* (Cambridge University Press, 1957).

[2] D. R. Benson, 'Halifax and the Trimmers', *Huntington Library Quarterly*, vol. xxvii (1963–4), pp. 115–34. On the whigs as trimmers, Miss B. Behrens, 'The whig theory of the constitution in the reign of Charles II', *Cambridge Historical Journal*, vol vii (1941–3), p. 71.

[3] *History of Whiggism* (1682) cited Behrens p. 52, n. 23.

in the king alone but in king, lords and commons.[1] 'Can king, lords and commons do an unlawful act?' asked Colonel Titus in parliament in February 1681. 'Must we not have a supreme power? To limit it to something is to say it is not supreme.'[2] The traditional answer had been that the law was supreme, but even whigs began to see the difficulty of determining what the law was and getting universal agreement on its constitutional bearing. A tract of 1692 on the 'fundamental laws' of the realm said that they were nowhere written down (save 'in the very heart of the Republic') and it was for parliament to declare them. In any case 'England in her polity is like Nature in instincts, who is wont to violate particular principles for public preservation'.[3] This was the view of the great Trimmer himself. 'I would fain know,' wrote Halifax

> whether the common law is capable of being defined, and whether it doth not hover in the clouds like the prerogative and bolteth out like lightning to be made use of for some particular occasion? If so, the government of the world is left to a thing that cannot be defined . . . so that the supreme appeal is we know not what.

As 'there can be no government without a stated rule', some authority had to be able to resolve perplexities. For Halifax this was parliament and so 'there is no fundamental, for the Parliament may judge as they please'. He commented

> Fundamental is a word used by the laity, as the word sacred is by the clergy, to fix everything to themselves they have a mind to keep, that nobody else may touch it.[4]

The whigs had to reconcile a belief that the law should be supreme with the need to have a sovereign and therefore arbitrary power in the state. They had more urgently to justify resistance to a ruler supposed to have flouted the laws, in a community which traditionally had thought such resistance wrong and which, after the civil wars, had a notably strong sense of its imprudence. The best remembered of the whig replies to Filmer's resurrected works is John Locke's *Two Treatises of Government*. It is perhaps the famous philosopher's long connection with Shaftesbury, the great whig leader, that makes this

[1] Behrens p. 66 n. 69.
[2] O. W. Furley, 'The whig exclusionists—pamphlet literature in the exclusion campaign 1679–81', *Cambridge Historical Journal*, vol. xiii (1957), p. 28.
[3] Behrens, p. 52 n. 24.
[4] Halifax, *Complete Works* (Pelican Classics, 1969), pp. 197–8.

work important for the historian of the Revolution period: it does not seem to have had much practical influence on whig fortunes. It is now thought to have been mainly written during the great crisis around 1680. But it was not published (with part omitted) until 1690 and it seems to have been a book more cited than read.[1] Locke attacked Filmer both by disposing of his proofs that men were born unfree and more importantly by arguing that to be born free 'is not a state of licence'. Even if no government existed, a man might dispose of his 'person or possessions' as he pleased, but would be 'bound to preserve himself' and 'as much as he can, to preserve the rest of Mankind'—and even lesser creatures also.

> For men being all the workmanship of one omnipotent and infinitely wise Maker; all the servants of one Sovereign Master, sent into the world by his order and about his business, they are his property, whose workmanship they are, made to last during his, not one another's, pleasure

(or, for that matter their own).[2] It was really to God that Locke attributed the sovereign power necessary for the safety of society. Like Filmer or Bodin, he believed that only the command of someone with unquestioned authority could make laws valid and effective.[3] But like the puritans he both laid stress on omnipotence among the divine attributes and believed strongly that God laid his commands directly on his individual creatures.[4]

Locke believed that it was by reason that man could discover God's will. Man's freedom

> is grounded on his having reason, which is able to instruct him in that law he is to govern himself by and make him know how far he is left to the freedom of his own will.[5]

Conversely,

> where there is no law, there is no freedom. For liberty is to be free from restraint and violence from others, which cannot be, where there is no law[6]

[1] See P. Laslett's edition of the *Treatises*, pp. 58–79 and J. Dunn, 'The politics of Locke in England and America in the eighteenth century' J. W. Yolton, ed., *John Locke —Problems and Perspectives* (Cambridge University Press, 1969), pp. 45–80.

[2] *Second Treatise* para. 6.

[3] See *e.g.* W. von Leyden, ed., *John Locke: Essays on the Law of Nature* (Oxford University Press, 1954), p. 111.

[4] Locke's family were puritans. Cf. J. Dunn, *The Political Thought of John Locke* (Cambridge University Press, 1969), chap. 18.

[5] *Second Treatise*, para. 63. The ensuing references to Locke are to the paragraphs or chapters of this treatise.

[6] para. 57.

Children, though 'we are born free as we are born rational',[1] could not use their freedom until they could use their reason: till then, they were subject to their parents. As for men who would not use their reason and transgressed the law of nature to which it was a guide, they were no better than wild beasts. It was everyone's duty to uphold the law of nature by restraining and punishing them, if necessary depriving them of their liberty or even killing them. Thus the ultimate basis of social organization was not the power of a government but 'reason, which God hath given to be the rule betwixt man and man and the common bond whereby humane kind is united into one fellowship and society'.[2]

Not only society but private property was anterior to government. God had given the earth 'to mankind in common', but no man could enjoy the fruits of the earth save by appropriating a portion of them to himself. This is done by labour: 'God and his reason commanded' man 'to subdue the earth'. So when a man cultivated a piece of land for his subsistence, the land was rightly his. Because 'nothing was made by God for Man to spoil or destroy', no man was entitled to more of the fruits of the earth than he could use before they decayed. But the invention of money removed this limitation because it allowed producers to exchange the perishable goods they produced for something imperishable. This allowed inequality in the distribution of wealth but it encouraged industry. Locke saw that money had no intrinsic value and he believed that it had existed longer than the state: so 'men have agreed to disproportionate and unequal possession of the earth' by 'a tacit and voluntary consent'[3] to regard money as valuable. This was Locke's answer to Filmer's contention of 'no king, no property' and he seems to have been especially satisfied with it. 'Property I have nowhere found more clearly explained,' he wrote.[4]

'Political society' was formed by individuals pooling their 'natural power' to enforce the law of nature[5] and putting themselves at the disposal of the state for this purpose. This gives far greater security against both disorder and foreign attack and also ends the dangerous system of each man being judge in his own case when acting in defence of his rights. Locke supposed that the change had taken

[1] para. 61.
[2] para. 172.
[3] chap. v.
[4] Laslett, introd. to *Treatises*, p. 15.
[5] para. 87; chaps. vii, viii.

place very early in human history, though he insisted that the 'state of nature' continued to exist in certain cases, such as international relations. He believed that government rested on the consent of the people, who had originally decided what form it should take, and he argued rather curiously that a child on coming of age could freely leave the state in which he lived and was not obliged to become a subject of it. But in general he insisted on the state's power. Everyone owed it obedience who lived within its borders and benefited from its operations, even to the extent of 'travelling freely on the highway'.[1] If a man suffered oppression he was to go to law, not resort to force. Locke even thought it salutary that the person of the prince should be sacred, though it might mean that those whom he had personally injured were without remedy against him.[2] Like Bodin and Filmer, Locke made the 'legislative' the 'supreme power of the Commonwealth', with the ultimate claim to obedience.[3] He did not deny that this power might be entrusted to a monarch, though he thought it safer to confer it on some sort of assembly.[4] If those who made the laws consisted at least in part of ordinary subjects who had afterwards not to enforce them on others but to obey them themselves, this was 'a new and near tie upon them' to make laws 'for the public good'.[5] Locke does not further answer Filmer's strictures on assemblies and majority voting: no doubt he hoped that reason, which makes God's law intelligible to man, would lead all the members in the same direction. Algernon Sidney, whose *Discourses Concerning Government* were a refutation of Filmer as famous in its day as Locke's, had more to say in defence of popular institutions of government. Where civic spirit was strong, they had promoted prosperity, justice and military strength in a way few monarchs had. Filmer's strictures on the Roman republic applied only to its declining years. But Sidney unlike Locke was a strong republican and his historical lore is often as questionable as much of Filmer's.

Though Locke's state is authoritative, limitations of a traditional kind remain. 'The obligations of the law of nature cease not in society ... the law of nature stands as an eternal rule to all men, legislators as well as others.'[6] The state could have no power beyond that once surrendered to it by individual men: the power, that is, to enforce the

---

[1] para. 119.
[2] paras. 207, 205.
[3] para. 134.
[4] para. 132. Cf. para. 94.
[5] para. 143.
[6] para. 135.

law of nature by preserving men's 'lives, liberties and estates'.[1] It followed that unlimited political power could not be rightfully attained by conquest. But likewise a rightful legislature, though its enactments superseded the unwritten law of nature, could not be 'absolutely arbitrary over the lives and fortunes of the people'.[2] It was bound to rule by 'promulgated standing laws' and not 'extemporary arbitrary decrees'.[3] It could not take away any man's property without his own consent, though Locke regarded taxation by a representative assembly as conforming to this principle.[4] Moreover, the legislature was 'sacred and unalterable in the hands where the community have once placed it.' Even the legislators themselves could not 'transfer the power of making laws to any other hands' because 'the people alone can appoint the form of the commonwealth'.[5] This was the only way in which independent 'umpirage . . . for a peaceable decision of all their controversies' could be guaranteed.[6] It goes without saying that all the lesser authorities in the state had to obey the laws and refrain from tampering with the legislature. Locke wrote in fairly abstract terms (Algernon Sidney, who did not, was executed on the strength of his as yet unpublished *Discourses*). But Locke's argument is carefully tailored to English conditions. It is plain that he thought that in England the executive power was vested in the king but that he shared the legislative power with the lords and commons.[7] If his officials acted contrary to the law, the people could resist them.[8] If the legislature abused its authority or if the king 'sets up his own arbitrary will in place of the laws' or if he altered the legislature in other ways— such as tampering with elections or failing to convene parliament when he should—the people might take power into their own hands.[9]

How could Locke justify this anarchic-sounding proposition to a conservative-minded public? His argument, like Filmer's, combined a moral appeal with worldly wisdom. He could point out that even strong partisans of monarchy believed that a king should rule according to law: James I is quoted at length.[10] 'Absolute monarchy' for Locke was 'inconsistent with civil society' because it failed to provide the impartial adjudication in all controversies which is 'the end of

---

[1] para. 123.
[2] para. 135.
[3] para. 136.
[4] paras. 138, 140.
[5] paras. 134, 141.
[6] para. 227.
[7] paras. 151, 213.
[8] paras. 202, 206.
[9] chaps. xviii, xix.
[10] para. 199 (the passage quoted from above, p. 13).

civil society'. Only an independent legislature and universal subjection to the laws could do this.[1] The relationship between a despot and one of his subjects was that between two men in the state of nature: with the corollary that the subject might, if he could, enforce the law of nature against the despot. 'Overturning the constitution and frame of any just government' is 'the greatest crime a man is capable of', but 'either ruler or subject' who forcibly invades 'the rights of either prince or people' is guilty of it.[2]

> Whosoever uses force without right, as everyone does in society who does it without law, puts himself into a state of war with those against whom he so uses it . . . every one has a right to defend himself and to resist the aggressor.[3]

When those in authority flout the laws and the established constitution they are themselves 'guilty of rebellion'.

> For when men by entering into society and civil government have excluded force and introduced laws for the preservation of property, peace and unity amongst themselves; those who set up force again in opposition to the laws do *rebellare*, that is, bring back again the state of war, and are properly rebels.

They may indeed be compared to robbers and pirates.[4] Since 'the society can never, by the fault of another, lose the native and original right it has to preserve itself',[5] the people may in such cases depose their rulers and set up others. Locke did not think in terms of a contract between ruler and subjects under which the parties had equal rights. Princes and legislators were trustees for the people. So in deposing them the people could properly act as judge in its own case: Locke does not share Filmer's objection here as might have been expected

> for who shall be judge whether his trustee or deputy acts well, and according to the trust reposed in him, but he who deputes him and must, by having deputed him, have still a power to discard him when he fails in his trust?[6]

Locke gives, though not very systematically, reasons for believing that the deposition of rulers could be done without too much danger to the social fabric in cases where it was right and desirable. He distinguishes between 'the dissolution of the society and the dissolution of the government'.

[1] paras. 90, 94.   [2] para. 230.
[3] para. 232.   [4] paras. 226–8.
[5] para. 220.   [6] paras. 222, 240.

The power that every individual gave the society when he entered into it can never revert to the individuals again as long as the society lasts, but will always remain in the community; because without this there can be no community, no common-wealth, which is contrary to the original agreement.

'Supreme power' when 'by the miscarriages of those in authority, it is forfeited . . . reverts to the society.'[1] Elsewhere[2] it is argued that in joining a community men implicitly agree to abide by the decision of the majority, because only if this is accepted can the community function. This makes it not entirely unreal to say that 'the community perpetually retains a supreme power of saving themselves from the attempts and designs of anybody' trying to subvert their rights.[3] Locke may have taken this idea from George Lawson, a puritan writer who had opposed Hobbes and in 1660 had considered what should happen when the government was dissolved but 'the community yet remains united'.[4] Both he and Locke concluded that the community should set up a new government, and of course both in 1660 and 1689 the English community retained enough coherence to do this.

With the idea of 'community' we may associate the belief that Locke held no less than Filmer—that man was a social animal and that social organization had grown quite naturally out of family ties.

God having made man such a creature that in His own judgment it was not good for him to be alone, put him under strong obligations of necessity, convenience and inclination to drive him into society.

The first society was the family, the first kingdoms were patriarchal, more advanced constitutional arrangements came later in response to popular pressure.[5] But while for Filmer the conclusion was that the king must be obeyed, what seems to have followed for Locke was that little harm would come if he was not obeyed—and that there was no danger of disobedience for trivial reasons: 'people are not so easily got out of their old forms as some are apt to suggest.' In England 'this slowness and aversion in the people to quit their old constitutions has, in the many revolutions . . . in this and former ages, still kept us to or . . . brought us back again to our old legislative of king, lords and

[1] paras. 211, 243. Cf. para. 149. [2] paras. 95–9.
[3] para. 149.
[4] Gough, p. 122. Laslett, note to *Second Treatise*, para. 211.
[5] chaps. vii, viii, esp. paras. 77, 94, 105–7, 111. See G. J. Schochet, 'The family and the origins of the state in Locke's political philosophy', Yolton, pp. 81–98.

commons'. Even the dynasty had never been changed. 'Great mistakes …will be born by the people without mutiny or murmur.' Only 'a long train of abuses, prevarications and artifices, all tending the same way', that is towards the subverting of the constitution, would make the people 'rouse themselves'—and this was as it should be.[1] Filmer thought that arbitrary power was more dangerous in the hands of the populace than in the hands of a tyrant. Locke thought the reverse because the resources at a tyrant's command gave him both a greater temptation and a greater power than other men to do harm: 'he being in a much worse condition who is exposed to the arbitrary power of one man who has the command of 100,000 than he that is expos'd to the arbitrary power of 100,000 single men.'[2]

Locke thought that men could organize society while remaining free because he believed that they could discover God's will concerning society by the use of reason. Elsewhere—notably in the essays of 1664 on the law of nature—he shows himself sceptical regarding simpler ways of achieving a consensus. The law of nature was not identical with tradition or self-interest or whatever men at a particular time happened to agree on. These led to precepts varying from man to man and from place to place—and which in some cases were downright wicked. Nor did Locke believe that men had an inborn knowledge of the law of nature, even though he said that it was plainly 'writ in the hearts of all mankind'.[3] Reason was the only means by which it could be known, yet Locke had no specially strong belief that men were rational and good. He says, for instance, that property 'is very unsafe' in the state of nature because 'the greater part' of mankind are 'no strict observers of equity and justice'.[4]

That the whig views represented by Locke could be at all credible probably owed much to the spread of an idea that he did not emphasize: namely that the public good was that of the individual citizens added together, so that the people's grievances were a reliable guide to what was wrong in the state.[5] An old-fashioned lawyer like

[1] paras. 223–5. Cf. paras. 208–10.
[2] para. 137.
[3] W. von Leyden's edition of the Essay of 1664 has already been cited. For the continuity of Locke's views, see Hans Aarsleff, 'The state of nature and the nature of man in Locke', Yolton, pp. 99–136.
[4] *Second Treatise*, para. 123.
[5] This paragraph is based on J. A. W. Gunn, *Politics and the Public Interest in the Seventeenth Century*, already cited.

Sir Matthew Hale could write (despite his parliamentarian sympathies) that 'the community considered as a community is a distinct thing from the particular persons that are integrals of that community'.[1] But Algernon Sidney was more typical of his age in making 'the safety of the people . . . consist in the preservation of their liberties, goods, lands and lives' and claiming that the people who 'smart of the vices and follies of their princes, knew what remedies were most fit to be applied'.[2] Richard Cumberland, a distinguished clergyman trying to confute the cynical egoism of Hobbes, achieved his end by downgrading altruism into something easy: 'The several kinds of public good are no other than (but exactly the same with) the good of individuals.' A society was happy when its individuals were happy. This meant that individuals must not injure each other, but Cumberland believed that providentially we promote the common good even when 'gratifying our brutal appetites'.[3] James Tyrrell, a friend of Locke who wrote an account of Cumberland's views for lay consumption,[4] said that each man was capable of seeking his own happiness and since all men were similar we could discover 'what things or actions will conduce not only to our own happiness and preservation but to all others of the same kind'.[5] It was the period of the civil wars that saw the growth of this kind of individualist thinking, with slogans like 'interest cannot lie'. In a time of confusion it no doubt becomes more natural so see society in atomistic terms.

Another thing that made whig views more credible was the whig belief that they represented not innovation but a defence of the status quo—what Tyrrell called 'the government as it is established and the just rights and liberties of all true Englishmen'.[6] Tory publicists might question the whig interpretation of English history and claim that the king was absolute. This in practice was not so and if, said the whigs, England was a

> regulated monarchy, then it is a fond thing with us to talk of an absolute monarch and what an absolute monarch is, or may do. And it is only the language of flattery that holds such discourses.[7]

[1] Gunn, p. 286, n. 1. Cf. below, p. 55.
[2] Gunn, pp. 301–2.   [3] Gunn, pp. 278–85.
[4] Cumberland had written in Latin.
[5] Gunn, p. 289.   [6] Furley, p. 29.
[7] Caroline A. Edie, 'Succession and monarchy—the controversy of 1679–1681', *American Historical Review*, vol. lxx (1964–5), p. 365.

Occasionally whiggish thinkers combined their respect for tradition with the more modern view that institutions cannot be changeless and might progressively improve. Algernon Sidney denied that there was 'one form of government established by God, to which all mankind must submit . . . having given to all men, in some degree, a capacity of judging what is good for themselves, he hath granted to all likewise a liberty of inventing such forms as please them best'. But

> the wisdom of man is imperfect, and unable to foresee the effects that may proceed from an infinite variety of accidents, which according to emergencies necessarily require new constitutions, to prevent or cure the mischiefs arising from them or to advance a good that at the first was not thought on. . . . Changes therefore are unavoidable,

limited only by certain 'universal rules' which 'ought always to be observed'. His emphasis tended to be on the repair of decay rather than on fresh advances. But, he said, 'there can be no reason why a polite people should not relinquish the errors committed by their ancestors in the time of their barbarism and ignorance'.[1] Sir Matthew Hale argued that the common law consisted of decisions applying a special technique of reasoning to changing circumstances. Since the changes would be reflected in the decisions, the continuing supremacy of law did not imply that everything must remain the same for ever. This evolutionary view of the state was the best answer to tory antiquarian polemics, but it only became central to whiggism with Burke.[2]

Just as the tories in the main did not wish to abolish parliament, so the whig belief that the royal power ought sometimes to be resisted did not necessarily imply that the monarchy ought to be destroyed. When Sir William Coventry asked a whiggish house of commons in 1679 if they wanted 'to drive the government to a commonwealth', in response 'the cry was universal, "no commonwealth, no commonwealth, we abhor the thought of it".' The whigs said openly that bad kings might be deposed, but they were careful not to mention the case of Charles I.[3] The typical whig view of the constitution was summarized thus in 1676:

> the legislative authority is in the king and the three estates, the power of levying money in the commons, and the executive power in the king, but to

[1] *Discourses concerning Government* (1763 edition), pp. 14–15, 136–7, 364.
[2] See J. G. A. Pocock, 'Burke and the ancient constitution, a problem in the history of ideas', *Historical Journal*, vol. iii (1960), pp. 125–43; Sir Matthew Hale's criticism on Hobbes's *Dialogue . . . of the Common Laws . . .* Holdsworth, vol. v, pp. 499–513.
[3] Behrens, pp. 60, 64 n. 62.

be administered by ministers sworn and qualified, which is the reason of those two grand maxims of the law of England: first that the king of England is always a minor and secondly that he can do no wrong.[1]

It is the attitude to the executive that is hard to fathom. Though they could be unrealistic about how it might work, the whigs did not want a weak monarchy. They shared the basic royalist view that the rights of king and people were complementary, not opposed. Henry Booth told the Cheshire freeholders 'that the king's prerogative when rightly used is for the good and benefit of the people; and the liberties and properties of the people are for the support of the crown and the king's prerogative'.[2] Locke too thought the executive required 'power to act according to discretion, for the public good, without the prescription of the law and sometimes even against it'. The only limit to the prerogative was that nothing should be done that was not beneficial to the people, 'for prerogative is nothing but the power of doing public good without a rule'. It is clear that Locke envisaged the prince as exercising this power, not parliament acting in his name. It was needed because parliament was 'not always in being' and 'too numerous and so too slow' for executive business. 'Prerogative was always largest in the hands of our wisest and best princes' because it was wisely used and so not questioned: hence a 'saying, that the reigns of good princes have been always most dangerous to the liberties of their people.' Alarmingly, Locke even thought that the prince might reform the legislature by sweeping away pocket boroughs.[3] The prerogative was regarded as 'part of the law' and whigs readily accepted that they had to obey the law even when it was harsh. Samuel Johnson said that 'when . . . it is made death by the law of the land to be a good Christian, then we are to lay down our lives for Christ's sake.'[4]

The whigs then stood for a 'mixed monarchy' and a royal executive. But if wicked ministers or a wicked king betrayed their trust, the ordinary laws had to be overridden: *salus populi suprema lex esto*. On such occasions parliament must exercise more power than usual. 'Take that power away of declaring treason in parliament and you may all

[1] Attributed to Lord Holles. Behrens, p. 51.
[2] J. R. Jones, *The First Whigs: the Politics of the Exclusion Crisis 1678–83* (Oxford University Press, 1961), p. 173. As Lord Delamere he led the northern revolt in 1688.
[3] *Second Treatise*, chap. xiv, esp. paras. 160, 165–6. Cf. paras. 157–8.
[4] See Figgis, pp. 224–6.

have your throats cut', Colonel Birch warned the commons.[1] Admitting that the king need not dismiss his ministers if parliament asked him to, a whig writer said that all the same because the commons 'are most likely to observe soonest the folly and treachery of those public servants . . . this representation ought to have no little weight with the Prince . . .' Therefore

> The best of our princes have with thanks acknowledged the care and duty of their parliaments in telling them of the corruption and folly of their favourites.[2]

The ultimate whig remedy if the king refused to keep the established ways was that defended by Locke. 'If a new monarchy, then a new conquest,' wrote Elkanah Settle,

> and if a conquest, heaven forbid we should be subdued like less than Englishmen, or be debarred the common right of all nations which is to resist and repel an invader if we can.

Another whig writer pledged his loyalty to the king

> so long as he lives and intends the public good, but when he declines from that, query, for then I am bound patiently to let him cut my throat if he will, which is repugnant to the law of nature, which commands my preservation.[3]

(III)

In the tory view of the state, the king was a proprietor, in that of the whigs he was a trustee. Tory thinking tended to make the monarch essentially a landowner, superior to other landowners but so much the same that an attack on monarchy was an attack on landownership. Whig thinking was more 'modern' in that it distinguished between the state and society: the state was the product of deeper social forces and its dissolution did not mean that society was dissolved. It is fair to say that the tories took a 'feudal' view of the state and the whigs a 'bourgeois' view—though to make Locke, for instance, an apologist of nascent capitalism is a little misguided because almost nobody was in opposition to it on the economic plane.[4] Tories and whigs were alike

---

[1] Behrens, p. 63.

[2] Behrens, p. 59.

[3] Furley, p. 34. Furley, pp. 29, 30, thinks Locke's views fairly typical of the whigs save in his analysis of the circumstances under which government is deemed dissolved.

[4] C. B. Macpherson, *The Political Theory of Possessive Individualism* (Oxford, 1962), examines Locke in this light and shows how he defines liberty in terms of property.

tending to accept that the state was given viability by the will of a sovereign power. For the tories it was the king's will, for the whigs that of parliament or the people. The whig view of human nature was more optimistic than the tory. For the tories, as for Hobbes, men were driven by conflicting selfish desires: only obedience to a superior would keep them working together in society. The whigs thought that men were capable of recognizing their common interests and God's purpose for them: free men were capable therefore of working together in unison. The whigs accordingly were not afraid of sovereignty being exercised collectively by a numerous body like parliament. The tories did not all agree with Filmer that republics were necessarily unlawful:[1] but with their view of humanity, the possession of sovereignty by one man was the only real guarantee of a united will.

The rival political doctrines were expounded by the more articulate members of the upper classes who dominated political life—the nobility and gentry reinforced by some well-to-do merchants and professional men. The attitude of those classes to the doctrines would largely decide which could prevail. After the Restoration the tide ran decidedly in favour of the King. It is true that even the 'cavalier' house of commons elected in 1661 was firm in defending the traditional privileges of parliament. But several legal pretexts and fictions which had been used to justify resistance to Charles I were swept away and it was made harder to challenge, with any show of legality, the King's own interpretation of what his powers were. The militia acts of 1661 and 1662 declared that the king had exclusive control of all the armed forces of the realm

> and that both or either of the houses of parliament cannot, nor ought, to pretend to the same; nor can nor lawfully may raise or levy any war offensive or defensive against his Majesty, his heirs or lawful successors.[2]

This was what the Long Parliament had done, and Cromwell's parliaments had always claimed a share in the control of the forces. An act of 1661 imposed the penalties of praemunire[3] on anyone maintaining that both or either of the houses of parliament had any

---

[1] Figgis, pp. 397–8.

[2] 13. Car. II St. I cap. 6. Cf. 14 Car. II cap. 3.

[3] Forfeiture of lands and goods, life imprisonment, incapacity, to sue for his rights at law.

legislative power without the King. During the lifetime of Charles II it was furthermore to be treason even to express, in writing or orally, any plan or intention to rebel or to depose or kill the king. Anyone found guilty of asserting that the King was a papist or a heretic or in any way stirring up hatred against the King or his government was to be disabled from holding office in church or state.[1] The Corporation Act of 1661 obliged municipal officers to take an oath affirming

> that it is not lawful upon any pretence whatsoever to take arms against the king; and that I do abhor that traitorous position of taking arms by his authority against his person, or against those that are commissioned by him.

(Again, this was what the Long Parliament had done.) This oath was successively imposed on militia officers, the clergy, schoolmasters and university teachers. When Danby became the chief minister he tried unsuccessfully to complete the process (1675) by having it imposed on the members of the two houses of parliament.

Besides using legal fictions to justify its assumptions of authority, the Long Parliament had managed to get an Act passed in 1641 which made it impossible to dispense altogether with parliamentary sessions. It provided for the automatic election of members and assembling of the two houses in case the King failed to order it. The Triennial Act of 1664 removed this guarantee for the voicing of popular grievances, though declaring still that parliament ought to meet at least every three years. In giving his assent to it, Charles II said that other countries would now believe that England was a monarchy. 'Farewell Magna Carta' was another contemporary comment. But it is interesting to see how the act of 1641—which even some royalists had originally thought moderate and statesmanlike—was now considered even by old parliamentarians like Prynne and Waller to afford cover for sedition. Sir John Holland, who had also been a parliamentarian and was to be a whig later on, confessed that he had changed his mind since 1641. 'I had rather never live to see a parliament called than to see a parliament to be called and sit contrary to the good will of the king', a situation from which 'greater and more desperate mischiefs have arisen both to king and people than ever have or possibly can arise through the long intermission of parliament, though those

---

[1] 13 Car. II St. I cap. 1. Other opinions that might not be expressed were that the Long Parliament was still legally in being and that the Solemn League and Covenant entered into by the parliamentarians in 1643 was still binding.

inconveniences be very great.'[1] In the same spirit the young Locke, not yet a friend of Shaftesbury, was writing:

> *Vox populi vox dei.* Surely we have been taught by a most unhappy lesson how doubtful, how fallacious this maxim is, how productive of evils, and with how much party spirit and with what cruel intent this ill-omened proverb has been flung wide lately among the common people. Indeed, if we should listen to this voice as if it were the herald of a divine law, we should hardly believe that there was any God at all.[2]

Because many of Charles II's measures and servants were unpopular, the tide of loyalty was succeeded by one of opposition. From 1673 two developments provoked an increasingly strong reaction—the rising power of Danby in the government and the knowledge that James, Duke of York, the King's brother and heir, was a papist. Danby attacked the crown's chief weakness, its poverty, by reforming the financial administration. He also augmented the supporters of the court in parliament by the judicious bestowal of favours and jobs. Both these developments were calculated to make the crown more independent in its dealings with parliament. The religious beliefs of the future James II, with all their repercussions, form a major theme of this book. Here we must simply and briefly note why the fear of popery did so much to intensify the suspicions respecting the monarchy. The tories in particular relied on the conscience of the King to keep him from infringing the law, even when he could do so with impunity. But protestants believed that catholics were bound not by their conscience but by their church: a catholic king would break all laws and promises if it would help to restore the old faith and get back the abbey lands, sure that if he sinned in so doing, the pope would absolve him. 'If the Duke comes to the crown a papist', Sir Francis Winnington told the commons, 'he brings *merum imperium* along with him.'[3] When the revelations of Titus Oates in 1678 seemed to show that there was a popish plot to seize power in the kingdom by force, the opposition reached its climax. Danby was impeached and spent several years in the Tower, though he was never brought to

---

[1] Caroline Robbins, 'The repeal of the triennial act in 1664', *Huntington Library Quarterly*, vol. xii (1948–9), pp. 121–40.

[2] von Leyden, p. 161: his translation of Locke's latin. These were apparently lectures by Locke to his pupils at Christ Church, Oxford.

[3] A. Grey, *Debates in the House of Commons from the Year 1667 to the year 1694* (1763), vol. viii, p. 326.

trial. The whigs, as they came to be called, set about getting James excluded from the succession.

Yet the strong feeling in favour of monarchy that had been in the ascendant at the Restoration had not expired, still less had the laws in restraint of rebellion to which it had given rise and the bad memories of the Interregnum from which it had gained strength. Not realizing this, James and the tories regarded the campaign for exclusion as an attack on monarchy itself:

> the same reason which people may think sufficient to exclude the right heir may (when they please) be deem'd valid enough also to depose and eject the lawful possessor of the crown.[1]

James was

> astonished that men of sense did not see that religion was only the pretence and that the real contest was about power and dominion, that it was the monarchy they designed to banish without which other banishments would give them little satisfaction.[2]

No doubt James was the more ready to believe this because, as he afterwards wrote,

> It had never entered into his heart or imagination that he should outlive the late King; for though he was three years and about four months younger, yet he always looked upon him as of a much stronger constitution and consequently never had the least fancy he should come to the crown.[3]

Others too were of this opinion. In 1681 James's master of the horse, Colonel Legge, told the commons that 'the King is a healthy man, the Duke is not'.[4] The younger Hampden thought that the papists were only interested in James's right because they planned to assassinate Charles.[5]

It is likely enough that the elimination of James would have been the signal for moves against Charles. 'The King', it was said, 'was sensible . . . that his chief security lay in having a successor they liked

[1] Edie, p. 361.

[2] J. S. Clarke (ed.), *Life of James II*, vol. i, p. 594. This work is a Jacobite compilation including extracts from James's own memoirs. Quotations in this book are from these except where there is a note to the contrary.

[3] *Life*, vol. ii, p. 5. But F. C. Turner, *James II* (Eyre and Spottiswoode, 1948), pp. 102–3, does not agree, citing the evidence of his second wife.

[4] Grey, vol. viii, p. 329.

[5] *ibid.*, p. 187.

worse than himself.'[1] This helps to explain why he would never agree to a change in the succession. But what the bulk of the whigs wanted was a king more to their own way of thinking, not the suppression of the monarchy or the curtailment of its powers. They seem to have believed both that the King was too strong to be attacked and also that by common consent he ought to be strong. The establishment of the Hanoverians eventually gave them something of what they wanted. We shall see them, before that, seeking the patronage of William III and even, as a last resort, that of James himself. Even at the outset, they remained monarchists while tampering with the monarchy: they wanted to change the succession by an ordinary act of parliament and so by agreement with the King. When Charles refused to agree, they did not dare to make good their claim that in the last resort parliament or the people might take the law into their own hands. Only a few of them were prepared to oppose the King by force and so the last word in the nation's affairs passed to him by default.

The monarchism of the whigs was apparent in their lack of interest in schemes for limiting the powers of the crown as an antidote to a popish successor. Suspiciously it was Charles who proposed limitations on the power of a popish king as an alternative to excluding James. Few people have ever supposed that he meant this seriously. He gave a foretaste of how it might work by his reconstruction of the privy council (1679) so as to admit the parliamentary leaders: by his own confession,[2] this changed nothing but appearances. The tories naturally did not like 'limitations'[3] but sometimes advocated them in preference to exclusion. We shall find them advocating something similar at the Revolution and some at least of them were not being disingenuous but really wanted to neutralize the popish James. It is interesting to see that in such a situation they considered the lawfulness of the king more important than his powers. What they wanted was an indisputable source of authority and this they thought that only a king with indefeasible hereditary right could provide. How much of the authority was to be exercised by the king himself was a less essential matter.

Some moderate opponents of the court were tempted by Charles's

---

[1] *Life of James II*, vol. i, p. 550. These are the words of the Jacobite compiler of the *Life* but he claims to be quoting contemporary letters.

[2] Ailesbury, vol. i, p. 35.

[3] Feiling, p. 185.

proposals to work with the government, but it is fair to say that they were deluded. Some who had formerly supported the Commonwealth, such as Wildman[1] and Neville, were attracted by 'limitations' because they looked like a step towards a republic. In *Plato Redivivus* (1681) Henry Neville proposed not a temporary but a permanent restriction of royal authority. The king was not to be deprived of his powers, but he was to exercise them according to the advice of four councils elected by parliament. Neville thought that 'it is needless to make any provision against a popish successor if you rectify your government'.[2] Republican inclinations may have helped Halifax to opt for limitations rather than exclusion.[3] James not unfairly remarked that his thinking was not 'calculated for the meridian of a monarchy'. The Trimmer said that 'monarchy is liked by the people for the bells and the tinsel, the outward pomp and gilding, and there must be milk for babes'[4]—remarkable words in a paper probably designed for the attention of Charles II. It should be stressed that even the republicans were not necessarily eager for rebellion, whatever James may have thought. Neville said that 'there cannot, nor ought to be, any change but by his majesty's free consent'. A war to take away 'the least part' of his rights 'could be justified by no man living. I say besides that, a civil war has miscarried in our days'. Though victoriously fought in 'defence of the people's own rights . . . yet could they never reap the least advantage in the world by it; but went from one tyranny to another'. He claimed to 'abhor the thoughts of wishing, much less endeavouring' to establish 'a commonwealth or democracy' since the nation was 'under oaths of obedience to a lawful king'.[5]

The bulk of the whigs abhored even 'limitations' as republican in theory and incapable of limiting a popish king in practice. They certainly resembled the paper constitutions of the Interregnum in dividing and weakening authority and so inviting overthrow by anyone who could get military backing. 'If you provide thus against the Duke of York, you take away all royal power and make the government a commonwealth,' said Vaughan in the commons. 'All that will

---

[1] M. Ashley, *John Wildman, Postmaster and Plotter* (Cape, 1947), p. 223.
[2] Edie, p. 361.
[3] H. C. Foxcroft, *Life and Letters of Sir George Savile, first Marquis of Halifax* (Longmans, 1898), denies it: see vol. i, pp. 152–5, 264–5.
[4] Halifax, *Works*, p. 55.
[5] C. Robbins, ed., *Two English Republican Tracts* (Cambridge University Press, 1969), pp. 173, 177.

signify nothing when, in effect, the crown is upon the Pope's head.' Such a scheme, said Boscawen in the same debate, 'would look like a commonwealth': allowing parliament to appoint 'clergymen and justices of the peace will signify nothing, a troop of horse and a file of musketeers will easily turn us all out of doors'. The entire personnel of government was unreliable: 'by being willows and not oaks, men have kept their places at court.' The commons thought that the resources and legal rights alike of a king were such that he could hardly be checked. One member thought that royal authority 'has ever over-balanced' that of parliament.[1] Colonel Birch said that for parliament to appoint the privy council would be 'such a breach of the prerogative, it will fall of itself'. The same objections applied to the more realistic suggestion made in 1681 that James's heir should rule in his stead as regent. 'Our law will not endure it, to divide the person of the king from the power,' said Sir William Pulteney. 'Both the person and the power will be courted.' Sir Nicholas Carew asked whether, if James would not accept the regency, 'those who fight against him are not traitors by law?' Sir William Jones, a distinguished lawyer, thought that if James were left with 'a title to be king, then without doubt all incapacities fail'. The whigs in short accepted the view that certain powers were 'inseparable' from the king's person. Vaughan summed up: 'this is perfectly to bring a war upon us and for the Duke to come in by conquest; and so farewell law, church and all.'[2]

The whigs wished to use the sovereign power which they claimed for parliament not to overturn the constitution but to conserve it by placing the crown for the future in safer hands. They could fairly claim that this was a sensible way of escape from what everyone admitted to be an impossible situation. Lord Russell 'thought it better to have a king with his prerogative and the nation easy and safe under him, than a king without it, which must have bred perpetual jealousies and a continual struggle'.[3] The bulk of the whigs hoped to preserve the lawful dynasty by sacrificing one member of it and transferring the succession to his lawful heirs: 'if an ancient family might possibly be ruined by the eldest son, it is not unjust to disinherit him,'[4] they said. James's elder daughter Mary, already married to the Prince

[1] Grey, vol. vii, p. 251; pp. 258–9; p. 244.
[2] Grey, vol. viii, p. 275; pp. 315–16; p. 321; p. 327.
[3] Edie, p. 354 n. 12.
[4] Sir F. Winnington, Grey, vol. vii, p. 453.

of Orange, was as things stood the person likeliest to succeed by this arrangement. It is wrong to suppose that any great number of the whigs were partisans of the Duke of Monmouth,[1] the senior royal bastard, or to take as typical such remarks as: 'the old rule is, he who hath the worst title ever makes the best king.'[2] The whigs could point out that parliament had often settled the succession before and that an Elizabethan statute had virtually made it treason to deny that this was lawful.[3] They could ask if Englishmen or Christians had to 'have that zeal for a corrupted leprous branch of royalty, that we must ruin both religion, government and Majesty itself to support him'.[4]

The interesting thing about the case against the whigs is the doubt it casts on the credibility of parliament's claim to be sovereign. This idea was really as unwelcome as the prospect of absolute monarchy. Either implied the overriding of received notions of right and justice, which was still felt to be both dangerous and wicked. 'I will not take away right where right is established,' said the moderate whig Sir Henry Capel.[5] But the disinheriting of James to safeguard the rights of the people was precisely this: it was doing evil, moreover, that good might come of it. James was to be condemned without a trial—unlike the regicides in 1660. It was inconsistent with the oath of allegiance, the formal safeguard of national obedience. 'When I swear allegiance, it is not only to the king but his heirs and successors and there can be no interregnum in our government,' said Sir Leoline Jenkins, secretary of state. Changing the succession, he further thought, was to 'change the very essence and being of the monarchy', to 'reduce it to an elective monarchy'.[6] It was not conservative at all. 'The succession of the crown to the next of blood is a law eternal and wrote with the immediate hand of God and nature,' wrote one tory. 'Kings are not the children of the most voices but children of the most high,' wrote another.[7] It was unfortunate for the whigs that they were attacking just at the point where princely rights (of inheritance) were just like those of an ordinary landowner. Lord Ailesbury might say in the house of lords 'I would not do an illegal thing to preserve my whole

---

[1] On this subject see J. R. Jones, *The First Whigs*, pp. 13–14 etc.
[2] Edie, p. 354 n. 11.
[3] Furley, pp. 26–7.
[4] Elkanah Settle: Furley, p. 30.
[5] Grey, vol. vii, p. 252.
[6] Quoted Feiling, p. 184.
[7] Edie, pp. 355, 357.

estate',[1] but more pertinent was the claim of Henry Coventry, another secretary of state, that the exclusion plan was 'the most ruinous to law and the property of the subject imaginable'.[2]

The whig plans were so horrifying that it was argued that parliament not only must not but could not carry them out. 'Acts of parliament,' went on Coventry, 'have not kept the succession out of the right line but brought in blood and sword . . . show me one man excluded . . . that had right of descent but has come in again.'[3] Lord Yarmouth told the lords that there was 'no law strong enough to fence out an indisputable title. It will entail a war to posterity'.[4] The fact was that if Tudor legislation respecting the succession had been observed, the Stuarts probably would not have come to the English crown. When the house of lords refused in 1680 to pass the exclusion bill sent to them by the commons, the danger that it might cause civil war bulked as large in the debate as the immorality of it—nowhere more than in the famous contribution of Halifax. He thought 'the parliament rather has a power than not' but 'if it occasions war, the duke will immediately fall on us'. Ireland and especially Scotland, which had once been strong enough to maintain its independence, were feared as providing him with resources and there was also the prospect of help from France. Laurence Hyde, brother of the Duke's first wife, warned the commons that 'notwithstanding this Bill, persons of loyalty will adhere to the Duke if he outlive the King'. He predicted a split among the whigs: a section would join the loyalists 'and there will be trouble in changing the succession'.[5] If exclusion were to be maintained, it could only be by that Cromwellian horror, a standing army.[6] Failure to maintain it when once asserted would be just as bad. Jenkins warned:

If the duke should try to cut this law with his sword, and he should overcome, the same power that can set aside this law will set aside all laws both of our religion and property; the power will be in the hands of a conqueror and he will certainly change the government.[7]

[1] The father of the memoirist: see report of debate in E. S. de Beer, 'The House of Lords in the Parliament of 1680', *Bul. Inst. Hist Research*, vol. xx (1943–5), pp. 31–6.
[2] Grey, vol. vii, p. 252.
[3] Grey, vol. vii, p. 243.
[4] For Yarmouth's and Halifax's views see De Beer's article just cited.
[5] Grey, vol. vii, pp. 402, 450–1.
[6] Grey, vol. vii, pp. 243, 313; vol. viii, pp. 318, 403, 408.
[7] Grey, vol. viii, p. 339.

So 'exclusion' would bring just the evils that the whigs expected from 'limitation'.

What is striking is that the whigs did not really disagree. 'I see nothing certain but our danger,' said Lord Cavendish in 1679, 'the remedies moved for are uncertain.' Colonel Birch thought 'we have no great reason to doubt' the danger of civil war.[1] An intelligent whig pamphlet of 1681 could only say 'if there must be a war, let it be under the authority of law; let it be against a banished excluded pretender'.[2] Paul Foley and Sir Thomas Player argued in the commons that war was at least better than popery.[3] The whigs insisted that exclusion would be no good without the organizing of an association to fight such a war.[4] It is in this context that something attractive can be seen in leaving the last word to the king and to his successors under the law. The misdeeds of a tyrant might be preferable to civil strife. 'When God gives us a king in His wrath,' said that old Roman-law pedant Sir Leoline Jenkins,[5] 'it is not in our power to change him: we cannot require any qualifications: we must take him as he is.' Many pointed out how Christians had obeyed heathen emperors like Julian the Apostate. 'Be subject to the higher powers,' said Lord Ailesbury, was 'required when Nero was Emperor.'[6] But possibly more would have said, with Sir Thomas Littleton, that Tudor monarchs had been able to change the nation's religion because there had been 'a general fermentation of religion all the world over; and these things go by tides and times', so that now even Louis XIV and the Sultan were powerless in this respect.[7] Whigs feared the royal power. Tories feared it less, not only because they believed that it should be great but also because they believed that in practice it was not as great as the whigs thought.

It is hard to gauge the relative popularity of the tory and the whig views. The King held three general elections in the years 1679–81 in the hope of getting a more tractable parliament but each time the whigs returned in greater strength. Charles was alone in his un-

[1] Grey, vol. vii, pp. 247, 405.
[2] *A Just and Modest Vindication of the Proceedings of the last two Parliaments*, Furley, p. 34.
[3] Grey, vol. vii, pp. 256, 406.
[4] Furley, p. 33.
[5] Quoted Feiling, p. 184.
[6] De Beer, *loc. cit.*
[7] Grey, vol. vii, p. 253.

wavering resistance to exclusion. The rejection of the whig bill by the house of lords when it finally reached them in 1680 may fairly be ascribed to royal influence, manifest in the King's physical presence at the debate. But the whigs were superior in party organization and they used this not only to maximize their own support but to cow and silence those who favoured the tories. Those who strongly opposed them were liable to find themselves under threat of punishment for collaboration with the papists. They were accused of exercising a sort of minority dictatorship. In 1680 the whig M.P. George Speke was warned of a widespread feeling that important parliamentary votes 'should not be carried by heats and a small number of the major party'—perhaps many of the wisest in the house and ten to one of the wisest outside against.[1] The tory writer John Nalson was prepared to concede that the king could not legitimately 'dissent to publick and necessary bills for the common good' but qualified this by saying 'the major part in either of the houses for passing bills so pretended may be but one or two voices or very few; and perhaps of no judicious men'.[2] There was some substance in the accusation. In a division of the house of commons on the exclusion bill in 1679, 207 members voted for it, 128 against and 174 did not vote. There was a large majority for the bill among the representatives from Wales and eighteen English counties. But among the members from the other 22 counties there was a small majority against. In the ensuing general election only 55% of those who had voted against were chosen again, as against 80% of those who had voted for. But 70% of those who had not voted were also returned.[3] It is not certain that the house was solidly whig and in any case who was to know if it was truly representative? Tory writers rather incongruously pointed out the deficiencies of the electoral system and said that it represented only a sixth of the nation.[4]

On the other hand there are plenty of signs of broad popular support for the whigs. Monmouth drew enthusiastic crowds on his tours of the country and so did William of Orange after the Revolution. Monmouth easily raised an army among the common people in 1685. The middle class electorate of the boroughs and counties contained a large whig element. The second Earl of Ailesbury recalled

[1] CSPD 1680–1, pp. 92–4, partly cited Behrens, p. 68, n. 73.
[2] Edie, p. 369.
[3] A. Browning, Doreen J. Milne, 'An exclusion bill division list', *Bulletin, Institute of Historical Research*, vol. xxiii (1950), pp. 206–7.
[4] Furley, p. 28.

in his memoirs that the parliaments of 1679–80 'were chosen contrary to the genius of a great part of the men of most worth in their several counties ... because the common unthinking people have a voice equal to a man of the best estate'.[1] In his own county of Bedford he seems to have thought that the 'many worthy and rich gentlemen of quality, and of the second form, and rich yeomen' were loyalists whereas 'those they called moderate men amongst the second sort, gentlemen and yeomen and farmers, were little addicted to monarchy'.[2] It was in the higher classes that the whigs found most opposition.

What was more important was that in practice most of the whigs behaved like tories: that is, when the King rejected their demands they did not dare to resort to violence. It is true that the whig parliaments did consider measures tending to the seizure of power, but they were ostensibly measures of resistance to the popish plot and to James should he take part in it: only obliquely did they threaten Charles and his control of the government. In 1678 the commons wanted the militia to be mobilized, a part at a time, to overawe the papists. This could not be done unless funds were voted and so they turned their plan into a parliamentary bill. Gilbert Burnet, later one of the strongest supporters of the whigs among the clergy but at this time fairly moderate, found that some hoped by this means to 'be more masters, and that the militia would not separate till all the demands of the two houses should be granted'. He warned the King, who vetoed the bill 'because it puts out of his power the militia for so many days. If it had been but for half an hour, he would not have consented to it'. This was the boldest measure ever attempted and it seems unlikely that it would have got through the two houses if subversion had been its main purpose. It was followed up by many demands, right down to 1681, that the militia and the other organs of government be placed in the hands of men less suspect to parliament. Charles occasionally sacrificed an unpopular servant, but we shall see that in 1680 it was decided, on the contrary, to get rid of many who were supposed to sympathize with the whigs.[3]

A more important proposal was to make it lawful for anyone to

---

[1] Ailesbury, vol. i, pp. 59, 60.
[2] Cf. Ailesbury, vol. i, pp. 61, 183.
[3] This and the next paragraph are mainly derived from my *English Militia in the Eighteenth Century* (Routledge and Kegan Paul, 1965), pp. 80–4.

resist a papist who was armed and to create an organization specifically for such resistance. It was popish troops in the government
service that were really envisaged as the danger here and what was
aimed at was to create a new excuse for resisting royal authority to
replace those which, as explained above, had been done away with
after the Restoration. In December 1678 it was proposed in the commons that it should be a felony for a papist to ride armed, even if he
held the king's commission, and that any protestant might lawfully
disarm or resist him. The 'non-resisting' oath first introduced in the
Corporation Act was to be abolished. Attention was called to the
Act of Association of 1585. This had been passed to enable the nobility
and gentry to form a defensive league against the papists: if Queen
Elizabeth had been murdered by them, the association was to have
avenged her death and preserved the ascendancy of protestantism. In
April 1679 there was a flat demand for a law giving the people the
right to take up arms against a king who tried to introduce popery.

These ideas continued to be canvassed right through the exclusion
crisis but, naturally, led to no legislation. It was hardly to be expected
that a king would agree to make rebellion lawful unless, like King
John in 1215, he had already been worsted by a rebellion. But the
whigs, who wanted to be able to rebel if the need arose, did not dare
to do it unless it was legalized. Sir William Jones warned them that an
association against James would be useless unless he was debarred
from the crown. 'The people will not come up so well to exclude a
person who by law has a title.'[1] The whigs thought the situation most
unfair. 'A popish successor may send popish guards,' complained Sir
Thomas Player in 1679, and the protestants would 'die like dogs and
have our throats cut; and I must not take up arms to defend myself
against such rogues.'[2] But most whigs thought that there was no help
for this. In January 1681, Sir Henry Capel asked that the commons
tell the King that the exclusion bill 'is our whole, our all' and went on

> we cannot subsist without it. All things will be in confusion, the monarchy
> lost. I would have the world see we have no intention to eclipse the monarchy,
> by meddling with the militia or the prerogative. When this is done, we have
> nothing to do but adjourn.[3]

This can stand as the whig swan song. In 1681, when Charles II dissolved the third parliament elected in two years without allowing it to

[1] Grey, vol. viii, pp. 268–9.   [2] Grey, vol. viii, p. 151.
[3] Grey, vol. viii, p. 265.

do any serious business, some of the leaders in the lords tried to go further. If we are to believe one of them, the shady Lord Grey of Warke, 'very many members' of the commons had resolved not to go home if there was a premature dissolution. But when the day came and the lords sent word 'to our friends' in the commons to remind them of their promise

> most of them could not be found, and those that were, answered us only with shaking their heads, and soon after we heard the commons' house was empty and so we went away.[1]

By the use of hindsight it is easy to see the whigs as the party of the future and the tories as belonging to the past. Neither the beliefs nor the behaviour of the two sides justifies this. The beliefs of tories and whigs were alike rooted in a God-centred view of the universe which is alien to modern thinking. It has been well said that Locke replaced the divine right of kings by the divine right of the freeholder. To a modern reader, Locke's proof of the divine origin of property is likely to seem just as much of a sophistry as Filmer's proof of the divine origin of kingship. Tories believed that the King ought to be obeyed in cases where whigs thought he should be resisted. It is possible to see this difference of opinion in terms of the spread of a more 'modern' view of human nature—to link Locke's politics with his educational views. But more immediately it was just a practical quarrel about how best to conserve a social order that both sides wanted to conserve. The whigs, like the tories, tended to see a strong monarchy and considerable restraints on the individual as necessary for the work of conservation: this will appear more fully in later chapters. In the last resort too, the whigs like the tories were prepared to allow the king to have the last word. The attitudes prevailing among the Englishmen who were active in politics in 1680 do not point to the inevitability of parliamentary government. They left the way perfectly open for the consolidation of a very strong monarchy and if anything this might seem the more natural development of the two.

[1] Behrens. p. 68, n. 72.

3

The Refurbishing of the Monarchy

CHARLES II was able to dispense with parliament in 1681 because he was a little stronger than his father had been forty years earlier. The work of his servants over the years, coupled with his own sagacity in avoiding political traps, meant that the crown revenues had improved and that there were no weakening commitments comparable to the Scottish and Irish troubles that faced Charles I. The King even had a few loyal troops at his disposal. Even so, the government remained essentially weak and Charles persisted in attempts to work with parliament until it was clear that he could no longer do so without total surrender to unacceptable whig views. What transformed the situation was the unwillingness of all but the extreme whigs to carry their opposition beyond a certain point: it was evidently safe—indeed the safest thing—to press forward with the strengthening of the royal government to which the whigs had objected. This was the keynote of Charles II's last years and of the reign of James II.

The first step was to reassert the King's traditional authority over the country's traditional institutions: notably the county magistracies, the judiciary and the municipal corporations. Charles had hitherto used his power over these in a fairly conciliatory way, but from about 1680 measures began to be taken that were to make them a good deal more submissive. This proved sufficient to crush the whigs, who were first deprived of their share of influential local offices and then harried by a judicial persecution under which many of them suffered death, exile, imprisonment or crippling fines. The whig extremists responded with plots and ultimately, on the accession of James II, with Monmouth's rebellion. But they were worsted each time.

More important, however, than the defeat of the rebels was the opportunity which the situation gave the King to build up new and more reliable instruments of government. Corresponding to the tory view of the state, the traditional institutions gave the sovereign authority rather than power. He was their undoubted head and the gentry, rich burgesses and lawyers who staffed the administration were his loyal defenders. But they expected to be allowed to do things in their own way and county government in particular remained only rather loosely under royal control. Behind the old institutions, however, the government was building up a new body of salaried servants with a more professional attitude to their work and stricter notions of obedience: naval officers, the little army that beat Monmouth, treasury and revenue officials. The crushing of the whigs and the thorough subjugation of the boroughs made possible an ultra-loyal parliament at the beginning of James's reign which completed by generous grants the long and slow process of financial reform. An augmentation of the forces was the result. The tory squires did not like this and they liked even less the religious revolution on which James embarked. Advancing from toleration for his fellow catholics to an outright attack on the anglican religious monopoly, James was increasingly governed by his own religious predilections. Nevertheless, we shall see that his religious policy was no mere aberration but complementary to the advancement of his secular power. James did not get much help from the squires in forwarding his religious measures, but he had both money and troops and he managed to find judges who would give legal countenance to most of the things he did. He did not have to worry too much about the murmurings of England's traditional local rulers.

Moral factors played a big part in the strengthening of the monarchy and this in turn had moral effects. Whigs who despaired of restraining the King made the best of things by seeking his favour. When James quarrelled with the tories he restored many whigs to local office: this offered prospects of perpetuating royal ascendancy by exploiting the enmity between the parties. If more whigs did not turn to James it was largely because they had another prince to turn to—William of Orange.

James never became an absolute monarch if by that is implied the power to change the laws and social structure of England (he would have had more chance in Scotland). Even the power of Louis XIV had many limits and the power of James was more limited still. But James was certainly absolute in the restricted sense of being independent: able to govern and interpret the laws to his liking despite the disapproval of most, perhaps, of his subjects. It took the coming of William with an army to alter this situation. How the royal power was built up is the subject of this and the next four chapters. The dramatic side of the story is perforce omitted—the execution of Lord Russell and Algernon Sidney, the murderous flogging of Titus Oates, Sedgemoor and the Bloody Assize. The present chapter considers what the crown gained, and what it failed to gain, from the reinvigorating of traditional institutions. Further chapters deal with the building up of new financial and military resources and with the religious revolution to which this forms the background. An attempt will be made in the course of them to estimate exactly how far the King managed to emancipate himself from the possibility of resistance by his subjects.

(I)

Royal control in the counties provided a broad, firm basis for the start of the royal recovery, though it was too circumscribed to be the basis of any sort of absolutism. County administration comprised a civil and a military arm, usually linked at the top by combining in one person the offices of *custos rotulorum* and lord lieutenant. The execution of the laws was the responsibility of the justices of the peace. Physical force in support of their orders was available from the militia and the officers and deputy lieutenants who controlled it formed the inner circle of the county magistracy. With the exception of a toothless Council of Wales, the prerogative courts that had overseen the work of the justices were no more. The habit of receiving and executing orders from the central government was well ingrained however. The crown retained also the power to appoint and dismiss (directly or indirectly) lord lieutenants, justices and militia commanders. The King could thus in principle place country affairs in the hands of obedient men. But he could not do this in a thorough and ruthless way without deeply wounding local feeling. The gentry believed that the country magistrates ought to be recruited from substantial county families: in the eighteenth century parliament was to establish property qualifications for deputy lieutenants, militia officers and justices of the peace. Moreover, it was felt that families with considerable property and influence in particular areas ought to have a commensurate share of administrative power in those areas. Certain families had an almost hereditary right to be lord lieutenant in certain counties—a fact most strikingly brought out by the making of temporary appointments when the head of the family concerned was a minor. In 1681 Lord Conway became regent, as it were, in Warwickshire for the young Earl of Northampton. In 1683 the Duke of Somerset came of age and took over Somerset from Lord Winchelsea.[1] The Earl of Bath controlled Devonshire for the young Duke of Albemarle after his father's death in 1670 and again in 1686 when he went to govern Jamaica. Bath assured Albemarle on that occasion that he would preserve his influence there and surrender the county when Albemarle was ready to resume it: the militia still bore Albemarle's name and colours and the deputy lieutenants drank his health whenever they met.[2] Lower down the scale, Sir Thomas Peyton was removed from the command of a Kentish militia regiment because he had sold his estates in the county: he was replaced by Sir Henry Palmer, a man of great 'interest'. Sir John Holland resolved to make Sir William Gawdy major of his Norfolk regiment of militia, his father having been so: each time he thus appointed a Gawdy, he ignored the claims of captains deriving from seniority.[3]

How awkward it might be if the government ignored claims of this kind is seen in the history of Norfolk under Charles II. After the Restoration, Sir Horatio Townshend had been raised to the peerage and made its lord lieutenant. He had built up a strong influence and seems to have served the crown well. In 1676 he was removed from the lieutenancy because he had quarrelled with Danby and thereafter worked with the incipient whig movement in the county. Lord Yarmouth, his successor, built up his power by alliance with the tories. Though Townshend's antecedents were parliamentarian and Danby's royalist, the quarrel between them was purely personal: Townshend had opposed Danby's attempt to get a parliamentary seat at King's Lynn for his son-in-law. Nor was Townshend ever an intransigent whig: in 1681 he abandoned the exclusionist cause and

[1] CSPD 1680–1, p. 638; 1683, January/June, p. 384.
[2] CSPD 1675–6, pp. 403, 450, 411. HMC *Le Fleming*, p. 67, no. 1114. HMC *Buccleuch/Queensberry* (*Montagu House*), vol. i, p. 345.
[3] Western, pp. 60–1.

seems to have wanted to make his peace. By failing to respect local interests, the government had lost a powerful supporter. Another interesting feature of the Norfolk scene was the suspicion aroused among the county gentry by the fanatical clergy who were the mainstay of the now triumphant tories. These zealots were men of low birth, it seems, and Dr Hylyard, the most influential with Yarmouth, was a 'carpet-bagger' from Yorkshire.[1] They too were a threat to local territorial interests, and again the moral was that the government might become dangerously unpopular if these interests were neglected. A practical difficulty often met with was that not enough active magistrates might be forthcoming to do the county business. Though many gentry were appointed to bench and lieutenancy, most of the work was done by a zealous minority. In a way this made purges easier, since the removal of a handful of active men might make a vital difference. But this would not work if the government was so unpopular in an area that it could not find other responsible, industrious gentlemen to take over. When Lord Lindsey purged the Lincolnshire justices after the exclusion crisis, the clerk of the peace complained that the active magistrates had been left out and replaced by others who refused to act: there had been no quarter sessions for six months in Holland and Spalding gaol was full of people awaiting trial.[2]

It was more prudent for the government to respect local prejudice and keep some at least of the respected local figures in power regardless of their views. This seems to have been the general policy followed from the Restoration until the exclusion crisis and it was not very popular with old cavaliers. In 1660 the deputy lieutenants of Hampshire asked Southampton, the lord treasurer (who was also their lord lieutenant) that the colonels of militia regiments should be appointed from among themselves, because the gentlemen who were not deputies were either inexperienced or politically unsound. But Southampton replied, while granting their request, that the government wished to avoid this duplication 'from the intent of engaging the more persons by the more plenty of employments, other countries abounding with persons of quality, whose interests were all fit to be engaged'.[3] From Oxfordshire Lord Falkland reported that he had to

[1] CSPD 1682, pp. 54–6, J. R. Jones, 'the first whig party in Norfolk', *Durham University Journal* NS vol. xv (1953–4), pp. 13–21.
[2] J. W. F. Hill, *Tudor and Stuart Lincoln* (Cambridge University Press, 1956), p. 186.
[3] Western, p. 64.

advise the appointment of a good many deputy lieutenants to avoid faction: there were many young men equally eligible in birth, fortune and loyalty.[1] In 1662 Sir John Prettyman complained to the King that he had been left out of the lieutenancy of Leicestershire despite severe losses in the royalist cause during the Interregnum.[2] By contrast, the government ordered the appointment of Sir Edward Harley to the command of the Herefordshire militia regiment of foot in 1667, though the Marquess of Worcester, lord lieutenant, objected that he was a 'presbyterian' and there was opposition to it.[3] The government seems to have been very loath to give county administration a partisan character. Even in September 1680 Sir George Fletcher, an ardent tory, was ordered to desist from acting as a deputy lieutenant in Cumberland and Westmorland and to resign his militia commission. Daniel Fleming, who expected to receive similar treatment, commented that neither of their fathers could be charged with being papists, traitors or fanatics.[4] Nor was the authority of royal officials always insisted on if it seemed likely to offend local opinion. In 1676 Secretary Coventry dissuaded the Duke of Newcastle from going to law because the Mayor of Nottingham had omitted some 'civility' to him as lord lieutenant: partly because the extent of militia officers' powers 'like other arcana imperii are not overhastily to be exposed', but also because it might attract parliamentary notice.[5]

Under growing pressure from the whigs the government at length became more authoritarian. At the end of 1679 a committee was appointed to inspect the commissions of the peace, with a view to removing undesirable persons.[6] By the end of 1680 the commons were complaining of undesirable appointments in the lieutenancies and in February 1681 Lords Suffolk, Manchester and Essex were deprived of their lieutenancies. In June came an order to remove from the lieutenancies all who had been dismissed from the bench:[7] by the end of 1682 a substantial purge had taken place though its character is not quite certain. Some had wished it to be purely

[1] CSPD 1660–1, p. 265.
[2] CSPD 1661–2, p. 519.
[3] HMC *Portland*, vol. iii, p. 306.
[4] HMC *Le Fleming*, p. 170.
[5] British Museum: Additional MSS 25124, ff. 87–90, 101–2.
[6] Ogg, vol. ii, pp. 623–4.
[7] Western, pp. 58–9, for most of what follows.

partisan. In 1678 Henry Layton had urged the government to confine the control of the militia to persons royal and episcopal in inclination and to this end suggested the compiling of a list of families who had formerly paid 400*l.* or more in composition for estates confiscated by the parliamentarians. In August 1681 the Earl of Lindsey, lord lieutenant of Lincolnshire, wanted the dismissal of those of his deputies who had failed to join in thanking the King for his declaration after the dissolution of the last exclusion parliament. He thought that unless this was done people would not believe that he enjoyed royal support. He hoped that it was now realized that the policy of courting 'presbytery' was a mistake and thought it would be 'an ill time to model' the militia 'when the enemy is in the field'. But the Marquess of Worcester, who was lord lieutenant of Wales and the neighbouring English counties, reported that he was not excluding those 'tolerable and possible to be reclaimed' as he understood that it was not intended to make a 'thorough reformation'. That this was still the government's point of view is suggested by the further history of Sir George Fletcher, mentioned above. In 1681 the government ordered his reinstatement in the militia organization. But the lord lieutenant, Lord Carlisle, refused to comply and both parties appealed to the King. Carlisle was the son of a Cromwellian and it is pretty plain that Fletcher and his friends did not think him trustworthy. But Charles showed himself less royalist than they. He said that those in 'prime stations' of service must live in good understanding and Fletcher had to apologize to Carlisle as a condition of being taken back.[1] Unity of the landed class, with only some necessary exception, seems still to have been the watchword. Men like Shrewsbury and Rutland who were whig-inclined retained office: to say nothing of outright renegades like Huntingdon. The government's main attack was against the municipal corporations, not the counties. We shall see that the attack on the corporations was congenial work for the upper class as a whole.

That county government remained somewhat independent of royal policy is to be seen in the activity of the ninth Earl of Derby, whose control of Lancashire and Cheshire inevitably resulted from his headship of a loyal and very ancient family and was further cemented by his marriage to a granddaughter of the Duke of Ormonde, the most distinguished of the veteran cavaliers. Derby seems to have

[1] Western, p. 61. CSPD 1680–1, p. 362.

wanted to remain friendly with all parties and he ended by infuriating everyone. During the exclusion crisis he supported opposition candidates for parliament, but opposed the signing of the petition which they instigated. In October 1681 he angered the King by appointing Lord Colchester colonel of militia and in May 1682 a loyal address, which he promoted in Lancashire, gave offence by speaking of the *King's influence over his successor* as the main security for the future against popery, schism and abritrary government. That autumn Derby showed up badly in a crisis of public order in Cheshire, when Monmouth visited it on one of his rabble-rousing progresses. Ormonde warned Derby to have nothing to do with him, but in reply Derby reported a rumour that Monmouth was reconciled to the court. Dr Fowler, the Rector of Whitchurch, warned Secretary Jenkins of the possibility of rebellion. The gentry were mainly loyal but the Delamere interest, on the other side, was stronger than theirs among the populace of the county. If the lord lieutenant was unfaithful, the militia might be surprised and the gentry disarmed.

The loyal party tried in vain to get Derby to call out the militia. In the end they staged a sort of surreptitious mobilization of it on their own, timed to coincide with their opponents' biggest demonstration. On September 12 Monmouth was entertained at a great race and sports meeting at Wallasey. On the same day there was a rival meeting in the Forest of Delamere, attended it was said by 80 gentlemen and 2,000 others, some coming in from Staffordshire. There was no rebellion, but some of Monmouth's supporters staged a riot when they got home to Chester and nothing could be done about it. The Cheshire gentry complained bitterly about Derby, but could get nothing beyond thanks for their zeal and a promise that he would be spoken to. In 1683 they asked permission to promote a loyal address from the Cheshire militia behind Derby's back, but were told not to do it as the King hoped to win Derby over by kindness.[1]

Demands continued for a more intolerant administration, which only a more thorough purge of the magistracy would have made possible. In July 1683 the quarter sessions of Essex ordered all the justices to bring all suspicious persons before them to give two sufficient sureties for good behaviour at least until the next sessions, on pain of imprisonment. Not only the known disaffected and those who

[1] Western, pp. 62–3.

went to conventicles instead of to church were deemed suspicious but all who had ever borne arms against the king or his father.[1] This was really an attempt to proscribe a section of the ruling class itself. The accession of James brought in a king who was prepared to go to such lengths. During Monmouth's rebellion orders were given to intern all who had formerly borne arms against the sovereign: Sir Edward Harley was one of the respectable victims.[2] But it was only James's religious policy that led eventually to measures which the traditional rulers of the counties would not implement. At first there was little difficulty, for magistrates were merely required not to persecute catholics, a thing which they had not been eager to do anyway. But in 1687 James decided to get a house of commons elected that would agree to the repeal of the laws protecting the anglican religious monopoly. He expected the county authorities to help him in the elections but found them predominantly hostile or unenthusiastic. He had already done something to make the counties more amenable by admitting catholics to the magistracy in defiance of the law. He now dismissed the more recalcitrant magistrates and replaced them with such whigs and dissenters as were willing to work with him. But the new recruits were not equal in social weight to those they replaced, and we shall see that James's election campaign had increasingly to be taken out of the hands of the county authorities. Before becoming unmanageable, however, they had done much to strengthen the royal position. The whigs had been subdued, the independence of the corporations was gone. There was no longer any organized movement of opposition to take advantage of their largely passive obstruction of the King's further measures.

(II)

The professional judiciary was brought under far stricter royal control than the county justices. The purge of the corporations brought the recorders into line and similar measures were taken with the twelve judges of Westminster Hall. As with the gentry, the government of Charles II at first tolerated some diversity among them, but under crisis conditions came to insist on judges who would

[1] CSPD July/September 1683, p. 103.
[2] Western, p. 69.

toe the line. Against James II the lawyers, like the gentry, eventually rebelled—but not before they had done valuable service.

After the Restoration, though most of the lawyers appear to have been parliamentarian in sympathy, a *modus vivendi* was established between crown and courts. The independence of the judiciary and the rights of the king were alike respected. At first most of the judges were appointed 'during good behaviour (*quamdiu se bene gesserint*)' as they are today: that is, they could not be dismissed when they displeased the king. One or two of Cromwell's judges also served Charles II, the most important being Sir Matthew Hale, an eminent authority on the history and theory of the law, who was chief baron of the exchequer in the sixties and lord chief justice from 1671 to 1676. Roger North said that his 'foible' was 'leaning towards the popular; yet when he knew the law was for the king . . . he failed not to judge accordingly'.[1] Similarly, Clarendon wrote of Vaughan, who succeeded Hale as chief baron, that he stressed those aspects of the law 'which disposed him to least reverence to the crown, and most to popular authority; yet without inclination to any change in government'. The same spirit was to be found in judges who were royalists. Lord Nottingham (lord keeper and then lord chancellor, 1673–82) defended in parliament the royal power to suspend statutes (1673) and his refusal to issue a writ of habeas corpus in vacation was one of the incidents which helped to provoke the Habeas Corpus Act. But even Burnet admitted that 'in his court [he] could resist the strongest applications even from the King, though he did it nowhere else'. Further, in an age when the chancellor might be a layman (Shaftesbury) or a lawyer entirely turned politician (Clarendon), he was very much a professional and began the process of turning equity into a system of rules and precedents rather than something in the arbitrary discretion of his court: he said that 'the conscience by which I am to proceed is merely *civilis et politica* and tied to certain measures'.

But political pressures led the government to mar this happy picture. Even in 1660 the judges of the court of king's bench, where most of the important 'political prisoners' were tried, had no guarantee to tenure in their patents[2] and the government took care to

---

[1] For this paragraph see Holdsworth, vol. vi, pp. 501, 539, 547, 580.

[2] For what follows see mainly A. F. Havighurst, 'The judiciary and politics in the reign of Charles II', *Law Quarterly Review*, vol. lxvi (1950), pp. 62–78, 229–52.

appoint strong royalists there. Lord Chief Justice Kelyng annoyed the commons in 1667 by calling Magna Carta 'magna farta' and by denials of writs of habeas corpus. In one such case he said that 'we must use a justifiable prudence and not strain the strict rules of law to enlarge those persons which will use their liberties to get the kingdom in a flame'.[1] From 1668 judges were appointed 'during pleasure' (*durante bene placito*). In 1672, the government did several things of doubtful legality (Declaration of Indulgence, stop of the exchequer, use of martial law): two judges were removed, apparently because they were not compliant. In the dismissal of lord keeper Bridgeman the government was within its rights, but Sir John Archer (another Cromwellian judge) was removed in defiance of his patent of appointment 'during good behaviour'. This was got round by allowing him to keep the profits of his office. In 1676–9 several judges were removed at the behest of politicians powerful at court. Danby raised his protégé, Sir William Scroggs, until he became lord chief justice, while the appointments of 1679 were influenced by the attorney-general, Sir William Jones, who sided with the whigs. The retiring judges were mostly due to go in any case by reason of age. But a sinister precedent was provided by Ellis, dismissed in 1676 and restored in 1679.

When the government began to oppose the whigs more firmly, it began more systematically to require compliance from the judges. Pemberton was dismissed in February 1680 and Sir Robert Atkyns was driven to resign for not concurring in certain measures which the courts were taking against the opposition. Pemberton's career is extraordinary. In 1681 he was brought back to replace Scroggs, whom Charles did not venture to employ after the commons had voted to impeach him. 1682 he was displaced as lord chief justice by Saunders, who was thought more likely to come to the right decision in the quo warranto case against the City. In 1683, he was removed from the bench altogether. Another dismissal was Dolben, replaced in 1682 by Wythens who had been chief prosecutor in some trials of the whigs. New appointments in 1683–4 brought in the two most notorious judges of the next reign—Sir George Jeffreys and Sir Robert Wright. Francis North, Lord Guilford (lord keeper, 1682–5), is an instance of a judge of more moderate temper who nevertheless survived into

[1] Helen A. Nutting, 'The most wholesome law—the Habeas Corpus Act of 1679', *American Historical Review*, vol. lxv (1959–60), p. 531.

the new era: but he was after all a tory, he was determined to keep out of trouble and he suffered much minor persecution which would have driven out anyone who had not made this unheroic resolution.

James II, like Charles II in 1672, needed judges who would not only enforce the law but sanction its being bent. They were most helpful to the crown in several cases, as will be more fully explained in due course. But there was less eagerness for this work than for the crushing of the whigs and only repeated purges kept it going. The judges inherited from Charles II are supposed to have been split 8 to 4 in favour of collecting the excise without new parliamentary authority and 7 to 5 in favour of giving military commissions to catholics. James decided on a test case to establish the legality of the latter and he interviewed some, if not all, of the judges to find out their views in advance. No less than six judges (and the solicitor-general) had to be removed in order to get a favourable judgment in the case of Godden v. Hales, in which all twelve were consulted. Even then, one dissented and four more claimed to have had misgivings.[1] Herbert, the lord chief justice, was certainly moved by conviction, not subservience, in finding for the royal dispensing power and the same may have been true of others. A matter soon arose on which he disagreed with the King and decided against him. In 1687 James refused a pardon to a soldier named Beale and ordered him to be hanged in front of his regiment at Plymouth. Herbert and Wythens ruled that the law required the execution to take place in Middlesex or the county of origin. To avoid losing the salutary example of a hanging on regimental discipline, James replaced Wythens by Allibone, a catholic, and exchanged Herbert with Wright, who had just been made chief justice of the common pleas. The continuing difficulty of keeping the judiciary in line was shown in the strongest way at the trial of the seven bishops. This represented a defiance of the king by the legal no less than by the clerical profession (the counterpart in both cases of the class solidarity which put the gentry against him). The counsel for the bishops included two dismissed judges (Pemberton, Levinz), the former attorney and solicitor general (Sawyer and Finch), two future chief justices of the common pleas (Pollexfen, Treby) and the future lord chancellor, Somers. In face of the leaders of their profession, the four judges at the trial did not dare to speak in favour of the

---

[1] For this paragraph see A. F. Havighurst, 'James II and the twelve men in scarlet', *Law Quarterly Review*, vol. lxix (1953), pp. 522–46.

King's power to dispense with the law which the bishops had impugned; one spoke to some extent against it and they were evenly divided as to the lawfulness of the protest which the bishops had made. Holloway and Powell, who believed it lawful, were replaced after the trial. James II never got a completely docile judiciary.

The government's power of patronage enabled it to tighten its hold on the legal profession. Traditionally the heads of it had been the serjeants and the judges had been promoted from among them. The rank of serjeant had been reached by successful work in the common law courts and the order was characterized by great respect for that law and suspicion of prerogative claims at variance with it. In the seventeenth century, however, the attorney and solicitor-general and the king's counsel overtook the serjeants: precedence and judicial office went to them. Nominated and paid a fee by the crown, though not paid solely by it, they represented the creation of a body of lawyers better fitted—both by inclination and by breadth of legal and political knowledge—to do the crown's legal work. The decay of legal education in the Inns of Court was another feature of the century. Based on lecturing and discussion, it began to seem old-fashioned with the multiplication of printed books. It never recovered from the disorders of the Interregnum, not least because the king's counsel established the right to be made benchers of their Inns. They had too much lucrative business to be willing to teach: student riots and the supersession of formal instruction by private study were the results.[1] An important strengthener of professional solidarity in the law had been removed.

The lucrative posts in its gift gave the crown a strong hold over the many lawyers with an urgent craving of money. Some of these were men of lowly origin—very lowly in the case of Saunders—who were seeking their fortune. Others were the younger sons of gentlemen, with no property and expensive tastes. Wright and Scroggs were of this type, and the gentry of Wales and the Marches seem to have produced many.[2] Jeffreys was one and another was Sir William Williams, who from being a whig Speaker turned into a catholic and James II's solicitor-general (prosecutor of the seven bishops). Another was Sir John Trevor, also a Speaker and master of the rolls.

---

[1] Holdsworth vol. vi, pp. 457–99.
[2] G. W. Keeton, *Lord Chancellor Jeffreys and the Stuart Cause* (Macdonald, 1965), p. 499.

North says that he was a great gambler and first attracted attention as a clever arbitrator of gamblers' quarrels: he also alleges that Pemberton began practice in a debtors' prison.[1] Some of the crown's legal tools were second-rate men who could not hope to make much money in any other way.

It would be wrong, though, to suggest that the only lawyers willing to serve the government were the needy, the profligate and the incapable. Of James II's appointments, Professor Havighurst classes four very low: Wright, Jenner and the two catholic appointments, Christopher Milton (brother of the poet) and Allibone. But he thinks that five would stand comparison with judges of other periods: Herbert, Edward Atkyns, Nevill and John Powell. Against Williams may be set a stauncher whig and post-revolution judge—Pollexfen—who acted as chief prosecutor in Jeffreys's 'bloody' circuit of 1685. What really made it possible for the government to tamper with the judiciary without, for some time, completely alienating the lawyers was that its demand for amenable judges was not considered entirely unreasonable. Judges had always been not just the guardians of the law but the asserters of royal authority when there were no police or regular troops to awe the populace. In a period of revolution, as this undoubtedly was, it was easy to see the judges' task as fighting for the King. Roger North, brother and biographer of Lord Keeper Guilford, discusses the rightness of appointing judges 'whose opinions were known beforehand; of which it is easy to say (as the anti-court party did) that judges were made to serve turns'. But

> here a government is beset with enemies ever watching for opportunities to destroy it; and having a power to choose whom to trust, the taking up men whose principles are not known is more than an even chance that enemies are taken into their bosom.
>
> ... The true distinction is, when governments use powers that do not lawfully belong to them (as high courts of justice)[2]; and when they use only such powers as are properly lawful, as the ordinary courts of the common law.

The idea that justice must be done and must be seen to be done was not lost sight of even by royalists. North claimed that when his brother suspected 'fraud, false dealing or forgery' in a case he would 'canvass the evidence to a scruple, giving all latitude to the counsel', in the hope of bringing it into the open.

---

[1] *Life of Guilford*, paras. 332, 339.   [2] *i,e*, the court that tried Charles I.

> For it was not enough that he, in his private opinion, thought a deed forged or the like; but he must have evidence by the force of which he might show it so plain as would satisfy the auditory as well as the jury.

If evidence was not forthcoming, he was careful to conceal his suspicions because in matters of fact

> he must have warrantable reasons for what he said or insinuated to the jury, who only were the proper judges; and the rather because they seldom found against his decisive directions.

In the cases which he tried on circuit

> (especially on the crown side) he was never easy till, by examining over and over and over again, asking parties questions, as attorneys, and everyone that he thought could help to clear up an intricate fact; and scarce gave over till he had brought it to so clear a state, as that the audience should think as he declared.

But these very circuits are the best illustration of the political role of the judges, for they provided the government with a valuable means of oversight over local politics and administration. The judges delivered political harangues to the gentry in court. They managed many of the surrenders of municipal charters—Jeffreys was especially famous in this work—and in 1685 they were among the government's agents in the parliamentary election. North records that when on circuit his brother 'took care always to declare the laws to the country' and while avoiding party distinctions

> as the tenour of our lawbooks run, he exhorted to loyalty and to support the royal prerogative by law; showing that the safety of the national religion and property depended on the people's dutiful and legal obedience to the crown: and for this purpose he used some short harangue at the entrance of his charges.

At first he found that 'factious gentlemen' came to 'sound and practise experiments upon him', especially 'if any factious cause was to be tried, as against a justice of the peace for disturbing conventicles'. But when he failed either to side with them or to say things that might be 'wrested to calumny, as if he favoured popery or arbitrary power', they ceased to come to the assizes. By contrast he made friends with the loyal gentry. He chose the western circuit 'because he knew the gentlemen to be loyal and conformable and that he should have fair quarter amongst them'. After a few circuits they found his measures and their desires consonant in all things; whereby he became not only well accepted but did also contract a sort of alliance and strict friendship with much the greater and most considerable part of them. And that interest stood him in good stead in time of need: for so considerable a body and so united as the Western gentlemen in parliament were, did so firmly ensconce him that his enemies could never yet get a clever stroke at him.[1]

The political bias of a man like Jeffreys was far greater than this. After his appointment as lord chancellor, he told his successor as lord chief justice in open court to

Be sure to execute the law to the utmost in its vengeance upon those that are known—and we have reason to remember them—by the name of whigs! And you are likewise to remember the snivelling trimmers![2]

But the difference between Guilford and Jeffreys was one mainly of style and we should beware of supposing that either did much that anyone then thought wrong. The political work of the circuit judges, for instance, went on under whig rule well into the eighteenth century.

(III)

Judges and local magistrates between them were able to suppress almost all political activity distasteful to the government because the law itself was authoritarian and there was pretty general agreement that it should be. This was another natural consequence of popular lawlessness and the absence of a police force. It was not compatible with the existence of free political life as we know it. Certain aspects of the law were criticized and even reformed without its general character being changed. Only the possession of some governmental power by opponents of the crown (in parliament, in local administration) did something for a time to redress the balance.

To modern eyes the censorship is the most blatant sign of the absence of freedom, though it was not the government's most formidable weapon against opposition, or even against criticism. Given statutory sanction for the first time in 1662, it had formerly been part of the work of the prerogative courts, and the crown continued to claim that the power to censor the press was inherent

[1] For the foregoing see the *Life of Guilford*, paras. 338, 166, 171, 189–91.
[2] Keeton, p. 334.

in the royal prerogative. Censorship was exercised on this basis both before the Act of 1662 and when it expired in 1679, at a time when parliament was hostile. A proclamation of October 1679 for the suppression of libels against the government[1] was followed in 1680 by another suppressing all news-books not licensed, after the judges had advised

> That His Majesty may by law prohibit the printing and publishing of all news-books and pamphlets of news whatsoever, not licensed by His Majesty's authority, as manifestly tending to the breach of peace, and disturbance of the kingdom.

In 1685 a more compliant parliament renewed the act of 1662, but not before a warrant had gone out to Sir Roger L'Estrange, surveyor of imprimery, to have the printers notified to have their products sanctioned in the same way as 'before the time of the late scandalous and intolerable liberties of the press'. Control of the press is here declared to be a prerogative inseparable from the sovereignty of the crown.[2]

The Stationers' Company had always been the government's chosen instrument in the management of the press and censorship was combined with the granting of copyright and the regulation of the trade. The Act of 1662 gave London (in the shape of the Company) and the two universities a monopoly of printing. At that time there were fifty-nine master printers in London, but the Act required that the number was to be allowed to fall to twenty and there were to be only four typefounders. Vacancies in both cases were to be filled by the Archbishop of Canterbury and the Bishop of London. Booksellers were to be licensed, imports of books were controlled: in at least one case a sale of second-hand books was stopped.[3] There was a blanket prohibition of books offensive to the church, any officer of the government, any corporation or any private person. Books had to be licensed before printing by certain high officials according to the subject-matter: the secretaries of state, for instance, had to license books about politics or history. Copyright was granted to persons entering their books at Stationers' Hall. The crown had always asserted the right to grant a monopoly in the production of certain books to whom it pleased. Some of these prerogative grants were confirmed in the act of 1662.

[1] F. S. Siebert, *Freedom of the Press in England, 1476–1776* (University of Illinois Press, 1956), p. 298.
[2] CSPD 1685, no. 694.   [3] CSPD 1686–7, no. 1096.

The censorship encountered a good deal of opposition and did not work well. It was essentially a monopolistic regulation of the trade, at variance with the tide of commercial expansion and with the less well regulated conditions of the Interregnum. The less privileged members of the trade resented the advantages conferred by royal grants on a favoured few and printers in general wanted more opportunities for expansion. The Stationers' Company seems to have been whiggish, as the City was in general. In 1668 it was ordered to admit three more dependable members to its Court of Assistants, and in 1669 it was threatened with a quo warranto, in the same way as refractory municipal corporations. Only in 1675 did it put in operation a number of regulations which the government had long demanded, reducing the numbers in the trade and ensuring more compliance with the licensing system.[1] For this was very far from working effectively: probably only half the output of the presses was licensed. It was hard, for one thing, to find staff for the work of censorship: one reader retired almost at once in 1675 'because of the tenderness of the employment and the vast expense of time it requires'.[2] L'Estrange, who was appointed surveyor in 1663, was at first given the main responsibility, under the secretaries of state, for seeing that the law was observed. He undertook much of the censorship himself but more importantly he and his assistants hunted for printers evading the licensers. From 1667 this work was done by messengers directly responsible to the secretaries, usually under the authority of general warrants like that which Wilkes was to win fame by resisting: the act was at any rate useful in clearly establishing the legality of these warrants. Arbitrary imprisonment and the taking of recognizances by the secretaries were summary weapons that could be used against the printers and booksellers.

The censorship does not seem to have prevented the spread of new ideas. It probably did hinder the organizing of regular political campaigns and in particular the emergence of newspapers. The expiry of the act in 1679 was followed by a flood of ephemeral writings which was not properly suppressed until 1682. But the government did not fully exploit the silencing of its opponents by establishing a powerful periodical press of its own. The Commonwealth and Protectorate had

---

[1] Siebert, pp. 258–9. L'Estrange, p. 256, believed that the crown rather than the company should control printing.
[2] Siebert, pp. 243–4.

had official newspapers and royalist successors appeared at the Restoration. But there was rivalry between different agents—Muddiman, L'Estrange and Under-Secretary Williamson most notably. From 1666 the territory was amicably divided between Muddiman, who circulated manuscript newsletters, and Williamson's *London Gazette*—which however carried no home news. The main rival to these was the gossip of the coffee houses: in 1675 therefore the government tried to suppress them by proclamation. The whig newsbooks were countered during the exclusion crisis by tory rivals such as L'Estrange's *Observator*, but when the crisis was over the monopoly of the *Gazette* returned.

Far more important than the censorship were the crown's wide powers under the law to put out of action any persons who made themselves obnoxious. The King still claimed the power to order the arrest and detention of whom he pleased, and the secretaries of state and privy council made extensive use of this power in the troubled years after the Restoration. This was partly because of the new Statute of Treasons (1661), which extended the offence to include seditious words. Two witnesses were required for conviction in a trial for treason, so if there was evidence of seditious words from one person, the suspect was imprisoned until a second witness could be found.[1] Parliament and indeed the judges had long sought to establish the power of the courts to deliver the imprisoned subject by writ of habeas corpus, notably in the Act of 1641 abolishing the court of Star Chamber.[2] But prompt obedience to the writ was not exacted after 1660, nor were the judges always willing to grant it—indeed there were doubts about which of them were competent to do so. The government created a further obstruction by sending political prisoners to remote places like the Channel Islands.

After the fall of Clarendon there began a series of attempts in parliament to have the transportation of prisoners without judicial warrant made illegal and to require the judges to issue the writ of habeas corpus speedily, the prisoner to be bailed if proceedings against him were not started within a reasonable time. The Habeas Corpus Act of 1679 was the fruit of these efforts. Even before this the court of king's bench, under the influence of judges like Hale, had come to make habeas corpus the 'usual' instead of the 'highest'

[1] Nutting, p. 537.
[2] Holdsworth, vol. ix, pp. 112–15.

remedy for imprisonment and to insist on prompt obedience to the writ. The government in any case was ceasing, in deference to public opinion, to order imprisonment by its own authority: after 1679 it relied mostly on warrants issued by justices of the peace. But though the Act of 1679 was unpopular in government quarters, it would be wrong to suppose that the crown's power was very much restrained. The unwillingness of the commons to restrict it too much was shown in 1674 when the bill then before them was amended to make 'detainer' rather than 'arrest' by the secretaries' orders illegal. This was after Secretary Coventry had said that without the right to imprison and interrogate suspects the royal system of intelligence would collapse. At least, he said, the act should specify 'what commitment the secretaries can make in case a man would kill the king'.[1] The act of 1679 did not require the release of persons arrested on charges of treason or felony. They could be held for a maximum of two law terms while evidence was being sought against them. It is true that the act required them to be bailed, but the judges got round that by demanding impossibly large sums as security.[2]

In any case, the law defined political offences so widely that arbitrary powers of arrest were hardly necessary. The Statute of Treasons has already been mentioned. In effect it made the intention to commit treason, evidenced by writing or speaking even if it was not in public, sufficient for conviction. Pemberton in 1681 laid down that words importing any malicious design against the government were treason. Thus it came about that Algernon Sidney was condemned on the strength of writings on political theory found in his study, and a nonconformist preacher named Rosewell was nearly executed for questioning the King's power of healing. It seems likely that any riot was treason. An apprentices' riot against bawdy houses in London was so deemed (1668) because by attempting 'public reformation . . . they take upon them the royal authority'.[3] For statements of political opinion that did not amount to treason the charge of seditious libel was available. The law relating to this offence had been developed in the Star Chamber. The ordinary courts now judged it in the same spirit. In 1679 Benjamin Harris was tried for this for having published

[1] Nutting, p. 534.
[2] Holdsworth, vol. ix, pp. 118–19.
[3] Ogg, *Charles II*, vol. ii, pp. 512–14. The act of 1661 was limited to Charles II's life, Holdsworth vol. vi, p. 399, but the trial and execution of the printer Twyn (1664) suggests that the judges could do as much even when they did not invoke it.

statements to the effect that if the Popish Plot succeeded, parliament could not be blamed if it had not been allowed to sit.[1] An obsolete statute *de scandalis magnatum*, which was put into force a good deal at this time, was of similar effect: it made it a grave offence to libel peers since they were the counsellors of the king. The punitive damages awarded for this offence were as good as imprisonment.[2]

It was the whigs whose political activity was disrupted by the use of the crown's various legal weapons after 1680, but we should not suppose that even the whigs had any objection in principle to the government's methods. The Long Parliament, to say nothing of Cromwell, had perpetuated the censorship of the earlier Stuarts with but little change. Milton himself had been a censor for a time. Commonwealth legislation on treason anticipated the statute of 1661.[3] Charges of *scandalum magnatum* were a weapon used by opposition peers. Both houses of parliament suppressed publications of which they disapproved and sometimes punished their authors. In 1667 the lords sentenced a man to the pillory and a 1,000*l*. fine for libelling Lord Gerard of Brandon.[4] As for seditious libel, Chief Justice Holt, a great whig lawyer, said in 1704

> To say that corrupt officers are appointed to administer affairs is certainly a reflection on the government. If people should not be called to account for possessing the people with an ill opinion of the government, no government can subsist. For it is very necessary for all governments that the people should have a good opinion of it.[5]

This was the natural doctrine at that time—perhaps is bound to be so in any age of great revolutionary upheavals.

The repressive character of the law was complemented by the character of the judicial process. In cases of felony and treason, the accused was not allowed counsel and had to conduct his own defence. He was usually allowed to receive legal advice outside the court but this was a favour. Stephen College, a whig agitator who was hanged in 1681, was not allowed to retain at his trial a paper of advice how to conduct his defence. Chief Justice North told him that he could not have counsel

---

[1] Siebert, p. 272.
[2] Ogg, vol. ii, pp. 465–6.
[3] Holdsworth, vol. vi., p. 426.
[4] Siebert, pp. 276–7.
[5] Siebert, p. 271.

unless matter of law arises, and that must be propounded by you; and then if it be a matter debateable, the court will assign you counsel, but it must be upon a matter fit to be argued. For I must tell you a defence in a case of high treason ought not to be made by artificial cavils, but by plain fact.[1]

In his biography of his brother, Roger North justifies this by the political situation: 'the defence was intended to be tumultuous.' The trial was to be turned into a political demonstration. The confiscated papers comprised

downright libels, most artfully and maliciously penned, to reflect upon the government, and tending to sedition, in the form of speeches, to be pricked in at the trial, as the cues were given . . . Criminals, of that sort should not have any assistance in matters of fact, but defend upon plain truth, which they know best, without any dilatories, arts, or evasions.[2]

Be that as it may, it hardly justifies the further rules that a prisoner received no notice of the charges and witnesses against him until the trial began and had no right to call witnesses in his own defence. In practice he was usually allowed pen and paper and a secretary (which enabled him to get a copy of the indictment). The court might allow him as a favour to see the list of jurors, so that he might challenge any that might be biassed, and to call witnesses. But if he called any, they were not sworn, and if they did not happen to be at hand he might have no opportunity to produce them. In two respects the accused was actually worse off than he had been earlier: he had to answer the crown's witnesses all at once after they had all testified, instead of one by one, and it was possible to interrupt the trial and remand the accused pending the collection of further evidence.[3] It is not surprising that trials were mostly short, a morning or afternoon sufficing for the condemnation of a traitor. Fortunately some political offences were not felonies but misdemeanours—seditious libel for instance—and in those cases the accused could have counsel.

It is true nevertheless that in some ways the law was evolving in favour of the accused. Bushell's case (1670) established that juries could not be punished for verdicts which the judges thought perverse. Juries were empanelled by the sheriffs, who were normally royal nominees. But where a municipal corporation had its own sheriffs, the

[1] Holdsworth, vol. ix, pp. 232–3.
[2] *Life of Guilford*, paras. 216–17.
[3] Holdsworth, vol. ix, pp. 196, 232–4. S. Rezneck, 'The Statute of 1696: a Pioneer Measure in the Reform of Judicial Procedure in England', *Journal of Modern History*, vol. ii (1930), pp. 5–13.

crown might be faced with whig jurymen. This was notoriously the case in London, where the City had the privilege of appointing the sheriffs of Middlesex. 'Ignoramus' juries made the capital a real asylum for the crown's enemies. Shaftesbury was preserved from a traitor's death and College was acquitted in London before an excuse was found to have him tried at Oxford. The purging of the corporations took care of this however—indeed the getting rid of 'ignoramus' juries may well have been the thing that rendered it essential. During the suppression of the whigs, loyal gentlemen even sat on petty juries themselves in order to be sure of the right result.[1]

The state of the law relating to evidence seems also to have been improving.[2] It was in the late seventeenth century that hearsay evidence gradually came to seem inadmissible. The political trials of the civil war period, though they seemed unlawful and unjust to the losing side, set new standards as to the evidence to be required. Witnesses had to be produced in court, written depositions being excluded; the prisoner might not be forced by questioning to incriminate himself. But these trends had yet to have their full effect—prevailing ideas as to evidence and proof were still hopelessly crude. There was a prejudice lingering from medieval times that evidence given on oath somehow had to be believed: that a row of sworn witnesses had to result in conviction, even though the prisoner could not swear his own witnesses or testify on oath himself. The testimony of one witness in any case could normally secure conviction. This seems again to result from a medieval idea, or rather situation: the jury had originally been persons with a knowledge of the circumstances of the case to be tried and their verdict of guilty was deemed equivalent to the evidence of a second witness for the prosecution. Two witnesses were required in a case of treason, but at the trial of the regicides in 1660, Bridgeman ruled that they could be to different alleged acts of treason.[3] The situation was aggravated by the prevailing low standards of honesty and fair dealing. Perjury and forgery were a common feature of the private quarrels and lawsuits of the period, and in view of the weight attached to oaths it was extremely unfortunate that perjury was not a felony.[4] There was

[1] CSPD 1682, p. 347.
[2] Holdsworth, vol. ix, pp. 217–18, 230–1.
[3] Ogg, *Charles II*, vol. ii, p. 513.
[4] *ibid.*, p. 510.

an eagerness to turn the crimes of others into a source of profit, well brought out by a curious episode in Sir John Reresby's memoirs. A Negro slave of his had died and he was unjustly suspected of having caused this by getting the man castrated. A nobleman thereupon tried to have Reresby prosecuted, in the hope of getting a grant of his estate if it was forfeited to the crown. When political passions were brought into play in a system already rife with error and dishonesty, there was little hope of justice. The worst cases of judicial murder were indeed during the Popish Plot scare, when the government was not particularly eager for convictions. The trial of Lord Stafford before the lords is especially notable, for the court protected him and he avoided most of the disabilities of the common prisoners of the time. Yet though he was almost certainly innocent, he did not escape.

Only when the judges were required not just to enforce but blatantly to twist the laws did the crown find itself fairly solidly opposed by the lawyers and by educated opinion. The royal courts could hardly command respect when the best lawyers could no longer be employed there as judges. Halifax wrote that his Trimmer 'thinketh men's abilities very much misplaced when the reason of him that pleads is visibly too strong for those who are to judge and give sentence . . . it is then that Westminster Hall might be said to stand upon its head'. This situation was virtually reached in the trial of the seven bishops. Many would have been ready to apply Halifax's prophetic words and say that the law had been 'thrown from the dignity of protecting mankind to the disgraceful office of destroying them'.[1] But it was late in the day to make this discovery when the workings of the law had already both destroyed organized opposition to the regal power and removed key restraints to its exercise.

(IV)

Of particular importance in the crushing of the opposition was the reduction to subservience of the municipal corporations. Not only did this increase royal authority in local administration but it opened the way to a more subservient parliament and so to the really firm establishment of royal independence. Returning four-fifths of the house of commons, strongholds in many cases of the parlia-

[1] Holdsworth, vol. vi, pp. 508–11.

mentary cause in the civil wars and of dissent and whiggery afterwards, the towns aroused the fear of the royal government, and any
signs of independence among their merchants and tradesmen were
resented by the nobles and squires. Even in 1661 the City of London
returned four undesirables to the 'cavalier' house of commons. In
some cases it was thought necessary after the Restoration to disarm
the municipalities by demolishing the fortifications of the towns and
confiscating their stocks of weapons.[1] The King was not too badly
placed to subjugate them more thoroughly. The granting of municipal
charters was a royal prerogative and a judicial means existed of
declaring existing charters forfeit: a writ of quo warranto, alleging
that the powers granted to the corporation had been misused or
exceeded. No corporation could avoid at least minor infringements
of its charter, so none was safe. Under the early Stuarts, a number
of charters were forfeited in this way and regranted on terms more
favourable to the crown. Cromwell too remoulded corporations, perhaps with a view to influencing their parliamentary representation.
During the period of troubles from 1640 to 1660, moreover, the
corporations had been repeatedly purged by whoever happened to be
in power and the legal title of those in possession in 1660 was often
doubtful and contested. The privy council found itself called on to
adjudicate between rival factions and the towns in general seem,
naturally enough, to have been very deferential to the crown.

It is fairly clear that the government took advantage of the situation
to increase its hold on the corporations.[2] In May 1661 it was decided
that when a new charter had to be granted, the King would reserve
to himself the initial nomination of the aldermen, recorder, town
clerk and common council, as too the appointment of future recorders
and town clerks. Further, the vote in parliamentary elections was to
be confined to the common council. As most of the corporations
recruited themselves by co-option, this would have kept elections in
the hands of a small body. In the course of 1661, the new 'cavalier'
parliament proceeded to pass a measure empowering the crown to
purge the existing corporations as well. Opposed in the commons by
the veteran parliamentarian Prynne, it was considered in the lords
by a committee headed by the Duke of York and meeting at his

[1] Western, pp. 32–3.
[2] For what follows see mainly J. H. Sacret, 'The Restoration government and municipal
corporations', *English Historical Review*, vol. xlv (1930), pp. 232–59.

lodgings. The amendments proposed by this committee to strengthen the bill may fairly be considered official policy. They provided for the surrender of all existing charters, the appointment of future recorders, town clerks and to some degree of mayors by the crown, and that county justices were to have jurisdiction in boroughs within their county—or else that borough justices were to be appointed by the crown. The commons refused to accept these amendments. But the Act as finally passed empowered the crown to appoint commissioners in each county who might remove any corporation officials as they saw fit and replace them by any existing or previous inhabitants of the town that they chose. The sacramental test by which the Act is best remembered was an afterthought: nobody was to be made a councillor or municipal official who had not within the year received the sacrament according to the anglican rite. The commissioners' powers were to last until March 1663 and they were not squeamish in using them. In Lancashire, Lord Derby proposed to turn out 'all who had ever been against the King, or given no testimony of loyalty before the Restoration'. At Chard and Kidderminster the corporations seem virtually to have been annihilated.

The Act indemnified corporations in respect of all offences committed before 8 May 1661, but the crown by no means intended to give up the future use of quo warrantos to keep the purged civic authorities in line. As early as March 1663 a privy council meeting at which the King and the Duke of York were present ordered quo warrantos to be issued against all towns that had not renewed their charters since the Restoration. This seems to have been done, not universally but on a fair scale, in the years that followed. The inclusion of the new religious tests and royal power over the appointment of recorder, steward and town clerk were features of new charters.

The results of the royal offensive were not, however, really lasting. There was a similar problem to that met with in county government. Where most of the solider men in a town were allegedly disaffected— meaning usually that they were 'fanatics' in religion—it was hard to replace them if they were purged from its government. At Reading the commissioners of 1662 removed fourteen members from the corporation but had great difficulty in finding others. Over half the new council had no experience of municipal office, one was a young man scarcely out of his apprenticeship, and the full number of twenty-five does not seem to have been made up for some time. Under these circumstances it is not surprising that the 'fanatics' crept back, by various dubious means. At Bewdley in 1673 nineteen voters at a parliamentary election were objected to: they had taken the required oaths but not the sacrament according to the rites of the Church of England. In a small town like Bewdley it was hard in any case to keep the corporation at its full strength. Oaths were doctored to make them more acceptable.[1] The practice of 'occasional conformity' or taking the sacrament merely to qualify for office had begun. At Leominster half the twenty-five members of the corporation were 'fanatics' by the 1680s.[2] A further problem was that a purge of the corporation, though politically very important, did not alter the parliamentary franchise unless this was confined to corporation members. Early in the century the commons had claimed jurisdiction over disputed elections and had accepted the principle that a new charter could not alter a franchise established by custom.[3] So it is not surprising that the offensive against the corporations did not prevent the exclusionists from winning the three general elections of 1679–81.

But the crown did not give up. In 1668 the sheriffs were told to warn the boroughs within their counties that the Corporation Act must be enforced and the lord lieutenants were ordered to find out if the corporations were readmitting officials turned out by the commissioners in 1662.[4] The exclusion crisis was the signal for a new offensive. In March 1680 the privy council told the corporations to enforce the Act and report their activity in doing so—removing members who had failed to comply with it and sending a list of their names.[5] The years 1682–5 were replete with the surrender and forfeiture of borough charters. This time the new charters represented a more radical break with the past. As was usual, they specified by name the members of the remodelled corporations and so were themselves a means of completely altering the personnel. The crown continued to claim the right to interfere in the appointment of steward, recorder and town clerk; professional lawyers might be

---

[1] P. Styles, 'The corporation of Bewdley under the later Stuarts', *Birmingham University Historical Journal*, vol. i (1947), pp. 98, 102. The Declaration of Indulgence of 1672 was partly responsible here.

[2] Ogg, *Charles II*, vol. ii, p. 635.

[3] Sacret, pp. 244, 259.

[4] Sacret, pp. 254–5.

[5] J. Tickell, *History of Kingston upon Hull* (1798), p. 550 n.

1 The Petition of the Seven Bishops, 21 May, 1688

2 A contemporary broadside giving a version of the Petition and the King's reply

June y 30 th 1688

Wee have great satisfaction to find by 35, and since by Mōn Zulestein that your Hi: is so ready and willing to give us such assistances as they have related to us. Wee have great reason to beleeve wee shall be every day in a worse condition then wee are, and lesse able to defend our selves, and therefore wee doe earnestly wish wee might be so happy as to find a remedy before it be too late for us to contribute to our owne deliverance but although these be our wishes yet wee will by no meanes put your Hi: into any expectation which may misguide your owne Councells in this matter, so that the best advice wee can give is to informe your Hi: truely, both of the State of things here at this

3 Facsimile of the first page of the letter inviting William to invade England, dated 30 June, 1688

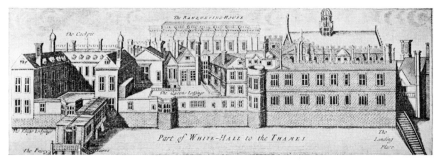

4 Whitehall from the Thames, from Ogilby's plan of London, 1677

5 Lambeth Palace, from an engraving by John Kip, 1697

6 An engraving by D. Marot, showing the order of sailing of William's invasion fleet

7 William and Mary taking the Coronation Oath, from an engraving by A. Schoonebeek

8 A satirical print of 1651 showing the Scots holding their King's nose to the grindstone

9 A mezzotint by G. Beckett depicting the Triumph of William III

10 James II, by an unknown artist

11 Prince William in Garter robes

12 Queen Mary, mezzotint by
A. Blooteling after Lely, *c.* 1677

13 Mary, James II's Queen, with her
infant son

14 The Seven Bishops, by an unknown artist

15 Counsel for the Seven Bishops at their trial, engraving by R. White

insisted on to do the work of the first two posts. But more striking was the power which the king often retained to remove any member of the corporation. Another new provision often met with was the power given to county justices to act within the boroughs. A memorandum in the 1682 state papers emphasizes this aspect of remodelling; it says that the ties between the inhabitants of a town were so close that it was impossible to get justice in its courts and cites a goldsmith of York who was acquitted of clipping coins.[1]

It was by utilizing the resentments of the gentry against the boroughs and their desire for influence there that the crown carried through the successive reorganizations. The commissioners of 1662 normally comprised the lord lieutenant and some leading gentlemen in each county. When the crown appointed a recorder, he was commonly a county potentate: Godolphin, Shrewsbury, Lindsey, Rutland are examples. The charters of the 1680s specifically allowed them to serve by deputy. Sometimes great lords would establish their hold over a town by threatening it with royal displeasure. After the Restoration Lord Gainsborough got Leicester to restore a friend who had been dismissed for royalism to the post of town clerk by threatening to get the King not to renew their charter. In 1676 Lord Huntingdon threatened the town with a quo warranto when his candidate was not elected to parliament.[2] But inducement played as large a part as threats. The paper of 1682 already cited says that towns willing to have a new charter could be given more extensive rights to hold markets and fairs and to try civil cases in their courts. Towns, on the other hand, that went to law in defence of their charters should lose such of their privileges as were 'inconvenient' if the case ended in forfeiture. Towns seem often to have taken a rather earthy attitude to the attack on their liberties and tried to make what they could out of it. At the prospect of a new charter in 1664, Leicester asked among other things for an extra horse market, the right to exclude strangers from the town on the evening of market day, and jurisdiction over neighbouring waste land.[3] Bewdley on surrendering its charter in 1684 asked for a toll of 1*d.* a ton on vessels passing the bridge over the Severn, two extra borough justices and the incorporation of the

[1] CSPD 1682, pp. 214–15.

[2] R. W. Greaves, in *Victoria County History of Leicestershire*, vol. iv (Institute of Historical Research, 1958), pp. 111, 113.

[3] H. Stocks, ed., *Records of the Borough of Leicester*, vol. iv (Cambridge University Press, 1923), pp. 490–1.

tradesmen into two companies.[1] Hull in the same year secured several concessions, including relief from the charge of maintaining banks and walls along the part of the river fronted by the royal garrison.[2]

In this situation the remodelling of the charters took on the forms characteristic of electoral management. Magnates would offer to secure the surrender of charters in order to show the extent of their influence and how useful they could be to the crown: Lord Ferrers, for instance, in the case of Derby.[3] Their agents then got to work on the townsmen, bestowing rewards and promising favours to come. The Earl of Huntingdon, who stage-managed the surrender of Leicester's charter in 1684, had an archdeacon as his agent, Dr. John Geary. He was instructed to hold out the hope of an 'enlargement of privileges' and to draw on the Earl for anything spent on 'wine, letters or other charges'. He duly sent the mayoress a gallon of sack: 'some others did the like' and the surrender was carried by 45 votes to 4. A 'wonderful loyal person' was elected mayor specially to head the delegation to bring the charter to the King: Huntingdon looked after them in London and gave them a feast.[4]

Many towns were prepared to surrender 'considering', as the Lincoln corporation said, 'how much it imports the Government of this Kingdom to have men of known loyalty and approved integrity to bear offices of magistracy and places of trust'.[5] Some of the larger towns were made of sterner stuff. Nine hundred citizens of Norwich petitioned against surrender.[6] Bristol surrendered, but only in 1684, after having once refused.[7] London in the end decided not to surrender. The government had not been eager to go to extremes against it. It was a powerful centre of opposition but it was also a source of loans, even when it was on bad terms with the crown. At the Restoration, the King confirmed its privileges, including the popular election of its aldermen, common council men and leading officials. He merely threatened, in 1662, that he would have to make changes if loyal men were not elected to the common council.[8] The loyal party

---

[1] Styles, pp. 111–13. [2] Tickell, p. 566.

[3] Ogg, *Charles II*, vol. ii, p. 634.

[4] R. W. Greaves, 'The Earl of Huntingdon and the Leicester charter of 1684', *Huntington Library Quarterly*, vol. xv (1951–2), pp. 371–91, esp. 376–9: and *Greaves, Victoria County History of Leicestershire*, vol. iv, pp. 114–16.

[5] Hill, p. 188. [6] Ogg, *Charles II*, vol. ii, p. 634.

[7] CSPD 1683 (i), p. 150; 1683–4, p. 259.

[8] R. R. Sharpe, *London and the Kingdom* (Longmans, 1894–5), vol. ii, p. 398, cf. pp. 394–5, 403.

was expected to gain control by its own efforts. One prop was afforded it by the militia. Normally the militia of a borough was under the control of the neighbouring county lieutenancy and was a further means of giving the gentry a chance to intervene in town affairs.[1] The City had a militia of its own but the commissioners who controlled it were royal nominees. In 1681, when the offensive against the corporations was opening, the militia commissioners were purged and they in turn purged the officers, removing those who were not members of the established church. When the corporation petitioned the King in favour of the frequent sitting of parliament, the lieutenancy presented a counter petition. This was a far cry from the days when the trained bands had fought for parliament against Charles I. In September 1681 Sir John Moore, a tory, was elected mayor after a line of whigs—apparently the citizens were unwilling to break the rule of electing the senior alderman. In 1682, two tory sheriffs were elected, after some very dubiously conducted elections ending in a show of force by the militia. But at the end of the year the loyal party failed to win the common council elections, despite a royal letter being read in each ward requiring the election of such as would conform to the Corporation Act. It was only then that a quo warranto action was begun, although a writ had been taken out a year earlier. When judgment had been given for the King, it was not entered until the citizens had been given a chance to surrender. In July 1683 they decided to do so, but in September they decided that it would be better to await the chance to get the judgment reversed. They were severely punished: the City did not lose its privileges, but it did not get a new charter, and there were no more elections. The king controlled the appointment of the mayor and aldermen and the common council ceased to meet.[2] A lesser town where civic liberty was very visibly extinguished was Poole. Grand juries of Dorset three times protested against its very existence as a borough. They regarded it as a sanctuary of debtors and criminals, dissenting in religion and containing no inhabitants fit to be magistrates. From 1684 it was governed by a body of royal commissioners.[3]

The more general result of this latest and greatest purge of the corporations was the dethroning of whig sympathizers and the infil-

[1] Western, p. 66.
[2] Sharpe, vol. ii, pp. 476–509. Western, pp. 66–8.
[3] CSPD 1683–4, pp. 215, 235.

tration of numerous tory country gentlemen into the municipalities. Indeed, according to Roger North, the demands of the gentry was the origin of the whole movement.[1] There was also greater boldness in tampering with the parliamentary franchise where this was annexed to the freedom of the borough. At Grantham the new mayor admitted his political friends as freemen and thus managed to beat the whig candidates in the parliamentary elections of 1685.[2] In London the livery companies surrendered their charters and the docile aldermen were told to admit only the very loyal to the livery: four leading City tories represented the capital in the 1685 parliament.[3] This great seizure of power was not without its hindrances and embarrassments. At Newcastle the admission of gentry as freemen was not entirely popular even with the loyal: it diminished the town revenue because freemen did not pay certain tolls and it annoyed the sons of gentry who had already become freemen by the orthodox but long and expensive method of serving an apprenticeship.[4] At Leicester the loyal party in the corporation would like to have withdrawn the parliamentary vote from the ratepayers at large but could not because it would have lessened the electoral influence of the neighbouring gentry.[5] Huntingdon for his part wanted the gentry to be able to act as justices in the town, but his parsonical agent warned him that this would foment opposition. 'Country gentlemen having little kindness for tradesmen may come and affront their Mayor and oppose them in all they do.'[6] At Bewdley the gentry had been infiltrating the corporation steadily since the mid-seventies, but whether from sloth or so as not to give offence, they confined their activities to parliamentary elections and did not interfere in the government of the town.[7] This may well have been the pattern elsewhere.

But any limitations there may have been to the process of remodelling the boroughs affected the influence of the gentry not that of the crown. This was shown clearly when James II tried to get a house of commons elected that would co-operate with him in his religious

[1] He cites the case of Poole. *Life of Guilford*, paras. 172, 320.
[2] G. H. Martin, *The Royal Charters of Grantham* (Leicester University Press, 1963), p. 22 n. 34.
[3] Sharpe, pp. 504–5, 509.
[4] CSPD 1686–7, no. 577.
[5] So thinks Greaves, *Victoria County History*, p. 116.
[6] Greaves, 'Huntingdon', p. 389.
[7] Styles, pp. 108–13.

revolution. The tories who had been placed in control of the boroughs would not work with him and so a new purge was began. In 1688 new charters were issued to thirty-five towns, most of which had gone through the same process only a few years before. In ten cases the old charter was disposed of by quo warranto, but in fourteen the first step was the exercise of the new power of removing corporation members—sometimes the entire corporation was removed. In nine cases quo warrantos and removals were used together. The new charters marked a further advance in royal authority. The royal claim to be able to dispense with statutory oaths was written into them, to facilitate the admission of catholics and dissenters. To the power of dismissal there was now added the power to appoint new members to corporations by letters mandatory. No squeamishness was now shown in restricting the parliamentary franchise to the members of the corporation in all cases.[1] Even where there was no new charter, there were incessant removals of corporation members and the appointment of new ones, whatever the crown's strict right in the matter. The objectives in town government which the crown had been pursuing since the Restoration may fairly be said to have been achieved: especially since the abased whigs were now willing, like the tories, to accept the king as the arbiter of power within the corporations. It was the popular leaders who had been ousted by the crown after 1681 who were restored by the prerogative in 1687. Sir Samuel Shorter, for instance, became Lord Mayor of London and in Bewdley a member of a leading whig family, the Soleys, became Recorder. The Bewdley whigs and their national leaders seem to have shown no reluctance after the Revolution in appealing to James II's (1685) charter when it suited their interests: the whig outcry against the new charters in 1689 seems to reflect only the fact that this was the best tactic at that moment for outing their opponents.[2] We shall see that in 1688 even this favourable situation did not allow James to win parliamentary backing for his policy. But that was because it was unwelcome not merely to the tories but to the whigs as well. If the King would but refrain from quarrelling with both at once, he had excellent prospects of achieving a docile parliament by encouraging competition in the country for his favour.

[1] R. H. George, 'The charters granted to English parliamentary corporations in 1688', *English Historical Review*, vol. lv (1940), pp. 47–56.
[2] Sharpe, pp. 476, 523. Styles, pp. 113–17.

(V)

At the start of his reign James managed to assemble a very docile parliament. It was not subservient in everything, but it gave the King the means to go further than his traditional resources would allow by building up his revenues and armed forces on a scale only matched in peacetime during the Interregnum. The repression of opponents and exploitation of the royal powers of appointment and dismissal worked as well with parliament as they did lower down. The upper house was scarcely a problem. Comprising 26 spiritual peers and about 150 temporal lords, its hereditary element of long standing was small enough to be dominated by the nominees of the crown—bishops and new creations. Thus in 1680 the lords had rejected the exclusion bill by the impressive majority of 70 votes to 30. But among temporal peers whose titles dated from before 1642—or from the Restoration years 1660–1, when the King was trying to conciliate all sections of opinion—the numbers were almost equal: 27 against, 24 in favour. The bishops on the other hand voted 14 against and none for and the lords whose titles dated from the Interregnum or the years since 1661 were overwhelmingly against (29 to 6, including royal dukes). Halifax's famous speech was hardly needed to sway a house so obviously composed of King's friends.[1] The only success of the opposition in curbing royal powers of nomination was the exclusion of catholics in 1680.

As for the commons, the elections of 1685 showed how the purges of magistrates and corporations had enhanced royal control. At least fifteen lord lieutenants were active in the elections. Some of these were in charge of several counties and they tried to influence the borough elections within their jurisdiction as well as the choice of county members.[2] The judges too, especially those on circuit, were busy in the campaign—notably Guilford in Suffolk, Jeffreys in Buckinghamshire and Levinz in Hampshire. The influence which the civil and military authorities of the county could exercise on elections, whether by coercion or by the distribution of local patronage, is well attested. Sir Thomas Littleton told the commons in 1678 that

[1] Computations of E. S. de Beer, 'The House of Lords in the parliament of 1680', *Bulletin of Institute of Hist. Research*, vol. xx (1943–5), pp. 22–31.
[2] The main source for what follows is R. H. George, 'Parliamentary Elections and Electioneering in 1685', *Trans. Roy. Hist. Soc.* 4th. ser. vol. xix (1936), pp. 167–95.

every man commanding the militia was a 'Bashaw' in his own county. Lord Townshend's management of elections in Norfolk provoked an address to the commons in 1675 against the long continuance of lord lieutenants and their deputies in office. His successor, and opponent, Lord Yarmouth, seems to have been just as forceful and in 1679 William Windham, with well grounded pessimism, said that 'to oppose an interest set up by the civil and military government of a county will be called faction by some, inconsiderate by others and very improbable to be successful by most'.[1]

This electoral influence was not unreservedly at the crown's disposal because in elections, as in other local affairs, the gentry to whom administrative power had been entrusted did not take kindly to dictation from the centre. In 1685 this prejudice was respected. Lord Sunderland, secretary of state, wrote twenty-six letters to prominent persons (including the lord lieutenants of eleven counties) urging them to attend the elections and help secure the return of 'good members' of 'approved' loyalty. But only in a few cases did he name candidates—this was usually left to local initiative. Lord lieutenants likewise found it advisable not to dragoon their subordinates. The Duke of Norfolk wanted the gentry in his three counties to agree on candidates for the county seats, whom he would then support. The earl of Rutland seems to have done much the same for the county and borough of Leicester.[2] This naturally left rather free play to local feuds within the loyalist ranks. At Lichfield there were four court candidates for the two seats. At Clitheroe, Derby (typically) opposed the nominees of Albemarle and they shared the representation. At Berwick the town was controlled by royal commissioners but they rejected a crown nominee as not royalist enough. Sometimes these disputes could be settled by mediation. A meeting of Shropshire gentry induced one candidate for a county seat to stand down so that they could unite behind two others.[3] The Duke of Norfolk found that in Surrey likewise there were three candidates for two seats. He caused a meeting of gentry to choose two of them by secret ballot and to these he gave his support in the election proper.[4]

With the loyalist party so amorphous, the whigs could not be kept out everywhere. In Hampshire the lord lieutenant and his son were

[1] Jones, 'Norfolk', p. 16, Western, pp. 64–6.   [2] Western, pp. 63–4.
[3] CSPD 1685, no. 427.   [4] Western, p. 63.

suspected of giving them covert support, in a 'cunning, trimming way'.[1] In Warwickshire, 'under the pretence of great loyalty', they sought election in order to be able to 'signify their repentance'. In Buckinghamshire they did quite well. Remarkably, the new charter for the borough of Buckingham named Sir Richard Temple, a leading whig, as recorder and it was his party that carried the day.

All the same, the elections were a disaster for the enemies of the new King and James declared that 'there were not above forty members but such as he himself wished for'. In the boroughs especially, it is evident that remodelling the corporations had placed control of the elections in safe hands. At places like Chippenham, Honiton, Lancaster and Berwick, the return of loyal candidates was ensured by the creation of new freemen—often from outside the town. At Scarborough the corporation claimed for itself the right to elect the members and the mayor arrested for riot a candidate who attempted to poll the freemen. At Sandwich, Pepys and the Governor of Dover were elected by those whom the corporation 'thought fit to own as freemen under the new charter'. The 'old' freemen, who were more numerous, held a separate poll. At St. Albans the new charter arrived just in time for freemen to be created for the election: previously the mayor had fallen back on threatening the opposition with prosecution for riot or (if they were innkeepers) with loss of licences or the quartering of troops upon them. At Reading the opposition candidates were refused the freedom of the town and their request for a poll was denied because they were not freemen.[2] Now that the government was asserting its right to supplant municipal officers at will, there was almost no limit to its power to meddle in elections.

The elections of 1685 were the culmination of the royal drive for greater control over the traditional institutions of government. The crown's new electoral power was used in a statesmanlike way. Local susceptibilities were not outraged and a house of commons was elected that was ultra but not totally subservient. The more knowing observers realized that it would not do the King's bidding in everything. The French ambassador, Barrillon, remarked that 'people believed to be the best disposed often change their opinions when assembled' and Bishop Fell thought that the new members 'if not

[1] CSPD 1685, no. 392.
[2] But the commons disallowed the election.

altered by the genius of the place will be very apt to comply with what is desired of them'. But before a parliamentary mutiny took place, the loyalty of the commons had led them to do so much for the King that he no longer had to worry very much about their dislike of his subsequent proceedings.

4

Royal Financial Independence

THE death of Charles II on 6 February 1685 gave a new impetus to the strengthening of the monarchy. Charles had never taken himself quite seriously as king, for all his determination 'not to go on his travels again'. He was popular but did not inspire awe, he liked intelligent company and disliked being at all under the sway of a powerful minister: he had able servants but kept them always squabbling for his favour. What was worse was his leaning towards extravagance, for the crown could not hope to be independent unless it was solvent. In emulation of Cromwell he fought expensive wars against the Dutch. Even in peacetime he had not been ruthless enough in checking waste. In short, he had been far more successful in preserving himself than in inspiring faith in the permanence of the Restoration.

The new king was far better qualified to do this, at least in the short run. In his youthful exile, while Charles grappled with the miserable burdens of titular kingship, his character had been formed and strengthened by three years' service in the French army under Turenne. This famous warrior James described in 1656 as 'one of the men in the world I am the most obliged to and have the greatest value for'.[1] He was to show his gratitude by making Turenne's not very capable nephew, Louis Duras, Earl of Feversham, the commander-in-chief of his own little army. Well might he say to the French ambassador in 1685 (if only in compliment)

> that he had been brought up in France and had eaten Your Majesty's (Louis xiv's) bread; that his heart was French, that he thought only of making himself worthy of Your Majesty's esteem.[2]

[1] Turner, p. 53. Cf. Turner, pp. 38–42.
[2] C. J. Fox, *A History of the Early Part of the Reign of James II* (1808), appendix p. cxxv. Cf. cv.

After the Restoration he played an important part in building up the army and (especially) the navy and his personality was that of an efficient but not very intelligent regular officer. Even the Jacobite eulogy which concludes his 'official' biography conveys this impression and cannot hide his faults.

> His outward carriage was a little stiff and constrained, which made it not so gracious as it was courteous and obliging . . . in his conversation and arguing, he endeavoured rather to convince with good reason than fine expressions, and having something of a hesitation in his speech, his discourse was not so gracious as it was judicious and solid.

He was brave, industrious and frugal. No 'diversion made him neglect his business, to which he had so great an application that it seemed to be of the number of his diversions too'. Though 'his temper was naturally hot and choleric', he mastered it in old age and even when young 'that fire or vivacitie appeared more in his comportment in the army than in the prosecution of his enemies'. He liked plain, honest dealing and was a poor judge of men

> so that for the time he was upon the throne, he was no less unsuccessful in detecting his enemies than he had been most part of his life in the choice of his friends.[1]

The same features appear in other portraits of him, but less sympathetically presented. Sir John Lauder of Fountainhall said that 'some wise men observed . . . that he had neither great conduct nor a deep reach in affairs but was a silly man'. Bonrepos, a special French envoy to his court, thought that 'he has all the faults of the king his father, but he has less sense and he behaves more haughtily in public'. Roger North wrote that

> so strong were his prejudices and so feeble his genius that he took none to have a right understanding that were not in his measures and that the counsel given him to the contrary was for policy of party more than for friendship to him.[2]

James II viewed politics in a simplistic and grossly materialistic way. There was a struggle between black and white. Anyone who was disobedient was an enemy who must be forcibly crushed. Anyone who was obedient (even venal renegades) was a friend to be cherished. He was implacably severe in the punishment of disaffection, but he

---

[1] See the eulogy that concludes the *Life of James II*, vol. ii, pp. 604–16.
[2] Turner, pp. 211, 235.

encouraged his opponents to recant and could show favour to those who did so.[1] He was entirely blind to the nuances of the whig position during the exclusion crisis. 'I hope now,' he told the Prince of Orange in June 1679,

> not only his majesty's eyes but all the honest men's eyes are opened and see that a commonwealth is what is driven at, and that they will take their measures accordingly ... He has yet the fleet, the garrisons, his guards, Ireland and Scotland firm to him, so that if he will yet stand by himself he may yet be a king, but for all that it cannot be without trouble and hazard; but firmness and good husbandry may carry him through all his difficulties; and I am very apt to believe that whensoever he shews he will be no longer used as he has been, and that they see he will be a king, that there will be a rebellion.[2]

In August 1680 Barrillon, the French ambassador, reported that James was 'persuaded that the royal authority cannot be established except by a civil war'.[3] James warned Charles

> not to imagine those men's good nature would be wrought upon by compliance, which was the fatal rock on which his father miserably split, and which by that means was so visible to him that if he shunned it not, his fall would be unlamented.[4]

Believing that 'nothing but his laying down his crown at their feet will satisfy them',[5] James told his brother not to hope for 'ease and happiness' in surrenders to parliament,

> remembering in what manner they made good to the late king his father that so oft repeated protestation that they would make him the most glorious king in Christendom.[6]

Of course James was here pleading against the sacrifice of himself—but we have seen that this probably was not his main preoccupation.[7]

James acknowledged that in 1680 'the monarchy ... has not vigour enough left to crush those who rise in opposition against it'. For this he blamed those 'who had the management of affairs at the Restoration'. Had 'that opportunity been prudently managed', the

---

[1] *e.g.* Scottish covenanters. Turner, pp. 185–6.

[2] Sir John Dalrymple, *Memoirs of Great Britain and Ireland from the Dissolution of the last Parliament of Charles II* (New ed. 3 vols. 1790), vol. i, Review, pp. 301–2.

[3] Turner, p. 180.

[4] *Life of James II*, vol. i, p. 555.

[5] *Clarendon Correspondence*, vol. i, p. 49.

[6] *Life of James II*, vol. i, p. 614.

[7] Above, p. 35.

crown could have gained so large an income that the 'republicans' would have been left with no weapon against it. Allowing the impeachment of Clarendon (his father-in-law) in 1667 had also been a bad mistake because it taught men to be afraid of parliament.[1] James therefore threw himself into the efforts to make the government strong and independent of popular pressure (especially in financial matters) and at the same time more completely dependent on the monarch's own will. He was far from having the political skill necessary for this great task, but his humdrum good qualities—and even some of his bad qualities—fitted him well for the direction of the mass of day-to-day work that it entailed. His frugality stood him in very good stead—both in running the government and in dealing with parliament. If he was haughty, he was also dignified. The shabby laxity of Charles II's court had not enhanced the prestige of the monarchy. Strict rules of ceremony were enforced at James's court and duelling and drunkenness were discouraged. James's lack of deeper wisdom was not made up for by any capacity to discern it in others and his reliance on unworthy followers was notorious. Halifax said 'that those which belonged to the Duke of York made him mad for there were few among them that had common sense'.[2] Charles deplored his brother's gullibility and contrasted it with the skill of Louis XIV in playing off Colbert and Louvois against each other.[3] But trusting subordinates is administratively sound, though it may sometimes be politically unwise. James tried, as Charles did not, to employ only men he could trust and to keep them marching in step under his direction. When the intelligent, sceptical and independent-minded Halifax was dismissed from the presidency of the council in September 1685—despite his famous part in defeating the exclusion of James from the throne—James said that

> he knew the inconveniences of a divided council and allowing his ministers to have opinions opposed to his own; that the king his brother had been injured by it and that his own conduct would be different.

Barrillon commented that James thought

> that it is even desirable for it to be known that the only way to be in favour at court, to keep his good opinion, is to follow his wishes blindly and have an attachment to his interests that is subject to no qualification or reserve.[4]

---

[1] *Life of James II*, vol. i, pp. 592–3.   [2] Turner, p. 211.
[3] Ailesbury, vol. i, p. 104.   [4] Fox, p. cxxii. Cf. p. cxxv.

Some of the men who rose to power under James II were incapable catholics (such as Dover, Melfort and Father Petre) to whom everything was forgiven on account of their religion but who contributed nothing to the strength of the government. Most of the others were capable but self-effacing administrators who acted on their own initiative only in departmental questions. Reinforcing the administrators were one or two men who were as capable as they but who also had, like the catholics, some personal influence with the King and therefore some voice in matters of broad policy. In 1679 Charles II had tried to appease the opposition by admitting some of their leaders to the privy council. To counterbalance them he appointed Laurence Hyde and Sidney Godolphin to the treasury board and the Earl of Sunderland secretary of state: reliable men but new to high office and so not yet odious to parliament. The 'three chits' emerged after 1681 as the most important political figures. Godolphin, 'never in the way and never out of the way', might almost be ranked with the administrators, but Hyde and Sunderland were imperious and passionate and rather contemptuous of administrative detail. Younger son of the great Clarendon and brother of James's first wife, Hyde not surprisingly was an unflinching supporter of the crown and one of the few who stood by James through the darkest days of the exclusion crisis. Created Earl of Rochester in 1682, it was he who presided over the crucial recovery in the royal finances. Robert Spencer, Earl of Sunderland, was also the son of a royalist, but his father had gone to war reluctantly and died on the field of battle while Robert was still a baby. Sunderland rose by attaching himself to whoever seemed to be the rising star in the court firmament and in spite of his cunning and intelligence he had picked a series of losers. During the exclusion crisis he identified himself with the interests of William of Orange, who in fact though not in law was the next heir after James. In the end both he and Godolphin voted for exclusion and were disgraced. But they wormed their way back into royal favour and in 1684 nearly managed to get Rochester 'exiled' to the lord lieutenancy of Ireland. Rochester was made lord treasurer on the accession of his brother-in-law and the others were almost ruined. But again they crept back, and at the end of 1686 Rochester was dismissed, Godolphin took control at the treasury (under a catholic first lord) and Sunderland established himself as the leading minister.

Sunderland survived because he was useful: he managed the general election of 1685 and he had a great grasp of diplomatic business. He rose to the top because his lack of principles, especially religious principles, enabled him to keep up with the twists in royal policy. Rochester could not shake off his family attachment to the Church of England when that became an encumbrance—nor could he dissociate himself as readily as Sunderland from the interests of William and Mary, for Mary was his niece. He did his best: in 1685, for instance, James decided that his principal officers should accompany him to the chapel door when he went to mass. Sunderland and Godolphin agreed, Rochester refused. Yet he was willing to go if ordered and James of all people had to tell him 'that it should not be an excuse for a thing that was bad in itself, that an order had been got for it'.[1] Sunderland was less hesitant in his subservience. The failure of the whigs seems to have convinced him that the royal power could not and therefore should not be withstood.

> He wondered anybody would be so silly as to dispute with kings; for if they would not take good advice there was no way of dealing with them but by running into their measures till they had ruined themselves.

In 1687 Bonrepos reported that

> the King is well aware of Lord Sunderland's character, that he is ambitious and capable of any sacrifice for ambition's sake; but though he has no great confidence in him he makes use of him because he is more devoted to him than others and because he unhesitatingly falls in with all his plans for the establishment of the catholic religion—though for himself he professes no faith at all and speaks very loosely about it.[2]

The administrators who kept the central government moving played a vital part in the strengthening of royal control. In government offices—as in the law courts to which they were still closely linked and as in local administration—business was carried on in the king's name, but the officials had become a privileged body who expected to be left to their own devices. Appointments for life were common, offices were looked on as a form of property and even became hereditary. At the same time, officials were increasingly bound by office custom and precedent, which governed their actions often to the exclusion of royal commands. Monarchical govern-

---

[1] Fox, pp. lxiii, lxiv.
[2] J. P. Kenyon, *Robert Spencer, Earl of Sunderland, 1641–1702* (Longmans, 1958), pp. 84, 155.

ment could not be a reality if this tendency was not checked. At worst it could even weaken the loyalty of administrators. In 1642 officials in those organs of government which had long been exempt from effective royal supervision seem to have been slightly less likely than the rest to adhere to the King.[1] Inefficiency and corruption were likely to result at all times. The exchequer was a ripe example in the Restoration period, with families entrenched in it like the Walkers, who had been ushers since the twelfth century, and the Fanshawes and Osborns who had been remembrancers since the mid-sixteenth. A securely entrenched official would appoint a few clerks to do his work and if he or they feathered their nests outrageously, he could not be dismissed from his office because it was looked on as his property. All depended on the system throwing up a few able and honest men.[2]

Reform of old-established offices was not completely impossible. In the middle period of Charles II's reign there was a trend away from appointments for life towards appointment during pleasure.[3] This made for servile judges but it may have made for better administrators. Another way of increasing efficiency was to substitute good salaries for the system of fees and perquisites, as had been done during the Interregnum. James II once said that a good salary could make officials

> value their employments and not subject them to a necessity of base compliances with others to the King's prejudice, by which to get one shilling to himself he must lose ten to the king . . .[4]

This principle was fruitfully applied in the excise and in various other cases, as when Pepys coupled a stern prohibition of private trading by naval vessels with an increase in the pay of their commanders.[5] But there was not money enough to do it generally. Mostly the crown had to rely on men who eagerly sought the traditional rewards of office

---

[1] G. E. Aylmer, *The King's Servants: the Civil Service of Charles I 1625–1642* (Routledge and Kegan Paul, 1961), pp. 405–12.

[2] S. B. Baxter, *The Development of the Treasury 1660–1702* (Longmans, 1957), esp. pp. 124–5, 139–40, 165.

[3] G. E. Aylmer, 'Place Bills and the Separation of Powers: Some Seventeenth-Century Origins of the "Non-political" Civil Service', *Transactions of the Royal Historical Society*, 5th series vol. xv (1965), p. 60.

[4] In 1667. J. R. Tanner, *Samuel Pepys and the Royal Navy* (Cambridge University Press, 1920), p. 41.

[5] In 1686. Tanner, pp. 72–3.

but were interested in the work as well: greedy pluralists yet zealous and able public servants. They made their way into established offices but often began and did much of their work as mere clerks of the regular officials. Here and there a little cluster of such clerks would be found which constituted the nucleus of a later great department of state. Several such secretariats grew up after the Restoration and they controlled or sidestepped, or even supplanted, old-established officials. This no doubt was held to be more practical than radical reform, but it had the drawback that the new administrative élite was out for the same sort of rewards as the old and exposed to the same temptations.

When James II dismissed Rochester from the treasurer-ship in 1686 he did so on the grounds that the charge was too great for one man. It is possible that there was a conscious desire to suppress great offices in order to place power in the hands of more pliable secondary figures; this is what Louis XIV did. But although this process was going forward, it would seem to have been as much by accident as by design. The periods when there were commissioners instead of a lord treasurer (1667–72, 1679–85, 1687 onward) were certainly periods when the treasury clerks developed more corporate identity and their office more formal organization: this was necessary in the absence of a personal head, which further enabled the secretary who headed the office (Sir George Downing in the first period, Henry Guy in the others) to become a powerful subordinate minister. The secretary at war advanced in a similar way. This office dated only from the civil war period and its holder was at first only the administrative arm of the general commanding the forces. There was really no such commander after the death of Monck (1670), though Monmouth had the title of General from 1674 to 1679, and so the secretary became responsible for routine administration. The secretary of the admiralty (Pepys) rose in just the same way, but certainly not entirely by royal desire. James, as Duke of York, had been made lord high admiral but had to resign because of the Test Act of 1673. Charles resumed some of the admiral's functions himself and for the rest appointed a commission of great officers of state to which Pepys was made secretary. This system was swept away in the crisis of 1679 and a commission of parliamentarians took over. But in 1684 James was restored in all but name as admiral and as king he kept the office in his own hand. Pepys was restored too as secretary and he was virtually minister of marine. Things were much simpler in the colonial field, for here there was no old great officer to displace: Robert Southwell and William Blathwayt built up a little secretariat for colonial business, initially under privy council direction. Lastly, there was one class of great officer that was not displaced (either in England or in France)—the secretaries of state who were traditionally the vehicles of the royal will. But the growing importance of their personal staffs is reflected in the fact that soon after 1680 their chief clerks came to be referred to as under-secretaries.[1]

The smallness of these secretariats must be stressed. The treasury in the eighties had five senior clerks and possibly four under clerks, with a domestic staff of eight. The board had a room next to the royal bathroom, which in 1683 was taken over to house the clerks![2] In 1684 Lord Middleton, secretary of state, had six clerks.[3] Blathwayt had three or four clerks in the plantation office and seems initially to have had only one in the war office.[4] In 1685 Pepys moved the admiralty into his own private dwelling by the river, and in 1689 Blathwayt in like manner was to bring the war office into Little Wallingford House which he had rented from the new king: other cases of this kind might be quoted. Even at that time, the country could not be run by this bare handful of men: their task was one of creative inspection, introducing new methods, making an orderly record and keeping the host of subordinate officials in the capital and the provinces up to the mark.

The members of this chosen band were often, fittingly enough, men of wide intellectual interests and thoroughly at home in the cultivated society of the capital. The expansive and expensive tastes of Samuel Pepys are well known. President of the Royal Society from 1685, avid collector of books and manuscripts, aspiring to write a history of the navy, he was also said to have the best harpsichord in England. Sent to help wind up the Tangier garrison, he took time off to visit Spain and enquire into its trade, administration, superstitions and mapmaking. But in much of this he was not exceptional and may well have been inspired by the example of older officials like Thomas

---

[1] F. M. G. Evans, *The Principal Secretary of State, 1558–1680* (Manchester University Press, 1923), p. 164 and n. 2. M. A. Thomson, *The Secretaries of State 1681–1782* (Oxford University Press, 1932), p. 129 n. 1.

[2] Baxter, pp. 19, 214–16.   [3] Evans, pp. 192–3.

[4] G. A. Jacobsen, *William Blathwayt, a late seventeenth-century English administrator* (Yale Historical Publications, 1932), pp. 407–8.

Povey, in whose company he met painters and virtuosi in the sixties and whose 'bath at the top of his house, good pictures and his manner of eating and drinking do surpass all that ever I did see of one man in all my life'. Sir Joseph Williamson, chief assistant and ultimate successor to Secretary Arlington, was an ardent bibliophile and when Blathwayt was posted to The Hague embassy as a young man, Williamson kept him hard at work searching for books, maps and medals. Blathwayt himself, who was an excellent linguist, developed the same tastes and in due course he too set subordinates rummaging in Dutch bookshops.[1] 'Political arithmetic' and in general the scholarly study of social questions which developed so much at this time were largely in the hands of men who were or had been government servants: Sir William Petty, Charles Davenant, Gregory King, William Lowndes.

Interested in the broader setting of their work, the best officials were also devoted clerks. They did a great deal of writing themselves and took care to follow the minutiae which might have been left to subordinates.[2] They started systematic records of letters sent, decisions taken, sometimes of the office routine: this gave their little offices a corporate character, with traditions and precedents that would outlast them and in some cases become eventually a new bar to efficiency. It was perhaps as well that they sometimes lapsed: Pepys took his records with him when he retired, and Williamson, who bought the life-keepership of the state papers in 1661, let these records of the secretaries of state get into such a mess that important treaties were missing and nothing could be found for want of a catalogue.[3] Yet despite these lapses there was a real pride in work accomplished and so the traditions founded were good traditions. Their almost puritanical attitude to business appears in Pepys' remarks to Lord Dartmonth, commanding the fleet in 1688, occasioned by the absence of a captain without leave

> I will have all the world to know that, as considerable as it takes the profit of my employment to be, and indeed by the King's favour it is, it should not, were it ten times greater, purchase my staying in it one day longer than I can see his service thrive as well as I.[4]

[1] Jacobsen, pp. 82, 198–9.
[2] See especially Jacobsen, pp. 413–14; A. Bryant, *Samuel Pepys—The Saviour of the Navy* (Reprint Society ed., 1953), p. 152.
[3] Jacobsen, pp. 26–7.   [4] Bryant, *Saviour*, p. 214.

Behind this administrative enterprise there is undoubtedly to be found an admiration for the France of Louis XIV. To some extent the problems of all the European monarchs were the same and in their solution Louis seemed to lead the way. Blathwayt strongly recommended

> one course which the king of France observes strictly in his plantations, and it is to give very large appointments to the governors out of his own coffers, not allowing them any perquisites or to draw any advantages or profits from the inhabitants.

When he became secretary at war, he asked the ambassador in Paris to send him all the printed or manuscript material he could obtain relating to the French army. He made extracts relating to his own office and later wished to study the regulations of the Invalides as a model for Chelsea Hospital. When Monmouth was dismissed from command of the army, James said with satisfaction that a secretary of state would now 'manage' it 'as M. de Louvois does in France'. Ambassador Montagu had already invoked this example in urging Arlington to assert his rights on the death of Monck. But though Charles Davenant expressed admiration of Richelieu who 'was eminent above the rest; he neglected no part of government; raising money was not his only care', most officials were content to limit themselves to the affairs of particular departments and leave high politics alone. Their importance in the political system varied widely. Some were (or had to be) content with a humble position where they had the honour of doing all the work. Such was William Bridgeman, a senior clerk in secretary of states' offices for over twenty years, who served Sunderland before the Revolution and Shrewsbury after it: two noblemen who agreed, whatever their dissimilarities, in shunning office routine.[1] Other officials rose to the very top but without ceasing to be officials, carrying out without question whatever orders they were given. This was the position of most of James's ministers (Secretary Middleton, for instance, or Lord Chancellor Jeffreys) but also of Sir Joseph Williamson or Sir Leoline Jenkins as secretaries of state to Charles II or Blathwayt when he acted as secretary of state to William III. Others again did not rise so high but exercised real power or influence in the fields in which they were experts: Pepys at the admiralty, for instance, or William Lowndes later as secretary of

---

[1] For the foregoing see Jacobsen, pp. 17, 99, 100, 212, 223–4; Evans, Thomson, index, s.v. Bridgeman.

the treasury (1695–1724). All these more eminent men, it may be noted, sat in parliament. But the contenders for real political power were normally men who outclassed the administrators in family connections and in influence either at court or in parliament and the country or both. There were hybrid types like Henry Guy, secretary of the treasury from 1679 to 1695 with a break in 1689–91. He was a political figure of some importance and he had worked his way up through various revenue posts and so was something of an administrator. But he had capital (he was a tax-farmer) and he became a friend of Charles II.[1] Administration alone would not have brought him so far.

The 'French' ideas of the administrators did not therefore necessarily make them partisans of despotism. Coupled with the administrators' lack of political influence, they meant rather that the officials would obediently serve whoever was in power. We shall see them loyally if sometimes reluctantly serving James but then, when he fled, reluctantly but firmly transferring their loyalty to William. Exactly the same was true of the 'chits', who all rallied to the new king, though characteristically Rochester was the least willing to have anything to do with him and he did not care for Rochester but got on well with the others. James's minions made the government stronger, but their ethos of order and obedience made it easier for a strong man to seize power by a coup d'état: this is an essential part of the story of 1688.

(II)

The first and greatest of the achievements of James's reign was the winning of financial independence. This had hitherto eluded English rulers in the seventeenth century, with repeatedly disastrous consequences. But the increase in economic activity was making an improvement possible, the beginnings of which go back to the civil wars. The development of trade and industry made it easier to raise taxes and easier also to devise taxes that did not fall directly on the owners of land and so were less likely to meet insurmountable opposition in parliament, where large landowners predominated. The customs had long been increasing in importance as a source of crown revenue. During the civil wars both sides levied excise duties. These were bitterly unpopular, especially when they fell on the neces-

[1] Baxter, *Treasury*, pp. 190–4.

sities of life, but proved indispensable in supporting the war effort—
particularly because they were an easy means of taxing individuals
and even districts that refused obedience to the authority imposing
them. Excise duties did not end with the war but in one form or
another have gone on ever since. At the Restoration, Parliament
sought to give Charles II an annual income of 1,200,000*l*.: a third of
this was to come from the excise and another third from the customs.
The only important direct tax on property was the 'hearth tax' or
'chimney money', which was expected to bring in less than half as
much as the excise. Despite the exemption of the poor, it was a
regressive tax and very unpopular and hard to collect. The abolition
of military tenures extinguished the fiscal burdens of wardship
which had been borne by the larger landowners. Half the excise was
intended as compensation for this and was voted to the crown in
perpetuity: thus the general body of consumers paid for the emancipation of their betters. Not too much should be made of this: the
feudal revenues given up amounted to only 100,000*l*. or about one-
twelfth of the annual revenue now agreed on all hands to be necessary for the crown. But it does appear to embody the fiscal philosophy
of the Restoration. The ordinary expenses of government were to be
met by indirect taxes falling on the general body of consumers.
Taxes on property—such as the Monthly Assessments of the civil
wars period or Ship Money before 1640—were to be imposed only
to meet extraordinary expenditure, that is to say primarily in wartime.

Charles II at first was in great financial difficulties: not only because
of extravagance, wars and unavoidable debts but also because trade
was bad and the taxes did not bring in as much as parliament expected them to. But by the eighties the situation had improved in
various ways. Trade had greatly increased. Professor Ralph Davis
has calculated that between the sixties and the end of the century,
exports and re-exports rose from 4·1 to 6·4 million *l*. annually and
imports from 4·4 to 5·85 millions. He believes that the main period of
growth was from 1677 to 1688 (when western Europe was mostly at
peace) and that the peak of activity was reached at the end of this
period and not reached again until the last years of the century,
owing to the disruptive effects of King William's war.[1] The growth in

[1] R. Davis, 'English foreign trade, 1660–1700', *Economic History Review*, 2nd series
vol. vii (1954–5), pp. 160–1.

imports and re-exports of tropical and colonial produce was the mainstay of this expansion. Characterized by falling prices and rising consumption, the trade in these products was well able to bear taxation. Sugar imports to London rose from 143,000 cwt a year in the sixties to 371,000 cwt at the end of the century and the price halved between 1630 and 1680. Virginia and Maryland exported 7,000,000 lb of tobacco in 1662–3 and 12,000,000 lb in the late eighties. The retail price per lb had fallen from 20 to 40s. before 1619 to 1s. in 1670 and the customs duty of 2d. per lb on colonial tobacco was over 100% of its sale price on the plantation. The import of calicoes, almost unknown until the Restoration, averaged 240,000 in the sixties and 861,000 a year at the end of the century. These commodities accounted for two-thirds of English imports from outside Europe and almost two-thirds of English re-exports to Europe.[1]

Agriculture does not seem to have prospered as much as trade, though lack of evidence and variations between commodities and districts make it hard to generalize. It seems likely that production was tending to rise faster than population, with a tendency in consequence towards falling prices, especially in the case of grain. Rents in some areas at least were stationary or tending downward. One student of the period speaks of a shift of the 'terms of trade' in favour of industry, *i.e.* more farm produce was now needed to buy a given quantity of manufactures and imports.[2] This situation may well have intensified the chronic suspicion with which the squires viewed the towns and great capitalists and helped to ensure that parliament took advantage of the opportunity to increase the revenue from trade. The prevailing economic ideas of the time worked in the same direction: the desire to protect native commerce, damage its foreign competitors and improve the balance of payments by restricting imports and discouraging the consumption of luxuries.

Of course gentry and merchants were all members of a single economic system and it was not really possible to tax one sector

[1] Davis, *loc. cit.*, pp. 151–3, 157.

[2] A. H. John, 'The Course of Agricultural Change', *Studies in the Industrial Revolution*, ed. L. S. Pressnell (Athlone Press, 1960), pp. 150–2. Although concerned with a longer-term trend, he seems to regard the 1680s as a bad time. Rents apparently were falling in Kent, tending to fall in Wiltshire and rising in the midlands in the period 1660–90; cf. C. W. Chalklin, *Seventeenth Century Kent* (Longmans, 1965), p. 65); E. Kerridge, 'Agriculture 1500–1793', *Victoria County History of Wiltshire*, vol. iv (Institute of Historical Research, 1959), p. 62; H. J. Habakkuk, 'English Landownership, 1680–1740', *Economic History Review* 1st ser. vol. x (1940), p. 13.

without any loss to the others. This objection was made to the various plans for a special tax on London and it was evident to all in the case of the excise. The most productive duties were those on ale and beer: an essential item of diet in those days and the source at one remove of a large part of the earnings from agriculture. In 1670 Sir Nicholas Carew told the commons that 'whatever excise you lay upon malt is an absolute land-tax' and Attorney-General Finch went so far as to say that 'everything by consequence is a landtax'.[1] In 1695 Charles Davenant, who had been one of James II's excise commissioners, remarked that many liberal-minded people feared that the excise might be the subject of an infamous bargain between crown and gentry.

> They say, land-taxes, polls, and customs lie so heavy upon the men of interest and figure in the nation that by such kind of impositions the gentlemen of England will never enable a king to live without a parliament.
> But excises being an easy way of contributing, insensibly paid and falling chiefly upon the common sort, they apprehend our representatives may some time or other, by the arts and power of the court, be prevailed upon to let them pass into a lasting supply to the crown, and they think so large a revenue would make the prince absolutely independent of his people . . .

(This of course relates to the greatly augmented excises resulting from King William's war.) Davenant conceded that

> some of our former princes have had designs to enslave this country, partly led into those measures by the gentry's flattery and corruption of their manners, who have been all along willing enough to traffic the people's rights.

But he did not think that the gentry would ever like the excise.

> All taxes whatsoever are in their last resort a charge upon land; and though excises will affect land in no degree like taxes that charge it directly, yet excises will always lie so heavily upon the landed men as to make them concerned in parliament to continue such duties no longer than the necessity of the war continues.

He felt obliged in fact to try and prove to the gentry that they would not suffer by the policy he advocated of relying more on excise and less on customs duties: the latter increased a gentleman's expenditure as seriously as the former reduced his income.[2]

[1] Grey, vol. i, pp. 273–4.
[2] *An Essay upon Ways and Means of supplying the War*, Works (reprint, Gregg Press, 1967), vol. i, pp. 31, 75–7.

It is certainly true that the gentry showed no eagerness before 1688 to increase the excise: there was only a temporary increase, from 1672 to 1680. It is also true that the excise was bitterly unpopular:

I wish long life may him befall
And not one good day therewithal,
And hell fire after this life here
Who first did raise this tax on beer.[1]

But the hope was never abandoned of so levying the taxes that they fell on the undeserving and spared the rest. The excise took in certain imported commodities, with the idea of making the foreigner pay.[2] There was also a belief that it could be compensated for by price controls, which would curb excessive profits of middlemen.[3] The beer tax was levied on the brewer and home brewing was exempt. This may have done something to hold down prices and it also favoured the substantial farmer or landowner, who brewed at home, and penalized the substantial capitalists with large breweries who at this very time were increasingly taking over the production of beer for sale.[4] It was only the land tax which the landowners were not in a position to shift,[5] and when it was mooted the response was not just aversion but panic. In 1670 Sir William Coventry told the commons that 'whoever would make a difference between the king and kingdom, such is he that moves for land tax'. Sir Nicholas Carew said that for the last land tax 'the poor woman turned her purse strings wrong side outwards'. Garroway called the land tax 'a mark of our chains'. Colonel Birch believed 'that day you give land-tax, you will sink land two years' value' and thought that they would take twenty years to recover from the 'wounds' already given.[6]

The country gentlemen in parliament might be persuaded to vote more taxes provided that the land was spared and provided that the political objections were not too great. Already in the early seventies, parliament had been willing to improve Charles II's ordinary revenue by extra duties on wine, vinegar, brandy and tobacco. Most of these

---

[1] But this was before the Restoration: E. Hughes, *Studies in Administration and Finance 1558–1825* (Manchester University Press, 1934), p. 122.

[2] Or colonist or capitalist. Coffee, chocolate, sherbet, tea.

[3] Davenant, *op. cit.*, p. 64; cf. Hughes, pp. 124–5.

[4] C. Wilson, *England's Apprenticeship, 1603–1763* (Longman's, 1965), pp. 199–200.

[5] But in the mid-eighteenth century landowners were able to make their tenants pay the tax.

[6] Grey, vol. i, pp. 314–16.

expired during the great struggle between Charles and Shaftesbury. Not surprisingly, parliament failed to renew them and it also damaged the customs revenue by prohibiting the import of certain French goods. In December 1680 an attempt was made to reach a financial compromise between king and parliament. Charles afterwards said that he would have given his assent to the exclusion bill if he could have got better terms.[1] As a bargain could not be made, Charles had to accept a loss of income and was further faced with a commons' resolution that anyone lending money on the security of the customs, excise or hearth tax 'shall be adjudged to hinder the sitting of parliaments and shall be responsible for the same in parliament'.[2] He just managed to make ends meet and thus the financial factor was crucial in the outcome of the exclusion crisis and the defeat of the whigs.

Charles's financial survival was partly due to the expansion of trade which kept the revenue buoyant, partly to a policy of peace at any price and the acceptance of growing French superiority in Europe. If old Lord Ailesbury is to be believed, Charles had forsworn foreign adventures for good, seeing at last that this was the way to keep peace at home.

I will have no more parliaments unless it be for some necessary acts to be passed that are temporary only, or to make new ones for the general good of the nation for God be praised my affairs are in so good a posture that I have no occasion to ask for supplies

. . . . .

I would have everyone live under his own vine and fig tree. Give me my just prerogative, and for subsidies I will never ask more unless I and the nation should be so unhappy as to have a war on our hands, and that at most may be one summer's business at sea.[3]

But better management of ordinary income and expenditure was essential. Payment of pensions and salaries had to be suspended for a time in 1681,[4] the costly garrison of Tangier was withdrawn in 1683. The influence of the frugal James was already great in his brother's last years. He used it to promote 'measures of vigour' and 'good husbandry'.[5] Though Charles had been feckless, some of his servants

[1] S. B. Baxter, *William III* (Longmans, 1966), pp. 173, 425, n. 37.
[2] Hughes, p. 154.
[3] Ailesbury, vol. i, pp. 21, 97.
[4] The last but not the first suspension of the reign. CTB 1681–5, pp. xxvi, xxvii.
[5] See *Life of James II*, vol. i, p. 661.

had long been working to improve the financial administration. Under the patronage of James (before and after his accession) they came into their own.

The treasury began its emergence at this time as a powerful watchdog of both revenue and expenditure. The lord treasurer, his secretary and the chancellor of the exchequer, were all important officials even at the Restoration and the treasurer's power in financial matters was in theory very great. But Lord Treasurer Southampton allowed his authority to be usurped and it was only after his death (1667) that the energetic body of commissioners to whom his office was entrusted began to make the most of its powers. An order in council of 1668, besides laying down that all appointments of revenue officers were to be by their recommendation, directed that they were to sanction the issues of money for departmental expenditure and report on requests for gifts and pensions. Control over the revenue-collecting agencies was centralized in their hands and they were also given power over the revenues of Ireland. This order was so important that it was hung up on a board in the treasury chamber. Attempts were also made by order in council to determine in advance the expenditure of the revenue for the coming year to produce something like a balanced budget. A scheme of this kind for 1676 could be altered by simple royal order to the lord treasurer, which meant that the treasury rather than the council was to exercise budgetary control. In 1676 also it was laid down that departments must have treasury permission to spend the money that they had received. The commissioners of 1667 called for weekly accounts of revenue received, money spent and what remained in the exchequer. As there was never enough to meet all the expenditure sanctioned, the treasury had each week to suggest how the money should be shared out. The treasury also tried to control such things as building projects and contracts for naval stores: the lord treasurer appointed his own inspector of stores and dockyard wages in 1677.

In all this work the treasury—lord treasurer or commissioners, as the case might be—had to go on fighting the other departments, not to speak of individuals, who wanted financial autonomy or just more money. Nothing could be accomplished without firm royal support and an end to royal grants behind the treasury's back. In 1669 and 1672 there were attempts to get the king to meet the treasury board once a week to sanction the distribution of available money and adjudicate between them and the spending departments (especially the navy). The unbusinesslike Charles II did not keep to this arrangement, but it is likely, though not certain, that the frugal James did have a weekly meeting with treasury officials. In James's reign treasury control was extended to the few sources of royal revenue hitherto free from it—such as those given to James as Duke of York—and in 1686 there was a reissue of an order in council of 1679–80 requiring all expenditures in excess of an establishment to be sanctioned by the treasurer. Since 1676, secret service funds had been paid out by the secretary to the treasury and so this department became virtually the sole channel for sanctioning expenditure.[1] Both a frugal king and an active treasury were needed to achieve the rough balance between revenue and expenditure characteristic of James's reign.

The collection of the revenue was a hard task in view of the unpopularity and comparative novelty of the taxes. If the royal judges at Westminster and on assize could be relied on to enforce the law, local juries or justices could not. Regular troops could occasionally be used in support, as in the well-known case of suppressing tobacco cultivation, but this was so reminiscent of Cromwell that the authorities dared not do it much.[2] The local militia was as unreliable in this field as the justices: at Hereford some of the militia actually joined in resistance to the hearth tax in 1666.[3] For the collection as well as the voting of the taxes, therefore, it was well that economic conditions made them not too onerous to pay. Customs and excise yielded badly in the sixties but never as badly as the regular direct tax, the hearth tax, and thereafter rising trade and more efficient collection combined to improve the yield. Farming was at first the rule for the permanent taxes but in 1671 the farming of the customs was abandoned in favour of direct collection. The remaining farmers were more and more closely supervised in the years that followed and direct collection was substituted for the excise in 1683 and for the hearth tax in 1684. There had long been a royal customs administration—the system of farming had simply been superimposed on it. There had been ample time for abuses and blocks to efficiency to grow up in the service—such as the office of Patent Customer in the several ports, the holders of which were absentees who executed their duties

---

[1] Baxter, *Treasury*, chaps. i–iv.
[2] *ibid.*, pp. 79–82.   [3] Western, p. 72.

through ill-paid and therefore corruptible deputies.[1] The treasury strove for efficiency and in 1684 ordered that all promotions in the customs service should go by merit.

The excise by contrast was a new tax and the collecting organization, which drew upon the best methods and men that had emerged under the farmers, was perhaps the most efficient state department. Headed like the customs service by a board of commissioners, it was staffed on principles far more characteristic of the nineteenth century than of the seventeenth. The excise officers were a conspicuous exception to the prevailing rule that officials were largely paid by fees and gratuities (licit and illicit) levied on the public. 'Their salary will be very good that they may be encouraged to do their duty well and unwilling to lose their places.' They were not allowed to hold other jobs outside the excise service. They were forbidden to serve in their place of birth and they were often moved from one place to another, to prevent their becoming too friendly with the local brewers. There was something approaching a system of apprenticeship to train new entrants in the 'art' of the exciseman—particularly the 'gauging' of beer at the brewery—and in 1686 a modest contributory pension scheme was started to provide for retirement after a life spent in this new profession. Commissioner Davenant confidently wrote that 'it may be presumed men of integrity and skill will act with as much vigour for the king as for themselves'.[2] The exciseman was certainly a much more reliable instrument of the monarchical state than the old type of fee-paid official, whose office was looked on as a piece of property. An even more striking contrast was with the collection of land taxes when parliament resolved to meet extraordinary expenditure in this way: it was left to amateur part-time officials in parish and county and the king was very heavily dependent on public goodwill.

Even when receipts and expenses roughly balanced, government finance remained a completely hand-to-mouth affair. There was no reserve to cover emergencies or failure of the revenue to come in at the time when payments had to be made. The banking system was still in its infancy and only the most primitive forms of short-term credit were available to bridge the gap. Government creditors had to

[1] On the customs, Baxter, *Treasury*, pp. 88–96. There were political purges in 1682 1687, 1689.
[2] Hughes, pp. 160–3, 211 n. 898.

wait for their money, or else they were given promises to pay which they sold at a discount to speculators with money to lend. To make matters worse, payments were usually ordered to be made out of a specific fund—customs, excise or what not. Money was only to be had when that fund was in credit and powerful creditors saw to it that they were assigned payment on some fruitful fund, leaving only the more uncertain revenues for the payment of poor tradesmen and the like. After the Restoration, Charles II had relied heavily on loans from goldsmiths (bankers) to bring more ready money into the system and tax-farming, with the system of large advance payments, was valued largely because it was a form of borrowing on the security of the taxes. During the sixties the treasury was trying to bring in changes which eventually, after the Revolution, were to give England a really strong financial system. Payment 'in course' from the exchequer was instituted: that is to say, creditors were paid in the order in which debts were contracted, instead of the more influential being paid first. This was not only fairer but it made the general public willing to consider advancing money to the exchequer. Still more so did Sir George Downing's innovation of 1665, when he induced parliament to appropriate the proceeds of an aid to paying for the Dutch war and to repaying loans contracted for this purpose. This device of a tax pledged by parliament as security for a loan was used in 1685 to raise the money to fight Monmouth and it became standard practice under William III. Downing's idea was that the public should lend to the exchequer and be able, at need, to sell the orders for repayment which would circulate as short-term government securities. The system worked fairly well when parliament fixed the amount to be borrowed but not when the royal officials tried to work it on their own authority without that restraint. In 1672 the government had to admit that it had overborrowed and the stop of the exchequer forcibly converted short-term debts of two millions into a long-term debt. Interest was paid on it but not very regularly, and the capital was never fully paid back.[1]

The subsequent striving towards solvency brought with it a slow reduction of indebtedness and restoration of the government's credit-worthiness: in 1680 Godolphin could make the rather modest claim that it was as good as a private person's. The ending of farming in-

[1] P. G. M. Dickson, *The Financial Revolution in England* (Macmillan, 1967), pp. 44–5.

volved some lessening of the abuse whereby receivers of government money kept it in their own hands and speculated with it instead of paying it into the exchequer:[1] this must have lessened the government's own need for credit. That the need was still pressing is shown by the curious anomaly that high officials of the financial administration were required on appointment to make substantial loans to the government, almost as if they were farmers. In 1683 three members of the new excise board advanced 30,000*l*., to be repaid in a year, and the same sum was lent by Lord Godolphin, then a lord of the treasury. The continued mixture of finance and administration did not promote efficiency and loyalty: this can be seen in the case of Charles Duncombe who was a thorn in the side of both James II and William III. Duncombe and Richard Kent had been appointed treasurers of the customs in 1677 and in 1679 they lent 160,469*l*. to the king. In 1683, Duncombe succeeded Kent as cashier of the excise and lent 20,000*l*.; at the death of Charles II he was owed 390,000*l*. In 1688 he demanded repayment of outstanding loans, refused to advance money for James's flight and was the first man to lend money to William when he took provisional charge of the government. James specially exempted him from a general pardon issued in 1692.[2]

It was when the crown was almost solvent but had nothing in hand that the prospect of financial help from Louis XIV was so attractive to the English kings. French subsidies never amounted to very much but they provided a reserve to cover emergencies. When Charles adopted a policy of peace at any price, it was of European importance as will be explained later. It was in the interest of Louis XIV that this policy should continue. But in subsidizing the English monarchy his purpose was not so much to strengthen it as to counter the growth of anti-French feeling in England. He was not therefore very generous. In the early seventies there had been a real alliance between the two crowns against the Dutch, and France paid England 8 million livres (over half a million sterling) for war expenses. But under parliamentary pressure, Charles II made peace with the Dutch in 1674 and Louis does not seem to have taken him seriously as a possible ally after that. He gave him a modest 1½ million livres in 1676 as a reward for proroguing parliament for fifteen months: this

---

[1] Hughes, pp. 150–5. For the continuance of the evil in the exchequer see Baxter, *Treasury*, pp. 157–164.

[2] Hughes, pp. 155 n. 635, 164–6; for his career in the nineties, pp. 173–4.

both muzzled anti-French opinion and kept England weak since only parliamentary votes could provide enough money for military preparations. But further extravagant requests for money by Charles came to nothing, especially since peace was established on the continent in 1678, leaving Louis so powerful that he cared less what England did. At the end of 1680, however, it seemed that Shaftesbury's great attack on Charles might end in a regency for William of Orange, Louis's great enemy. So Louis was again willing to offer Charles money just when Charles was most in need of it. By the secret agreement of 1681 Charles promised to call no more parliaments in return for a subsidy of 2 million livres in the first year and $1\frac{1}{2}$ million in each of the two following years: upwards, that is, of 100,000*l*. a year.[1] Louis was sure of continued English inactivity during that time and Charles had something that helped him keep afloat while financial reorganization was taking effect.

When James II came to the throne, he very soon advanced from a precarious financial equilibrium to the achievement of a solid balance in his own favour. His first care was to establish a position of strength from which to bargain with the parliament that he proposed to call. He gave a highly sinister significance to the improved system of revenue collection by ordering that the customs and excise duties should continue to be paid even though parliament had granted the bulk of them only for his brother's lifetime. Collection of customs revenues without parliamentary sanction had been a practice of James I and Charles I to which the Long Parliament no doubt thought it had put a stop by the Tonnage and Poundage Act of 1641.[2] But the intermission of the duties would have disrupted trade: cheap Dutch goods would have flooded the market and merchants who had already paid duty would not have been able to dispose of their stocks. So uneasy were the authorities as to the legal position that the treasury and customs boards each tried to place on the other the responsibility of deciding what could lawfully be done; the customs commissioners refused to act and Lord Keeper Guilford suggested collecting the dues but not spending the money. But for the reasons explained the merchants, even those thought to be 'fanatical', were

---

[1] C. L. Grose, 'Louis XIV's Financial Relations with Charles II and the English Parliament', *Jol. of Modern History*, vol. i (1929), pp. 177–204. He makes a *l.* sterling = 12 to 15 livres.

[2] 16 Car. I cap. 8, sect i.

willing to pay. The case of the excise is more interesting. The act granting it to Charles II had sanctioned the farming of it for up to three years. 'Most fortunately,' as a correspondent of the Duke of Ormonde put it, a three-year farm contract had been signed the day before Charles died. The government contended that the contract remained in force in spite of the King's death before its expiry: farmers paid a large part of their rent in advance and they could not be expected to do so unless they were sure of being able to collect the duties for the full three years. The judges upheld the validity of the contract. What makes the affair sinister is that farming the excise had been abandoned, as we have seen, in 1683. The three 'farmers' of 1685 were all servants of James before his accession. The excise board appointed (with little change of personnel) in the new reign was empowered to appoint and pay all the collecting officials, with the approval of the farmers, and to reassume the farm if the rent was not paid. The whole thing was an imposture designed to allow James to collect the excise till 1688 without parliamentary approval. Four of the judges saw through it and would not join the majority in approving: some people said that those who did approve were not the best lawyers.[1]

Another ticklish moment in the financial struggle had been reached at which reserves from France might turn the scale. James explained to Barrillon, the French ambassador,

> I have decided to call a parliament at once to meet in the month of May. I will publish at the same time a declaration continuing for me the enjoyment of the revenues which the king my brother had. Without the summoning of a parliament, I would risk too much by taking possession at once of what had been fixed for the lifetime of the late king. It is a decisive stroke for me to enter into possession and enjoyment of it because subsequently it will be very much easier for me to dismiss parliament or to maintain myself by such other means as may seem to me to be more convenient.

He also said, 'I know the English; you must not show yourself afraid of them at the start.' Barrillon wrote later that the 'secret murmuring'

[1] Turner, p. 245. E. S. de Beer, ed., *Diary of John Evelyn* (Oxford University Press, 1955), vol. iv, p. 417. HMC *Ormonde*, new series vol. vii, pp. 322, 324. *Lives of the Norths*. CTB 1685–9, pp. 10–11. Dr. W. A. Shaw in the index to this volume describes the farm as 'inoperative'. The farmers were Sir Peter Apsley, Sir Benjamin Bathurst and James Grahme: the first two Receivers General for the Duke of York and respectively his Treasurer and Trustee. Col. James Graham was Keeper of his Privy Purse and *pace* Dr Shaw is surely the person meant here.

against the illegal collection 'is very great' and some said this was not the way to get parliament to be generous.

> However, possession creates a sort of right and His Britannic Majesty seems very determined to maintain it at all costs, believing it impossible to maintain himself without it.

Louis was very willing to help the new king and sent over half a million livres at once, without being asked. Later he brought this up to two million: Barrillon was to hold it for use in a crisis, such as the refusal of parliament to vote the King a revenue. James and his ministers did not initially ask for money at all and were mainly concerned to justify to Louis the decision to summon parliament, which they expected him to resent. But James wept for joy when he heard of the arrival of the first half million and thereafter they pressed constantly for the continuance of the subsidy to Charles (the last part of which had in any case not been paid). Louis agreed with the policy of summoning parliament and forcing it to do the King's bidding: Barrillon's opinion was always that this could be done.

> the exploit of taking possession of the customs and excise revenues . . . will make the more thoughtful realize that the king of England wishes to bargain from a strong position.

At worst

> the King of England will content himself with first obtaining the confirmation of his revenue for three years because he believes that he would be able to obtain it afterwards for his life and that he would have time to put himself in such a position that it would be impossible to disturb him in the enjoyment of what he peacefully possessed . . . the wisest would be afraid of annoying the King of England and giving him a pretext for establishing a more absolute government and obtaining by force what parliament had refused him, in which case it would be easy for him to augment what he had once established contrary to the laws.

It was therefore unconvincing when James said that 'uncertainty' about the continuance of the subsidy 'would not allow him to act with the necessary firmness' and when Rochester warned

> that at the moment it was a question of establishing his authority and giving a stable [assurée] form to the government; that I knew well enough how important it was here to be in a position to give the law and not receive it.

Louis was optimistic and events bore him out: James got nothing in the end beyond the payment of Charles's arrears, though Louis remained willing to give something if the King decided that forcible action was necessary to protect the catholics.[1]

After such preparations it is hardly surprising that James's manner towards his parliament was forthright to the point of brutality. But most of the loyal men who sat there seem to have accepted this as honest bluntness. At his first meeting with the privy council after his brother's death, James made a brief impromptu speech in which he displayed some tact:

> I have been reported to be a man for arbitrary power but that is not the only story that has been made of me and I shall make it my endeavour to preserve this government in church and state as it is now by law established.

The ensuing line of reasoning was a little ominous:

> I know the principles of the Church of England are for monarchy and the members of it have shewed themselves good and loyal subjects, therefore I shall always take care to defend and support it. I know too that the laws of England are sufficient to make the king as great a monarch as I can wish

(he might well say this)

> and as I shall never depart from the just rights and prerogative of the crown, so I shall never invade any man's property.

But the councillors were so overjoyed by the speech that they begged leave for it to be published and James agreed: it seems that later he regretted the publication of the pledges it contained.[2] Even more useful to the government than these pledges was the fact, so vividly attested in Lord Ailesbury's memoirs, that in financial matters the King's approach was just what the country gentlemen could wish. He was frugal:

> a perfect economist and not of a giving temper. Not only his guards and garrisons were paid exactly but his household each quarter and all tradesmen whatsoever that furnished the king's and the queen's court.

He was eager to promote trade:

> even when Duke, when he saw the East India Company or other at an ebb, he would put in a good sum to revive the stocks. Trade he had much at

---

[1] Fox, pp. xviii–xxii, xxxvii, xliv, liv, lv. Cf. lvii, lix, lxvi. R. H. George, 'The Financial Relations of Louis XIV and James II', *Journal of Modern History*, vol. iii (1931), pp. 392–413.

[2] Turner, p. 240. *Life of James II*, vol. ii, pp. 3–5. 'Mr Finch' wrote down the spontaneous words from memory and made James promise to 'preserve' rather than 'not attack' the Church. James recalled he had 'often ventured my life in defence of the Nation'.

heart and his topic was, liberty of conscience and many hands at work in trade.

His views on taxation were impeccable:

> he would not have one farthing laid on land. 'That,' said he (and like a true English king) 'is the last resource if God Almighty should afflict us with a war.' . . . 'Lay it,' said he, 'on luxury, as chocolate, tea, coffee, East Indian commodities as not necessary for the life of man and' (with warmth) 'on wine' (for he was a most sober prince).

It would be wrong to attach importance to these roseate ramblings of Ailesbury's old age were it not that in 1685 (when he was Lord Bruce and sat in the commons) he had been selected to put forward tax proposals on the government's behalf. The King's remarks on taxation represented part of his instructions. He had been chosen for this work because he did not hold office and so his support of the crown would appear disinterested, as no doubt it was.[1]

The first step was to get the revenues which had been conferred on Charles II for life granted to James on the same terms. By now there was a school of thought that favoured a temporary grant, 'to be renewed from time to time that parliaments might be consulted the oftener'.[2] But on the first day of the session, May 19, the commons decided on a grant for life almost without discussion. Ailesbury had prepared the way by convening in advance a private meeting of M.P.s to which he says that over 250 (a majority of the house) came. The polite message which he says that the King sent to them explaining his wishes may perhaps explain why the commons were not offended by the bluntness of the speech from the throne. James warned them not to try and oblige him to summon them often by

> feeding me from time to time by such proportions as they shall think convenient . . . this would be a very improper method to take with me . . . the best way to engage me to meet you often is always to use me well.[3]

Rebellion first in Scotland and then in England provided an excellent opportunity to ask for more money and in the course of June parliament voted new duties on tobacco, sugar, French linen, brandies, calicoes and wrought silks, some for five and some for eight years. They also restored for eight years the temporary wine and vinegar

---

[1] Ailesbury, vol. i, pp. 100–1, 104–5. Cf. pp. 103, 107. But 'liberty of conscience' would not have been his 'topic' in 1685.

[2] *Memoirs of Sir John Reresby*, ed. A. Browning (Jackson, 1936), p. 362.

[3] LJ, vol. xiv, p. 10.

duties that had expired in 1681, removed the prohibition on importing these commodities from France, and empowered the King to borrow up to 400,000*l.* on the security of some of the new duties. James's revenue was now calculated to bring him a million and a half each year for life and another 400,000 a year for the rest of the eighties. But when parliament met again in the autumn, he told them that he needed a larger standing army in order to prevent further rebellions and asked for more money still. 700,000*l.* was voted, to be levied on wine, brandies and the linens and stuffs imported from France and the East Indies. At the same time, though, parliament began to show decided hostility both to the maintenance of an army and to the King's religious policy and James prorogued it before it could complete the voting of the money.[1]

The existence of rebellion in 1685 probably accounts for the ease with which extra money was voted. In the autumn Sir John Ernle, the chancellor of the exchequer, at first asked the commons for 1·2 millions and Sir Thomas Meres, supporting this, said that 'the principle of the rebel party is never to repent' and 'if so much be given, I would have you, gentlemen, to remember that the fanatics are the cause of it'.[2] But there are clear signs that parliament—'such a landed parliament was never seen',[3] Ailesbury recalled—went to work the more eagerly because it did not need to tax the land. In November, Ernle proposed extra import duties specifically 'to avoid a land tax' and the commons rejected such a tax when it was proposed by Sir Richard Temple, one of the few whigs in the house.[4] It was no doubt with the same end in view that the cost of putting down rebels was not met by a once-for-all grant of extraordinary revenue but by allowing the king to borrow and increasing his ordinary revenue so that he could repay his creditors. To produce enough money at once without borrowing would almost certainly have involved a land tax or its equivalent.

Still more striking is the animus against London and its commercial wealth shown in the debates on taxation. London had long had a great preponderance in the lucrative foreign trade of the country and the provincial towns and the country districts alike had been jealous of her prosperity. There was a long history of attempts to limit her

[1] The bare bones of revenue history are conveniently given in Dr W. A. Shaw's introductions to the CTB 1681–5 and 1685–9.
[2] Grey, vol. viii, p. 367.   [3] Ailesbury, vol. i. p. 98.   [4] Grey, vol. viii, p. 368.

growth—latterly in the form of proposals to tax new buildings. When the commons debated this idea in 1670, one member said that the country towns were getting poorer unless they were ports and another claimed that the growth of the capital depopulated the nation because wealthy families living there did not need so many servants as in the country. Against this it was said that it was unfair to lay a tax on a single area and that the prosperity of the capital brought prosperity to the regions too.[1] Ailesbury, however, proposed in 1685 to place a tax for one year on the rents of houses built on new foundations within the Bills of Mortality since 1660 and to prohibit further building in this area. His immediate purpose was to avoid further tax burdens on the trade of the 'outports'.

> I had this notion from what I had heard for years past from men that understood perfectly the good of our nation. They termed it that the head was too big for the body, that the counties were dispeopled by lazy and idle persons leaving the plough and cart for to run up to London and there to take little and idle ale-houses, and much more to this purpose.

Sir John Reresby spoke very much in the same vein:

> this one county drained all England of its people, especially the north, our tenants all coming hither, finding by experience that they could live here better in a cellar or a garret than they could live in the country for a farm of 30*l*. rent; that hereby this little piece of England had laid a tax in a manner upon all the rest of England and was a nuisance to all the rest and therefore it was not so improper that it should be taxed separately, and the rather because it was never taxed before or but once very little.

The commons approved the tax in principle, but the committee appointed to investigate it reported 'that it would require a long time to perfect' and it went no further. It was not popular at court, which after all was a part of the capital: government and big business were linked in many ways and court nobles might own metropolitan land. Ailesbury's career as a court spokesman was ended by this episode and Reresby found himself in bad odour with his patron, Lord Halifax, 'he having a deep concern therein'. The affair shows the readiness of the country gentlemen to impose taxes on another class whose prosperity they envied.[2] The crushing of municipal inde-

---

[1] Grey, vol. i, pp. 301–2.

[2] Ailesbury, vol. i, p. 106. Reresby, pp. 375–8. To be fair, London probably was depopulating the provinces. Deaths exceeded births and the population must have been kept up and increased by massive immigration. The unemployed may have congregated there as in modern under-developed countries, to which seventeenth-century England is sometimes compared. See further an interesting article, Caroline A. Edie, 'New Build-

pendence yielded a pretty direct financial dividend in the form of new taxes on trade.

James's efforts won the unstinted praise of the leading European autocrat. 'Never has a king of England acted with more authority in his parliament than this prince does at present,' wrote Louis XIV in June, and he expressed his satisfaction in July that James had

> entirely dissipated by his own forces all that could disturb his reign and simultaneously reestablished his revenues and his authority at a higher point than any of his predecessors had been able to attain.

He even began to fear that James wanted to be friends with the Dutch (this was true as we shall see) and that he might use his new-found wealth to pursue an independent foreign policy:[1] at the end of the year he was thinking of countering this, as he had before 1681, by subsidizing the parliamentary opposition. But James had now no reason to fear such opposition. Sir John Reresby remarked of the prorogation in December 1685

> Some said the king had so good a revenue and was so good a manager that he would be able to subsist and maintain both his fleet and army without more money and therefore would scarce have occasion for more parliaments; and the rather because he had refused 700,000*l.* by this dismission, which the commons were preparing to give him.[2]

Like his continental counterparts, the English King had gained a large income and consequent political independence on the tacit understanding that the upper class would be largely exempt from taxation.[3] Commercial expansion is usually associated by historians with the growth of the middle classes and of liberal political movements, but it was also the basis of absolute monarchy. It enabled James to raise with little friction a revenue sufficient for his maintenance and administered entirely by his own paid servants. Unless he wished to go to war, he would not need to meet parliament again. His subjects could not dictate to him and there was a fair chance that he would be able to dictate to them. An English king who was solvent might well have power as well as authority.

---

ings, new Taxes and old Interests: an urban Problem of the 1670s', *Journal of British Studies*, vol. vi (1966–7), pp. 35–63.

[1] Fox, pp. lxxv, xcv, cx.

[2] Reresby, p. 399.

[3] Compare in particular the establishment of an excise in Brandenburg in the 1680s. It fell on the towns alone and such activities as the nobles' home brewing escaped it. F. L. Carsten, *The Origins of Prussia* (Oxford University Press, 1954).

5

The King's New Weapons

JAMES II had an ordinary peacetime revenue of some two millions a year. The equivalent figure for Charles I's period of personal rule (*i.e.* leaving out extraordinary taxes like Ship Money) was about 600,000*l*. at the start, rising to some 900,000*l*. by 1640.[1] Charles II was supposed to have 1·2 millions. He did not manage to collect so much at first, but in his later years he was receiving 1·3 to 1·4 millions a year. This shows the progress that the English monarchy was making—though it may be mentioned that Davenant estimated Louis XIV's peacetime income as equivalent to 12 million sterling a year.[2] To the English national revenues there should really be added the revenues of Scotland and Ireland, some of the taxes raised by local authorities, and the very considerable amount paid in fees by the public to royal officials.[3]

The King now had money enough to maintain substantial armed forces and overawe his subjects with them. In the longer run his solvency was calculated to underpin this purely physical power by consolidating the royal influence which the King exercised through being an employer—in particular, an employer of members of the upper class. The more the leading families looked to the King for a livelihood, the greater the possibility of local magistrates who would willingly do his bidding and parliaments that would vote him still more money.

Services to the crown had always been a tradition and a source of

---

[1] See figures and authorities cited in Aylmer, *The King's Servants*, pp. 64–5.

[2] Cf. Dickson, p. 42 and Davenant, *op. cit.*, p. 13.

[3] Prof. Aylmer estimates the annual total of these fees under Charles I at 250,000*l*.– 400,000*l*., p. 246.

profit for the nobility and part of the gentry. It is possible that it attracted them more after the Restoration than it had done earlier. The improvement in the crown's financial management had its parallel in the class immediately below it. Towards the middle of the century, the device of contingent remainders was invented, which made it easier to enforce the rule of primogeniture: the head of a family could be reduced to the status of a tenant for life of his estates, with no power to divide them by sale or bequest. At the same time there was a change in the law relating to mortgages, which made it easier to borrow in this way without risk of foreclosure. Loans could be raised and the money given to the daughters and younger sons of the family in lieu of a share in the land. Large estates henceforth were less likely to disintegrate, though like the crown they had to shoulder an increasing weight of debt. The greater landed families might be hard up but their economic basis had been made a little more secure. This in itself was likely to strengthen the position of the crown, for most of these families had ties with the court. But it seems too that the younger sons, with a little money but no estates to manage, would be more likely than before to try and improve their position by entering some profession—which sooner or later would probably mean seeking a government job.[1] Thus the bond between the crown and the greater families would be tightened.

It would be valuable to know more precisely if the Civil Wars had any effect in modifying this situation. The idea that they caused a revolution in landownership had not stood the test of enquiry but there can be no doubt that taxes, fines and confiscation caused heavy losses to many. In Kent, for instance, most of the old-established gentry families still had their estates in 1688—though most of the newcomers since 1600 had proved less soundly based and had lost theirs. But Sir George Sondes had to pay 3,500*l.* to get back his confiscated estate and claimed that 20,000*l.* worth of stock and goods had been lost as a result of the confiscation. On emerging from prison in 1647, Sir Thomas Peyton found his

> whole time swallowed up in the business of farming which notwithstanding will never repair the breaches made in my fortunes by the evil of persons and times.[2]

[1] See H. J. Habakkuk, 'Marriage settlements in the eighteenth century', *Transactions of the Royal Historical Society*, 4th series, vol. xxxii (1950). pp. 15–30.

[2] Chalklin, pp. 200–2. The general statement is based on a survey of 180 families (out of some 800) by Prof. A. M. Everitt.

At a lower level it might be asked if the burdens of these wars did not begin the decline of the small landowner which was so marked a feature of the century after the Restoration.[1] At all events many, great and small, must have dreamed of getting on the right side of the tax-gathering process and recouping their losses in crown employment. Personal military service too may have shaped the attitude of some towards the governmental machine, in terms both of loyalty and of career expectations. In 1688 Bishop Compton caused something of a scandal by taking up arms in the Revolution, but it is interesting to note that several of his colleagues had fought for Charles I in their youth: Archbishop Dolben of York and Peter Mews of Winchester are examples. This was a royalist church militant with a vengeance!

The royal revenue, greatly though it had increased, was still trivial by the standards even of the next century, amounting perhaps to 5% of the national income. But the political influence generated by spending it was enhanced by the fact that government servants, though few, were well paid and the highest officials were the wealthiest men in the country. This both whetted the appetite for royal favour and gave immense prestige and social influence to those on whom it was bestowed: the crown benefited both ways. Curiously enough, it seems to be Macaulay who makes this point best, despite the amount of work on both administrative and economic history that has been done since his time.

> The average income of a temporal peer was estimated by the best informed persons at about three thousand a year, the average income of a baronet at nine hundred a year, the average income of a member of the house of commons at less than eight hundred a year. A thousand a year was thought a large revenue for a barrister. . . however, the stipends of the higher class of official men were as large as at present, and not seldom larger. The lord treasurer, for example, had eight thousand a year, and when the treasury was in commission the junior lords had sixteen hundred a year each. The paymaster of the forces had a poundage amounting in time of peace to about five thousand a year on all the money which passed through his hands. The Groom of the Stole had five thousand a year, the commissioners of the customs twelve hundred a year each, the lords of the bedchamber a thousand a year each.

Moreover

> Titles, places, commissions, pardons, were daily sold in market overt by the great dignitaries of the realm; and every clerk in every department imitated,

[1] A. H. Johnson, *The Disappearance of the Small Landowner* (Oxford, 1909).

to the best of his power, the evil example. . . . It is probable that the income of the prime minister during his tenure of power far exceeded that of any other subject. . . . This is the true explanation of the unscrupulous violence with which the statesmen of that day struggled for office . . . and of the scandalous compliances to which they stooped in order to retain it.[1]

Macaulay's view is not contradicted by recent research. His figures for large landowners' incomes are probably too low: 5,000*l.* for a peer, 1,200*l.* for a baronet and 400*l.* and upwards for the gentry are perhaps fairer guesses.[2] Of the incomes from high office, those of the two secretaries of state are almost as striking as the treasurer's. The nominal salary was 100*l.* a year, payment of which normally continued for life. But from 1660 there was also an annual allowance of 1,850*l.* Another allowance was in lieu of lavish free diet at court, which had been customary. At the end of Charles II's reign this amounted to 292*l.* for one secretary and 121*l.* 13*s.* 4*d.* for the other each year. From 1675 they had respectively 3,000*l.* and 2,000*l.* a year in secret service money and a fairly early stage this came to be treated as extra salary, more money being issued for actual secret service. A large though irregular income came from fees paid by those who needed documents from a secretary's office. Getting a charter for St. Albans in Charles II's reign involved three payments to Secretary Bennet, of 5*l.*, 6*l.* and 20*l.* respectively. A new source of funds was the profits from the *London Gazette*, which the secretaries shared. The fee income was high in wartime, because of the issue of commissions, and in the first year of each reign, when all patents of office had to be renewed. It was said that William III repaid the loan of 30,000*l.* which Lord Shrewsbury made him for the Revolution by making him secretary of state and so giving him the boom profits of his accession year. As secretary of state from March 1689 to November 1693, Lord Nottingham received 5,867*l.* 9*s.* 2½*d.* in fees and 4,376*l.* from the *Gazette*.[3] There can be no doubt that the earnings of a secretary of state were equivalent to the income of a wealthy nobleman.

[1] Macaulay's famous 'third chapter' on the state of the country (see Charles Firth's ed., vol. i, pp. 299–300).

[2] G. E. Mingay, *English Landed Society in the Eighteenth Century* (Routledge and Kegan Paul, 1963), pp. 20–3; cf. Aylmer, pp. 326–31. Gregory King's estimate is the starting point of calculation in our time as in Macaulay's. Aylmer notes his calculation of the national income as amended by Colin Clark is 49,200,000*l.*

[3] Evans, pp. 206–21, 358. Thomson, pp. 145–50, 170. H. J. Habakkuk, 'Daniel Finch, Second Earl of Nottingham, his House and Estate' in J. H. Plumb, ed., *Studies in Social History, a Tribute to G. M. Trevelyan* (Longmans, 1955), p. 161.

The higher government offices could all enable their possessors to live like gentlemen or even like noblemen. Even the humbler offices could provide very comfortably for their possessors. Henry Guy (who died worth 150,000*l.*) admitted to receiving some 2,570*l.* a year in fees, New Year's gifts and 'casual profits' as secretary to the treasury in 1679–84. The real figure was probably at least 3,500*l.* The six members of the board of customs established in 1671 had salaries of 2,000*l.* (later 1,000*l.*) a year. Excise commissioners had 1,000*l.* a year.[1] An under-secretary of state could aspire to 500*l.* a year and a senior treasury clerk to that or more.[2] The collector of customs at Bristol got 400*l.* The collectors of excise were paid 100*l.* a year, their subordinates the supervisors and gauging officers 80*l.* and 50*l.* respectively: the last were better off than most curates, indeed had more than most livings in the church were worth, though here pluralism had to be allowed for.[3]

Government service had its drawbacks. Payment, as already explained, could be badly in arrears—though this was probably less the case in James II's peaceful and thrifty reign than under his predecessor or successor. Office involved expense as well as profit. Sometimes a principal had to defray the cost of his subordinates' salaries and of housekeeping for his department. The secretaries of state had to pay some of their clerks, though others lived exclusively on fees. A memorandum in Sir Robert Southwell's papers quotes the normal scale of fees as 5*l.* to the secretary, 'to his secretary twenty shillings, to the entering clerk five shillings, and to the office keeper half-a-crown'. In Secretary Middleton's office in 1684, John Cooke, who was in effect the under-secretary, received the fees and paid another clerk beside himself. The other four clerks were paid by the secretary: their salaries came to 300*l.* a year or more.[4] There could be other important expenses, such as the high cost of living at court. Nottingham seems to have spent little on office housekeeping and clerks' salaries, but it has been estimated that during his first term as secretary he spent some 9,000*l.* more than he might otherwise have done.[5]

[1] Baxter, *Treasury*, pp. 193–4. B. R. Leftwich, 'The Customs Revenue in England, 1671–1814', *Transactions of the Royal Historical Society*, 4th series, vol. xiii (1930), p. 192. Hughes, p. 163 n. 669.

[2] Thomson, p. 139. Baxter, *Treasury*, p. 231.

[3] Leftwich, p. 192. Hughes, pp. 161, 218.

[4] Evans, pp. 192, 210.   [5] Habakkuk in Plumb, p. 162.

Office holding was thus a sort of commercial speculation and enterprise and importunity were needed to make the most of it. Everyone clamoured for pensions, gifts and allowances to supplement their pay (not to speak of additional offices). Then, besides the regular fees, there were 'perquisites of office' which, not to put too fine a point on it, were bribes. As deputy to Secretary Arlington, Joseph Williamson received many offers of from 50*l.* to 100*l.* for himself and 50*l.* to 500*l.* for his chief as soon as a certain piece of business should be completed.[1] The tradition that an office was a form of property meant that offices could be lucratively disposed of. Holders was often allowed to sell them, though the King did not relinquish his rights of appointment and dismissal. On becoming secretary of state in 1668, Trevor paid his predecessor Morrice 8,000*l.* Arlington received 10,000*l.* from Williamson on handing over his secretaryship in 1674. Williamson was less lucky, receiving only 6,000*l.* on his own resignation in 1679. Sunderland, his successor, had to sell another office (in the royal bedchamber) and an annuity in order to pay and he left office under a cloud after less than two years and was not permitted to sell. Thanks however to his skill as a courtier, he again became a secretary in 1683—gratuitously.[2] Lord Conway, whom he displaced, received a pension from the crown—another accepted way of making loss of office lucrative. Rochester got 4,000*l.* a year on ceasing to be lord treasurer in 1686, Danby had tried for 5,000*l.* and even the widow of the catholic Lord Belasyse, first lord of the treasury after Rochester's fall, got 2,000*l.* a year from William III.[3]

Although offices could not be inherited, as in France, it was possible informally to establish something like dynasties of officials. Officeholders pulled strings to get jobs for their friends and relations and some officeholders were left to appoint their subordinates. The secretaries of state appointed their own clerks, and the more important of these clerical subordinates themselves appointed clerks to assist them.[4] The Poveys are an example of an 'official' family. Justinian Povey had been accountant-general to James I's Queen and held various other financial offices. The civil war ended his prosperity but his son Thomas, who seems to have been a skilful trimmer, served both Charles II and Cromwell and held a variety of

[1] Evans, p. 215. [2] Evans, p. 216.
[3] Baxter, *Treasury*, p. 18.
[4] Evans, pp. 191–3. This at any rate was the case with Williamson and Cooke.

offices after the Restoration, specializing in colonial affairs. He also sat in parliament and married a rich window. (His brother Richard became secretary and commissary of Jamaica but did not do well.) Childless, he did his best to promote the fortune of his sister's son, William Blathwayt: he looked after his education and helped to get him first a post in an embassy and then a clerkship in the little office concerned with colonial affairs. Blathwayt did so well that his elder son was a country gentleman with no need of office. The younger became an army officer. Blathwayt seems to have passed on one of his offices to his son-in-law, Edward Southwell, as part of his daughter's dowry. The patronage of his little colonial department soon came into his own hands and in 1680 he brought in John Povey, probably a cousin, who married his step-sister. He failed to have him made secretary to the board of trade and plantations when it was set up to replace his office in 1696: that post was to be the making of another official family, the Popples. But John Povey became a clerk to the privy council and other Poveys served as secretary to the victualling board and lieutenant-governor of Massachusetts.[1]

Royal servants came from a diversity of backgrounds and their fortunes too diverged. The treasury clerks of the seventies and eighties ranged from Arthur Fleetwood, who was a first cousin of Treasurer Danby, to William Lowndes who does not seem to have had any patron when he entered the department. Some rose to political significance, like Lowndes or like William Shaw who was an M.P. in 1685. Some prospered but more moderately: Philip Lloyd's advance to the top was arrested by failure to win Danby's favour but he became a knight, a council clerk and (1685) a hearth money commissioner at 600*l.* a year. Some did badly: Roger Charnock was dismissed in 1671 and apparently reduced to living on his two other jobs worth only 150*l.* a year.[2] But if entering crown service was not to bet on a certainty, it nevertheless offered a path to fortune for the relatively poor and valuable extra income for the relatively well-to-do: Sir Edward Dering estimated in 1680 that if he ceased to be a treasury lord, he would have to cut his expenditure from 1,300*l.* to 600*l.* a year.[3]

The social and political effect of royal patronage of which con-

[1] Jacobsen, index s.v. Povey, Southwell.
[2] Baxter, *Treasury*, chaps. 9 and 10.
[3] Chalklin, p. 198. Dering took only his 1,600*l.* salary: Baxter, *Treasury*, p. 48.

temporaries were probably most conscious was its preservation from ruin of improvident members of the upper class who henceforth would find it awkward ever to disobey the King. Two important figures of James II's reign come into this category: Sunderland who emerged as the leading minister and Henry Hyde, second Earl of Clarendon (elder brother of Lawrence), whose humiliating tenure of the lord lieutenancy of Ireland and eventual emergence in opposition symbolize the alienation of the staunch anglicans from the throne. Sunderland was an able man but he was a compulsive gambler, at least until middle age, and confessed himself a bad manager of his estates, the rents from which fell heavily in his time. Secretary of state and president of the council from the end of 1685, he also had 6,000*l.* a year in pensions, not to speak of another 7,000*l.* a year from Louis XIV and 21,000*l.* charged on Ireland, payable in instalments. Yet when he was forced to flee at the Revolution, he had so little ready money that only a loan from Sir Stephen Fox enabled him to make good his escape.[1] Clarendon appears to have had no property except what belonged to his wife. He needed his Irish job to keep him afloat and in particular to make a good marriage for his son. This helps to explain why he submitted to being stripped of authority to the benefit of Tyrconnel and the catholics—though even so he was removed in the end and complained that he had been a loser financially.[2]

Very different was the case of enterprising men who used office to rise in the world. Heneage Finch, first Earl of Nottingham, inherited estates worth 1,900*l.* a year from his grandmother. He rose to be lord chancellor (at 4,000*l.* a year) and not only became a peer but also enlarged his estates and made a very good marriage for his son. Daniel, the second Earl, who succeeded his father in 1682 and was prominent in the politics of the Revolution period, came into estates worth 5,000*l.* a year. His tenure of a secretaryship from 1689 to 1693 has been estimated to have yielded a net profit of 25,000*l.* In 1693 he bought the estate of Burley in Northamptonshire for 50,000*l.* and soon began to build a great house there. He held office twice again, in 1702–4 and 1714–16, which would seem to have been of particular help in educating and providing for his children. His estates were worth about 9,000*l.* a year in the end. This is a case

[1] Kenyon, pp. 10–11, 74–7, 86 n., 144 n., 226, 232.
[2] *Clarendon Correspondence*, vol. i, pp. 195, 303–4; vol. ii, p. 144.

in which profitable official careers complemented good estate management.[1]

A humbler case is that of William Blathwayt (1649–1717) who, as he said, 'never pretended to any estate', being sprung from two families of merchant origin, turned lawyers and officials. He started in Whitehall as a clerk in the office of Sir Robert Southwell, himself a privy council clerk who was acting as secretary to the council committee on trade and plantations. In 1679 Southwell sold his clerkship for 2,500*l.* on being sent as envoy to Brandenburg and Blathwayt took over his job, though under the nominal supervision of the council clerks in rotation. In 1680 he became in addition the first surveyor and auditor general of plantation revenues and in 1683 he purchased the further office of secretary at war. From 1681 to 1683 he also acted as under-secretary to Lord Conway, secretary of state. He had also become an 'extraordinary', *i.e.* second-rank council clerk. In 1687 Evelyn correctly guessed his income at 2,000*l.* a year. He was paid 1,095*l.* as secretary at war, 500*l.* as auditor, 250*l.* as an 'ordinary' council clerk and 350*l.* in connection with his work for the plantations committee. Under William III he acted as secretary of state and a member of the board of trade: he was not paid the full secretarial emoluments but at the most he was getting over 4,000*l.* a year. He had to pay his subordinates in some of his offices and his colleagues levied fees on his own pay, which in the nineties was sometimes thousands in arrears. On the other hand he was not backward in taking fees: so much so, that when he was desperately trying to get officers to rejoin the army in order to face William of Orange's invasion, he was suspected of doing it for the sake of the fees he could charge on the absentees. Gratuities too came his way: 50 guineas from St. Kitts for help in procuring convict labour, 200*l.* offered from Virginia in 1692 for getting council sanction to a port bill—not to speak of sturgeon, bricks of tobacco, marmalade from Barbados and ermine from New York. He was elected to parliament in 1685 and in 1686 his friend Southwell found him a wife, Mary Wynter, whose family house and estate at Dyrham Park near Bristol came into his possession and were suitably embellished. He died there a prosperous country gentleman.[2]

Though it was not unknown for families who had made their pile in

---

[1] Habakkuk in Plumb, pp. 142–4, 158, 160–7.
[2] Jacobsen, esp. chaps. ii, xiii.

the employment of the state to retire into independence and opposition, the wealth and social distinction that flowed from service to the crown were calculated to keep society as well as government monarchical. The King was at the apex of the social as well as of the political pyramid, distributing rewards as well as commands and punishments. The solvency of the crown safeguarded the social bases as well as the political system of monarchy.

(II)

Of more immediate importance were the revitalized and expanded army and navy. Permanent land and naval forces, like the tax on beer which was raised to pay for them, were something that came to afflict England in the civil war period and have never since been got rid of. Charles I, it is true, had tried always to have some ships in pay but on land he had nothing much beyond a few gunners in his forts. When civil war broke out his opponents had the little navy on their side and were as well able to raise armed forces as he was. At the Restoration Charles II found Cromwell's army and navy in being but nothing towards their maintenance except debts. The army was almost abolished: indeed it was only the impossibility of finding enough money to pay them off that prevented more stringent reductions of both ships and men in pay.[1] Despite royal interest in it, the navy languished for want of money and discipline. But in the eighties both services experienced a great revival, made possible by the financial and administrative progress. This really meant that it was no longer possible to start a great rebellion against the King. Ironically, James was to be overthrown all the same and the armed forces which had supported his throne were even more important after 1688 in preventing his return.

The rebuilding of the navy was of great importance for the Revolution, for it alarmed the Dutch, spurred them therefore to help in the overthrow of James, and kept off the French afterwards. Colbert had just created a great fleet for France and the course of the Revolution might have been different if the English had not kept pace. This was a question in which the crown could hope for support even from a rather hostile house of commons. In 1675 Pepys warned the house of 'the condition of our neighbours' the French and Dutch,

[1] W. A. Shaw in introduction to CTB 1681–5, p. xii.

'who never till now since the memory of our dominion at sea ever had pretended to any equality, but now do to a considerable superiority to us in naval force'. In 1677 the lord chancellor told parliament that 'there is not so lawful or commendable a jealousy in the world as an Englishman's of the growing greatness of any prince at sea', and parliament voted 600,000*l.* for the building of thirty warships of the first three rates.[1] But parliament was not always interested. For some years it was the King's own money that paid for new ships and the navy went to ruin in the years (1679–84) when the admiralty was entrusted to commissioners acceptable to parliament. The continuing interest of James and Charles was vital and the regeneration of the navy at this time is perhaps the most striking manifestation of the vigour of royal government. Especially interesting for us is the special commission of 1686 by which Pepys corrected the damage done during his years of eclipse. At his request, Sir Anthony Deane, an eminent shipbuilder, reported on the state of the ships. He found 142 out of 179 unfit for service but thought that he could repair them all in three years and maintain a proportion in actual service at a cost of 400,000*l.* a year. But he and his associates would need power to 'suspend any officers' who did not co-operate, reward those who deserved it, and dismiss idle workmen. The existing senior officials, known when acting together as the navy board, had been too lax in doing this. The remedy was to set them aside in favour of the special commission, though the better ones were included on it. But in accord with the prevailing spirit, the old officials were not dismissed but bypassed and confined to routine tasks. Deane and his colleagues did even more than he had promised and just before the Revolution they retired and the old gang were restored.[2] This radicalism from above, overturning traditional authority, could achieve much in the field of administration. Whether it was salutory to apply it, for a political purpose, to the church, the universities, or the municipal corporations is less certain.

Charles and James raised the number of first, second and third rate ships from thirty in 1660 to fifty-nine in 1688; the total tonnage of the fleet rose from 62,594 to 101,032.[3] Perhaps even more important

---

[1] Ninety ships had been built since 1660 yet the French were twenty-four, the Dutch forty-four ahead in ships of over twenty guns. Bryant, *Samuel Pepys: The Years of Peril* (Reprint Society Ed., 1952), pp. 122, 130, 133. Tanner, p. 31.

[2] Bryant, *Saviour*, ch. vii and pp. 206–7. Tanner, pp. 34–6.

[3] Tanner, p. 75.

were the steps taken to build the naval officers into a regular profession with a code of conduct: this is only one branch of the reforming activity associated with Pepys and James, but it is the one that needs emphasis here because it was so directly calculated to strengthen the authority of the crown by creating obedient servants. Offering more jobs and more continuous employment, the navy was being invaded as never before by the sons of the upper class, and if the 'gentlemen' were more likely to be royalists than the 'tarpaulins' they were certainly less likely to give ready obedience to orders. Pepys lamented in 1674 'the universal loss of discipline amongst the seamen of England' and complained that

> little care goes to the making officers of the navy for their own preservation to put in very wholesome words and cautions in their orders for any service to be done, such as words of dispatch, efficacy, good husbandry, etc.

He waged an interminable struggle against absence without leave, intemperance and disobedience of every kind, and if Charles did not always support him, James did: against drunkenness, for instance, 'for the restraining which, as well in the navy as in every other part of the service, I well know he has immoveably determined to have the severest means used'. But at the same time the general rules governing officers' careers were altered in a way likely to improve their behaviour. The increase of pay as an incentive to cease private trading has been mentioned; the introduction of half-pay for senior officers demobilised after the two last Dutch wars and of pensions to old and wounded officers (1672–3) had a similar tendency. The officer could at any rate hope to be well provided for throughout his life and it was therefore in his interest to serve faithfully.

Lower down, the most important move was the 'establishment' of 1677 'for ascertaining the duty of a sea-lieutenant, and for examining persons pretending to that office'. Three years' service at sea, one of them in the hitherto plebeian rank of midshipman, certificates of good conduct and proficiency, and passing an examination in navigation and seamanship, were required of aspirants. Pepys wished to prevent youths 'having passed some time superficially at sea, and being related to families of interest at court' from obtaining 'lieutenancies before they are fitted for it'. But at the same time he hatched a plan, not made effective till 1686, for encouraging 'families of better quality...to breed up their younger sons to the art and practice of navigation'. This was to allow such youths to serve as 'volunteers' (*i.e.* cadets) at sea under conditions that would prepare them for commissioning and to give berths as 'midshipmen extraordinary' to lieutenants and commanders for whom there was no employment in their proper rank.[1] From Pepys's work there sprang a body of officers recruited from the class whose natural ties were with the King but with professional standards of conduct and competence that do not always come naturally to an aristocracy. But it was late in the day: too many senior officers in King James's navy were in the bad old Restoration tradition. Arthur Herbert, for instance, who was to desert it and command the invading fleet in 1688, was both corrupt and ignorant. 'Haul up that whitchum there' was his style of orders to his ship's company.[2]

The army was of much more direct importance than the navy in maintaining royal authority and its growth, efficiency and loyalty preoccupied James as much as anything during his reign. Of the force with which Monck restored him, Charles II had retained only one regiment of foot and one troop of horse, adding to them a few units formed largely from his own followers. In 1663 he had 3,574 men in standing regiments and 4,878 more in garrisons and independent companies scattered through England. Extra forces were raised for his various wars but soon disbanded: there was no money for peace-time augmentations. In 1680 there were 5,690 men in pay in England and 3,010 at Tangier. The withdrawal of that garrison began an improvement of the military position. The regiments in England at the end of the reign totalled 9,215 men, besides twenty-four independent companies in garrisons. It must also be noted that Charles's other kingdoms had armies, larger in proportion to their revenues than England's. There were 3,268 men in pay in Scotland in 1685 and 9,703 in Ireland. These countries were already fully exploited and James could do little to increase the forces there. He could increase the efficiency of the Irish army, which had been organized mainly in independent companies and troops, by forming it into regiments. He also tried to increase its loyalty by placing it under the command of his friend Tyrconnel, who turned out protestant officers and

---

[1] Bryant, *Peril*, pp. 100–10, 149–50; *Saviour*, pp. 133–4. Tanner, pp. 66–74 and on half-pay, pp. 55–6.

[2] Bryant, *Saviour*, p. 53. In fairness it should be said that the very idea of a distinct naval profession was new. Herbert and many others held military posts too.

soldiers and replaced them with catholics. Five thousand men were displaced, often with considerable hardship, but protestant observers did not rate the efficiency of their successors very highly.[1]

In England, James could do much more, Monmouth's rebellion giving him the means and justification. He inherited a force of one regiment and three large troops of horse, one regiments of dragoons (mounted but intended to fight on foot) and seven regiments of infantry. Disregarding temporary additions, the augmentation of 1685 amounted to eight regiments and one large troop of horse, two regiments of dragoons and nine of foot. The actual number of men in pay varied according to circumstances, but in principle the size of the army was more than doubled. Charles II spent about 200,000*l.* a year on it in peacetime: James about 530,000*l.*[2] But as with the navy, there was no guarantee that an increase in size would be matched by a due maintenance of standards of loyalty and efficiency. The army was basically a raw, untested force, though it had a very fair leavening of men who had seen active service—in the civil wars, the Dutch wars, at Tangier or in foreign service. Also, it had, like the navy and the civil service, an element of private property and private enterprise in its organization that militated against efficiency and reliability. The instant infection of this new service with the old vices was probably due in the first instance to the shortage of money during its formative years. Insufficient and irregular pay meant living on credit and the search for profits to pay debts. It also meant endless conflicts over the available money, with fraud as a prime weapon. When he took charge of Ireland in 1686, Lord Clarendon found that the pay of the army there had commonly been six months in arrears and that there had not even been a system of advancing subsistence

[1] C. Walton, *History of the British Standing Army, 1660–1700* (Harrison, 1894), pp. 496–8. C. Dalton, *English Army Lists and Commission Registers, 1660–1714* (Eyre and Spottiswoode 1892–1904, reprint 1960), vol. ii, pp. xii, xiii, 37–8: The Irish army had consisted of a regiment of guards (twelve companies), some twenty-four troops of horse and seventy-four companies of foot. These became six regiment of foot and three of horse, plus a dragoon regiment from England. CSPD 1685, nos. 335, 1092.

[2] CTB 1685–9, pp. xciii xciv. Shaw's figures for the augmentation are different but his comparison seems to be with an earlier point in Charles's reign. The 'large troops' were the precursors of the Life Guards and were almost regiments: each had about 200 'private gentlemen', plus a horse grenadier troop of fifty to sixty. Dragoon regiments had six troops of fifty men each, raised to sixty in September 1688. Horse regiments were mostly similar, but with forty (fifty) per troop. Foot regiments mostly had thirteen companies in this reign. One hundred strong in Monmouth's rebellion, the companies fell to fifty but rose to eighty in 1687. Walton, pp. 418–9, 422, 424–8.

money—the part of the pay required to cover the housing and feeding of the troops. It was hardly surprising that when he refused to allow company commanders to draw pay for men shown by the musters to have been non-existent, some said that they could not pay their debts unless this was permitted.[1]

To prevent the English army collapsing for want of money, it had been provided with a banker—the paymaster general of the forces. He raised money on his private credit, advanced it to the army and in return received not only a salary but a commission deducted from the soldier's pay and interest on all sums not repaid after four months. Sir Stephen Fox, first holder of the office (1661–79), made a great fortune and it was said to be worth 10,000*l.* a year to him.[2] The regiments were regularly inspected by commissaries of musters and pay was only issued for the number of men shown on their rolls. But the responsibility for seeing that each troop or company was complete was left to the captain, who drew pay for the number of men that he could produce. False musters were the result: captains presented men who were not bona-fide soldiers of their company or they forbore to fill vacancies until just before the muster day. Either way, they drew pay for non-existent men and the real strength of the army was therefore never as great as its paper strength. Of the pay issued, only a part ever reached the soldier. Some of it was quite lawfully withheld to pay for his clothing: the regimental colonels received it and supplied the uniform. This system both led them to connive in false musters and allowed them to make profits at the expense of the troops. The clothing contract was sold to the highest bidder without regard for consequences. In Dublin in 1686, tradesmen were offering colonels 600*l.* for their clothing rights and in 1689 Schomberg reported to William III from Ireland that 'the whole concern of the colonels is only to live off their regiments, without doing any thing else for them'.[3] There were other stoppages from pay besides that for the clothing, and the officers were always tempted both to invent more and to stop the money from the 'subsistence' set apart for the soldier's daily needs, rather than from the remainder of his pay. The gross pay of the foot soldier was 8*d.* a day; the sub-

[1] Clarendon, 7 December, 30 November 1686 in Walton, pp. 675, 677. Cf. p. 686 and n. 1995.

[2] Walton, pp. 640, 641.

[3] Walton, pp. 391 n. 905, 394 n. 913. But in the first case the colonels reported it indignantly, Clarendon, 10 April 1686.

sistence money was supposed to comprise 6*d*. of this, but in 1686 Clarendon found that many Irish soldiers were only getting 'twopence a day to live upon'. He called a council of war which 'agreed to a rule' to ensure that 'each man should have fourpence a day in money for every day in the year'.[1]

The financial system of the army was calculated to make the soldiers ragged and hungry as well as depleted in numbers. It goes without saying that mutiny, desertion and disorder were likely consequences. The soldiers for the most part did not live in barracks but were billeted. They were given their subsistence and with it paid for their board and lodging. The government specified in orders where each unit was to be quartered and the civil power was called on to help in finding quarters. Normally they were in public houses, but occasionally these were insufficient and orders were given to use private dwellings. The requisitioning of billets seems to have been regarded as illegal and in 1677 an act of parliament declared it to be so and also required payment of quarters to be made by the paymaster-general and stopped from the soldier's pay. This act appears to have been ineffective and the soldier's lack of money made him a dangerous as well as an unwanted guest. As early as 1673, innkeepers were paying soldiers (to go away) instead of the reverse. Bad behaviour and extortion from civilians kept fresh the national hatred of armies.[2]

Rather than seeking to improve the situation, the authorities tended to be too willing to exploit it. They sanctioned the bearing of fictitious men on the books, sometimes to meet a particular expense, but usually (at this time) to give extra pay to officers. They allowed officers' servants to be paid as soldiers. Fees were exacted from the officers by the various officials with whom they dealt, thus adding to the financial pressure. Pluralism was allowed. Colonels were also captains of companies and the practice was beginning whereby colonelcies were conferred on senior officers whose real work lay elsewhere. Naval officers were still being provided for by being given military posts: natural enough in view of the amphibious services of

---

[1] Clarendon, *ibid.*, in Walton, p. 678 n. 1975; cf. 12 January at p. 660 n. 1933a.

[2] Walton, pp. 712–15 and appendix lxxx: see commons' debate, 3 November 1673. At Exeter in 1688 they were astonished that the Dutch troops were civil and paid for what they had, *ibid.* p. 481 n. 1209. The Petition of Right had asked that billeting should stop but did not say it was illegal. Carts were regularly pressed (*ibid.* p. 706) which was statutory for the militia. In wartime (1666 and 1673) men were pressed (*ibid.* p. 481).

Monck or Prince Rupert or King James himself. James's friend, Lord Dartmouth, who was really an admiral, was not only master general of the ordnance but colonel of the Royal Fusiliers.[1] The bad practice had already begun of giving commissions to children: even under the meticulous James, Percy Kirke junior served as an ensign at the age (apparently) of three and Lord Ettrick was a captain at eighteen months.[2] The generous allowance of leave should also be remembered when considering how many officers can actually have taken their profession seriously: a third of the officers in a regiment might be absent at a time and the theoretical limit of two months' leave a year does not seem to have been enforced. In April 1686 Lord Bath complained that two regiments quartered near him lacked all their field officers and one was without most of its captains.[3] For the lower ranks, too, the army had something of a part-time character. Men were allowed to supplement their meagre pay by working, either on the upkeep of government property or at ordinary jobs in the town.[4] It should be stressed that the English army was not the only one to have the various peculiarities mentioned above: they were common enough everywhere. But they were especially serious in a new army, not much hardened by war.

It was fully in keeping with the way that the army was organized that posts in it should tend to become a species of private property. The purchase of commissions was not new and it flourished in this period, both in the entirely evil shape of bribes to superiors in order to procure appointment and in the more respectable form of an outgoing officer receiving an indemnity from his successor. This practice may be said to have received official recognition in 1684 when a percentage was levied from buyers and sellers towards the cost of Chelsea Hospital. Though Charles II later declared he would allow no more sales, and James disliked the practice, it was never stopped or even really prohibited. In 1672 the Duke of Buckingham had bought a regiment for 1,500*l.* and in 1684 a colonelcy of guards changed hands for 5,100*l.* In 1686 Clarendon reported that colonels in Ireland were selling 'their quartermaster's, adjutant's and clerk's places for whatever they can get'. Even private's and gunner's places

---

[1] Because the Fusiliers were raised to guard the artillery.
[2] Dalton, vol. ii, pp. xv, 22, 135 n. 22, 195. Kirke was appointed in 1684.
[3] CSPD 1686–7, no. 372. Walton, p. 691.
[4] Walton, p. 648. G. Davies, 'Letters on the admin. of James II's army', no. 12, *Jol. Soc. Army Hist. Research*, vol. xxix (1951).

were sold, for the ranks of the army had not yet become solely a refuge for the destitute.[1] The members of the troops of horse guards were styled gentlemen. All cavalrymen had to provide their own horses or have money enough to buy one from the government, and even the better infantry regiments were joined by sons of yeomen.[2]

Appointments within a regiment commonly went by recommendation of the colonel, although appointments at all levels were striven for by applicants from every quarter and anyone with good connections and a long purse might hope for success. Not only did this system give no very notable reward to military merit, it made it possible for units of the army to become something like family possessions. A glance at army lists suggests that many companies and troops were little family concerns: two of the three officers will often be found with the same name and sometimes the third man is a relative of the other two. At a higher level, a regiment might resemble a pocket borough, its higher ranks dominated by members of influential families in alliance. The Duke of Beaufort's regiment of foot was raised in 1685 in the huge area (Wales and the Marches) of which he was lord lieutenant. His lieutenant-colonel (by royal recommendation, as were two captains)[3] was Sir John Haumer of the well-known Flintshire family and the captains included, for instance, Edward Games and William Winter, both from prominent Brecknockshire families. The Earl of Bath also raised a regiment of foot in 1685. He was lord lieutenant of Devon and Cornwall and among his captains figure such well known west country names as Wyndham, Granville and Godolphin. The Princess Anne's dragoons were raised in Somerset at this time and again local families were prominent in it.[4] Raised at a time when the landed class was fairly solidly behind James against Monmouth, the new regiments seem to have been largely of their creation and to have reflected the traditional territorial loyalties of rural England. Completely loyal while the landed families were well affected, they might not be so reliable in more difficult times.

---

[1] Walton, pp. 449–55. Illegal by a statute of Edward VI.

[2] Walton, pp. 419, 481,708. He offers no evidence *re* the infantry. One of the 'gentlemen', Anthony Heyford, became colonel of the Royal Dragoons in 1689 (Dalton, vol. i, p. 307).

[3] CSPD 1685, no. 959.

[4] Dalton. Cf. Davies, 'Letters', no. 3. Walton seems unreliable when stating areas where regiments were raised: but it is easier to speak of officers than men.

James, in short, had a regular army with a built-in tendency to degenerate into a ramshackle feudal host. His task was not only to expand it but to see that it became an efficient and reliable instrument of his rule. His influence was probably already at work in Charles II's last years. It is certainly seen in the reform of the board of ordnance which, besides controlling the artillery and engineers, supplied munitions both to the army and to James's special concern at that time, the navy. Like the admiralty, the ordnance had in effect been handed over to a body of parliamentary commissioners at the time of the popish plot. In 1682 it was placed instead under the control of James's naval friend, Lord Dartmouth, and in 1683 a book of instructions was adopted for it which remained the constitution of the department until its abolition after the Crimean War and was praised by the Duke of Wellington. The master general was assigned a salary, to obviate 'those undue means formerly practised'[1] to pay him, and so were the other officers. A system of issuing stores and money was established which required the principal officers to countercheck each other and prevent fraud. In 1682 also, the gunners, who seem previously to have been little more than sinecurists attached to the different forts, were subjected to military discipline and ordered to be regularly exercised.[2] This was the feeble beginning of a regiment of artillerymen.

James's wider attempts to improve his army comprised better training and stricter discipline on the one hand and rewards and fairer treatment for officers and men on the other. The two things were complementary, for it was the troops who were fairly treated that could be kept in the strictest obedience, as the Dutch example particularly showed. The most spectacular and best remembered training measures were the camps of instruction held each year during the warmer months. They were of particular importance at that time because the system of billeting meant that the troops might otherwise be dispersed in very small detachments indeed. In camp not only could large bodies of troops be taken out on ambitious exercises but the individual regiments were together all the time and could perfect their drill. Even in 1684 a camp at Putney Heath contained some six thousand five hundred men. The camps at Hounslow Heath in 1686, 1687 and 1688 held much larger numbers: thirteen thousand

[1] O. F. G. Hogg, *The Royal Arsenal* (Oxford University Press, 1963), vol. ii, p. 1051.
[2] Walton, pp. 732–3.

at least in 1686.[1] They were intended to be a permanent annual event: Shales the commissary general was granted the right to hold a market at Hounslow in perpetuity. It was to operate daily during the encampment and every Thursday at other times.[2] The overawing of the capital and the concentration of force ready to overwhelm an uprising are the purposes of this encampment usually stressed, but its training function was certainly no less important, and James devoted much time and effort to the personal supervision of this work. An official drill-book was published in 1686, and in 1687 there was 'a person appointed to exercise the forces and visit the garrisons'.[3]

Measures to make the army a more attractive career comprised firstly an increase in the number of top jobs. This was necessary anyway in view of the greater size of the army and the drive to make it more efficient. Until 1685 there was no regular staff of general officers, but James II appointed three lieutenant-generals, three major-generals and four brigadier-generals. There were also two adjutant-generals (instead of one) and a quartermaster-general: these posts were held by colonels.[4] A measure not immediately connected with efficiency was the conferring upon the captains of the two regiments of foot guards the additional rank of lieutenant-colonel.[5] The creation of these 'plum' jobs gave the King a chance to encourage and reward both efficiency and fidelity. For the less aspiring, army service now gave the prospect of secure provision for life. Half-pay was being used to provide for officers temporarily unemployed: soon it was to be paid as a pension to officers too old to serve.[6] Already care was being taken of old soldiers in this position. For Ireland, which had long possessed something like a standing army, Charles II ordered in 1679 the creation of a hospital for men 'grown aged, or otherwise unserviceable' but 'continued in our pay for want of some other fitting provision for their livelihood and maintenance'. Kilmainham Hospital was opened in 1684 and occu-

[1] 10,144 privates according to the list in Dalton, vol. ii, p. 92. 16,000 according to *The Ellis Correspondence* (ed. Hon. G. A. Ellis, 2 vols., 1829), 26 June: this must be too much even for all ranks.

[2] CSPD 1686–7, no. 107.

[3] Walton, pp. 46, 629.

[4] Walton, pp. 619–20, 622–4. Dalton, vol. ii, p. 89.

[5] Dalton, vol. ii, pp., xv, 114. The officers of guards' troops ranked from colonel down but these troops was really regiments.

[6] Walton, pp. 688–90.

pied by 10 officers and 100 men. Soldiers were eligible for admission if they were disabled by wounds or had served for at least seven years and become too old or infirm to earn their living. For the English army, Chelsea Hospital was begun in 1682 and finished in 1689: pensions were paid meanwhile to those eligible for admission, and though twenty years' service was required except for those actually maimed, the number in 1689 was 579. Nell Gwynn is said to have inspired the founding of Chelsea; certainly Sir Stephen Fox made some amends to the army by a lavish contribution to it. It was built on the ruins of a theological college which James I had tried to found: an interesting commentary on the changing basis of royal power. Both hospitals were financed by stoppages from army pay and in the case of Chelsea, at least, the government made a large profit! Though they were not the first homes for old soldiers, the establishment of these two large hospitals was a tangible sign that the standing army had really come to stay.[1]

Pending retirement or advancement, the daily life of the military man was made more tolerable by the repression of abuses. The foundation of this—as of every other military development, of course—was the improvement in the crown's financial position. In 1684 the government ceased to borrow the money to pay its troops from its own paymaster and his remuneration was cut accordingly: it was the revenue so saved that was diverted to pay for Chelsea Hospital.[2] In 1686 Clarendon settled all the Irish army's arrears of pay, made monthly advances to each unit for subsistence and paid everyone in full at less than two-monthly intervals.[3] In November 1687, captains of foot in England were ordered to pay subsistence to their men twice a week. They were allowed, however, to retain a day's pay a week for providing 'necessaries' (underclothing, etc.). They had, however, to account with each man for the expenditure of this money every two months. For the balance of the gross pay, each man was to be accounted with each time the regiment was reclothed.[4] James II further abolished some of the fees which his officials exacted from the army, though in this he was not very successful and it was only the officers who were the immediate beneficiaries.[5]

[1] Walton, pp. 593–607 and app. lxix.
[2] Walton, p. 641. The old arrangement continued in Scotland till at least 1699. See app. lxix for similar financial basis of Kilmainham.
[3] 7 December in Walton, p. 675.
[4] Walton, pp. 652–3.   [5] Walton, p. 662, app. lxxv, lxxvi.

In return for such benefits as these the government sought a higher standard of conduct both towards itself and towards the community. From 1687, musters were taken once a month instead of once in two months.[1] King James gave 'strict order' that the troops should produce certificates from the local magistrates that they had behaved well and paid for their quarters in the places through which they had passed, and when a certificate was refused, an enquiry by a gentleman of the locality was ordered.[2] Public warning was given to the townspeople where soldiers were quartered not to give them credit (the King would not allow soldiers to be arrested for debt).[3] The troops were not allowed to accept money in lieu of quarters and officers were to see to it that quarters were paid for by their men.[4] Royal proclamations in 1685 and 1688 gave publicity to these orders.[5] That James was doing a little more than applying good standard rules is suggested by some individual cases. Militant whigs were protected from plunder and insult. In 1685 the King regretted that the army had not hanged some rebels at Frome, but would have nothing taken from the people without payment.[6] Save for public houses, there was to be no quartering without the householder's consent. Two soldiers who beat a constable at their officers' command were to be court-martialled,

> His majesty esteeming that as it was a great fault in the officers to employ soldiers to beat any person, so it is no excuse for the soldiers to say they were commanded by an officer so to do, which they could not think to be any part of their duty as soldiers.[7]

Unfortunately James had to concentrate forces at key points on the coast in 1688, in the expectation of attack. He could not do this without placing some in private houses. He also, for some reason, exacted some free quarters in public houses.[8] So the army's reputation continued rather black; the proclamation of 1688 admitted that abuses continued. It is only fair to add that we hear of civilians

---

[1] Walton, p. 643. [2] Davies, 'Letters', no. 6.
[3] CSPD 1686–7, nos. 45, 1185. [4] Davies, nos. 10, 11, 15.
[5] R. Steele, *Tudor and Stuart Proclamations* (Oxford University Press, 1910), nos. 3815, 3871 (vol. I, pp. 461, 469).
[6] Davies, 'Letters', nos. 5, 9. CSPD 1685, no. 1113.
[7] Davies, 'Letters', nos. 14, 17, 18.
[8] *ibid.*, nos. 19, 20, 26, 29. He had already insisted on concentration despite its unpopularity in 1686. CSPD 1686–7, no. 39.

abusing soldiers and of soldiers living in friendship with the people and protecting them from brigands.[1]

The maintenance of military discipline requires the punishment of offenders: we must consider what success James had in providing for this. It was already normal for armies to be governed by a military code administered by military courts. There was general agreement that this was the right system for the navy and soon after the Restoration, parliament had given statutory sanction to it there. But ashore such a system was regarded as a serious threat to the authority of the law of the land. The Petition of Right had asserted in particular against 'martial law' a statute of Edward III 'that no man shall be forejudged of life and limb against the form of the Great Charter and the law of the land'; also that no offender was exempt from punishment by the normal course of the law. The objection was not only to the setting up of a new legal system but to exempting anybody from the authority of the existing one. There was a traditional view that martial law could be made use of in time of war, but this was interpreted very narrowly, as meaning when the ordinary courts had ceased to function or 'when an enemy is really near to an army of the king's'[2]. Articles of war laying down a scale of punishments for military offences and establishing a system of courts-martial were in fact issued whenever the country was at war. Both sides did this during the civil war and the Earl of Northumberland's code of 1640 for the army fighting the Scots was reissued with relatively little alteration in 1673 for the Dutch war, in 1677 when there was an expedition against the French, and in 1692. There were also articles issued in 1666 and a very detailed code for the Tangier garrison, while martial law was certainly used during Monmouth's rebellion. In Ireland, too, there was 'a greater latitude of punishing soldiers'. By contrast the articles issued in 1663 in England (peacetime) were chiefly concerned to provide for dismissal or stoppage of pay in certain cases 'because my Lord General (Albemarle) is wary of going further'.[3]

But this does not mean that there was no legal provision for the maintenance of military discipline. In the first place there was the

[1] CSPD 1686–7, nos. 139, 1066.
[2] Holdsworth, vol. vi, p. 226.
[3] Walton, app. liii, lix, lx, p. 532. On Ireland *Journal of the Society for Army Historical Research*, vol. xxiv (1946), p. 63.

doctrine that soldiers were in no way exempt from the ordinary operation of the law: this was energetically upheld by the judges and with certain exceptions the government fully accepted it, in particular leaving to the civil courts all cases where both soldiers and civilians were concerned.[1] Next, old statutes provided punishments for certain military offences such as the purloining of clothes and equipment and in particular for desertion, which had been declared a felony in Henry VI's reign. Lawyers were not agreed as to whether this applied to troops at home as well as those overseas, but the government had won an important case in 1601, and under James II deserters were tried in the civil courts and hanged.[2] For the remaining military offences the government since the Restoration does not seem to have hesitated to order courts-martial and instruct them to judge the case 'according to military discipline' or some such rule.[3] Albemarle's commission as captain general empowered him to try 'all capital and criminal offences whatsoever' by court-martial or summarily. But the general tenour of this document suggest that it was intended mainly to meet the circumstances of a civil or other war. More significant is a memorandum on the powers which Albemarle had had which was drawn up by Sir Joseph Williamson in 1678. It says that major offences were tried and punished by general courts-martial 'provided that the same extended not to the taking away of life or limb' and that lesser offences were punished by regimental or garrison courts-martial.[4] This seems to have been the government's policy and in 1686 it was given more public and regular expression. A full set of articles of war of the wartime pattern was issued but with a proviso that 'no punishment amounting to the loss of life or limb be inflicted upon any offender in time of peace'. This system, legal or not, seems to have functioned without interference from the civil courts. It was clearly adequate to punish minor offences and the major ones were mostly either punishable by ordinary law or only likely to happen in time of war (desertion in the face of the enemy, for instance). But an important gap remained: it is not clear that there

---

[1] Holdsworth, vol. vi, pp. 227–8. Walton, app. lix. Davies, 'Letters', no. 7, 11.

[2] Walton, pp. 531, 533, app. xxiv s. 8. E. Samuel, *Historical Account of the British Army and of the Law Military* (1816), pp. 70–4. Holdsworth, vol. vi, pp. 228–9: he does not consider 18 Hen. vi cap. 19 which seems to have been the statute invoked by the government.

[3] Walton, app. xlix, lxi.

[4] Walton, app. i, xxi.

was anywhere an adequate power to punish mutiny or lesser offences tending that way. Collective action to demand arrears of pay may especially be mentioned as something only too likely to happen.[1]

A general feature of seventeenth-century armies which James II tried to exploit in order to strengthen his military position was their cosmopolitanism. Of the seven regiments of foot which James inherited from his brother, two had originally been in the service of other states and had been transferred. The 'Holland Regiment', as it was still called (later famous as the Buffs), had been formed in 1605 from the companies of English volunteers that had been raised by the Dutch during their revolt against Spanish rule. When Charles II went to war with the Dutch in 1665 he ordered all his subjects in their service to come home and the Dutch cashiered all those who would not swear loyalty to them. The English officers came over and the King gained a fine, seasoned regiment.[2] The first or Royal Regiment was a Scottish regiment claiming extreme antiquity, but first heard of in France in 1633 and built up from Scots who had been serving with Gustavus Adolphus. Charles II borrowed it from Louis XIV in 1661 and again in 1666. Henceforth he regarded it as his own regiment and it returned to the English service for good in 1678.[3] Three temporary regiments were raised for French service in 1672 and only recalled in 1678: many of their officers and men served thenceforth in the English army, including such leading figures as Churchill, Kirke and Trelawny.[4] Meanwhile there continued to be two British brigades in the Dutch army. The three regiments of the Scots brigade had disregarded the call to come home in 1665 and three new English regiments had been created after the conclusion of peace with the Dutch in 1674.

These 'international' regiments were useful to the English crown in various ways. They were a means of training Englishmen in the art of war and providing materials for a more seasoned army than could be created at home. Secondly, they might be a very effective military reserve: a force for which the King did not have to pay but which he could borrow in emergencies. Parallel to the financial reinforce-

[1] Walton, app. liii.

[2] I have conflated Walton, p. 13 and J. W. Fortescue, *Hist. of British Army* (Macmillan, 1910), vol. i, pp. 296–7.

[3] England and France being at war in 1666 and almost in 1678.

[4] C. T. Atkinson, 'Charles II's regiments in France, 1672–1678', *Journal of the Society for Army Historical Research*, vol. xxiv (1946), pp. 53–65, 129–36, 161–72.

ment from France was the military reinforcement which Charles and James arranged for from the Dutch. An Anglo-Dutch treaty of 1678, following the marriage of William and Mary, required each country to assist the other with troop and ships in the event of attack. The two British brigades could therefore be summoned home whenever the King needed them, and in 1685 they were brought over to fight Monmouth. Although they did not have to be used, the six regiments formed a most impressive strategic reinforcement, both in quantity and quality. 'They are the best men and best prepared for service that ever were seen,' said Blathwayt of the Scots.[1] A final reason why such troops might be especially useful was that service away from home might lessen their ties with the community and make them a more dependable instrument for a despotic ruler. James always sought the removal of officers not politically reliable from the British brigades in Holland,[2] and when his relations with William became strained, he tried to transfer his reserve force from Dutch to French service. In October 1687, Sunderland sought French financial help for a plan to establish a regiment of catholics from the English troops then in Holland. It was the King's intention to recall all these troops but most of the protestants were expected to remain behind. The new corps would normally be stationed in France and by that means it would be 'better kept up and better disciplined' than the other English troops and would be

> a nursery to educate and form catholic soldiers who will not be informed of the dangerous maxims to monarchy which are spread throughout all England and from which even the catholics are not entirely exempt.[3]

Attempts were similarly made to detach the troops actually in the British Isles from their local roots. English regiments were deliberately stationed in some part of the country other than that where they were raised.[4] We have seen that the English army included a Scots regiment and in 1686 a battalion of the Scots foot guards was brought south.[5] In 1685 a regiment was raised in England for the Irish establishment[6] and James planned to exchange regiments between

[1] Davies, 'Letters', no. 1 and n. 10.
[2] Case of Lt.-Col. Babington, CSPD 1685, nos. 1682–4.
[3] Dalrymple, vol. ii, appendix to bk. v, pp. 134–7. Cf. pp. 138–9.
[4] Davies, 'Letters', no. 3.
[5] Walton, pp. 45–6.
[6] Dalton, vol. ii, p. 13.

England and Ireland, so as to have the whole force under his own eye.[1]

In the upshot, the 'cosmopolitan' factor did not help James and even worked against him. In 1688 he was able to bring the whole Scots army to help in England and also four Irish regiments and Irish recruits at least enough for a fifth.[2] But a revolution in Scotland was made possible by the removal of the former, while the terror and distaste aroused by the latter was out of proportion to their usefulness. Louis refused to pay for as many troops as the Dutch had and most of the officers at least refused to return from Holland when they were called for early in 1688. Three regiments were formed from them —one English, one Scottish and one mainly from the recruits provided by Ireland. Only the last seems to have been strongly attached to James. The other two served William right through the long war that followed the Revolution. The British troops remaining in the Dutch service were brought up to full strength and took part in the invasion: two of the English regiments were thereafter permanently transferred to the English army. William put his British troops in the vanguard and thereby made his arrival look less like a foreign attack. Another way in which these Anglo-Dutch regiments may have helped William was in creating a tradition of service with the Dutch among English officers and courtiers. Many of the officers were men of considerable social or military standing. The most notable was the Earl of Ossory (died 1680), the eldest son of the Duke of Ormonde, who had commanded the whole contingent in 1678. It was perfectly respectable in normal times for English officers to leave the royal service and resort to the Prince of Orange.

Nothing annoyed James's subjects more than his employment of catholics in the army and it was on this issue that he quarrelled with his very loyal parliament. This was another way in which he could recruit soldiers who had every reason to be loyal to him through thick and thin. He certainly took advantage of this possibility and it helped him to build up the strong body of loyalists within the army which will be described in conclusion. But first it should be said that he probably did not make the most of his chances. The catholic officers whose appointment caused so much concern in 1685 seem to have numbered about ninety. There were no doubt others already

[1] *Clarendon Correspondence*, vol. i, p. 339.
[2] J. G. Simms, *Jacobite Ireland 1685–91* (Routledge and Kegan Paul, 1969), pp. 45–8.

concealed in the army. Lord Dunbarton, who was appointed by James to command the Royal Scots foot regiment, had commanded it when it was in French service and apparently was not replaced when it came to England: perhaps he had retained the command informally.[1] Certain regiments had a strongly catholic tone among the officers but this does not seem always to have extended to the men. Lord Dover raised a regiment of horse in 1685, which was disbanded, and a troop of guards in 1686. These were intended to be definitely catholic units and the latter at least was in an important strategic position, helping to guard the sovereign. But according to Ailesbury, the principal officers were so corrupt that it was heavily infiltrated by protestants. Lord Lichfield's regiment is the subject of a famous story from 1688: it was asked in the presence of the King if it would support him in the repeal of the religious tests and bodily showed its refusal by laying down its arms. Almost all its field officers and captains were catholics or last-ditch loyalists and it had been raised by the Duke of Norfolk, who had catholic relatives thought he was himself a protestant. The personal incapacity and lack of social influence of the catholics is shown in this sort of episode. A famous attempt to infiltrate catholics into the ranks of a protestant regiment was also without avail. James gave a regiment of foot to his illegitimate son, the Duke of Berwick, who in 1688 tried to put in five Irish catholics per company in place of existing men. The lieutenant-colonel and five captains allowed themselves to be cashiered rather than accept this: although they afterwards volunteered to defend James against the invasion and although one of them, Thomas Orme, had been a gentleman pensioner at James's coronation and came of a family severely mulcted by Cromwell.[2]

(III)

The new instruments of royal power made it possible for James to govern much as he pleased without having to face new rebellions. By embarking on a policy of catholic emancipation and attacks on the Church of England he made his rule so unpopular that his subjects

---

[1] Dalton, vol. ii, p. xi and note says 'about two score' catholics were recommissioned after parliament objected and he seems to list thirty-four, also six specifically removed in 1689 as papist. But CSPD. 1686–7, no. 101, yields another fifty. Dunbarton was a French major general.

[2] Dalton, vol. ii, pp. xvi–xvii summarizes these incidents.

deserted him almost with one accord when the country was invaded by a foreign prince. There is this to be said in defence of what he did —that only the combination of invasion and desertion was fatal to him. Unlike his father, he seems to have been safe at home as long as he was not exposed to attack by a foreign state. The national fear of revolution, so important in promoting the growth of royal power, was not extinct. Some previously loyal people experienced a change of heart, like Edward Butterfield, rector of Middle Clayton, who was led by the events of the reign to a more serious study of the nature of government than he had hitherto made. He decided 'with the rest of the clergy to give up non-resistance, and resolved that no authority is sacred nor claims submission but legal'.[1] But in September 1687 Barrillon reported

> there is a great deal of general excitement and there is considerable activity among the opposition groups in London; but the English are not easily moved to rebellion and they keep themselves within legal bounds so as not to run the risk of losing their property. This fear prevails in general over every other consideration in this country and their zeal for religion is not violent enough to lead them into enterprises which would make them liable to legal penalties.[2]

In the central government, administrators who were out of sympathy with royal policy tried to make the best of things as they were. The Ellis family, who all seem to have been in government or church service, were lucky in including a monk among their number. When the monk came into favour at court in James's reign, his protestant friends and relations took full advantage of it. 'St Paul refused not to go in the ship, though dedicated to heathen gods,' they said, and 'pray bow a little to Baal.' One of them told John Ellis that 'an honest, senseless monk' had got him to write a letter of recommendation 'and I durst as well be hanged as not do it' but it was to be ignored if the person recommended was unworthy. In May 1687 H. Aubrey, who was an Irish revenue commissioner and an English M.P., reported to John Ellis that office-holders unwilling to support the government's religious measures in parliament would be dismissed. 'I am told I must pass the fire ordeal. I am provided for it and resolved, as every honest man should be, to serve the King as far as

---

[1] Cited in Margaret M. Verney, *Memoirs of the Verney Family*, vol. iv (Longmans, 1899), pp. 409–11 and thence by G. Davies, *Essays on the Later Stuarts* (Huntington Library Publications, 1953), pp. 85–6.

[2] Turner, p. 365.

with a good conscience I may.'[1] This time-serving coupled with a refusal to do anything utterly base was found also among the nobility and gentry who were the natural leaders in the counties. They needed royal favour to keep ahead of their local rivals and they were reluctant to give up all chance of it, even when treated badly. Lord Ailesbury recalled that his 'maxim' was

> not to make one step against my conscience, on the other hand to be silent and to keep my place in Court as long as I could for to do good if possible and to keep the Earl of Peterborough from the lieutenancies I enjoyed.[2]

We shall see that when called on in 1687 to help in the election of a more pliable parliament, they often preferred evasion or perfuntory compliance to outright refusal.

Passive resistance accorded more with the national mood than rebellion. By itself it could not destroy the government now that standing armed forces had been created. Within the forces there was discontent, plotting, even secession to William. But relatively few were ready to take positive action against James and a good number showed positive loyalty to him. The concentration of troops at Hounslow to overawe the capital had a boomerang effect—it gave discontented officers a good opportunity for plotting. Ailesbury said that 'many chief officers so empoisoned the others that in process of time they were the instruments of all the King's misfortunes'. The camp was broken up in the summer of 1688, none too soon. But Ailesbury also said that 'most subalterns and private men continued firm to the King'.[3] An association of protestant officers were formed and the defection of (mainly) senior officers in face of the invader was crucial in crippling resistance and deciding James not to fight. But the deserters entirely failed in their attempts to take large bodies of troops with them. In the navy, there had been a near mutiny in 1687 when the catholic admiral, Sir Roger Strickland, had ordered the saying of mass on board his ship. Strickland was superseded by Dartmouth in September 1688, apparently because of the unpopularity of his religion. The fleet likewise came to have its informal association of protestant officers, perhaps inspired by the example of the army.[4] The naval officers did not get beyond the discouraging of battle and

---

[1] *Ellis Correspondence*, vol. i, pp. 83, 89, 299, 302–3.
[2] Ailesbury, vol. i, p. 153.   [3] Ailesbury, vol. i, p. 150.
[4] E. B. Powley, *The English Navy in the Revolution of 1688* (Cambridge University Press, 1928), p. 68.

their role even here was not decisive, as we shall see. Two well-placed observers thought that if it had come to a battle, most of the captains would not have fought,[1] but William was very lucky not to have to put this to the test.

Some idea of the amount of positive loyalty in the army can be gained by considering how many officers remained loyal to James after his fall, at least to the extent of refusing to serve his successor. If we take the English army as it stood in November 1687, and add together the officers then serving who fought for James after the Revolution, those who resigned or were dismissed at the time of his departure, and those whose service ended about that time for reasons unstated, we find that for the higher ranks (captain and above) the total is about a hundred—roughly a quarter of the establishment of 1687. For the junior officers (lieutenant and below) the figure is much more modest: about 160 out of roughly 800. Moreover, two-fifths of these are merely known to have left the service about the end of James's reign and many of them must represent natural wastage: only a few of the seniors are in this uncertain category. These figures do not bear out the idea that the juniors were more loyal than the seniors. On the other hand, the juniors were probably humbler people, who could less easily afford to defy authority. They were also less experienced and more easily replaced than the seniors. There were over a hundred new officers (mostly junior officers) who were appointed to the already established regiments after November 1687 and were dismissed or resigned at the end of the reign.[2]

The loyal officers were not evenly spread through the army but certain regiments seem to have been more loyal than the rest. After the Revolution, the winners paid certain regiments the compliment of disbanding them—apparently because they were thought to be too loyal to the outgoing monarch. McElligott's Irish regiment has already been mentioned. All the new regiments of horse that James had raised to meet the invasion and half the new-raised regiments of foot were likewise got rid of. So were some of the older units: Dover's troop of guards, Werden's regiment of cavalry and Prince George's regiment of infantry. It is to be doubted if all of them deserved it.

---

[1] Burchett and Byng. Powley, pp. 87–8.
[2] These figures and most of what follows are based on Dalton. But although he collected much information, his account is sketchy for many of the officers, and he sometimes contradicts himself.

Some were supposed to be bodies of catholics: Dover's, McElligott's, two new horse and two new foot regiments. Another horse regiment had been raised by Lord Salisbury, a catholic. Prince George's regiment was almost certainly disbanded because of its history: originally raised for sea service when James was lord high admiral, it had been called the Duke of York's regiment till 1685 and had long been suspected of infiltration by catholics. In fact almost all the officers seem to have been loyal to the new order of things. One regiment that was not disbanded gave far more tangible evidence of Jacobitism by a famous mutiny when it was ordered to fight in Flanders: the Royal Regiment of Foot. It was Scottish, it had served Louis XIV until ten years before, and on both counts it was no doubt most unwilling to be sent against the French. Werden's horse does indeed seem to have had a very large bloc of men loyal to James among the senior officers, as did Montgomery's,[1] Lichfield's, Huntingdon's and Hales's foot. A good share of such men was found in Peterborough's and Fenwick's horse, the Holland Regiment and the Royal Fusiliers. Some regiments definitely had 'rebels' at the top, but loyalists among the junior officers, like the Royal Dragoons (Cornbury's) or the Queen's Regiment of Foot (Trelawny's). Some seem to have had both 'rebels' at the top and at least no opposition to them lower down, like the Princess's Regiment of Horse (Scarsdale's). But how little all this might count, the case of Lichfield's regiment on one side and several on the other amply show. The separation of colonels from their regiments and regiments from their home areas may have counted for something here. The Earl of Bath, governor of Plymouth and lieutenant of the surrounding counties, joined William. His regiment of foot was stationed in Kent and seems to have been very loyal.

King James's soldiers cheered the acquittal of the seven bishops but in the main they would not rise against their master. There was a body of rebellious officers who doubtless enjoyed a great deal of sympathy but well-placed loyal officers seem to have outnumbered active rebels. Where these gained military ascendancy in 1688 it was by an energetic coup (as at Hull and Plymouth) rather than a general movement of opinion. It may be guessed that the soldiers did not rebel for the reason that the people did not: rebellions had been suppressed, political consciousness was at a low ebb and a lead was

---

[1] Son of Lord Powis, catholic rival of Beaufort in the west: took over his regiment.

expected from above. The officers may have achieved a degree of professional loyalty, disinterested or otherwise:[1] many were outright loyalists, most were steadily obedient to both old and new governments, as the civil servants were.

Even assuming some readiness to rebel in the country, and that some army units could not be relied on, the chances of beating James without massive foreign aid were slim. In 1685 the little force which James inherited in England was able to vanquish Monmouth's army (to which it was slightly inferior in numbers) before any reinforcements became available. Even at the bitter end, in December 1688, Ailesbury could tell the King that the officers who remained loyal pledged themselves to have 3,000 or 4,000 horse ready to march wherever he wished. Ailesbury urged him to march to Scotland, brushing aside Danby's 'broomsticks and whishtail militia' which had risen in Yorkshire. After the Revolution, Danby told Ailesbury that in that case there would have been no alternative but to submit and 'crave his pardon'.[2] Not only had there been a great increase in the royal standing forces but the physical capacity of the civil population to take up arms, whether for or against the government, was steadily diminishing. It was still commonly felt that respectable citizens ought to be allowed to have arms, both to assist in national defence and to protect themselves against malefactors in the absence of a proper police force. Country houses often contained miniature arsenals. In times of crisis the authorities seized the weapons of those whom they saw reason to mistrust, but they were expected to give the weapons back when things quietened down. Sir Robert Atkyns, a former judge suspected of opposition sympathies, complained of the confiscation of his arms in 1683. Not only was this a blow to his dignity, but he felt himself defenceless against the enemies which his judicial career had brought him and was afraid to leave his house.[3]

There had, however, been a steady decline for a century or more in the number of arms kept and of men proficient in their use. The civil wars may have reversed the trend for the time being but it was not permanently halted. There are signs that the disarming of the people for good was an integral part of the crown's measures for destroying

---

[1] Dalton lists many officers achieving good promotion in late 1688 and leaving or being driven from the army at the Revolution.

[2] Ailesbury, vol. i, pp. 193–6.

[3] Western, p. 69. On possession of arms cf. pp. 3, 4.

whig powers of resistance. At the time of the Rye House Plot (1683), the customary disarming of the opposition was ordered, but the arms were not afterwards restored: they were handed over to the militia or the ordnance. Moreover, an Act of 1671 for the preservation of game had substantially raised the property qualification entitling a man to hunt and had authorized the confiscation of sporting gear (including guns) belonging to persons without the qualification. The further disarming of the people seems to have been one result of this measure and James II's government took advantage of it: in 1686 Secretary Sunderland ordered the seizure of guns kept by persons without legal qualification on the pretence of taking part in shooting matches.[1]

The disarming of the people was accompanied and intensified by the decline of the militia. This comprised the 'trained bands' of former days, placed on a statutory basis at the Restoration and recruited by obliging property owners to hire and equip the soldiers. Parliament would have liked it to be the mainstay of national defence, but they made it so big that it could not be maintained in an efficient state with the funds available—or likely to be available. It numbered some 90,000 foot and 6,000 horse and the financial provisions of the militia act sufficed to pay for a few days' training each year, a certain amount of guard duty, and the mobilization of the whole force for about a month in an emergency. It could not really be made fit to fight in battle but it was very useful for police work in times of trouble. The disarming of opposition in the manner described above was its chief task, along with the arrest of suspects and the breaking up of conventicles. After the Restoration, when the civil wars had left ample material for rebellion in the form of disbanded soldiers and caches of arms, it was an important prop of monarchy. At the end of Charles II's reign it was the means of drawing such 'sting', in the way of arms, as the whigs possessed. Against Monmouth's army the militia could do little—the regiments that tried to fight him mostly ran away —but they contained his revolt by disarming and holding down his supporters in other parts of the country and their continued activity on his flanks and rear prevented him from effectively occupying the territory through which he passed. As long as many civilians possessed arms, something like the militia may well have been necessary.[2]

---

[1] CSPD 1686–7, no. 1212. Western, pp. 71, 72. Cf. pp. 119–20.
[2] Western, part 1.

Under James the militia was steadily superseded by the army, though it does not seem quite true to say that he got rid of them because he did not trust them. When Monmouth landed, Sunderland optimistically said that the militia in the south west was 'very affectionate', and orders went out to keep them together as long as the acts allowed and to take into royal pay those who were willing to serve longer.[1] Even when the news came that they were not fighting well, the King continued to urge their use to stop supplies and men reaching the enemy. He thought that they could do good service if well governed and recommended that they be stiffened by contingents of regulars or volunteers.[2] On July 16 he told the French ambassador that he would not be able to do without regular troops 'knowing how little value he could place on the militia'.[3] At the end of the month a circular was sent to the lord lieutenants asking what was the annual cost of keeping the militia together for as long as the law would allow.[4] There was a plan to use part at least of this money towards the expense of Chelsea Hospital.[5] But it does not seem to be until the spring of 1687 that instructions were issued to some lord lieutenants that there were to be no more musters of the militia without special order.[6] We shall see that this was the moment when the king was nerving himself to break with the loyal gentry, who controlled the militia, and forward his religious policy through an unholy alliance of catholics and dissenters. The disarming of the people and the building up of the army made the King less dependent on the militia—if he chose not to depend on it—and so more independent of the landed class. The clumsiness of the militia and the costliness of trying to make it work better made it natural for him to turn to the army. When his relations with his subjects worsened, he could afford to 'stand down' the only people outside the army who were organized for appearing in arms. This was troublesome when invasion came and the heavily burdened army needed reliable auxiliary forces on which lesser tasks could be devolved. But for the time being it meant that physical force was monopolized by organizations under the King's immediate control.

An important reason why James did not have to fear a rebellion like that which destroyed his father was that there was no longer any

[1] CSPD 1685, nos. 854, 992, 1138. [2] CSPD 1685, nos. 1154, 1159, 1161.
[3] Fox, p. cii. [4] CSPD 1685, no. 1368.
[5] Western, p. 48. [6] CSPD 1686-7, nos. 1807, 1808.

prospect of national insurrection in Scotland or Ireland.[1] It was the rebellion of the Scots that had led to the crisis in England in 1640. The subsequent rebellion of the native Irish and the fears and disputes to which it led in England were most important in the heightening of the crisis into civil war. Cromwell, however, had crushed the Scots and the Irish and made them totally subject to England. In this, as in other respects, the restored monarchy was the heir of Cromwell. Irish and Scottish turbulence was not extinct, but when the next great crisis (the popish plot) came along, both countries were kept in check. Nothing happened there this time to tip the balance against the crown in England. On the contrary, Ireland and Scotland emerged as a source of strength. They had been reduced to such subservience that the King could tax them more readily than he could tax England. As already noted, they made a significant contribution to the growing regular army.

In Scotland the King occupied a very strong position in the legal and governmental system. Scots law gave even less protection to the subject than English. It allowed, for instance, arbitrary imprisonment, torture and the punishment of juries whose verdicts displeased the authorities. The (single chamber) Scots parliament lacked power and independence. Some of the functions of the English parliament were performed by other bodies in Scotland. The parliamentary representatives of the Scottish commons were mostly small-town tradesmen, easily bullied. Legislation was initiated by a commission (the Lords of the Articles) nominated in effect by the crown. However, royal control of the government was not always accompanied by governmental control of the country. The territorial magnates had a tradition of rebellion and disorder to a degree no longer obtaining in England. The presbyterian party in the church likewise outdistanced the English puritans in rebelliousness, believing as they did that the lay power should be subordinate to the spiritual. Charles I's government had been overwhelmed by these rebellious elements and when Charles II briefly reigned in Scotland in 1650–1, it was almost as a captive.

The Restoration in Scotland, however, gave the king effective control of the country to a far greater degree than in England. Cromwell had driven the presbyterians from power and the Scottish

---

[1] This brief summary follows Ogg, Simms and G. Donaldson, *Scotland—James V to James VII* (Oliver and Boyd, 1965).

nobles had tired of their ascendancy and were ready for a partnership with the King. In contrast to the respect shown for the legislation of the Long Parliament, an Act Rescissory annulled all Scottish statutes passed since 1640. English-style taxes were voted on a scale generous for so poor a country and the king was able to keep up a substantial militia to support his authority. Episcopacy was restored and in 1669 an act of supremacy gave the king power to 'remove and transplant' bishops and clergy at will. Many presbyterians refused to accept the new ecclesiastical system, though it was a compromise which would probably have satisfied their more moderate English brethren. Attempts at toleration (1669–72) only strengthened the party, and Lauderdale, the most powerful Scottish minister, veered from conciliation to repression. Persecution had already led to revolt in 1666 and in 1679 it did so again. In 1680 some extremists even renounced their allegiance to Charles II. Scottish rebellion seemed admirably timed to help the exclusionists and the supporters of the crown bestowed on Shaftesbury's followers the nickname borne by the Scots presbyterian rebels: whigs. This was unfair in most cases yet very apt. But the Scottish whigs were not able to help the English parliamentarians as they had in 1640. The Scots militia proved unreliable, but the Scots parliament voted considerable funds and a little regular army was raised. The rebels of 1679 were defeated (ironically) by Monmouth, savage military repression kept the presbyterian south west in order thereafter and Argyll's attempt to rise in 1685 in support of Monmouth was a failure.

Lauderdale retired in 1680 and his place was taken by the Duke of York, who went to Scotland as his brother's commissioner in 1679 since England was too hot to hold him. Thanks to Lauderdale's work, James was able to rule Scotland almost as an absolute monarch and to show how he would wish to rule in England. The acts which he made the docile Scottish parliament pass are a notable pointer. In 1681 parliament declared that the religious beliefs of the heir to the throne in no way affected his right to succeed, and they imposed an unusually wide-ranging 'non-resisting' oath. Everyone had to promise not to try and bring about changes in church or state—not even to the extent of attending meetings on such subjects. In the spring of 1685, when James had become King, the Scots parliament made the excise (the main source of revenue in Scotland) perpetual and instituted the death penalty for attendance at conventicles. They further gave protection to royal officials against prosecution for their mis-deeds and placed the lives and fortunes of all Scots aged between sixteen and sixty at the King's disposal. Though whigs and moderates in England were horrified at Scottish developments, there was one aspect of James's rule there which greatly reassured the tories. He stoutly supported the episcopal church and showed no signs of under-mining it to the profit of presbyterians or catholics. But in this respect James's behaviour in Scotland was no reliable guide to what he would do in England. He was no way inclined to help the presbyterians, since they were rebels. He rightly regarded the Scottish bishops as docile tools of monarchy (any who were not could be instantly dismissed). He expected to find the Church of England just as pliant, and when he found that it was not, his attitude towards it changed.

Ireland was a larger and richer country than Scotland, better able to provide resources that would strengthen the monarchy elsewhere. Charles II and James II had less to fear than their predecessors from the catholicism and national feeling of the Irish—they believed their main problem to be the political unreliability of the dominant British minority. Cromwell had completely subdued the Irish and the royalists who had taken refuge with them. The greater part of the land had been divided among the 'soldiers and adventurers' who had helped the reconquest with their swords or purses—fit companions for the Scottish presbyterians already settling in the north. Their leaders willingly restored Ireland to Charles II in 1660, but he did not trust them and tried to build up a counterweight to their influence. Initially he attempted to win support in Ireland by promising both that the Cromwellians might keep their land and that the deprived loyalists (including loyal catholics) should be restored to the land that they had lost. The Irish parliament passed an Act of Settlement (1662) and an Act of Explanation (1665) to resolve the contradiction. The Cromwellians had to surrender some of their land—not, as a rule, directly to the former owners but to the King, who bestowed it on men who were thought to be reliable. Much went to English courtiers but Irish catholics were given a certain amount. Cromwell had reduced their share of the land from 60% to under 9%. It rose again to 25% by 1685. The main agent in begging land from the crown for catholics was an Irish friend of the Duke of York named Richard Talbot. The catholics of course were not satisfied with the meagre extent of their restitution. Former landowners haunted the districts where their properties had been situated and some took to brigandage. The name of tory bestowed on these brigands was to achieve wider currency.

The good financial position of the crown in Ireland should be viewed against this background. The protestant minority who dominated the Irish parliament[1] needed the King's protection if they were to keep their land and hold down the papists. (Parliament moreover could not legislate without the prior leave of the English privy council.) After the Restoration the Irish parliament followed the English pattern in extinguishing feudal dues and voting taxes instead—seemingly on a generous scale. Sir William Petty, the eminent economic expert (himself an Irish 'adventurer'), computed that England had fifteen times the wealth of Ireland, but paid only six times as much in taxes. Eventually topping a quarter of a million a year, the Irish revenue sometimes yielded a surplus—even as early as 1670—and provided the King not only with troops but with a small reserve of ready cash. Moreover, it had been voted in perpetuity. After 1666 therefore the Irish parliament ceased to be summoned.

The crown was strong enough in Ireland to prevent anyone stirring there in the years of the popish plot. This was important: any activity among the Irish catholics might have so intensified the panic in England as to make civil war possible. But though the events of 1641–2 were not repeated, the precarious equilibrium in Ireland was disturbed and not thereafter restored. First catholics and then protestants suffered: eventually English opinion was to be seriously upset, and though King James believed himself to be further strengthening the crown's position in Ireland, it is doubtful if he was really compensated in this way. For most of Charles's reign Irish affairs were roughly in a state of balance, thanks to the prudence of the Duke of Ormonde and the Earl of Essex who between them governed the country for twenty years. They restrained both protestants and catholics. Employment under the crown and in local government was almost exclusively reserved for protestants but the catholics were protected from persecution. The popish plot, however, obliged Ormonde to repress the catholics in order to keep them quiet. They were disarmed, catholic bishops and regular clergy were expelled, some religious institutions were dissolved. Once the crisis was over

[1] Catholics were not excluded.

it was the turn of the protestants to suffer. The repression of the whigs in England tended to bring all old roundheads under suspicion. Since the protestants in Ireland were very largely of this character, a renewed strengthening of the catholics was thought to be desirable. In June 1684 James's friend Talbot presented a report on Ireland to the King. In October it was decided that Rochester should replace the elderly Ormonde and inaugurate a new policy. Rochester told him that the King was doubtful of the loyalty of the Irish army. In December the King told Rochester that he would remove the Irish troops from the control of the lord lieutenant and place them under a lieutenant general responsible directly to a secretary of state in London. All officers who had borne arms against his father or himself would be removed. Charles told Barrillon that he would begin to appoint catholic officers in Ireland, beginning with Colonel Justin Maccarty who had served Louis XIV. Sunderland as secretary of state was to preside over this reorganization and the idea may even have been his. It was the beginning of his liaison with James and the catholics that was to bring him to power.

James's accession set the seal on these plans. Talbot was the first catholic to be given a military commission. Raised to the earldom of Tyrconnel, he went to Ireland in May 1685, and though in subordinate command, he was able to begin the removal of protestant officers. The post of lord lieutenant, which seems to have become a sort of booby-prize for unsuccessful leading courtiers, was temporarily vacant: the King had promoted Rochester. Sunderland was proposed for the post by his rival, which would have removed him from the seat of power: he retaliated by proposing Rochester's brother, Clarendon. Tyrconnel regarded this appointment as a defeat and at once left Ireland, but the new policy continued: no doubt things might have been different if the English parliament had continued to sit.[1] In March 1686, Sunderland told Clarendon of a comprehensive plan to bring catholics into the council, the magistracy and the municipal corporations; three judges were also removed. Clarendon was humiliatingly informed that his advice had not been asked because as yet he did not know as much about Ireland as the King's other advisers.[2] Even before official word had reached him, Clarendon had protested and in particular urged that any catholics that were

[1] Kenyon, pp. 101–3, 120. Turner, pp. 379–87.
[2] *Clarendon Correspondence*, vol. i, pp. 293–4.

employed should be English, not Irish. James replied that employing Irish catholics would not damage

> the true English interest there, so long as the Act of Settlement is kept untouched, which it must always be, though many ill and disaffected people are secured in their possessions by it; which makes it the more necessary for me to secure myself and the Government against such, for you cannot but be sensible that there are but too many of the old leaven amongst the English there.[1]

The Irish privy council was remodelled in May and Clarendon ordered the corporations to admit catholics in June.[2] Tyrconnel returned to expedite the remoulding of the army and to take command of it. He also tried to interfere extensively in civil business and he soon began to press for more radical measures still, involving at least a tampering with the Act of Settlement. At the end of August he went back to court to press his case, leaving general alarm behind him.[3] Clarendon thought that over 2,000 catholics had been brought into the army even before Tyrconnel's visit and these men were making bloodcurling boasts.[4] Protestants were threatened with denunciation for having taken part in whig plots. They saw good officers and soldiers turned out and ragamuffins put in. Clarendon told his brother that

> if the King will but hear his English subjects, and consider, what he did believe when I left England, that the contest here is not about religion, but between English and Irish, which is the truth, all will do well.[5]

But in January 1687 Clarendon was recalled and Tyrconnel appointed in his stead.

Further Irish developments belong intimately to the story of the Revolution. They were just the thing to arouse a panic fear of popery that would neutralize the great weight of veneration for the King's authority. The gradual eclipse of Clarendon's loyalty should probably be viewed in this light. Actually the government's aim seems always to have been the restraint rather than the ruin of the supposedly dangerous protestants. James had no wish to emancipate Ireland from English tutelage. Even Tyrconnel proposed to leave the protestants with half their land (the better half) and in the towns likewise there

---

[1] *Clarendon Correspondence*, vol. i, pp. 298, 339.
[2] *ibid.*, pp. 399, 400, 417–18, 461–2.
[3] *ibid.*, pp. 560–3.
[4] *ibid.*, p. 514.
[5] *ibid.*, p. 559.

was an attempt to hold a balance between protestant and catholic traders. It was above all the army that gradually became a catholic stronghold. Many protestants fled from Ireland in alarm but economic activity, in which protestants predominated, did not seriously begin to flag until late in 1688. This of course meant that Ireland continued to be a source of strength to James, even if an embarrassing one.

The general situation in his three kingdoms suggests that James would not have lost his throne if William of Orange had not come over. This is clear enough even from the terms of the invitation on which William insisted. The 'immortal seven' English leaders who signed it were anxious not to mislead the Prince and so avoided optimistic statements. Even allowing for this, the document they sent him showed clearly how desperate they were. They believed that 'nineteen parts out of twenty' of the people were 'desirous of change' and

> would willingly contribute to it if they had such a protection to countenance their rising as would secure them from being destroyed before they could get to be in a posture able to defend themselves;

The same applied to 'much the greatest part of the nobility and gentry' while the army and still more the navy were thoroughly disaffected. Yet they warned the Prince that it was doubtful if he could make his preparations sufficiently secret to avoid the arrest and disruption of his friends before his landing. Nevertheless, they hoped that he would risk an attempt that year because (as they said at the outset) 'we have great reason to believe we shall be every day in a worse condition than we are and less able to defend ourselves'. They expected within a year to see a purge of the army and further purges calculated to produce a subservient parliament:

> if things cannot then be carried to their wishes in a parliamentary way, other measures will be put in execution by more violent means; and although such proceedings will then heighten the discontents, yet such courses will probably be taken at that time as will prevent all possible means of relieving ourselves.[1]

In other words, England would go the way of Scotland.

There could therefore be no revolution without William, and William was a Prince and half a Stuart. He would not intervene

---

[1] Dalrymple, vol. ii, bk. v, pp. 107–10.

unless he had good reason of his own for doing so and he was highly unlikely to join in any plan for lessening the power of the monarchy. This meant that the Stuarts had done enough to secure the permanence of their work. The legitimate dynasty was to be overthrown but not the army, the navy, the taxes, the new methods of administration. The Stuarts had inherited the shadow of these things from Cromwell, had restored their substance and endowed the nation with them in perpetuity, whether it would have them or no. Religious toleration, which in retrospect seems like the jam that accompanied all this governmental powder, was likewise initiated during the Interregnum, revived by James and not thereafter abolished—though that is not to say that James deserves sole or even much credit for it. It was the ramifications of the religious question that enabled William to intervene in English affairs. The Revolution was not really a popular uprising but nor was it a military conquest. William would not have come over with an army of 12,000 men to fight a king at the head of 40,000 if religious developments had not produced a situation in which the people could be expected to be on his side. Why, though, should he have any desire even then to embark on such an enterprise? Religion was in evidence here too, but for him it was also a diplomatic and dynastic question. The revolution was made by a confederacy with both British and foreign components, of which William was the centre—a surprising alliance of elements not usually combined, heavily reliant on people who normally abhorred revolution. The character of the Revolution reflected the nature of the confederacy that made it. To understand that we need to consider both religious developments in England and the European position of William of Orange.

NOTE

Though without influence on the power struggle in England, the attempts of Charles and James to decrease the autonomy of some of the American colonies deserve mention since they were so much of a piece with what was being done elsewhere. Englishmen of all parties believed in the subjection of the colonies to the home country, especially in matters of trade, but whigs like Shaftesbury thought that the colonists should be allowed a good deal of local self-government. The royal authorities, however, regarded autonomous colonies as potentially dangerous, like municipal corporations. The New England colonies had been allowed more independence than the rest and campaigns were waged against them closely parallel to those against the English boroughs. In both cases there was an abortive offensive immediately after the Restoration followed by a more sustained effort in the 1680s. Massachusetts had managed to preserve its charter on the earlier occasion, but a royal commissioner enquired into its government in 1676 and presented an unfavourable report. Legal proceedings eventually led to the forfeiture of its charter in 1684 and the government further decided to annul the charters of Rhode Island and Connecticut and merge New England, New York and New Jersey into a single large colony. There was to be no elective assembly, as had hitherto been the practice. Sir Edmund Andros was appointed governor of this great province in 1686 and succeeded in bringing it fully into being by the following year. The colony of New York was a precursor of this scheme. In 1664 Charles had empowered his brother James to conquer New Amsterdam from the Dutch and to make himself its proprietor. It has borne his ducal title as its name ever since. James tried to rule through a governor and nominated council without an elective assembly. Andros was his governor from 1673 to 1682, when the colonists, by threatening to pay no taxes, obliged the Duke to convene a sort of constituent assembly. On becoming King, James rejected the constitutional charter which they had drawn up. But through he ruled autocratically, he had established religious freedom—in contrast to the intolerance which prevailed in Massachusetts. The medley of national and religious groups in the ex-Dutch colony made this essential. Autocracy and religious freedom—which he believed would be good for trade—were eventually to become the keynotes of James's government in England too.

6

The Religious Question

THE place of religion in seventeenth-century politics is paradoxical. It was considered essential to the well-being of society and yet it was also the most obvious threat to social stability. Almost everyone believed that God was the ultimate source of political authority and relied on the fear of God to make men perform their social duties. This is particularly seen in the extensive use of oaths, not only in the courts of law but also to ensure obedience to the government and upright conduct by officials. But just because religion was so important, the claim could be raised that the secular power ought to subordinate itself to the spiritual. The calvinists and the papists in particular, though normally they regarded obedience to the established government as a religious duty, were inclined to justify revolt against rulers who were not of the true faith. It was obvious how much the strength of the rebellion against Charles I had owed to the puritans and the Scottish Kirk. The Irish rising of 1641 was a telling example of rebellion from the other religious extreme. Educated people further remembered the French wars of religion in the sixteenth century, when calvinists and papists in turn had attacked the monarchy.

Nobody was more conscious of the political dangers of religion than the advocates of strong government. Hobbes listed among the seditious doctrines weakening the commonwealth the beliefs 'that every private man is judge of good and evil actions'; 'that whatsoever a man does against his conscience is sin'; 'that faith and sanctity are not to be attained by study and reason but by supernatural inspiration'; and above all that the church is independent of the state, 'another kingdom, as it were a kingdom of fairies, in the dark'.[1]

---

[1] *Leviathan,* chap. 29.

His response was to give state authority a primarily secular basis. But the older idea of the divine right of kings had equally originated as a means of defending lay rulers from clerical interference: it derived from the medieval quarrel of empire and papacy. Filmer said that 'the main and indeed the only point of popery is the alienating and withdrawing of subjects from their obedience to their prince' and *Patriarcha* opens with an attack on the famous Jesuit writer Bellarmine.[1] John Nalson in 1678 equated the 'spirituo-temporal monarchy' of Rome and the 'democratical presbyterian' as 'utterly inconsistent with the safety and very essence of monarchy . . . as also with the peace, happiness, liberty and property of the subjects'.[2] Innumerable sermons on the anniversary of Charles I's death took this as their theme. In 1685 Evelyn heard the Bishop of Ely 'perstringing' the 'pretended reformists' who

> favour'd the killing of kings whom they found not complying with their discipline; among these (after he had deduced that wicked doctrine of divers popes and their doctors etc.) he reckoned *Calvine* who implicitly verges that way; and observed that not one of all the regicides executed for the murder so barbarously perpetrated this day shewed any signs of remorse.[3]

'Sure the hand of Joab the Jesuit with his king-killing doctrine was in all this,' explained another preacher, 'and every one of the regicides had a pope in his belly to give him a dispensation and absolve him from his oath of allegiance.'[4]

The problem with religion as with secular politics was to discover what was the most conservative system: to organize religious teaching and observance in such a way that it supported rather than disrupted the state. After the Restoration, the Church of England regained its religious and educational monopoly. Charles I and parliament had failed to agree on a replacement for it before the civil wars; Charles II and parliament did agree (at least after the 1661 elections) in wanting it back. The anglican system was an attempt to reconcile uniformity of worship in a politically dependable church with freedom of conscience. The king appointed the higher dignatories of the church and had extensive powers of interference within it, as we shall see. The law required attendance at the official church services and (more important) acceptance of the royal supremacy in church matters. Severe penalties might be imposed in default by both lay and

---

[1] Figgis, pp. 180, 184.   [2] Figgis, p. 188 n. 1.
[3] Evelyn's Diary, vol. iv, pp. 404–5.   [4] Figgis, p. 380.

ecclesiastical courts (with excommunication, for instance, leading to imprisonment). It is true that the court of high commission had been abolished in 1641 and was not revived. But as with its secular equivalent, Star Chamber, its loss was partly made up for by the increasing political reliability of the other courts. On the other hand the conformity required was increasingly external and political rather than truly religious. The Elizabethan Act of Supremacy had finally repealed the medieval statutes which enabled the ecclesiastical courts to require the burning of all those convicted of heresy.[1] The crown retained the power to impose the death penalty on heretics in special cases. But the last burning of heretics in England took place in 1612 and when in 1677 a judge in Wales threatened some quakers with the flames it caused such a stir that the government rebuked him and parliament abolished all temporal penalties for heresy.[2] The Act of Supremacy had moreover limited the definition of heresy to what was so adjudged by the authority of scripture or of the first four general councils.[3] Increasingly anglican apologists repudiated the idea of interfering with a man's private beliefs or personal worship.[4]

In the same spirit, the penalties imposed on religious dissent were proportioned to the amount of political danger supposedly represented by the people in question. The maximum penalties were extreme. To maintain the supremacy of the Pope and to refuse the oaths acknowledging that of the King could lead to outlawry and forfeiture—sometimes to death. Conversion to the Roman church was high treason for both converter and proselyte. Non-attendance at anglican worship could entail the forfeiture of two-thirds of a man's estate. It was the catholics who were most likely to incur these and other severe penalties. But protestants who would not go to church and attended conventicles might forfeit all their goods and be required on pain of death to promise, under oath, to leave the realm forever.[5] As a rule, though, the severest laws were not put in force after the Restoration. The authorities thought it sufficient to muzzle non-anglicans and keep them out of positions of influence. The Act of

[1] 1 Eliz. I cap. 1, s.6.
[2] C. E. Whiting, *Studies in English Puritanism 1660–1688* (Church History Society, 1931), pp. 145–6.
[3] Or so declared by parliament and convocation together. Sect. 20.
[4] *e.g.* Whiting, pp. 498, 503. For the development of this position see W. K. Jordan, *Development of Religious Toleration in England* (Allen and Unwin, 1932–40).
[5] Convenient summary in Whiting, pp. 441–2.

Uniformity (1662) excluded nonconforming clergy from the church, the schools and the universities. The religious side of the Corporation Act was strengthened by the Act of 1665 which obliged such teachers and clergy to remove five miles from any corporate town, or any other town where they had ministered. Significantly, they were allowed to stay if they would take the 'non-resisting' test. Meetings of dissenters for worship were suppressed on the ground that they were a cover for plotting. The government first ordered suppression after Venner's futile rising in January 1661.[1] Further plots brought a temporary (1664–7) Conventicle Act which punished attendance at a conventicle with transportation for the third offence. Because 'seditious sectaries . . . have or may at their meeting contrive insurrections', a permanent Conventicle Act was passed in 1670. But its penalties did not go beyond stiff fines. Neither Conventicle Act applied to family gatherings with not more than four outsiders present. It was the propagation of dissent that was attacked rather than dissent itself.

This system was simply the application to church matters of what was still the most popular doctrine concerning the extent of political authority: that there were certain 'fundamentals' which formed a law that ruler and subject alike had to observe but that in 'things indifferent', undetermined in this way, it was for the ruler to decide and the subject to obey him. What the religious fundamentals were was suggested by the restricted definition of heresy in the Act of Supremacy. Some anglicans would have wished to add a few more points, particularly the government of the church by bishops. On other matters it was not claimed that the church of England could infallibly pronounce, but merely that the anglican way was one among several that might be lawful and that it should be followed because the ruler commanded it. Opposition to the system was hampered and limited by the fact that hardly anyone dared contemplate complete religious freedom. In particular, most of the protestant dissenters did not dissent in fundamentals but 'only desired that such things might not be pressed upon them in God's worship which in their judgment who used them were acknowledged to be matters indifferent and by others were held unlawful'.[2] The presbyterians among them even wished to preserve uniformity, but in their own way. Indeed their

---

[1] F. Bate, *The Declaration of Indulgence, 1672* (Constable, 1908), p. 16.
[2] Bate, p. 6 (some dissenting ministers to Charles II at Breda in 1660).

main objection against the church was that it was not strict enough: the bishops and their courts were too lax in repressing vice. They would retain bishops, but wanted 'only things necessary to be the terms of union' and 'the true exercise of church discipline against sin'.[1] Anglicans maintained that it was frivolous to reject the established rule in matters which neither side thought were fundamental. Schism was sinful and lack of uniformity in worship was not merely indecorous but set a dangerous example of disobedience. Some anglicans procured 'testimonials' from foreign presbyterians to the effect that they would conform to the Church of England if they were English. Nonconformist teaching sometimes seems to bear out the anglican contention that their dissent indicated a general propensity to disobey. A writer against the Five Mile Act in 1669 said that laws not made for the public weal did not bind the conscience.[2]

The fact remained that under Cromwell an entirely different religious system had been in force. Although religious practices considered dangerous to the state had been repressed, a considerable diversity had been officially allowed. The powerful new army rather than the power of a traditional religious faith had been relied on to maintain the authority of the state. Religion had contributed to this result by sustaining the morale and discipline of the army, but it was the religion not of the nation but of the minority possessed of military power. The conjunction of a standing army and religious diversity was found elsewhere in Europe in the later seventeenth century: most notably in the Dutch Republic but also in France (till the revocation of the Edict of Nantes) and in the Elector of Brandenburg's territories. The conjunction was not accidental: it was a new formula for stability and power in the state. Money was needed to pay for armies: trade and industry had to be encouraged if the necessary revenue was to be forthcoming, and it was in the trading and industrial part of the community that religious dissent flourished, explain it how you will. It is worth emphasizing that both constituents of the formula were likely to be anathema to English squires. In most areas both church and militia were strongly under their influence and the militia was very much the secular arm of the church, the main instrument in breaking up large conventicles. The Cromwellian system threatened the power of the squires in two closely related

[1] Bate, p. 9 (Baxter to Charles, Clarendon etc. in June 1660).
[2] Whiting, p. 505.

fields. In 1668 opponents of toleration in the house of commons argued that it was only possible in France and Holland because there was a standing army to keep order:[1] this was an important reason for the squires to support the anglican monopoly.

But though Cromwell's legacy might be repudiated, the religious effects of his rule could not be entirely undone, except on paper. The protestant sects had been allowed freely to expand and could not readily be broken up. The anglicans had ceased to be the established church and they acquired in consequence some of the characteristics —strengths as well as weaknesses—of a sect. The dynasty in exile had had an opportunity for religious rethinking. From all this grew great changes in the triangular relationship between king, established church and nation.

The religious fruits of the Interregnum seem to have been a greater diversity of belief and a greater stiffness in maintaining the different points of view. Most of the extremer sects fell on evil days after the Restoration and served only to provide the persecutors with evidence that toleration would be socially dangerous. But the Cromwellian period had seen the beginnings of the quakers and they continued to develop under persecution. With their reliance on the 'inner light' and highly informal way of worship, they represented a radical new departure in religion that was as distasteful to puritans as to anglicans. In their early days they testified to their faith by breaches of decorum, ranging from refusal of 'hat honour' to noisy demonstrations in church and going about naked. Even more seditious were their refusal to pay tithes and, above all, their refusal to take oaths: a traditional form of social protest. This aroused such horror that a special Act was made against refusing oaths in 1662. It also meant that the quakers were at a disadvantage in all legal actions and that they were liable to be punished, like catholics, for refusing the oath of supremacy. The quakers were the most persecuted of the sects and the other dissenters complained that but for the horror they inspired there would have been less persecution.[2] But they were also the staunchest in resisting persecution and active in organizing themselves to meet the distress which it caused. Quaker sufferers may well have numbered 15,000, deaths as many as 450, with a pecuniary loss of a million pounds under Charles II and James II.[3] This more than

[1] Western, p. 49. [2] Whiting, p. 153.
[3] Whiting, p. 218.

anything made it impossible to regard persecution as the correction of some over-scrupulous people who had got slightly and temporarily out of step with the church.

But the gap between the bulk of the puritans and the anglicans was also getting wider, with the same effect. The independents and baptists, who wanted freedom for the individual congregations, had gained in strength during the Interregnum. The presbyterians, who wanted to maintain much uniformity, were forced by their exclusion from the church in 1662 to behave like independents. As time went on, the younger and less socially influential members of the group tended to accept their dissenting status as permanent and try to improve it; their more conservative brethren never lost their loyalty to the church to which they had once belonged. Secretary Williamson nicknamed this section the Dons and the more radical group, the Ducklings. It was the Five Mile Act which revealed the difference: the Dons were willing to take the 'non-resisting' oath, the others were not.[1] Within the Church of England an analogous development was taking place. A party of militant anglicans[2] had emerged who were hostile to the idea of compromise for the sake of comprehensiveness which was attractive both to more moderate anglicans and to the Dons. Though they may not have wished to drive their adversaries out of the church,[3] they resembled the more sectarian dissenters in their strong belief that their opinion in matters generally held in doubt was the right one, and in stressing the differences rather than the similarities between the church and non-anglican protestants. This point of view had been emerging under the early Stuarts but was much more characteristic of the Restoration. Perhaps the most striking manifestation of it was the insistence for the first time in the Act of Uniformity of 1662 that all beneficed clergy of the Church of England must be episcopally ordained.[4] This was one important reason why the presbyterians left the church, even though many of them had received episcopal ordination. There was also a growing reluctance to worship in foreign

---

[1] Whiting, p. 60. Dons included Baxter, Bates, Jacomb, Manton. Ducklings included Watson, Janeway and Samuel Annesley, cousin of Lord Anglesey.

[2] A trend rather than a party. Such terms as 'Laudian' and 'High Church' which can be applied to definite groups do not fit all the people here concerned. What follows relies heavily on R. S. Bosher, *The Laudians and the Making of the Restoration Church Settlement* (Dacre Press, 1951).

[3] This is a controversial point: see Bosher, pp. 270–3.

[4] sect. 13.

protestant churches. In the sixteenth century the English ambassador in Paris had attended Huguenot worship. Under the Stuarts this was discouraged.

Anglican militancy reflected a growth of popularity and so of self-confidence in the church. The English reformation had been imposed from above and the Laudian régime likewise had depended on royal support. But in time protestantism, in its puritan guise, had become a great popular movement and now anglicanism underwent a similar transformation. During the Interregnum it was no longer the official religion. It retained the loyalty of those who really believed in it and attracted many who were opposed to the new régime. It became and henceforth remained the religion of the ordinary squire who loved the King but was jealous of his local independence. In 1661 a strongly anglican house of commons was elected for the first time. The anglicans now occupied a position similar to that of the bulk of the puritans in 1640—men who had not been dissenters excluded from established institutions, but on the contrary occupied a strong position in church and parliament. Anglican political attitudes evolved accordingly. The Laudians had always repudiated the view that the church was a mere creature of the state. They believed that bishops like kings held their authority by divine right and that it was the duty of the ruler to defend the church against those who would alter its character. The anglican doctrine of non-resistance to royal authority was balanced by that of passive obedience: unlawful[1] commands were to be disobeyed and only the punishment for disobedience passively endured. After the Restoration the anglicans in no way kowtowed to the King. The house of commons, in passing the revised prayer book of 1662 without discussion, were careful to record that they had a right to discuss it. The new bishops, too, were of sterner temper than their predecessors, who when dethroned by Cromwell had slunk into obscurity and given almost no lead to the anglican faithful. Any hint that the King might not support the church now brought strong episcopal protest. In January 1663 Gilbert Sheldon, the strongest of the bishops, reproved Charles for seeking to end persecution.

> By your act you labour to set up that most damnable and heretical doctrine of the church of Rome, whore of Babylon. How hateful will it be to God

[1] That is, contrary to the 'fundamentals'.

and grievous to your good subjects . . . that your majesty . . . should now show yourself a patron of the doctrines which your pen hath told the world, and your conscience tells yourself, are superstitious, idolatry and destestable. Besides, this toleration . . . cannot be done without a parliament, unless your majesty will let your subjects see that you will take unto yourself liberty to throw down the laws of the land at your pleasure.[1]

In 1660 Dr Herbert Croft, later Bishop of Hereford, had warned the King, referring to his alliance with the presbyterians in 1650,

that for the guilt he had contracted in Scotland and the injuries he was brought to do against the Church of England, God had defeated him at Worcester and pursued his controversy with a nine years' exile; and yet He would further pursue him if he did close with His enemies.[2]

Sheldon's rebuke in particular prefigures closely the attitude of the bishops in 1688. The Church of England was becoming more intransigent both towards the dissenters and towards the government. On both counts it was becoming less well suited to the role of a comprehensive, monopolist state church for which the Elizabethan settlement had designed it.

It is hard to say what was the strength of the different religious groups in Restoration England. In 1676, when he was trying to restore the waning alliance between church and king, Danby had a religious census made with the object of proving that the dissenters were too few to be bothered with. It showed that there were nearly $2\frac{1}{2}$ million conformists over the age of sixteen, against only 108,000 protestant nonconformists and under 14,000 papists. These figures disregard the leverage the dissenters could exercise through being concentrated in London and the other towns; also the fact, officially noted in the returns, that conformity increased as soon as it was known that the census was to be made.[3] There were undoubtedly many laymen and even many clergy who belonged to the Church of England without sharing the militant anglican view that it was the one true church in the land and that its system was better than any other. Some idea of the strength of the militant anglicans among the clergy during the Interregnum can be gained from the number of clergy expelled from their posts by the victorious Roundheads. Out of about 8,600 livings in England, 2,425 are known to have been

[1] Bosher, p. 264, n. 3. [2] Bosher, p. 155.
[3] CSPD 1693–4, pp. 448–50.

sequestered; in the cathedrals and universities, 1,479 deprivations are recorded. There may have been more expulsions, but on the other hand the total must be scaled down to take account of pluralism. It is clear that at least half the clergy carried on under Cromwell. Likewise most of the clergy who occupied livings at the end of the Cromwell era carried on under the Restoration. The number of those who either left in 1662 or were turned out in order to restore the old incumbent was about 1760.[1] It seems unlikely that the clergy were less devoted to anglicanism than the influential laymen who appointed them, or indeed than the general body of the laity. Probably the bulk of the nation should be thought of as simply protestant. The militant anglicans exercised a good deal of control over the church but they were a minority like the dissenters. There are many instances of clergy who were really out of place in the church, some having conformed in 1662 only after much heart-searching.[2] As for the dissenters, the compilers of the 1676 census in the province of Canterbury noted that many, especially of the presbyterians, came to church and that many belonged to no sect. They believed that the chief sects—presbyterians, baptists, independents and quakers—were of roughly equal strength. But when the King issued licences for dissenting worship in 1672, many more were given to presbyterians than to baptists and independents combined.[3]

In this situation the relatively mild form of persecution in force was not an appropriate policy. It hurt the dissenters without liquidating them. It fell upon some who were heterodox from the militant anglican point of view but inoffensive to moderate opinion. It therefore promoted discord in the nation instead of uniformity. There was a growing reluctance to enforce the law, evident in the penalties imposed by the Conventicle Act of 1670 on officials who failed to do so. This reflected the sympathy with puritanism, still strong among gentry and town officials, but also the growing dislike of persecution even on the part of sincere anglicans. During a big drive against conventicles in the City in the summer of 1670, men were heard to

[1] A. G. Matthews, *Walker Revised* and *Calamy Revised* (Oxford University Press, 1948 and 1934): discussed by Bosher, pp. 5, 266 and Miss Whiteman in G. F. Nuttall and O. H. Chadwick, *From Uniformity to Unity* (S.P.C.K., 1962), pp. 34–5.

[2] Whiting, pp. 28–30, 404. N. Sykes, *From Sheldon to Secker* (Cambridge University Press, 1959), pp. 27–9.

[3] Quakers would not take licences. F. Bate, *The Declaration of Indulgence 1672*, appendix vii.

say that they loved the liturgy but not this way.[1] The political in-offensiveness of most of the dissenters must have become increasingly apparent. The presbyterians had helped in the Restoration and remained loyal under persecution. The quakers, though they were the most dynamic and radical of the sects, were also the leading practitioners of the passive obedience preached by the official church. In 1685 some of them published a 'testimony against all plots, conspiracies and rebellions' and the few who joined Monmouth were disavowed.[2] We shall see that the other sects too were interested in protection from the powers that be, not in reviving the kingdom of the Saints. The increasing preoccupation with worldly prosperity, of course, did much to change the religious climate. The argument that toleration was good for trade became a main instead of a sub-ordinate part of the case for more religious freedom. Economic experts such as Sir William Petty joined in the debates of the theo-logians.[3] The trade depression resulting from the second Dutch war may have stimulated this line of argument. The example of foreign countries, important in the economic debate, had a wider effect in showing the viability of toleration. Life in Cleves as secretary to a mission to the Elector of Brandenburg helped to turn Locke from a supporter into an opponent of intolerance. 'They quietly permit one another to choose their way to heaven,' he said, 'for I cannot observe any quarrels or animosities amongst them upon the account of religion.' He gave credit both to 'the power of the magistrate' and 'the prudence and good nature of the people'.[4]

The search for the secret of prosperity went along with the new emphasis on 'interest' as a human motive and the belief that men's interests harmonized helped to make liberal views credible in religious matters no less than in politics. The tory Sir Roger L'Estrange in 1682 could still say of the dissenter

he deserves to be expelled humane society that narrowly prefers his little, dirty interest.

But Dr John Owen, the greatest of the independents, had written that 'to surmise the acting of multitudes, contrary to their own interests

---

[1] Western, p. 50. Whiting, pp. 414–24 for Puritan gentry; pp. 432–5 and G. R. Cragg, *From Puritanism to the Age of Reason* (Cambridge University Press, 1950), pp. 221–2 for anglican sympathy.

[2] Whiting, p. 181.   [3] Petty devised a new catechism. Whiting, p. 537.

[4] H. R. Fox Bourne, *Life of John Locke* (1876), vol. I, pp. 103–4.

. . . is to take away all assurance out of humane affairs'. Toleration would 'preserve industrious men in a peaceable way of improving their own interests' and this would ensure national strength and unity.[1] This argument was especially favoured by the two religious extremes—the quakers and the papists. Quakers would not take oaths and protestants did not believe that papists were bound by them. So both needed a means of proving that they could be trusted and the idea of 'interest' supplied this. In 1651 John Austin, a catholic lawyer, had argued that catholics, if given freedom, would be 'bound by their own interest (the strongest obligation amongst wise men) to live peaceably'.[2] William Penn wrote in 1688 that

> whatever be the morality of any party, if I am sure of them by the side of interest and necessity, I will never seek or value an ensurance by oaths and tests.

Later in life he reflected that 'interest has the security though not the virtue of a principle'.[3] Though Penn was an oddity—or at any rate an anachronism—in being both a dissenter and a courtier, it is fair to say that there was nothing illogical about a quaker lining up behind James II with papists and with extreme anglicans who were to be non-jurors. Oaths were a stumbling block to all three, and passive obedience a practice common to quakers and consistent churchmen.

The critics of intolerance were mostly conservative in aim, like their opponents. By relaxing persecution, they hoped to enable men of good will to unite against those who really needed to be repressed. But there was disagreement as to who must be accounted enemies and advocates of change differed greatly in the amount of freedom they were prepared to grant. Penn had abandoned puritan theology but not the puritan ethic. For him, criminals, vagabonds and loose livers were 'the evil-doers that violate those laws which are necessary to the preservation of civil society'. Government had been established because of human wickedness, its tasks were 'to terrify evildoers' and 'to cherish those that do well': it was 'a part of religion itself, a thing sacred in its institution and end'.[4] Penn therefore wanted to unite all the righteous against the sinners. He wrote in 1675 that religious presecution could not be beneficial 'unless some

---

[1] Gunn, p. 160, cf. pp. 193–4.
[2] Gunn, p. 158. [3] Gunn, pp. 186–7.
[4] V. Buranelli, *The King and the Quaker* (Pennsylvania University Press, 1962), pp. 140–5.

one party have the wisdom, wealth, number, sober life, industry and resolution on its side, which I am sure is not to be found in England'.[1] Freedom and equal political rights for all denominations was his solution. At first he had excepted the papists, but by James II's reign he had ceased to do so. He had two reasons for believing that neither anarchy nor renewed persecution would result from religious freedom. On the one hand, 'though all parties would rejoice their own principles prevailed, yet everyone is more solicitous about its own safety than the others' verity'.[2] On the other, toleration would establish a balance of power between anglicans, papists and dissenters which none would allow to be disturbed for fear of being swamped. At one time Penn spoke of the Church of England holding the balance between the other two. At another, he said that dissenters and papists would combine against the church until its monopoly was destroyed, but then split. The papists, being few in number, would need to behave with moderation to prevent a protestant coalition against them.[3]

Penn wanted real religious freedom, but his views seem better suited to the eighteenth century than to the passionate seventeenth. More immediately popular were schemes which recall, and to some extent were inspired by, the original spirit of the Elizabethan settlement before it had been denatured by intolerant groups in control of the church. Comprehensiveness and mutual tolerance among moderate men were here combined with the repression of more extreme opinions. One important purpose of such schemes was indeed a religious truce so that all could fight together against immorality. The lax morals of the Restoration period were often attributed to the disunity among the upholders of religion. But the spread of popery, unbelief and gross unorthodoxy was seen as part of the same disease, and it was thought that extremists in doctrine needed suppressing, as well as the merely wicked. We have seen that the presbyterian 'Dons' wanted a settlement of this kind. They were ready to share control of the church with the upholders of prelacy, but they wanted strict discipline over the laity and would not contemplate toleration for papists and socinians.[4] Ironically, many of the men who supported from within the church the plans for greater tolerance were representatives of a trend that had emerged in reaction against calvinist

---

[1] Gunn, p. 178.   [2] Gunn, p. 181.
[3] Gunn, pp. 182–5.   [4] Bate, p. 13.

rigidity when the calvinists had seemed likely to succeed in imposing their own narrow system on the Establishment. Cambridge had been the metropolis of English calvinism and with the Cambridge Platonists[1] it became likewise the most important anti-calvinist centre. These men were really the English equivalent of the Arminians (Remonstrants) in Holland: there was similarity of ideas and, as the century advanced, personal contact as well. They rejected the doctrine of predestination and went on to reject rigid schemes of dogma in general. Cudworth could not 'ascribe to God those dreadful decrees by which He inevitably condemned innocent men out of pure arbitrariousness to guilt and sin'. 'If He makes a creature intelligent and voluntary,' said Whichcote, 'He must use him as such.' 'He that is most practical in divine things hath the purest and sincerest knowledge of them,' wrote John Smith, 'and not he that is most dogmatical.' Sound religious instinct was the essential thing and reason, not dogma, should be its guide. 'I oppose not rational to spiritual,' said Whichcote. 'for spiritual is most rational.'[2] Scientific enquiry was welcomed as leading to a better understanding of the divine plan, though the ideas and findings of the scientists were not always very welcome to the Cambridge men. But there was a clear link between the new science and the new departures in theology, very apparent in the large clerical contingent in the Royal Society. Indeed that body had originated in a group formed during the Interregnum, so Bishop Sprat explained, to hold discussions 'without the wild distractions of that passionate age'. He claimed that it had produced 'a race of young men . . . who were invincibly armed against the enchantments of enthusiasm'.[3]

The pupils of the Cambridge men formed the nucleus of a new church party whose watchwords were an emphasis on ethical teaching and a further reduction of the essentials of the faith (Whichcote had reduced them to two verses of the Bible[4]). The Cambridge Platonists were unworldly and mystical. The next generation, however, fell in with the growing fashion of making self-interest the incentive to good behaviour. For all these reasons they were accused of abandon-

---

[1] Ralph Cudworth (1617–85), Henry More (1614–87), Benjamin Whichcote (1609–83) and John Smith (1618–52) were the best known.

[2] E. Cassirer, *The Platonic Renaissance in England* (Nelson, 1953), pp. 79, 82, 29, 38

[3] Cragg, p. 88.

[4] Titus ii: 11–12. Cragg, p. 39 n.

ing Christian orthodoxy: the name of Latitudinarian was in consequence invented for the Cambridge Platonists and inherited by the
younger men. It might at least have been expected that they would
have championed the right to secede from the church: this cause had
been won in Holland, thanks to Arminian resistance to the calvinists.
But though the Cambridge men were in good odour with Cromwell's
government, they and their disciples were equally so under the
restored monarchy and all were loyal members of the church. Like
the 'Dons' they wanted greater comprehensiveness while avoiding
the dangers to doctrine and morals that came from schism. Cudworth
thought that 'just as in Noah's Ark were all sorts of animals', so 'in
our English church' there were 'all kinds of protestants: Calvinists,
Remonstrants, and I believe even Socinians'.[1] But the principle of
uniformity was to be respected, as Stillingfleet laid down in orthodox
terms in 1660: 'it is not the difference of opinion formally considered
that is punishable but the tendency to schism which lies in the divulg-
ing of it.'[2] Opposed from the outset to the fanatical puritan spirit,
the Latitude-men naturally defended the anglican position against it.
Simon Patrick in 1668–70 wrote three pamphlets rebuking the self-
righteous exclusiveness of the dissenters and beseeching them to
rejoin the church.[3] Stillingfleet wrote again of the *Unreasonableness of
Separation* in 1681. Both stressed the gains to the papists from protestant divisions. It was the same in politics: in 1683, Burnet and
Tillotson preached to Lord Russell, condemned for treason, the
orthodox doctrine of non-resistance.[4]

How this very mild form of intolerance could develop into a
limited form of toleration can be seen in the development of Locke's
ideas after 1660. Locke had close links with the Latitude men, though
his basic ideas were far from Cambridge platonism. Even in 1660 he
believed that 'the common principles of religion all mankind agree in
and the belief of these doctrines a lawgiver may venture to enjoin;
but he must go no farther if he means to preserve an uniformity in
religion'. He bewailed, too, 'the unlimited power of the modern
priesthood' who 'look the civil government in the face and have raised

[1] Rosalie L. Colie, *Light and Enlightenment—a Study of the Cambridge Platonists and
the Dutch Arminians* (Cambridge University Press, 1957), p. 40.
[2] Cragg, p. 199.
[3] Whiting, pp. 498–500.
[4] Cragg, pp. 162–3.

such convulsions in the latter ages as were unknown to the ancient world'. But the experience of the Interregnum had convinced him 'that a general freedom is but a general bondage, that the popular asserters of public liberty are the greatest engrossers of it too, and not unfitly called its keepers' and that religious liberty 'would prove only a liberty for contention, censure and persecution'. So, pleased at 'the approaches of a calm' after a 'storm' which had lasted as long as he could remember,[1] he concluded that it was the traditional remedy of state control that was the antidote to the political dangers inherent in religion.

An unpublished essay of 1667 still defined the state's power in religious matters in fairly orthodox terms, but this was tempered by the very explicit statement that the purpose of the state was purely secular: 'to preserve men in this world from the fraud and violence of one another; so that what was the end of erecting government ought alone to be the measure of its proceeding.' The magistrate in deciding whether to persecute and the believer in deciding whether to submit had to be guided by their understanding of God's purpose and He would punish them if they wilfully misunderstood it: as in the *Treatises of Government*, God's sovereignty is the real guarantee of harmony in society. Religious belief and even worship were as such no business of the civil magistrate. He 'ought not to tolerate at all' beliefs and actions 'absolutely destructive to human society, as that faith may be broken with heretics, that if the magistrate doth not reform religion the subjects may, that one is bound to broach and propagate any opinion he believes himself ...'. Papists deserved repression because their allegiance was to a foreign ruler and dissenters because their common worship was the distinguishing mark of a political faction. But 'force and compulsion' were 'the worst, the last' means to be used against them because they contravened the purpose of the state—the prevention of violence. The repression of the papists should continue: there was no danger of it arousing sympathy for them and it might even be effective since this was a religion that had been propagated by a well-organized, state-supported clergy. The dissenters, however, were better left alone. They were very numerous, but hopelessly divided: it was persecution that made them unite into a party. All the same, Locke's emphasis was still on comprehension.

[1] Fox Bourne, vol. i, pp. 149, 151, 155–6.

Christian religion hath made more factions, wars and disturbances in civil societies than any other, and whether toleration and latitudinism would prevent those evils

he asked, adding

that toleration conduces no otherwise to the settlement of a government than as it makes the majority of one mind and encourages virtue in all, which is done by making and executing strict laws concerning virtue and vice but making the terms of church communion as large as may be; *i.e.*, that your articles in speculative opinions be few and large, and ceremonies in worship few and easy, which is latitudinism.[1]

(II)

The events of the Interregnum and Restoration which altered public thinking on the religious question affected the King and his ministers no less. Charles I had died a martyr for the Church of England and some cavaliers indentified the cause of church and king. But others concluded that the crown should not be too closely linked to one religious party because this might be a threat both to its popularity and to its independence. From the start of his exile, Charles II had with him a party of conjoined papists and maverick protestants opposing the staunch anglicans. Bristol was at first their leader and Henrietta Maria their great patron. The Duke of Buckingham was a member from the start and throughout his disreputable and otherwise inconstant life he remained an enemy of religious exclusiveness, greeting the accession of James II with a pamphlet in favour of liberty of conscience. Even royalist clerics did not always identify the King's interest with their church. John Gauden put into the *Eikon Basilike*, which was fathered on Charles I, the sentiment that 'connivance and Christian toleration often dissipates' the strength of religious factions 'whom rougher opposition fortifies, and puts the despised and opposed parties into such combinations as may enable them to get a full revenge'. Jeremy Taylor, sometime chaplain to Charles I, made a very similar point in his *Liberty of Prophesying*, on the authority of the French politique historian De Thou (d. 1614).[2] Dissenters were not above using this kind of argument to pay court to the ruler. The presbyterian John Humfrey wrote (1667)

[1] Fox Bourne, vol. i, pp. 174–94. Locke would not have tolerated atheists.
[2] Gunn, pp. 154–5.

If such factions are considerable and equal, a neutral kind of unconcernment and indifference makes the chief magistrate strong, while he keeps his interest in all of them.

Sir Charles Wolseley wrote in 1668 that

> so many divided interests and parties in religion are much less dangerous than any, and may be prudently managed to balance each other and to become generally more safe and useful to a state than any united party or interest whatever.[1]

Penn made use of Gauden's remark and knew the work of De Thou. In 1675 he told the Elector Palatine, who was persecuting quakers, that toleration 'rendereth the prince peculiarly safe and great ... because all interests, for interest's sake, are bound to love and court him'. At home in 1675 he advocated 'superiors governing themselves upon a balance, as near as may be towards the several religious interests'.[2]

Charles II was not a religious man and had no noticeable sympathy with anglicanism, still less with puritanism. He died a catholic and all through his life there were rumours of his tending that way. But soon after his nominal accession he was given timely lessons in the way that both papists and presbyterians could treat a king. In 1650–1 he reigned in Scotland on terms agreed with the presbyterians and for most of that time suffered appalling humiliation from the kirk. In France his mother attempted to bring her youngest son over to Rome without his consent and more or less by force. Thereafter he supported the religious policy of men like Hyde and Ormonde and so his restoration led to the triumph of the church. But he did not owe his return entirely to anglicans, and accordingly wished to make some concessions to other parties. The anglican outcry against this has already been mentioned: it gave a clear warning that restored priest was likely to prove old presbyter writ large. Charles was hardly likely to turn back to the presbyterians after the way that they had treated him. He told Lauderdale in 1660 that presbyterianism was no religion for a gentleman[3] and in his later years 'always lamented that common and ignorant persons were allowed to read' the Bible, thinking that 'this liberty was the rise of all our sects, each interpreting according to

---

[1] Gunn, pp. 163–4, 167–8.
[2] Gunn, pp. 177–8.
[3] G. Burnet, *History of My Own Time, The Reign of Charles II*, ed. O. Airy (Oxford University Press, 1900), vol. i, p. 195.

their vile notions and to accomplish their horrid wickednesses'.[1]
But his pardon saved a number of dissenters from the hands of anglican persecuters. With the catholics he was anxious to go further, for
they had provided the royal cause with many loyal servants and it was
not in the royal interest that they should be weakened. There took
place in consequence the revival of an old quarrel between crown
and nation that had begun in the previous century.

Royal leniency to papists had long been a grievance, not only in
itself but also because it involved a strikingly wide use of the royal
prerogative. At the Reformation all the authority which the pope had
exercised in England passed to the crown. Legislation of the 1530s,
renewed in 1559, empowered the archbishop of Canterbury, with
royal authorization, to exercise the same dispensing powers as the
pope, 'not being contrary or repugnant to the holy scriptures and
laws of God'. The crown's legal advisers had drawn up a list of all the
different sorts of papal dispensation, not forgetting to specify the
customary fee in each case.[2] In the Conventicle Act of 1670, parliament confirmed to the King and his successors 'all powers and
authorities in ecclesiastical affairs as fully and as amply as himself or
any of his predecessors have or might have' exercised them.[3] These
powers, moreover, were not conferred by parliament. They had been
given some statutory recognition and embodiment, but they were
believed to be inherent in the crown. 'In ecclesiasticals,' wrote
Secretary Williamson in 1671, 'it is apprehended that the king has all
power, he is supreme, the parliament has no part of it. In civils it is
otherwise.'[4] There was therefore something like an arbitrary royal
despotism within the church. This was if anything heightened when
the clergy lost in 1664 the power to tax themselves through convocation. The bishops apparently thought that they would not have to
pay so much if it was left to parliament to tax them but they lost a
means of corporate pressure on the crown. No debates were allowed
in convocation hereafter until the brief unsatisfactory session of
1689.[5]

[1] Ailesbury, vol. i, p. 93.
[2] E. F. Churchill, 'Dispensations under the Tudors and Stuarts', *English Historical Review*, vol. xxxiv (1919), pp. 409–15.
[3] 22 Car. II cap. 1, s. 17, cited E. F. Churchill, 'The Dispensing Power of the Crown in Ecclesiastical Causes', *Law Quarterly Review*, vol. xxxviii (1922), pp. 432–3.
[4] CSPD 1671, p. 563 cited *ibid.*, p. 428.
[5] Sykes, pp. 36–43.

The power of the crown to bind and loose in ecclesiastical matters is well seen in the life of the universities, then essentially a part of the church. They were subject to royal visitation, the statutes of universities and colleges were amended and undesirable persons were removed. At the same time, those whom the King wished to favour were rewarded: mandates were issued to require the appointment of royal nominees to chairs, headships of colleges and fellowships and dispensations were given when an appointment was against the terms of the statutes. Each of the religious revolutions of the sixteenth century was followed by a purge of the universities and parliament conducted another during the civil wars. At the Restoration there was a visitation to remove those intruded by parliament and all who refused to worship in the anglican way had to withdraw, even before parliament had decided on a new Act of Uniformity. Academic advancement became something of a political free-for-all. Loyal cavaliers and their children were rewarded with university posts. The upheavals of the Interregnum had meant that some deserving men had failed to complete their studies: the royal power was exercised to require the bestowing of degrees on such men—even in medicine. Further dispensations allowed favoured dons with other preferments to be non-resident. Charles II later admitted in a letter to St John's College, Oxford, that dispensations to loyalists had 'produced ill effects in causing deserving persons to leave the college and younger men to seek interest at court rather than proficiency in learning'. But nothing seems to have come of his promise that aspirants would have their attainments properly tested in future.[1] Orthodoxy was as likely to suffer in this system as scholarship. In 1669 Daniel Scargill was expelled from his Cambridge fellowship for Hobbist opinions (which he appears to have got secondhand) and dissolute living. He managed to get a royal order for his reinstatement. By appealing to Sheldon, Corpus Christi College was able to get this set aside. Significantly for the future, they argued that it was without precedent that his legally chosen successor 'should be outed of his fellowship (his freehold) by his majesty's royal letters'.[2]

One use which successive monarchs had consistently made of their plenary ecclesiastical powers was to nullify the acts of parliament

---

[1] See Churchill, 'Dispensing Power of Crown', pp. 309–15.
[2] J. L. Axtell, 'The Mechanics of Opposition—Restoration Cambridge v. Daniel Scargill', *Bulletin of the Institute of Historical Research*, vol. xxxviii (1965), pp. 102–11.

against popish recusants.[1] Whatever the theoretical danger of popish beliefs to the state, the fact was that most catholics were harmless and even useful to the government. Leniency towards them might also facilitate good relations with the catholic powers. Even Elizabeth had offered in 1586 to commute the drastic new statutory penalties against recusancy into a sort of income tax levied at the rate of 6s. 8d. in the pound. A memorandum of 1626 by Attorney General Heath shows that the catholics at most had to pay a moderate levy on landed income, those without land paying a modest sum to avoid the confiscation of their goods. Priests and those harbouring them were left alone, though they should have suffered capital punishment. The only innovation made by Charles II, and subsequently by James II, was to suspend the execution of the laws publicly, by a royal declaration. James I had prudently refused to do this when the Spanish government requested it in 1623.

The English gentry did not really differ much from their kings in their attitude to catholics. Protestant squires were on good terms with their catholic neighbours, recognized their loyalty and had no wish to persecute them. The middle and lower classes no doubt felt more strongly. An important feature of whig propaganda, on which a good deal of money was spent, was spectacular pope-burning processions at which a costly effigy of the pontiff, stuffed with live cats to make him squeal, was consigned to the flames. But even whig justices seem to have been reluctant to imprison popish gentry.[2] It was, however, rightly believed that there was a considerable difference between ordinary English catholics and the supranational hierarchy to which they owed obedience. Under the promptings of pope and Jesuits there was no knowing what they might do. 'I do not, I will not, say all our Romanists are inclined to rebellion', declared one preacher on Guy Fawkes' Day, but 'if papists be good subjects, no thanks to their popery; and I fear, 'twill be hard for 'em to be good catholics at Rome and good subjects at home.'[3] The fear of popery was fear of the hierarchy and of what it might achieve in league with menacing foreign powers and a sympathetic English king looking for ways to increase his authority. 'Whilst the papists have a prospect of a Popish

[1] See Churchill, 'Dispensing Power', pp. 422–3.

[2] Western, pp. 69, 70 on reluctance to persecute. O. W. Furley, 'The Pope-burning Processions', *History* NS. vol. xliv (1959), pp. 16–23.

[3] Figgis, pp. 377–8.

successor, they will never be quiet', Sir Thomas Player told the commons in 1679.[1] Colonel Titus in 1680 warned that 'they will burn us and damn us. For our estates, they will take our lands, and put monks and friars upon them. Our wives and children must beg . . .'[2] A pamphleteer of 1681 thought that 'our nobles are sentenced to be peasants and our peasants to be no better than slaves'.[3] Swynfen, a whig leader, in 1679 expected that 'in case of a popish successor, all that are considerable persons will either go out of the Kingdom and those that remain about the king will adore the rising sun' (sic).[4] Much play was made with the supposed threat to take back the abbey lands and James found it advisable when speaking in the City in 1679 to say that it was in his own interest to defend all rights of property.[5] The King's protection of popery was seen as an adjunct of plans to increase royal power and so even when parliament came to favour toleration, it would not accede to the royal wish that catholics too should be tolerated.

(III)

During the reign of Charles II there was an endless stream of rival plans for a more liberal religious settlement. Each plan represented a particular alliance of religious parties and was intended to benefit some groups and damage others. Each time the groups that did not benefit were strong enough to prevent the implementation of the plan. In the autumn of 1660 the government promoted a conference at Worcester House at which terms were agreed with the presbyterians for their inclusion in the restored church. But the Convention Parliament, though there were many puritans in it, did nothing to ratify the scheme before its supersession by the intolerant parliament of 1661. It seems that the independents in the Convention, out of spite against the presbyterians, worked with the more militant anglicans against comprehension. At the end of 1662 Charles II appealed to parliament to acknowledge his right to circumvent the Act of Uniformity by the use of his dispensing power. Parliament refused, and as the King was known to desire toleration for the papists he did not even have the full support of the presbyterians.

---

[1] Grey, vol. vii, p. 140. [2] *ibid.*, pp. 400–1.
[3] Furley, 'Pamphlet Literature', pp. 23–4.
[4] Grey, vol. vii, p. 249. [5] Furley, 'Pamphlet Literature', p. 24.

The catastrophe of the second Dutch war and the fall of Clarendon led to the ascendancy of the anti-anglican trend at court in the persons of the 'cabal'. It was now that the most important plans for greater tolerance emerged: the one that was to be tried again by James II before the Revolution and also the one that was to be tried again by his opponents after it, with incomplete but more lasting success. The latter plan evolved from the work of lawyers and liberal churchman. Sir Robert Atkyns produced an abortive Bill for Comprehension in 1667 which was significant for the future in requiring those who were to benefit to assent to all of the Thirty-Nine Articles that were concerned with doctrine. This was derived from the Act of 1571 which laid down the conditions—not then including episcopal ordination— on which foreign clergy might be admitted to preferment in the church.[1] It came to be interpreted as meaning assent to all the articles except three and a half.[2] In 1668 Lord Keeper Bridgeman established contact with the presbyterians and independents through Hezekiah Burton, his chaplain, and Dr John Wilkins, brother-in-law of Oliver Cromwell, a founder of the Royal Society and soon to be Bishop of Chester. The advance was now made of preparing both a Bill of Comprehension to benefit the presbyterians and another for toleration to satisfy the independents. Sir Matthew Hale drafted the former. But the opponents of the existing system were still too divided and parliament was still too hostile for progress to be made. The commons rejected both Bills, showed some sympathy for comprehension, but called for the stricter enforcement of the laws against dissenters. The presbyterian 'Dons' showed little sympathy for toleration: Manton thought that comprehension might have been accepted by parliament if it had not been linked to this wider issue. In this they differed not only from the independents but from the rest of the presbyterians, the 'Ducklings'. None of the groups really had the same aims as the court. Wilkins' comprehension plan provided for only a rather vague test of orthodoxy and his Toleration Bill contained no such test at all. But even the leaders of the independents wanted to confine toleration to those who in doctrine were orthodox and to deny it to the papists and the licentious. On the other hand Dr

---

[1] 13 Eliz. cap. 12. This proposal had first been made in 1663, when the Lords considered a bill to implement Charles's declaration.

[2] Arts. 34, 35, 36 and part of Art. 20. Plans of comprehension are less fully treated in this chapter than toleration plans because they all proved abortive.

John Owen, the leading independent, warned the Dons that comprehension would 'neither do the King's business nor ours'. The last
phrase can only indicate some willingness to connive at the great
royal objective—the protection of the catholics.[1]

This was the central religious feature of the plan which Charles now
tried and which James tried again in due course. It was in 1669 that
the Duke of York became a catholic and desirous of the right to
profess his new faith openly. He found that his brother was of the
same mind and at a secret meeting with two catholics (Lord Arundel
of Wardour and Sir Thomas Clifford) and a crypto-convert (Arlington, the author of the 1662 declaration) it was decided to enlist the
help of France for restoring the Roman faith.[2] Charles admitted to
the envoy of Louis XIV that the project would seem rather absurd
to anyone who knew England well, but that

> the presbyterians and the other sects had a greater aversion to the English
> church than to the catholics; that all the secretaries desired only the free
> exercise of their religion and provided they could obtain it, as it was his
> design they should, they would not oppose his intended change of religion:
> that besides, he has some good troops strongly attached to him and if the
> deceased King his father had had as many, he would have stifled in their birth
> those troubles that caused his ruin; that he would still augment as much as
> possible his regiments and companies under the most specious pretexts he
> could devise . . . that he was sure of the principal places in England and
> Scotland; that the governor of Hull was a catholic; that those of Ports-
> mouth, Plymouth and many other places . . . would never depart from the
> duty they owed him:

Charles was also fairly sure of the army in Ireland. As for his motives,

> he told me that he was pressed both by his conscience and by the confusion
> which he saw increasing from day to day in his kingdom, to the diminution
> of his authority, to declare himself a catholic; and besides the spiritual advan-
> tage he should draw from it, he believed it to be the only means of re-
> establishing the monarchy.[3]

Seemingly, Charles had found the role of a parliamentary and anglican monarch insupportable and was returning to the policy of
Cromwell: a standing army to maintain both state power and religious toleration, but with the papists not the Saints as the ideological
backbone of the new order.

[1] R. Thomas, 'Comprehension and Indulgence', Nuttall and Chadwick, pp. 196–206.
Sykes, pp. 71–5.
[2] *Life of James II*, vol. i, pp. 440–2. This part of the work is not in James's own words.
[3] Dalrymple, vol. i, Review, pp. 89, 90.

Charles eventually secured an alliance with France, but it had a political as well as a religious objective—the isolation and defeat of the Dutch. Eventually it was the political objective that gained priority. The French did promise, by the secret Treaty of Dover in 1670, to aid the catholic project with troops and money. But they wanted to fight the Dutch first: they were afraid that their military and diplomatic plans might be upset by the religious enterprise. Now a war was bound to make Charles more dependent financially on parliament and so less able to defy them in religious matters.[1] Charles at first pressed for the religious scheme to be given priority, but he gave way and eventually became less interested in it than were the French. The outbreak of war in 1672 was preceded by a Declaration of Indulgence which gave royal permission to catholics to worship in private and royal leave to worship in public to protestant dissenters who applied for a licence. The dissenters duly applied for licences and the King was thanked by deputations of their leaders: the Dons showed reluctance but not so the Ducklings and independents.[2] The war, however, went badly, the royal finances duly deteriorated and parliament had to be asked for help. Royal policy had had the effect of greatly enhancing fears of 'popery and French interest' which, as the ultra-royalist Bishop Parker put it, 'like Circe's cups bewitched men and turned them into brutes'.[3] The commons voted 'that penal statutes cannot be suspended but by act of parliament'[4] and Charles had to withdraw his Declaration. Parliament further forced upon the King the Test Act of 1673 which barred papists from holding office under the crown. This was an interesting new departure and showed clearly the nature of opposition to popery. It was not a measure of persecution—it was instead the limitation of one of the most essential of the royal prerogatives, the king's right to make use of the services of any of his subjects. The danger it guarded against was not the spread of popish beliefs but the presence of papists in high places and the threat of rule by a religious minority. It is significant that its passage was preceded by an address of the

[1] As noted by the compiler of the *Life of James II*: see vol. i, pp. 443, 449, 450.

[2] Thomas in Nuttall and Chadwick, pp. 207–10. The government was reluctant to license large and conspicuous meeting places for dissenters, Bate, p. 96.

[3] Quoted in H. Horwitz 'Protestant Reconciliation in the Exclusion Crisis', *Jol. of Ecclesiastical History* vol. xv (1964), p. 202.

[4] In 1663 they had merely said that it was without precedent. Churchill, 'Dispensing Power', pp. 430–1.

two houses requesting the expulsion of foreign Jesuits, the execution of the law against Jesuits who were native-born and the tendering of the oaths of allegiance and supremacy to all officers and soldiers.[1] In 1674 Arlington admitted to parliament that popish officers had been employed in the troops raised for the Dutch war 'because they were thought to have more skill'.[2]

The commons further concluded that it was too dangerous to drive the dissenters into the arms of the catholics by measures of intolerance. They adopted in 1673 the liberal policy which they had rejected in 1668. A bill for the ease of protestant dissenters was passed which removed some stumbling blocks that kept presbyterians out of the church; to all who might still decide to remain outside it, freedom of worship was to be allowed if they would subscribe to the doctrinal part of the Thirty-Nine Articles and take a 'non-resisting' oath. Together with the Test Act, this was in large measure the religious settlement adopted in 1689. But on this occasion the relieving Bill was amended by the lords in such a way as to bring back the King's dispensing power. The commons objected and were still discussing the lords' amendments when the session ended—we shall never know if they would finally have accepted them.[3] Charles could never have had much use for the Bill as it first stood, for it would have meant protestant solidarity against his catholic friends. Many anglicans, too, could not stomach it. Archbishop Sheldon had sent out a sort of whip to ensure that the bench of bishops was well filled and the bishops voted with the courtiers to amend the Bill and rejoiced at their success in wrecking it.[4] Bishop Morley felt that it would have meant

> an establishment of schism by a law, and that would have been much worse than any connivance, nay than any toleration can be by the king's dispensation and declaration only.[5]

The King having failed to advance his interests by leaning on the dissenters and catholics, it was natural to return to the policy of alliance with the church. Danby accomplished this in his rise to power and it remained more or less royal policy until reversed by James in 1686. At the behest of a meeting of bishops which he had summoned

---

[1] Bate, p. 123. [2] CSPD 1673–5, p. 106 cited Churchill, *ibid.*
[3] Thomas, *loc. cit.*, pp. 212–13.
[4] Bate, pp. 106, 127. [5] Thomas, *loc. cit.*, p. 215.

to advise him, Charles in February 1675 formally revoked the licences which he had granted to dissenters and ordered the suppression of conventicles.[1] He urged his brother to resume attendance at anglican worship and later countenanced an attempt to reconvert him.[2] He no longer dared to continue the old tradition of issuing dispensations to catholics and catholic officers retired from the army.[3] But in spite of parliamentary addresses against them, the catholics remained largely unmolested and in spite of renewed persecution the dissenters were stronger than before their spell of freedom. Renewed persecution seems moreover to have made them work more closely together. The Ducklings were in the ascendant among the presbyterians and union was almost achieved between presbyterians and independents.[4] It will be remembered that at the same time the dissenters were recovering their power in the municipal corporations. The elections for the three exclusion parliaments were a triumph for dissent as well as for the broader whig movement.

The attempts to grapple with the religious problem in Charles II's last years were accordingly coloured by dissenting militancy and anglican fears resulting from it. The main religious preoccupation of the exclusionists was, of course, with the catholics, who in 1678 were disabled from sitting in parliament. But in 1680 the commons voted for the repeal of the Corporation Act and a bill to annul the Elizabethan statute requiring dissenters to abjure the realm passed both houses, though it never received the royal assent.[5] There was just a chance that the dissenters might achieve outright emancipation and it was tory anglicans who now took the lead in proposing toleration and comprehension in order to forestall this. Sir Edward Dering proposed a 'bill for uniting his Majesty's protestant subjects' to the commons in November 1680. A committee was appointed to draw it up under the chairmanship of his cousin, Daniel Finch, the son and heir of Lord Chancellor Nottingham, and better known by the title which he was soon to inherit. This was the effective start of his career as a political champion of the church, which was to extend into the reign of George I. Not only the religious legislation but the political settlement of 1689 was to owe a great deal to him. With his pious

[1] Bate, pp. 140–1.
[2] *Life of James II*, vol. i, pp. 482–3, 539, 701.
[3] Churchill, *loc. cit.*   [4] Thomas, *loc. cit.*, p. 229.
[5] To the fury of the commons the text was purposely 'lost'. Thomas, *loc. cit.*, p. 224. What follows is derived mainly from Horwitz, 'Protestant Reconciliation', pp. 201–17.

respectability and prolific wife, 'dismal' Nottingham seems almost a displaced Victorian. His intelligence and probity were respected at court and in parliament, but he was too much of a pedant to be thoroughly successful in politics.

Finch believed that comprehension 'was the most likely and effectual way to lessen the number of dissenters', though he thought that those remaining should have enough 'limited exercise of their religion ... that so we might be united, at least in interest and affection'. This strategy of dividing the dissenters might well have worked in the sixties but they were too united for it to accomplish much now. Roger Morrice, an associate of Baxter the leading Don, noted that all who wanted comprehension wanted 'indulgence' too for those who could not be comprehended; further, that there were many who wanted 'indulgence' and did not want comprehension at all. The committee, nine of whose twenty-eight members were dissenters, quickly drew up a Bill for Comprehension but decided that there ought to be a Toleration Bill as well and the commons agreed. Thereafter the dissenters concentrated on perfecting the Toleration Bill and left work on the Comprehension Bill to the anglicans. This was an alarming revelation to the anglicans of how the dissenters were drifting away from them and it also meant that the Comprehension Bill was not drafted in terms likely to attract wavering dissenters. The presbyterian, Dr Humfrey, eventually offered amendments to remedy this and to show that some dissenters were still interested in Comprehension. But the attempts of the Dons to keep in touch with churchmen at this time seem to have been rather unsuccessful. The situation of 1689, when Toleration was carried but Comprehension was not, was clearly foreshadowed.

The proposals of 1680 foreshadow the legislation of 1689 not merely in principle but in detail. Finch drafted both Bills and he was to see one of his drafts become the Toleration Act after the Revolution. The Comprehension Bill, among other things, would have relieved clergy from subscription to the contentious three and a half articles, from assent to the prayer book, and from the use of the surplice and of the cross in baptism. An amendment would have admitted to the church those who had received presbyterian ordination in the years 1644–60. The Toleration Bill as originally drafted exempted all those taking a declaration against popery from certain penalties. They were to be allowed to worship publicly and the reasons for the prevailing intolerance are well brought out by the stipulation that they might not meet 'arm'd with fire arms, nor ... with the doors shut during all the time of prayer and preaching'. They were to continue to pay tithes and serve in parish offices. Amendments carried in the commons sanctioned teaching by dissenting schoolmasters and tutors but excepted from toleration all who denied the doctrine of the Trinity and required dissenters to take the oaths of allegiance and supremacy and dissenting clergy to subscribe all of the Thirty-Nine Articles save the contentious three and a half. (The quakers, however, were not to be obliged to take the oaths, and baptist ministers did not have to subscribe to part of Article 27, respecting baptism.) These amendments seem to have been acceptable to dissenters and anglicans alike and they show that though comprehension was dying, there was still agreement in upholding a definite standard of orthodoxy and denying toleration to those who would not accept it.

Churchmen nevertheless were alarmed at what was proposed. Even a liberal like Stillingfleet wanted something far more restrictive. Comprehension in the form proposed would, he said, create two classes of churchmen, those who accepted the existing liturgy and those who did not. What was required was a reform of the liturgy to make it more widely acceptable. Anyone who could not accept the revised version would have first to appeal to his bishop, so that his scruples might be examined and removed. If he remained unreconciled, he might worship apart but only on payment of the statutory weekly fine of one shilling imposed in 1558 on those not coming to church. Nor were the dissenters to have their own schools. The crushing of the whigs ended for the moment any prospect of changes in the law and was a relief to many anglicans. It was accompanied by a savage renewal of the persecution of dissenters. New currency had been given to the belief that they were all seditious: grand juries pressed for the execution of the laws against them on those grounds. By way of diminishing their influence in local life, it was proposed both in Devonshire and Northamptonshire that religious tests should be imposed on innkeepers.[1] There was also a strengthening of anglican militancy within the church. From 1681 to 1684 a small

[1] Cf. Essex and Kent, CSPD 1682, pp. 179–80; 1683 pt. i, pp. 86, 103; pt. ii, pp. 103, 262–3. Grand juries at assizes and quarter sessions not only initiated prosecutions but drew attention to offences that were prevalent.

commission, with Blathwayt as its secretary, was given power to advise the King on ecclesiastical preferment. It was dominated by Archbishop Sancroft, Compton the Bishop of London, and Lawrence Hyde. Influential tories at court, like Clarendon, or in the provinces, like Beaufort, worked with it. The King seems to have taken its advice in most of the higher church appointments and its active members retained their influence in this matter after its demise. For Sancroft this was a step towards making the church more centralized and authoritarian in its government, following the example of Laud.[1] For the government it was clearly a means of making churchmen, like local magistrates and municipal councillors at this time, more dependent upon its will. The church was strengthened against the dissenters but the government was strengthened within the church. The government, moreover, might hope to exploit the renewed hostility between church and dissent if the church would not do as it pleased.

This was the situation when James II came to the throne. Friends and foes alike have always depicted James as a naive enthusiast whose religious policy was totally out of step with the ruling ideas of his generation. His defenders portray him as in advance of his time—a pioneer of religious freedom. His detractors present him as a preposterous reactionary—a would-be restorer of the old faith and perhaps even of persecution for protestants. The main purpose of this chapter is to suggest that both these views are wrong—that James's ideas about the place of religion in the state were typical of his generation, not exceptional, and that his religious policy consisted partly of traditional elements (protection of catholics, high-handed interference within the established church) and partly of the continuation of policies current in his brother's reign (alternation between alliance with the church and alliance with the papists and dissenters when the church would not do as the King wished). James of course lacked the finesse of Charles and could afford anyway to be much rougher because his general position was much stronger. He also appears to have become increasingly preoccupied with the religious, as opposed to the practical, political significance of what he was doing.

[1] R. Beddard, 'The commission for ecclesiastical promotions, 1681–4: an instrument of tory reaction', *Historical Journal*, vol. x (1967), pp. 11–40. He notes similar activity after the Restoration and also by the archbishops in Scotland from 1676.

James seems to have believed what most educated Englishmen believed—that religious persecution in itself was wrong but that for political reasons it might be necessary to forbid dissenting religious groups to organize and worship publicly. As his natural inclination was to think the worst of anyone who was not entirely obedient, he probably tended to exaggerate the political danger from religious dissent and the need to suppress it—but this might vary according to political circumstances. Thus in 1669, when the government was trying to conciliate the nonconformists, James told Dr Owen (at least according to his memoirs) that he

> had no bitterness against the nonconformists, he was against all persecution merely for conscience sake, looking upon it as an unchristian thing and absolutely against his conscience.

His secretary Coleman admonished a Norfolk parson zealous against 'the fanatic nonconformists' that his master 'was very much troubled that any persons should be troubled for serving God that was within conscience that they thought they ought to do'.[1] But by his accession the political situation had altered and he referred to the dissenters as 'true republicans' while the churchmen were 'the royal party' who had 'showed themselves so eminently loyal in the worst of times'.[2] He told the bishops that

> he would never give any sort of countenance to dissenters, knowing that it must be faction and not religion if men could not be content to meet five besides their own family, which the law dispenses with.

Despite his friendship with Penn, he wrote to Queensberry that he had 'not great reason to be satisfied with the quakers in general'. It was only in March 1686 that he relieved quakers of recusancy fines, as he had long been doing for catholics, and only in 1687 that 1600 of them could thank him for release from prison in accordance with 'what some of us have known to have been the declared principle of the King, so well long before as since he came to the throne'. By that time the political situation had changed again and a Declaration of Indulgence was issued. But it is not surprising that when some (mostly pliable) bishops were called together and invited to thank the King for the Declaration, White and Sprat 'could not but remember how vehemently the King had declared against toleration and said he

[1] Turner, pp. 307–8.
[2] Kenyon, p. 112.

would noever by any counsel be tempted to suffer it'.[1] James's reluctance to tolerate politically suspicious protestants, and how political exigencies might overcome that reluctance, are both visible in the discussions of April 1686 which led to the first abortive attempts to alter the religious system in Scotland. Barrillon reported that the King and the Scottish lords were considering freedom of worship for both catholics and sectaries: the latter, however, were to observe certain rules

> which are necessary for the maintenance of monarchy and the government and which restrain and set some limits to the excesses of the fanatics and Quakers. They will not be able to meet in the fields (*à la campagne*) as they did.
> This liberty accorded to the nonconformists has caused great difficulty and been much debated for several days. The King of England had greatly wished that only the catholics should have been allowed to practise their religion.

But the Scottish lords believed that this could not be done if the persecution of the presbyterians continued.

> At length the King of England agreed that liberty should extend even to the sectaries, provided that necessary restrictions that had been agreed on were imposed.[2]

Rejecting the ruler's authority in the name of religion, the extreme Scottish presbyterians were perhaps the only substantial body of James's subjects whose behaviour to some extent justified his fears of 'republicanism'.

It may well have been political reasons that originally led James to become a catholic. He seems to have had little religious feeling in his youth[3] and what he wrote about his conversion suggests that like his brother he was attracted to catholicism because it represented lawful authority and a barrier against disorder.[4] He says that in his youthful exile, though not tempted to apostasize,[5] he admired the

---

[1] Turner, pp. 307–10.

[2] M. V. Hay, *The Enigma of James II* (Sands 1938), pp. 226–7. James refused a new statutory guarantee of protestantism, 'a faith that he believes false and erroneous'.

[3] Turner, pp. 95–7. His evidence is rather thin.

[4] Cf. Turner, p. 98 n. citing Lord J. Russell, *Life of Wm, Lord Russell*, pp. 37–8. Cf. account of his conversion in the *Life*, vol. i, pp. 440–1: he wanted to go on worshipping as a protestant, thought that catholics could easily get dispensations for this sort of thing, but was told that it was an 'unalterable doctrine' of his new church 'not to do ill that good might follow'.

[5] But there were constant suspicions that he had.

devotion of the catholics, their seemly worship and munificence in charity, and the many instances in which catholic friends had abandoned loose living. The several days of public prayers, confession and receiving the sacrament in the French army before the relief of Arras in 1654 was an incident that may well have impressed him.[1] Later, he was led to read about the history of the Reformation, and the more he did so, the more convinced he became that the reformers had been guilty of schism. Eventually he came to believe that the Roman church was infallible and that

> without submission you cannot be a Christian. It was that consideration chiefly which made me embrace the communion of the Roman church, there being none other that pretends, or could pretend, to infallibility than it, for there must necessarily be an infallible church or otherwise what our Saviour said could not be, and the gates of Hell would prevail against it. The practice of the anglican church confirmed me in that belief, it having always acted since the Reformation as if it believed itself infallible, although it does not wish to admit it.

What else could justify the laws against papists and dissenters? James, like Charles, was hostile to the free interpretation of the scriptures by the individual, which he thought left 'Christianity in a state of dissolution'. He thought that protestantism had led both to immorality and to the proliferation in England of 'Socinians and Latitudinarians'.[2]

James wanted to safeguard the authoritarian state that he was building by placing the key positions in the hands of men with sound religious views: only these could be expected to be completely reliable. In the 'Advice to his Son' written soon after he had been driven from the throne, he warned the infant, if he became king, not to let

> any loose liver or atheistical persons insinuate themselves into your confidence or pleasures, none such are to be trusted, no more than those who make their gold their God, they will all fail you in the time of trouble . . . whosoever is true to his God, will, nay must be so to his king. Employ such, rely on such and let none but such have your confidence and favour. And tho' 'tis impossible for a king to make use of none but such, let such always have the preference, have a care how you trust a Latitudinarian, they are generally

---

[1] *Life*, vol. i, pp. 209–10.
[2] James to Princess Mary, Nov. 1687, in Mechtild, Countess Bentinck (ed.), *Lettres et Mémoires de Marie, Reine d'Angleterre, épouse de Guillaume III* (The Hague, 1880), pp. 4–9.

atheists in their principles and knaves in their nature, as for Trimmers they are generally cowards . . .[1]

James recognized the loyalty of catholics and wished like previous sovereigns to protect and employ them. He did not believe that only catholics were loyal and he found it hard to accept that loyal anglicans would not regard them as allies. At the time of the Declaration of Indulgence in 1672, he had believed

> that none but catholics and protestants of the church of England made a conscience of submitting to their kings; to which my lord Halifax replied, his highness would soon see the contrary as to the latter, who he was sure would roar out against this declaration with all their might, which proved accordingly.[2]

Despite this, during the exclusion crisis, he dismissed hatred of popery as a mere pretext for treason on the part of republicans. To those who urged him to change his religion he replied that

> all the world sees that it is not religion they drive at so much as the destruction of monarchy, and if this handle were taken away another would soon be found.[3]

He told the Prince of Orange that 'they that pretend to lay aside one for his religion may as well lay aside another for some fancy or other'.[4] In 1685 he could still tell Barrillon optimistically that he intended to 'grant' the catholics

> entire liberty of conscience and the free exercise of their religion; this is a work of time and it can be brought about only step by step. His Britannic Majesty's plan is to achieve it by the assistance of the episcopal party which he regards as the royalist party.[5]

But he could not be entirely oblivious of the massive English hostility to catholics, not excluding himself. He only concluded, however, that self-preservation required his giving the catholics a strong position in the state, regardless of anglican objections. He told Barrillon at his accession that 'he could never be in entire safety till the catholic religion was established in England in such a manner as not to be ruined or destroyed'.[6] In July 1685 Sunderland told Barrillon that

---

[1] *Life*, vol. ii, p. 620; cf. p. 638. He thought Clifford had been Charles II's only loyal minister.

[2] *Life*, vol. ii, p. 137. [3] *Life*, vol. i, p. 632.

[4] Dalrymple, vol. i, Review, p. 300. [5] Turner, p. 258.

[6] Dalrymple, vol. ii, bk. ii/iv, p. 38.

'good sense and right reason' required this: 'without it he will never be in safety and always exposed to the indiscreet zeal of those who will heat the people against the catholic religion as long as it is not fully established.'[1]

James does not seem to have imagined that the catholics would ever be more than a minority in England,[2] but he became increasingly bent on making them a powerful minority by reason of their position in the royal service. Monmouth's rebellion and the consequent expansion of his forces gave him, as he told Barrillon, an opportunity that might never recur for arming and employing catholics. Catholic soldiers and officers were accordingly enlisted and James commented that freedom of worship for catholics would thus be established before parliament legalized it and that the prospect of government employment would effect more conversions even than freedom of worship.[3] In November 1685 he told parliament that the 'officers in the army not qualified according to the late Tests for their emploments' were

> most of them well known to me, and having formerly served with me in several occasions and always proved the loyalty of their principles by their practice, I think them fit now to be employed under me and will deal plainly with you, that after having had the benefit of their services in such time of need and danger, I will neither expose them to disgrace nor myself to the want of them, if there should be another rebellion to make them necessary to me.[4]

In February 1687 a habitué of the court recorded that 'the King says he will dispense his favours equally between his Church of England subjects and his Romish' and was able to give a list of appointments in which this principle had been applied.[5] The further building up of a catholic contingent within the army has already been described.

James's desire to buttress his position by arming a religious minority harks back, like so much else at this time, to Cromwell, though his arraying of the catholic Irish recalls rather the continental rulers who crushed popular resistance by employing foreign mercenaries.[6]

[1] *ibid.*, pp. 106–7.
[2] James's 'Advice to his Son' urged protection of the Irish catholics 'that at least in one of the kingdoms there may be a superiority of those of that persuasion'. *Life*, vol. ii, p. 636. Cf. vol. i, p. 656.
[3] Turner, p. 285. [4] LJ, vol. xiv, p. 73.
[5] *The Ellis Correspondence*, vol. i, pp. 240–1.
[6] Cf. V. G. Kiernan, 'Foreign Mercenaries and Absolute Monarchy', *Past and Present*, no. 11 (April 1957), pp. 66–86.

As he was increasingly forced to struggle against the anglicans in order to complete the emancipation of the catholics, the Cromwellian parallel became closer. While an embattled religious minority stiffened the ruling élite, religious toleration would fragment the people and damp down opposition. In the 'Advice to his Son', James said

> be never without a considerable body of catholic troops, without which you cannot be safe, then people will thank you for liberty of conscience. Be not persuaded by any to depart from that

(*i.e.* liberty), he continued, but

> I make no doubt if once liberty of conscience be well fixed, many conversions will ensue, which is a truth too many of the protestants are persuaded of . . .

This was the nub of James's policy and he made a few more detailed recommendations to his son. The secretary at war should be a catholic, the secretary of the navy protestant. There should be a secretary of state of each religion. The treasury board should contain three anglicans, one catholic and a dissenter. Irish regiments should serve in England and 'as many Catholics as can be in the army, some church of England and dissenters'.[1]

But it would be wrong to depict James as a thorough machiavellian. This would be to ignore his naivety and streak of honesty. Unlike Charles, he had not waited till his deathbed to profess his conversion and he had upheld his new faith at great risk. Of his change of religion he said in 1679 that

> what I did was never done hastily, and I have expected many years and have been prepared for what has happened to me and for the worst that can yet befall me.[2]

The original motive for the change may have been largely political. But like Louis XIV he grew more pious as he grew older and increasingly the protection and propagation of his faith became his main concern.[3] The driving force of his later years was not the restless ambition of a thrusting absolute monarch but remorse for his sins and the desire for personal sanctity. Women (or rather sex) obsessed

---

[1] *Life of James II*, vol. ii, pp. 621–2, 637, 641–2.

[2] *Clarendon Correspondence*, vol. i, p. 45. For similar remarks, Turner, p. 209.

[3] He once told d'Adda, the papal envoy to his court, that he recognized that he might have been safer on his throne had he not raised the religious question. Davies, *Essays on the Later Stuarts*, p. 52, citing L. Ranke, *History of England*, vol. iv, p. 279.

him—he strove in vain to curb his desires. It is commonly supposed that a syphilitic infection intensified his pride and stupidity in later life.[1] After his accession, much of his time was taken up with prayers —ten hours a day sometimes—and this preoccupation helps to explain his failure in politics.[2] But in 1687 his promiscuity still continued and he envied Louis XIV (who was younger) his self-control in this respect.[3] The greater part of his 'Advice to his Son' is devoted to religious exhortation and above all to the need to live chastely. James points to the practical disadvantages of royal mistresses and bastards—the waste of money and the intrigues at court which they caused—and no one certainly had more cause to do this than he had. But above all he was conscious of his own grievous sins of the flesh, for which God had chosen to punish him even in this world, in order to reclaim him and make him 'an example and warning to all the world'. He gave thanks for all the 'mortifications and punishments' inflicted on him since the Restoration, 'which had He not been pleased to repeat often, I have but too much reason to apprehend I should not have been awakened out of the lethargy and insensibility I was in. . . .' The deaths of relatives, children and friends had been followed by his expulsion from his kingdoms by his own daughters and son-in-law: 'for all which I praise God, and look on myself as much happier than ever I was in all my life, having that quiet of mind and inward peace which cannot be understood or enjoyed' save by the truly repentant sinner.[4] In exile, he was able to devote himself almost entirely to works of piety. 'I was never truly happy,' he told the Abbot of La Trappe in 1695, 'till I was convinced that it is impossible to have content in this world but by despising of it.[5]

Lauderdale (who died in 1682) once gave his chaplain a remarkably prophetic characterization of James II.

'This good prince', said he 'has all that weakness of his father without his strength. He loves, as he saith, to be served in his own way and he is as very a papist as the Pope himself, which will be his ruin', and when the Doctor replied 'My Lord, will he venture the loss of three kingdoms for his religion?', the Duke answered 'yes, if he had the empire of the whole world he would

[1] But there seems no evidence beyond hearsay. Turner's discussion, p. 234, is unconvincing.
[2] *Ellis Correspondence*, vol. i, p. 91. Ailesbury was of this opinion.
[3] Turner, pp. 300–2.
[4] *Life of James II*, vol. ii, p. 631; cf. what follows and precedes that page.
[5] *Life of James II*, vol. ii, p. 614.

venture the loss of it, for his ambition is to shine in a red letter after he is dead.'[1]

James wanted power but he did not want it above all else. His religious policy was not kept within the bounds of the politically prudent and so it became a threat to his position instead of a source of strength.

[1] From an unpublished life of the chaplain, Dr George Hickes, a noted scholar and nonjuror, cited in W. B. Gardner, 'the Later Years of . . . Lauderdale', *Jol. of Modern History*, vol. xx (1948), pp. 121–2.

7

James's Religious Campaign

THE extent to which James could implement his religious policy was clearly shown in the first eighteen months of the reign. Thanks to the generally improved position of the monarchy, there was nothing to prevent his emancipating the catholics by means of the huge royal prerogative in religious matters. But not even a carefully packed parliament was prepared to set the seal of permanent legal sanction upon what he had done. He was in the position characteristic of an absolute monarch: he could bend and flout the laws but he could not change them and sooner or later they would resume their empire. He could get no further without popular support, and in the second half of his reign he tried rather reluctantly to win this by resuscitating the whigs and exploiting the divisions between protestants. But the protestants managed to unite and to demonstrate their solidarity in defence of the law. James could not get further than his initial half-victory. Only the birth of a son to him in 1688 gave some hope of permanence to his work.

He began his reign cautiously. Against the advice of his ministers, he decided to worship publicly as a catholic because he thought

> that if he had shown fear, the people ill-disposed to him would have had him at a disadvantage; that though he took some risk in his action, his conscience obliged him to make open confession of his religion.[1]

But catholics were not at first given office: instead, a council was established to look after catholic interests. It comprised two elderly catholic peers, Arundel of Wardour and Belasyse, and two cronies of

[1] See Turner, pp. 246–7. For what follows see further pp. 243, 251–2, 258–9. Louis XIV thought the same.

the King, Richard Talbot and Henry Jermyn (soon to be ennobled as Tyrconnel and Dover). The auspicious beginnings of the reign encouraged James to go further. Although there was some murmuring at his public profession of his faith, the many prophecies that he could not come to the throne peacefully were completely falsified. James began to think that parliament would at once sanction the ending of persecution and would only object to the employment of catholics in the royal service from fear that eventually only catholics would be so employed. By the end of April the favourable outcome of the general election had strongly confirmed this impression. On 11 May came the first of several orders to the lord treasurer to stop the recovery of fines due from specified 'loyal' recusants for failure to go to church.[1] Monmouth's rebellion provoked, as we have seen, the employment of catholics in the army and James's avowal to parliament in the autumn that he was determined to keep his catholic officers. The uncongenial Halifax was dismissed when he refused to promise support for the repeal of the Test and Habeas Corpus Acts.[2]

Parliament disappointed James's hopes. On 26 May the commons' grand committee on religion passed two resolutions pledging them to defend the 'reformed religion' of the Church of England and calling for the enforcement of the laws against all dissenters from it whatever. James was very angry, sent for the leading members of the governmental party and reproved them. Next day the commons rejected the resolutions on report and instead expressed satisfaction with the royal pledge to defend the Church of England, 'which', they ominously added, 'is dearer to us than our lives'. Barrillon thought that this was a moral defeat and that another time the King would be 'neither able nor willing to exercise authority'. His supporters' resentment against him was inflamed by the taunts of the whigs. They proceeded to bring in a draconian bill making into high treason 'anything said to disparage the King's person or government'. But an amendment was carried exempting preaching and teaching against the errors of Rome from the penalties of the Act. James suspended the session soon after this, and perhaps because of it.[3] When parliament reassembled in the autumn, he surpassed himself in tactlessness. The demand that

---

[1] Turner, p. 306.   [2] Foxcroft, vol. i, p. 454.
[3] G. Davies, 'Tory Churchmen and James II', *Essays on the Later Stuarts*, p. 48. Turner, pp. 272–4.

catholic officers be permitted in the forces was coupled with the assertion that 'a good force of well-disciplined troops in constant pay' was essential to future security. The King asked for more money to pay for them.[1] An army and popery combined was more than even this house of commons could swallow though their opposition was muted. A debate rather hostile to armies ended in a decision to make the militia more effective. By one vote they decided not to consider supply until they had considered the other parts of the King's speech. But they only made a tactful remonstrance and afterwards voted him, as already mentioned, 700,000*l.* Their address promised an indemnity for catholics who had been serving and asked, but without saying so directly, that no more should be appointed. The King's reply was a stinging public rebuke, such as he had already threatened in the summer.[2] He was present when the lords debated the message and heard Halifax's ironic thanks for his plainness and speeches against the employment of catholics from such anglican stalwarts as Lord Nottingham and Henry Compton, Bishop of London. The last

> spake long, calmly and with great respect and deference to his majesty, yet very full and home; and when he ended he said he spake the sense of the whole bench, at which they [the rest of the bishops] all rose up.[3]

This was the first sign that, with the whigs smashed and the tories thrown into confusion by the government, the anglican hierarchy might be able to emerge as a focus of political leadership. Next day (20 November) James prorogued parliament and lost his money. Compton was removed from the privy council.

Parliament would probably have done a certain amount to meet the King's wishes, given time and preparation. James did not despair. Barrillon found him 'in excellent spirits and he congratulates himself on having taken a dignified and firm part'. The prorogation was only until February and James told William of Orange that he hoped 'when they next meet they will be in better temper and consider the true interest of the nation'.[4] The cowing of members by threatening the dismissal of placemen had already begun and not only James but

---

[1] LJ, vol. xiv, p. 73.
[2] '. . . he would reply to the commons in such firm and decisive terms that they would never so offend again.' Quoted Turner, p. 272.
[3] Turner, p. 295. Convenient summary, Davies, pp. 54–8.
[4] Turner, p. 296.

Lord Treasurer Rochester expected parliament to relent. But government action was hampered by the rivalry of Sunderland and Rochester. Sunderland was gaining ground by wooing the catholics at court (from the Queen downward) and by pandering to the King's catholic sympathies. In July 1685 James told Barrillon that he had confided more of his religious plans to Sunderland than to his other ministers. In September it was through Sunderland that he established official relations with the Pope. In December Sunderland was given the office of lord president from which Halifax had been removed. Jeffreys, who had already been made lord chancellor, was his creature. By 1686 an unofficial council of catholic courtiers was meeting regularly under his direction and as he was the only capable politician among them, their influence was at his disposal. His position at court was now stronger than Rochester's but he could hope for no sympathy in the anglican-dominated parliament. Whether for this reason or not, he maintained that parliament could not be bribed into submission and that the King, having seemingly broken the law, could not allow it to meet without exposing himself to attack.

Parliament was therefore further prorogued and the prerogative was used to give the catholics what James wanted them to have. In March 1686 he told Barrillon that 'having already risked the loss of three kingdoms by declaring himself a Roman Catholic, he would not belie his own past' but use his authority 'for the establishment of the true religion'.[1] In the same month, a collusive action (Godden v. Hales) was brought at Rochester assizes to test the legality of the commissions that James had given to catholics contrary to the Test Act. Sir Edward Hales pleaded that he had a royal dispensation from taking the necessary oaths: he lost the case and appealed. In June the twelve judges with but one dissentient concurred in the judgment for Hales in the court of king's bench. Although a purge of the judiciary was needed to produce this result, it was not necessarily bad law. Chief Justice Herbert pointed out that dispensations had constantly been used in the appointment of sheriffs despite an express statutory prohibition and that the courts had constantly upheld the King's right to do this. The judges ruled that

'tis an inseparable prerogative in the kings of England, to dispense with penal laws in particular cases and upon particular necessary reasons.

[1] For the foregoing, Kenyon, pp. 122, 127–8.

This was

the ancient remains of the sovereign power and prerogative of the kings of England, which never yet was taken from them nor can be.[1]

In July four catholics (Lords Dover, Belsayse, Arundel and Powis) were admitted to the privy council. On 22 October a commission of the council, including catholic members, was set up to revise the commissions of the peace: the infiltration of catholics into local government began. At court it was remarked that 'the Irish are the happy men here'.[2] Meanwhile, public catholic worship was spreading under the state's protection. Catholic propaganda poured from the presses and convents of Jesuits, friars and monks were established in London, to the scandal of the citizens. In Ireland, the catholic bishops were in expectation of state pensions.[3] Diplomatic representatives were exchanged with Rome.

The only opposition to these measures that James could not readily suppress came from the anglican church. He could hardly forbid protestant worship, even at court. Not surprisingly, sermons everywhere came to concern themselves with the danger to the church and the errors of Rome. The King became increasingly annoyed and gave orders for the restraint of the preachers, but the bishops would not go beyond requiring them to moderate their tone.[4] In March 1686 James repeated some instructions for preaching which his brother had sent to the archbishops: preachers were to confine themselves to expounding the doctrines to be found in the catechism and they were to avoid politics and controversial theology.[5] In May things came to a head when a notable London preacher, John Sharp, Dean of Norwich and later Archbishop of York, spoke on the forbidden topic in answer to an anonymous letter from a parishioner in spiritual doubt. Compton was ordered, as Bishop of London, to suspend him from his function as rector of St Giles in the Fields. Compton refused to do so without judicial process and thus increased the odium which had already led to his removal from the privy council. In July an ecclesiastical commission was created by royal fiat, the purpose of

---

[1] D. Ogg, *England in the Reigns of James II and William III* (Oxford University Press, 1955), p. 168. Turner, pp. 319–20.

[2] *Ellis Correspondence*, vol. i, p. 64: March 1686.

[3] *Clarendon Correspondence*, vol. i, p. 529.

[4] L. von Ranke, *A History of England, Principally in the Seventeenth Century* (1875), vol. iv, pp. 293–4.   [5] CSPD 1686–7, nos. 227–8.

which was made sufficiently plain by its first act, which was to suspend Compton from his functions and place his see under the control of the docile Bishops Sprat and Crewe. The commission has been commonly regarded as illegal. The Court of High Commission which had been such a terror to the puritans in the time of Laud had been abolished by the Long Parliament, with confirmation at the Restoration. But the royal supremacy in ecclesiastical matters remained and it can be argued[1] that the commission merely exercised the powers of visitation inherent in that supremacy. It never claimed to be a court of law; its authority was confined to ecclesiastics and did not go beyond suspending or at most depriving them. There was thus no resemblance to the old high commission and, of course, the purpose was entirely different—not to defend the church by punishing laymen but to attack it by cowing churchmen. James told Barrillon

> that God had permitted that all the laws which have been passed for the establishment of the protestant and to destroy the catholic religion should now serve as a basis for what he wished to do for the re-establishment of the true religion

and he pointed out that his ecclesiastical powers were greater than those of other catholic kings. The irony of a catholic king's using powers that had been usurped from the Pope was not lost on contemporaries.[2]

The appointment of the commission carried forward, in a very different form, the policy already initiated of restoring central control in the church. It undertook routine control activities that the bishops could not manage: in October 1686 it stopped three London clergy exempt from episcopal jurisdiction from solemnizing marriages without licence and heard petitions against simony and incontinence.[3] In the typical manner of absolutism, it was an instrument for reducing a powerful organization to obedience by bypassing its great officers (the bishops in this case) and placing it under the control of a body more subservient to the royal will. It seems that the original idea had been to make Sunderland vicar general in spirituals, like Thomas Cromwell under Henry VIII. But James had no wish for overmighty ministers and a commission was thought preferable.[4] Composed mainly of reliable royal instruments, it included two staunch anglicans

[1] Ogg, *James II and William III*, pp. 175–8.   [2] Turner, p. 317.
[3] *Ellis Correspondence*, vol. i, pp. 172–3.   [4] Ranke, vol. iv, p. 298.

for show. There were three bishops and four great laymen. Archbishop Sancroft balanced Sprat and Crewe among the former and Rochester was joined to Jeffreys, Sunderland and the new chief justice, Herbert, among the latter: it is noteworthy that the archbishop and the treasurer dared not refuse to act, though Sancroft stayed away.

James threatened the independence of the church but did he threaten its existence? It was natural to suspect that he intended gradually to place it under the control of catholic priests.[1] When Edward Sclater, perpetual curate of Putney, became a catholic, he was indeed given permission to retain his living. But this was an isolated instance: no vacant parish was bestowed on a catholic. James appointed some highly unsatisfactory bishops. Samuel Parker (Oxford) he described to d'Adda, the papal envoy, as a sympathiser with the catholics who would bring round his clergy. Thomas Cartwright (Chester) co-operated with the priests at court. Watson of St David's was ultimately deprived for simony. With Sprat of Rochester and Crewe of Durham they formed the beginnings of a party for James within the episcopate. But though some of them might fairly be called worldly courtiers, none was a catholic. The church in the main was left to the protestants.

It was otherwise with the universities and schools which then formed part of the church. Education and in particular educational endowments had been placed completely under anglican control. This was bound to be resented by catholics and not by them alone. 'I have always declared my opinion,' William Penn told the fellows of Magdalen College, Oxford when they sought his help,

> that the preferments of the church should not be put into any other hands but such as they at present are in; but I hope that you would not have the two universities such invincible bulwarks for the church of England that none but they must be capable of giving their children a learned education.[2]

James tried to undermine the anglican educational monopoly and it is interesting that his most arbitrary measures were taken in 1687, when

---

[1] Macaulay, vol. ii, pp. 739–66, presents the case for being suspicious. The long vacancy of the see of York (April 1686–November 1688) may not have been as sinister as was thought: Crewe was offered and refused it in May 1686, Ogg, *James II and William III*, p. 164.

[2] J. R. Bloxam, ed., *Magdalen College and King James II, 1686–1688* (Oxford Historical Society 1886), p. 105. This collection of documents is the source of what follows on Magdalen College.

he was trying to arouse the dissenters against the church. There was an unsuccessful attempt to make Cambridge confer a degree on a catholic. The governors of Charterhouse school were ordered, also without success, to give a papist a scholarship. But it was in Oxford that something was achieved. In 1686 Obadiah Walker, Master of University College, who had apostatized, was allowed to keep his place and set up an oratory for his followers in the college. John Massey, a known catholic, was appointed by dispensation to be dean of Christchurch. In April 1687 the King ordered the fellows of Magdalen College to elect Anthony Farmer, another reputed catholic, as their president. Magdalen, like Christchurch, was a very rich foundation. Burnet thought that it might well be the richest college in Europe, with an income from its estates of 4,000*l*. or 5,000*l*. a year at least[1]—as rich, in short, as a peer of the realm.

The fellows of Magdalen were a loyal body who had raised a company for service against Monmouth. They acknowledged the King's right to tell them whom to elect as president, but with the reservation that the nominee should be of good character and eligible under the college statutes. Farmer was neither and so the fellows set him aside and elected one of their own number, John Hough. They contended that they could not have waited for a further royal nomination because the college statutes required the vacancy to be filled within a certain time. The government did not press the claims of Farmer but refused to regard Hough's election as valid. The fellows were told to elect the Bishop of Oxford instead and when they refused, some ecclesiastical commissioners were sent to hold a visitation and install him. The fellows agreed to 'submit' to the new president as far as it was 'lawful', but the King then required them to admit that they had been in the wrong and to ask his pardon. On refusing, most of them were turned out and replaced by catholics.

James made an example of Magdalen even though the fellows' objection to Farmer proved well founded. No doubt the immediate reason was, as Penn said, that 'Majesty did not love to be thwarted',[2] but other considerations of wider interest were involved. Magdalen seems to have had the reputation of being troublesome. 'Ye have been a stubborn, turbulent college,' the King told the fellows, 'I have known you to be so these six and twenty years.' Bishop Cartwright,

---

[1] G. Burnet, *History of His Own Time* (1818 ed.), vol. ii, p. 321.
[2] Bloxam, p. 105.

one of the commissioners for the visitation, reproached them with having quarrelled with their presidents, with the college visitor and with each other.[1] Chastisement was no doubt felt to be overdue. The form it took, however, involved a sinister extension of the powers of the ecclesiastical commission. The fellows claimed that Hough had been regularly installed as president and was 'invested with a freehold under the protection of his majesty's laws'. When he was turned out at the visitation, Hough appealed to 'the King in his courts of justice'. He thought himself the only instance of a man 'deprived of a freehold . . . without being summoned or heard'.[2] The commissioners were beginning to trench on matters felt to appertain to the common law. When they had suspended Compton, they had not deprived him of the temporalities of his see. By laying hands on Magdalen, on the other hand, they 'shew'd the King a way to put into every place; not to say, that in its consequence it affects every man's property in England'.[3] Nor was there anything accidental about this. When the commission was first set up, Barrillon reported that it was to enquire into misappropriations of ecclesiastical property and that there were hopes of 'considerable sums' passing to the crown.[4] The visitation of Magdalen was in this spirit: the King contemplated quo warranto proceedings[5] such as had destroyed the independence of all other types of corporation. The management of college property, especially charitable funds, and the non-observance of college statutes were enquired into—rather as Thomas Cromwell's agents had investigated the monasteries prior to their dissolution.[6] The fellows of Magdalen had many powerful friends—headed by the King's daughters and the Duke of Ormonde—who took care of them after their deprivation. This must have stiffened their resistance and also ensured that it had a wide impact and that the importance of the issues involved was understood. 'The more popular you become,' Cartwright rightly told them, 'the more pernicious will you be in encouraging your deluded admirers.'[7]

---

[1] *ibid.*, pp. 85, 186.

[2] *ibid.*, pp. 60, 121, 136.

[3] Thomas Tramallier of Jesus College to Lord Hatton, *ibid.*, p. 167.

[4] F. A. J. Mazure, *Histoire de la revolution de 1688 en Angleterre* (1825), vol. ii, pp. 132–3.

[5] Bloxam, p.183.

[6] Cartwright complained of bastards resulting from disobedience of the statute requiring college servants to be males. *ibid.*, p. 189.

[7] *ibid.*, p. 116.

The use of his prerogative enabled James to pose an almost limitless threat to the established order and already in 1686 he had managed to put catholics on a footing of equality with anglicans in the fields of governmental activity and propagation of the faith. But his achievement depended on the continuance of his own life. He was an ageing man and his heirs were protestants and sure to reverse what he had done. He does not seem to have worried much about this at first but the catholic party as a whole naturally did. Once their initial emancipation was accomplished, they turned their attention to means of making it permanent. The extremists, like their whig protestant counterparts, inclined to a revolutionary solution: the exclusion of the lawful heir. For some time they had been interesting themselves in the possibility of converting James's younger daughter, Anne, and altering the succession in her favour. The French and Danish ambassadors (Anne's husband being Danish) were also interested. Even if the succession was not changed, the fact that William and Mary were childless would make Anne's conversion an important gain: even the Pope, who was cautious, was eager for it. In the summer of 1686 a curious document called 'a remonstrance made to the King of England by his council' leaked out from catholic circles. It suggested a change in the succession together with a French alliance and a war against the Dutch.[1] The Irish catholics had even wilder ideas. According to Clarendon, the bulk of the people believed that the Pope could still bestow Ireland on whom he pleased. He reported a rumour that the Pope had legitimized Mr Fitzjames, the King's natural son later made Duke of Berwick, and that he was to seek foreign aid and then be 'sheltered' in Ireland till his time came to claim the three kingdoms.[2] Tyrconnel did in fact propose that Fitzjames should be appointed lord lieutenant with himself as deputy and should marry his daughter. A heightened version of this proposal reached the ears of William of Orange.[3]

James would have nothing to do with such plans: whatever their religious advantages, they contradicted everything he had stood for in politics. 'It is God who bestows crowns,' he said to Barrillon, 'and it is far from my intention to do anything against justice and law.' Two possibilities remained: renewed efforts to gain parliamentary ratifi-

[1] Mazure, vol. ii, pp. 161–4. Cf. Kenyon, p. 135; Baxter, *William III*, pp. 205, 216–8.
[2] *Clarendon Correspondence*, vol. ii, pp. 81–2, 124–5, 476.
[3] Baxter, *William III*, pp. 218, 430 n. 5. Kenyon, p. 142.

cation of his religious policy and, partly as a means thereto, persuading the lawful heirs to the throne to accept it. A change in the law was deemed necessary in any case, to remove a further weakness in the catholic position. Despite the royal protection which they enjoyed, they never managed to add significantly to their number by conversions. This was put down to the unattractiveness of conversion while legal immunity could be promised for the present but not for the future. As Halifax was to point out to William, persons likely to be converted for worldly reasons would hold back as long as there was a danger that at a later stage they might be held to have acted illegally. In May 1686 Sunderland made the remarkable claim to d'Adda that if the Test Acts were repealed, there would be no protestants left in England after two years.[1]

In the winter of 1686–7, therefore, there was a fresh attempt to cajole those who sat in parliament into a change of heart on the religious question. Once again the rivalry of Sunderland and the Hydes spoiled such chances of success as there were. Sunderland argued that parliament was recalcitrant because his rivals had not been disgraced. He pointed out that 200 M.P.s depended on the King for their livelihood and that opposition in the lords could be overcome by new creations. The Hydes had not opposed royal policy, but they obstructed it where they could, and their impunity was bad for discipline. The catholic council came to the same conclusion in September 1686: they were especially concerned at protestant strength in the lords. But James could not bring himself to the necessary shock action of an abrupt and complete ruin of the Hydes—especially as Sunderland was so obviously eager to ruin them, insinuating that even if Rochester changed his religion he would not be sincere, and so could not be trusted. Instead there was a long campaign of fairly amicable persuasion. To allow time for it, parliament was further prorogued in the autumn until February, and then again until April. The King began by trying to persuade his personal friends at court—Rochester was the most eminent—to become catholics. He failed, and with great reluctance dismissed Rochester at the end of the year. In January Tyrconnel superseded Clarendon in Ireland. Next James demanded from those in his service who sat in parliament an undertaking—at first he tried to get it in writing—to support the repeal of the Test Acts and penal laws. Although he interviewed a great

[1] For this paragraph, Kenyon, pp. 131, 136, 139, 146–7. For the next, pp. 133 *et seq.*

many of them in person ('closeting', they called it) he found that they would accept dismissal rather than comply.

The second line of attack, through the lawful heirs, had been opened up at the same time as the first, through parliament. In November 1686 James sent his friend William Penn to Holland to persuade William and Mary to declare themselves in favour of the repeal of the obnoxious laws. Sunderland tried to improve relations with the Dutch by transferring the incompetent Bevil Skelton from The Hague to Paris and replacing him by his own friend Albeville: not an improvement as it turned out.[1] Penn may have been authorized to offer help against France as an inducement to William, and in the spring of 1687 Albeville was told to commend James's policy to him on the grounds that it strengthened the royal prerogative and was in imitation of the Dutch policy, so advantageous to commerce. William told Penn that he would consent to the toleration of both papists and dissenters and even help to get such a measure through parliament, but he would go no further. Alarmed, however, by the uproar and new developments in England, culminating in the elevation of Tyrconnel, he sent over a special envoy, Dijkvelt, in February 1687 to investigate the situation and discuss with James both the religious question and that of the succession. James was indignant about the latter:

> he was aware of the rumours about the succession but they had no founda-
> tion in fact but were invented by the factions in order to alarm the heirs; he
> was incapable of intention to interrupt the succession, such an intention
> would have been contrary to justice and to the affection he bore to his
> children, especially the Princess of Orange.

But he asked in vain for 'entire submission to his judgment' in the religious question.[2] Sunderland was now in something of a panic. It was apparent to him that parliament was not going to obey the King, but he had induced James to dismiss the Hydes by arguing that opposition would crumble if this was done. He therefore offered Dijkvelt not merely a firm alliance against France but a voice for William in all civil and military appointments in Ireland and England if he would declare his approval of repeal. This, as Lady Sunderland pointed out in a remarkable letter to William, was a trap. William could not convincingly retract a submission made to James, but

---

[1] But Kenyon defends Albeville, p. 136 n. For Skelton, Turner, p. 265.
[2] Turner, pp. 352–5. On Tyrconnel, Kenyon, p. 150.

James could evade the performance of promises made in return. Dijkvelt seems to have hesitated, but he did not close with the offer. The second line of attack petered out like the first (though James later attempted the conversion of Mary). Sunderland was under a cloud.[1]

Bolder and more radical measures were needed if the catholics were to win legal emancipation. Such measures were already under way in Scotland, where the King's position was much stronger. 'Measures need not be too nicely kept with this people', Lord Chancellor Perth told James.[2] The Earl of Perth and his brother (created Earl of Melfort in 1685) were rivalled in the Scottish government by Queensberry, the treasurer. Perth became a catholic in 1685, while Queensberry's political and religious position approximated to that of Rochester, to whom he was distantly related by marriage. Perth's conversion appears to have been sincere and at first without political significance: he expected to lose his offices. Melfort, who eventually followed his example, began by being angry at what he had done. A catholic political offensive was made possible by anti-catholic rioting in Edinburgh in January 1686. James was very angry and blamed Queensberry, who was governor of Edinburgh Castle. After debate in the catholic council attended by Rochester and Sunderland, he demoted and eventually dismissed Queensberry and gave his governorship to the catholic Duke of Gordon. He summoned the Scots parliament to meet at the end of April and asked them to give 'ease and security' to the Scottish catholics in return for some degree of free trade with England. But all that was forthcoming was a measure allowing catholics to worship in their own homes and even that only passed the Lords of the Articles by 18 votes to 14 and was heavily defeated in parliament. A still milder measure was drafted, but James prorogued parliament and instead used his prerogative. Orders to the privy council in September and November required them to protect private catholic worship and to admit catholics to civil and military offices and even to church livings.

James had refused, as already remarked, to link the presbyterians with the catholics in his measures for toleration in Scotland. But he was given reason to reconsider this. When in March 1686 he first outlined his new policy to the Scots privy council, he found them so

---

[1] Kenyon, pp. 149, 151–2. Sunderland has ever since been accused of plotting with William, but Kenyon has shown this was not so. It is not clear if he had James's authority for what he did. [2] Ogg, *James II and William III*, p. 171.

unenthusiastic that three of them were summoned to London. They told the King that they would support a measure of toleration for catholics if the unreconciled presbyterians were also included. One of these men was the Duke of Hamilton. He was a presbyterian at heart, but he was a staunch royalist, was well thought of by James and had been working with Perth and Melfort against Queensberry. James pressed Hamilton hard to support his policy. Hamilton made an equivocal reply and seems to have played some part in the drafting of the second abortive Toleration Bill. James and his ministers were apparently under the impression that he was friendly. It was in this situation that a Declaration of Indulgence was issued (12 February 1687) in which James took full advantage of the enthusiastic declarations of royal pre-eminence formerly made by the Scots parliament. Invoking 'our sovereign authority, prerogative royal and absolute power, which all our subjects are to obey without reserve', he gave catholics and quakers leave to worship publicly. Presbyterians were allowed only to worship in private and were reminded of the terrible penalties attached to their practice of open-air meetings. To the disappointment of the government, Hamilton failed to join in an address of thanks for the Declaration, but even so they do not seem to have given up hope. The Declaration was defective in form and a second one was issued on 5 July 1687.[1]

In Scotland therefore the government had revived the policy of allying catholics and protestant dissenters against the protestant episcopalian establishment. The experiment was not initially fruitful, but it seemed the only hope in England also. The disgrace of the Hydes and the approach to William and Mary pointed the same way. William was a calvinist and the invitation to him was to help in ending the anglican monopoly. Gradually, and without much confidence or enthusiasm, the King and Sunderland began to make an alliance with the dissenters. In November 1686 a licensing office was established in London where for 50s. a dissenter could buy a dispensation for his family from the laws by which they were constrained. Early in March 1687 James decided to establish toleration by decree, on the same lines as in Scotland.[2] The official purpose of

---

[1] Turner, pp. 366–77. Sir J. Mackintosh, *History of the Revolution in England in 1688* (1834), p. 290.
[2] Kenyon, p. 153. He thinks that Arthur Herbert's desertion was the last straw for James.

the Declaration of Indulgence issued on 4 April was to 'make our subjects happy and unite them to us by inclination as well as duty'. The 'free exercise of their religion' was to be added 'to the perfect enjoyment of their property, which has never been in any case invaded by us since our coming to the crown'. (The owners of former church lands were given a special reassurance.)

> We cannot but heartily wish, as it will easily be believed, that all the people of our dominions were members of the catholic church, yet we humbly thank almighty God it is and hath of long time been our constant sense and opinion (which upon divers occasions we have declared) that conscience ought not to be constrained nor people forced in matters of mere religon. It has ever been directly contrary to our inclination, as we think it is to the interest of government, which it destroys by spoiling trade, depopulating countries and discouraging strangers; and finally, that it never obtained the end for which it was employed.

To 'all our loving subjects' permission was given to meet for worship 'after their own way and manner', provided only that the meetings were peaceful and not clandestine or seditious. The imposition of religious tests on office holders was suspended, 'as we are desirous to have the benefit of the service of all our loving subjects, which by the law of nature is inseparably annexed to and inherent in our royal person'. The Church of England was promised protection and the concurrence of parliament was confidently looked forward to. The King had not quite given up hope of the anglicans. The existing parliament was prorogued again, not dissolved. 'Closeting' and negotiations with William went on until June. Sunderland apparently told James that new elections fought in alliance with the dissenters would produce a parliament only slightly better inclined on the religious question and much less inclined than the old one to support the government in other respects. The current worsening of international relations would make this a dangerous situation.

James eventually 'judged all other advantages far inferior to the principal one, which was the advancement of the catholic religion'.[1] Parliament was dissolved on 2 July and next day d'Adda, who had already been enthroned as a titular archbishop, ceased to be an unofficial envoy and was publicly received as papal nuncio. Preparations for a general election began with a series of addresses of thanks for the Declaration, intended of course to impress public

---

[1] Kenyon, p. 159.

opinion. Nearly 200 were received in the course of ten months. Over a third were avowedly from dissenters and as many from corporations and grand juries where no doubt dissenters had been given a large voice. But the few servile anglican bishops and some of their clergy also petitioned.[1] On 7 August a new purge of the London livery companies was ordered which restored the City to whig control. On the 11th there began the removal of lord lieutenants who were obviously going to be unhelpful in the elections—precursor of the thorough purge of county magistracies and municipal corporations in the autumn. On 21 August James and Sunderland began what was in effect an election tour of the western counties.

To give James a real chance of success there could be no substitute for a male heir educated in his own religion. On his western tour he prayed at the shrine of St Winifred, Holywell, for a son, and the Queen took the waters at Bath for the same purpose. To the general astonishment, rumours of the Queen's pregnancy began to circulate in mid-October. The news was officially confirmed on 14 November. Whatever further benefits this might promise for the King, its immediate effect was to make it harder than ever for Sunderland to implement the ticklish new political strategy. Once the catholics had achieved a place in the government, the extremists among them had begun to undermine Sunderland's position, believing that they no longer needed him. Tyrconnel in particular was his foe because he would not help in plans for greater Irish independence. With the help of the moderate catholics, Sunderland had been able to keep the extremists in check. When Tyrconnel was placed in charge of Ireland it was with the inferior title of lord deputy and two protestant advisers, Fitton and Sheridan, to check him. But Tyrconnel ignored all limitations and in August 1687 he met James at Chester and induced him to confirm the catholicizing of the municipal corporations that he had carried through and to authorize the raising of the Irish army to 10,000 men and the drafting of a new Act of Settlement, to be put before an Irish parliament in 1688. The repercussions of this on English opinion were likely to be disastrous.

As for the extremists in England, they took leave of reason when they heard of the royal pregnancy. They were sure—suspiciously sure, the protestants thought—that a miracle had happened and that the child would be a boy. They demanded a general election at once,

[1] Mackintosh, pp. 175–7.

expecting another miracle, whereas Sunderland knew that only lengthy preparations gave any chance of success. The moderate catholics, who usually supported him, agreed this time with the extremists—they hoped that the pregnancy would enable them to do a deal with the anglicans. This tactic was opposed by Sunderland at a meeting of 'those that are upon the secret of affairs' on 10 November and he secured the elevation of Father Petre, a leading extremist, to the privy council. He thus joined the extremists, but by dividing the catholics put himself in a position to delay the election. His personal position was safeguarded to some extent by the dearth of able men among the catholics, but it began to be threatened by the rise of Melfort to a leading position among the extremists. An inept politician, he was a skilful courtier and threatened to eclipse Sunderland in royal favour. Sunderland had for some time been currying favour by holding out prospects of his own conversion and his eldest son had actually been converted. At the end of 1687 he told James that he was ready to declare himself a catholic whenever it would be for his service. For him the pregnancy was not a miracle but a great gamble. He was likely to win lasting power if catholic rule endured and be grievously punished for his apostasy if it did not. He tried hard to get an augmentation of his already substantial pension from Louis XIV 'which would enable him to contemplate with less uneasiness the revolutions so frequent in England'.[1] James for his part fortified Portsmouth on the landward side. He needed a secure bolthole from which he could, if need be, make a rapid retreat to France. Tyrconnel fished for French support, hoping that in such an emergency Ireland could escape from English control.[2]

(II)

Sunderland's attempt to get a tractable parliament in 1688 was a pretty desperate stroke. But it was not quite as hopeless as it seems in retrospect, nor was its failure necessarily very damaging to the royal position. Had it not been possible to launch an invasion at that moment, the outcome might simply have been an uneasy equilibrium.

The year-long electoral campaign began in earnest in September

---

[1] Dalrymple, vol. ii, bk. v, app., p. 147. Kenyon, p. 178. For general developments after the dissolution see Kenyon, pp. 153–63, 171,

[2] Mazure, vol. ii, pp. 288–9,

1687 when it was decided to conduct a general purge of the municipal corporations.[1] To ensure that local administrators in general would support the government, Sunderland, on 25 October, asked every lord lieutenant to 'call before him' all his deputy lieutenants and justices of the peace, 'either jointly or separately, as he shall think fit', and ask them three questions:

1. If in case he shall be chosen knight of the shire or burgess of a town when the King shall think fit to call a parliament, whether he will be for taking off the penal laws and the Tests.
2. Whether he will assist and contribute to the election of such members as shall be for taking off the penal laws and the Tests.
3. Whether he will support the King's Declaration for liberty of conscience by living friendly with those of all persuasions, as subjects of the same prince and good christians ought to do.

The lord lieutenant was to write down in each case 'whether he consents, refuseth or is doubtful'. With a view to the replacement of those whose replies were unsatisfactory, he was also to send in lists of catholics and dissenters fit to be appointed deputies or justices. In December it was announced in the *London Gazette* that 'being resolved to maintain the liberty of conscience and to use the utmost endeavours that it may pass into a law', the King had 'thought fit to review the lists' of deputies and justices, 'that those may continue who are willing to contribute to so good and necessary a work and such others added from whom he may reasonably expect the like concurrence'.[2]

From the answers to Sunderland's questions it is possible to form some idea of how the politically active classes were reacting to the government's new strategy and what its chances were of winning an election.[3] Not that the magistrates who were questioned were a very representative sample even of the landed class from which they mostly came: the magistracy had been purged of whigs by Charles and diluted with catholics by James with the object of making it a docile body. These men would not lightly say 'no' to a royal request. In any case, few men of any kind were keen to offend the powerful royal govern-

[1] Kenyon, p. 166.
[2] Mackintosh, pp. 190–1.
[3] The answers were printed by Sir George Duckett, *Penal Laws and Test Act* (2 vols., 1882–3). For the questions see vol. i, pp. 26–9. Missing from the returns are Cheshire, Hertfordshire, Lancashire, Middlesex, Rutland, Suffolk, Surrey, Warwickshire and the City of London. Further references to the survey are all to Duckett,

ment. For these reasons, the result of the poll has commonly been accepted as highly disappointing for James. It would be pointless to give numerical totals since so many shades of opinion were expressed and also because it was the leaders of opinion that were being polled and some had much greater local influence than others. But if an attempt is made to sort the replies into the government's own categories of 'consent', 'refuse' and 'doubtful', the result is three groups of roughly comparable size. The 'consents' seem to have been slightly the largest group and the refusers the smallest. But it was the inclusion of catholics that put the 'consenters' ahead and even supposing this to be proper, their wealth and local influence was almost certainly below the average of their class. The 'consenters' were numerically strong in some outlying and midland counties usually thought of as conservative strongholds: Northumberland, Cumberland, Westmorland, parts of Yorkshire, Worcestershire, Herefordshire, Monmouthshire, Flint, even Gloucestershire. They were also numerous in some parts nearer London, such as Kent and Hampshire—possibly because the influence of the court was more felt there.

The outright refusers were weak in the north and in Devon, Cornwall and Somerset (no doubt the memory of Monmouth's fate affected these counties). But they were strong almost everywhere else and some were outspoken. Sir John Packington in Worcestershire said in answer to the first question:[1]

> The principal intent of the Test and penal laws . . . being to secure the protestant religion, till I am convinced that it is now in less danger than when those laws were enacted, or some better security shall be proposed than they offered us, I humbly conceive they cannot be taken off without eminent hazard (if not ruin) to the church of England, of which I profess my self a member. I can neither in conscience nor honour (if a parliament man) consent to the releasing a title that relates to its protection and support.

Equally significant was the presence among the 'doubtfuls' of a large body who were not simply avoiding commitment but who on the contrary voiced a perfectly clear opinion of their own, that of the more enlightened anglicans. As Sir Faire Medow Penyston put it in Oxfordshire:

> I ever was and still am of opinion that no human laws whatsoever either ought or can exercise an absolute dominion over the judgments and con-

[1] vol. i, pp. 238–9. He counted the Act of Uniformity among the penal laws.

sciences of men, and therefore ought not to inflict any manner of punishment for that over which they neither have nor can have any jurisdiction, wherefore I shall willingly assent to the taking off all such penal laws which debar people from the free exercise of their consciences in the religious worship of almighty God. But the Tests which I humbly conceive is at present the greatest security the Church of England by law hath, of which I profess myself an unworthy member, I cannot consent to repeal without an equivalent security for them established in a parliament.[1]

Sir Humfrey Forester in Berkshire said that

he cannot be for repealing the Tests, but as for the penal laws that are not absolutely necessary for the support of the Church of England, he is willing to have them repealed, having been sixteen years in commission without ever having persecuted any one for their opinion. [2]

A more tactful way of voicing this view was to offer to vote for repeal if 'convinced that the King's equivalent proposed for the security of the protestant religion may be sufficient'[3] or else 'provided his religion and property may be secured'[4] or in another case if 'secure provisions were made' that all benefices, college fellowships and other preferments should go to 'those of the Church of England and none else'.[5] If these moderate but firm anglicans are moved from the 'doubtful' column and added to the 'refusers' they greatly outnumber those who were willing simply to follow the King: indeed they are almost a majority of those expressing an opinion.

Linked in particular with the tolerant anglican strain of opinion was something even more sinister from James's point of view: there were signs of an attempt in some counties to form a united front, not so much to oppose the King as to intercede with him. In some counties a large section of the magistrates presented a joint answer, or else answered separately but in more or less identical terms. An identical answer came from the bulk of the magistrates in Devon and Cornwall: they were 'doubtful' as to the first two questions 'till it be debated in parliament, how the religion by law established may be otherwise secured' and they would wish to see the election of members who would 'most faithfully serve his majesty in all things, with security to our said religion'.[6] In Cumberland and Westmorland, sixteen individuals wrote almost identical letters to the effect that in an elec-

[1] vol. i, p. 340.   [2] vol. ii, p. 165.
[3] vol. i, p. 185: John Baker, Sussex.
[4] vol i, p. 181: John Machell, Sussex.
[5] vol. i, p. 354; Sir Thomas Taylor, Kent.   [6] vol. i, pp. 374–8.

tion they would support 'loyal and well affected' candidates and if elected themselves would be guided in their opinion by the reasons advanced in debate.[1] Half those who replied in Lincolnshire sent in a collective negative response.[2] Eleven of the Somerset magistrates replied alike that they were opposed to repeal but might change their opinion on hearing the debates.[3] The bulk of the East Riding answers, though individual, were identical and to much the same point as those in Cumberland.[4] The collective answer of Merioneth is noted below and the numerous moderate anglican replies in Norfolk and Sussex seem to have a common inspiration.

To some extent the existence of collective or identical answers may have been due to the initiative of lord lieutenants. They seem usually to have called meetings at which the answers were received and this gave an opportunity for concerted replies. At the Penrith meeting Lord Preston, the lord lieutenant of Cumberland and Westmorland, asked those present to give their answers in writing or orally to his secretary. The meeting then resolved that each man should retire and write his own answer. But the protestants retired to one room and the catholics to another: they returned with their answers after about an hour and it seems reasonable to suppose that they spent this time in trying to agree what to say.[5] Some lord lieutenants tried to secure uniformity in the answers in order to produce a more intelligible result. The Duke of Beaufort reported that he had strictly obeyed the instruction to

> write down particularly of every individual deputy lieutenant and justice of the peace (whom I took singly one by one), whether he consented, refused or was doubtful, which I at last reduced all their several discourses to.[6]

In some counties it was possible to give the replies in the form of a simple table.

Reasons of administrative convenience are enough to explain why the lord lieutenants acted as they did, but it is tempting to wonder if they were not also trying decorously to put pressure on the government. Many lord lieutenants resigned rather than help in the survey and it must not be supposed that those who did not resign were any

---

[1] vol. i, pp. 32–42.
[2] vol. i, pp. 155–6.
[3] vol. ii, pp. 12–13.
[4] vol. i, pp. 61–9.
[5] Sir Daniel Fleming of Rydal's account quoted by Duckett, vol. i, p. 50, from J. Nicolson and R. Burn, *History and Antiquities of the Counties of Westmorland and Cumberland* (1777), vol. i, pp. 165–70.
[6] vol. i, p. 288.

more sympathetic towards the King's policy. Rochester, who was 'thought more zealous then was necessary' in Hertfordshire, certainly was not. The Duke of Beaufort, who feared supersession by the Marquis of Powis, toured his huge lieutenancy—but only in December and his report was negative.[1] Of the fourteen lord lieutenants who continued in office and put the questions, half subsequently rallied to the Revolution, and it is notably in their counties that there were strong and more or less collective manifestations of negative or moderate anglican opinion. Devon and Cornwall, with their striking solidarity in the 'moderate' cause, were in the care of the Earl of Bath: he protested against the canvass and we shall see that his defection was of crucial importance to William in 1688. Norfolk, another 'moderate' stronghold, was the lieutenancy of the Duke of Norfolk—a protestant but head of a great catholic family. 'Negative' Lincolnshire was the domain of the Earl of Lindsey, a relation of Danby's. From Dorset came a tabular, largely negative, result: its lord lieutenant was the Earl of Bristol, whose family seem to have been unable to decide whether to be catholic or protestant. Even among the lord lieutenants appointed in place of those who had resigned, Jeffreys and Huntingdon sent in tabular and rather negative returns for their counties (Buckinghamshire, Shropshire, Leicestershire, Derbyshire) rather similar to that produced in Dorset. Jeffreys, whatever else he was, was no papist, and Huntingdon was a turncoat who had once been a whig and was to rally to the Revolution.[2] Not only, then, are there indications of a dominant block in the magistracy made up of outright and moderate defenders of anglicanism but there are also signs of some organization among them and of continuing support in high places. The Austrian ambassador pointed out in April 1688 the bad moral consequences of this for the government: previously 'everyone suspected his neighbour of being a partisan of the King and people suppressed their disaffection, which now they express without fear'.[3]

But the picture presented by the returns was not quite as gloomy for the government as is often supposed. What would interest a political realist like Sunderland was not what men would ideally

[1] Kenyon, pp. 172-3.
[2] But the tabular returns, especially in Jeffreys's case, may simply reflect lack of influence of the lieutenant in his lieutenancies. Peterborough, who was very loyal and a catholic convert, sent similar returns for Northamptonshire.
[3] Turner, p. 331.

prefer but what they could be bullied into accepting and sticking to. Viewed in this light, the returns provide some encouragement for supporters of the King. To the affirmative replies there might be added a numerous 'soft centre' of men who were not merely doubtful but did not qualify their doubts with any firm pledge to maintain the ascendancy of the Church of England. These two groups together seem to have formed a numerical majority of those expressing an opinion, though a preponderance of influence almost certainly lay with the supporters of anglicanism. Moreover, many of the magistrates failed to express an opinion at all. A good many absented themselves from meetings and could not be traced. Quite a few said simply that they would not stand for parliament or even that they would take no part in elections. Age and infirmity were reasons commonly given. It could be argued that this was an element capable of being bullied into submission.

It is very hard to estimate the strength of the 'soft centre'. The commonest attitude taken up among the 'doubtfuls' was that it was wrong to prejudge the issue before the subject was debated in parliament. Thus John Hill in the North Riding said that if elected to parliament

> 1. I will endeavour to serve his majesty faithfully and dutifully, and regulate my votes according to my judgement upon the arguments of the house.
> 2. When I assist in the choice of any parliament men, I will promote the election of such as I believe will act according to the foregoing answer.[1]

Such an affirmation might spring from a strong belief in free enquiry and debate as the proper basis for legislation. Robert Apreece in Huntingdon said

> He thinks it a great presumption in any person to promise or engage the making or abrogating laws, because when he comes into the house of commons (where every man hath free liberty of speech), he may hear such reasons as he could never imagine for or against the same. Therefore if it be his fate to be chose to so eminent a trust, upon the debate of the whole matter I (sic) will do that which I judge to be most for the honour of almighty God and the service of my King.[2]

But the rejection of pre-engagement had other, rather different connotations. The belief that parliament was free to debate and determine every question on its merits went along with the belief that the rest

---

[1] Duckett, vol. i, p. 99.
[2] vol. ii, p. 68.

of the country was not free and must do whatever parliament in its wisdom decided. Sir George Fletcher in Cumberland thought

> that the first question is more proper for the consideration of a parliament than a private meeting of country gentlemen who not having liberty to debate, are unable to arrive at a true understanding of the conveniences or inconveniences that may attend this question.[1]

Thomas Waite of York promised if elected to parliament to 'use all my skill to find out that which is equal and good and most convenient for common safety and society' and added

> that we must submit ourselves to what the parliament shall ordain by majority of voices, according to their discretions, nor can we oblige them to act otherwise, though they tell us they are for taking away those laws and Tests.[2]

Three Lincolnshire magistrates

> humbly conceive where the legislative power (being king, lords and commons) have concurred in the making of acts, it were a presumption in men of our private stations to arraign or censure the same, but as to their being prejudicial or not prejudicial to the nation is wholly to be left to the determination and judgment of a succeeding parliament.[3]

This attitude could modify considerably the effect of a doubtful or negative reply. Apreece, for instance, promised to try to 'choose' candidates 'no ways obnoxious to the government, and in their judgments I shall acquiesce'. Myles Staveley of Ripon could not bring himself to assent to the repeal of the obnoxious laws, but he promised to 'vote for such men as I think loyal to the King, and capacious upon the debate to determine in that matter'.[4] As already noticed, a group in Somerset qualified their negative by saying 'they know not how they may change their opinion upon hearing the debates'. Dr Aldworth of Magdalen College, Oxford, could not

> in his conscience declare himself for the taking away of all penal laws and Tests, yet shall submit to such laws, and repeals of such laws, as the king with his parliament shall think fit.[5]

---

[1] vol. i, p. 31. [2] vol. i, p. 74.
[3] vol. i, p. 157. Cf. Sir E. Smith, Essex, p. 394.
[4] vol. i, p. 81.
[5] 'Dr Allworth', vol. i, p. 329 and n. Cf. Hon John Darcy, North Riding, p. 96; Sir E. Norreys, Oxfordshire, p. 340. Sir George Blundell, Bedfordshire, said 'that he cannot pretend to a capacity of determining beforehand what his thoughts and actions shall be in progress of time, as to affairs of this nature'. (vol. ii, p. 48.)

Deference was sometimes more apparent than real. A 'doubtful' answer to question 1 might be balanced by an undertaking in the reply to question 2 to work for candidates who were firm for protestantism or the Church of England.[1] Deference could also work against the King instead of for him. Affirmative answers as well as negative ones were qualified by a pledge to hear the debate before finally deciding. Sir John Cotton in Bedfordshire said that he would 'come into the house with a design to be convinced with the best argument, which he hopes may be given for the repealing [of] the laws'.[2] But there was a strong note of deference to the King's wishes, both among those who supported and among those who opposed him. The Duke of Beaufort reported

> in general of those I have put down refusing, or doubtful, that there were very few of them that did not show to be much troubled that they could not comply with what the King desired and that did not declare, they would always be ready to venture life and fortune in his service; and would never refuse to comply with any intimation of his, as far as their consciences would give them leave; that as to this, they did apprehend the consequences of the repeal now desired would be destructive to the religion they professed, which fear they said, tho' possibly groundless, yet to them that could not help being possessed with it, made it, they conceived, sin in them to contribute towards it.[3]

A collective negative answer from the West Riding began boldly by saying that there seemed to be no legal obligation upon them to answer the questions at all but went on

> we think ourselves under no obligation to reply to them, otherwise than to show our willingness to express our obedience wherever, and by whomsoever, the King's name is made use of.

James Herbert in Oxfordshire gave a negative answer 'tho' he should be ready to serve the King in anything else'.[4] Protestation of loyalty could be a polite way of evading an answer, as when four Northumberland worthies said that if elected to parliament

> it shall be our chiefest care and study to do nothing there contrary to our duty to God or our loyalty to our dread sovereign.[5]

---

[1] As with the three Lincolnshire men mentioned above and the corporations of Doncaster, Leeds and Pontefract.

[2] vol. ii, p. 49: cf. Chas. Bull, West Riding, vol. i, p. 85, Sir C. Heron, Northumberland, vol. i, pp. 133–4; H. Bull, Somerset, vol. ii, p. 11.

[3] vol. i, pp. 288–9.   [4] vol. i, pp. 88, 339.

[5] vol. i, p. 128: Delaval, Jennison, Bickerstaffe, Lambton.

But many of those who gave a negative or doubtful answer qualified it by promising to work for the election of 'loyal' candidates. The corporation of York, who answered 'doubtful', promised to vote for honest, loyal men who 'I believe will very well please the King'.[1]

The effect of submissiveness was heightened by the fact that almost everyone answered 'yes' to the third question. It was framed in such a way, with emphasis on personal behaviour towards neighbours, that it was almost impossible to answer 'no',[2] and the general tone of the replies was a wholehearted repudiation of persecution even where the first two answers were 'no'. Charles Wythers in Hampshire who 'refuses the two first. Answers to the third, he will be upon the defensive, not offensive'[3] was uncharacteristic in his coolness. Sir Ralph Carr in Northumberland, after two negative answers, went on

> for the third question, when I was in authority I used all the mildness imaginable to those which differed from me in judgment, always thinking that conscience neither ought nor could be forced. I intend always to live in obedience to the established laws of the nation and in loyalty to my King.[4]

The general attitude of Sir Hugh Cholmely in the North Riding was doubtful.

> As I never used previous meetings to lead my votes, so I always voted as I thought upon hearing the debate, and therefore cannot give a certain answer to the question undiscussed.

But he added:

> No man can differ more in opinion from myself than I differ at the same time from him, and in equal causes, the living fairly seems to me a debt so justly due to human nature, I must think meanly of any one [who] should either slacken his kindness or other friendly office merely on account of religion or opinion.[5]

Sir George Fletcher and Sir Richard Musgrave in Cumberland gave a similar reply to Cholmely's to the first two questions, but to the third Fletcher replied:

---

[1] vol. i, pp. 78–9. Cf. the answers of Cumberland and Lincolnshire mentioned above. Nottingham Corporation (vol. ii, pp. 126–7) simply said they would elect loyal persons.
[2] Exceptions vol. i, p. 167; vol. ii, p. 104. The only cases I have found and those reported as answering no to all three.
[3] vol. i, p. 424. Cf. vol. i, p. 213; vol. ii, p. 148; Ric. Cross (Somerset), vol. ii, p. 11.
[4] London, 5 April 1688, vol. i, p. 136.
[5] vol. i, p. 95.

> I have ever been of the King's opinion that conscience ought not to be forced and when I was a member of parliament did act accordingly, and it is my desire, as it shall be endeavour, to live friendly with men of all persuasions.[1]

and Musgrave:

> I do very well approve of the King's Declaration of Indulgence and shall endeavour to live friendly and peaceably with men of all persuasions, as becometh every good Christian, provided they demean themselves in no wise contrary to law.[2]

The fact that there was general sympathy for the King's ostensible aims made this a good opportunity for those with really high notions of royal power to voice them. Lionel Copley in the East Riding thought that

> The King is the head and spring from whence all our laws do flow and consequently the most proper judge of the conveniency and tendency of all our laws . . . therefore do think my self engaged in duty . . . to endeavour . . . the making void the penal laws and Tests, they being by his majesty esteemed affrontive to himself and injurious to his subjects.[3]

It is also interesting to find a certain acknowledgement of the dispensing power even among those who did not fully support the King. York Corporation, who were 'doubtful', nevertheless admitted a

> duty to support the King's Declaration and will do it by living peaceably with all men of what persuasion soever they may be, as becomes a good Christian and a loyal subject to do.[4]

Thomas Charleton in Nottinghamshire could not consent to the repeal 'in general' but would 'endeavour to support the King's Declaration for liberty of conscience'.[5] It is unusual to find anything as strong as the Dean of Ripon's answer, that

> to support the King's Declaration was against his conscience; but as for living peaceably and quietly with all men of any persuasion whatsoever, he was ready to do it.[6]

[1] vol. i, p. 31.
[2] vol. i, p. 32.
[3] vol. i, pp. 67–8. Lord Richardson (Norfolk) was for repeal, 'the Tests having been made out of invectiveness to the King's person'. vol. i, p. 300.
[4] vol. i, pp. 78–9.
[5] vol. ii, p. 126.
[6] vol. i, p. 82. The dean, like all the clergy asked, was able to evade question (1) by pointing out that he could not be an M.P. He evaded (2) by saying he had no vote and was loath to answer (3).

A reply that deserves mention for its ingenious hint at protestant fears of Louis XIV was made by William Cartwright of Ossington in Nottinghamshire:

> I highly honour the King for his gracious declaration for liberty of conscience and wish all foreign princes would imitate him in that particular.[1]

The prevailing mixture of deference to the King and sympathy with his professed objects is perhaps best brought out in a letter from the magistrates of Merionethshire to the Duke of Beaufort. Owing to a misunderstanding they had failed to attend a meeting he had called and they submitted their written response 'as the real dictates of our consciences'. They thought

> that the Test is a law not to be abrogated, as being the sole support and defence (together with his majesty's gracious assurances of protection) of the established religion and church whereof we are all members, to the abolishing of which should we assent, we think that thereby we tacitly condemn one of the greatest tenents (sic) our church maintains, and that in the blessed sacrament. As for some of those laws that were enacted at the first establishing of this national church, and some later acts concerning dissenters from the same church, we will leave them to the wisdom of a parliament. . . . As to the last question, we think we should much degenerate from the principles of our religion if we did not live peaceably with our fellow subjects, being what the first founders of our religion and church (the primitive Christians) did with those very heathens that persecuted them; much more we think it our duty to live in peace and charity with those that profess Christianity, though of different persuasions, as long as they live obediently under his majesty's government, as we are resolved ever to do; as well out of a just esteem for his sacred person, as out of a principle of duty; whose reign that it may be long and happy over these nations we daily pray for.[2]

Two distinct but not quite opposite conclusions can therefore be drawn from the canvass: that the preponderant part of the upper class wanted a different religious policy from that of James but that they were sufficiently in sympathy with it and sufficiently inclined to be deferential for it to be possible to push them along in his direction. This helps to explain why Sunderland could tell d'Adda in March 1688 that they were 'morally certain of victory'.[3] But the pushing would have to be done largely from the outside. So many influential men were hostile that the government could not work simply through the

[1] vol. ii, p. 124.

[2] vol. i, pp. 290–1: they also hoped never to 'want the good influence of Your Grace's lieutenancy in the Welsh counties'.

[3] Kenyon, pp. 191–2.

natural leaders of county society as it had done in 1685. The behaviour of the lord lieutenants over the survey showed this clearly enough. Only half a dozen put the questions promptly and conscientiously. Some were recalcitrant from the start and others temporized and had to be faced early in 1688 with the choice of putting the questions or removal.[1] Altogether over half (17 against 14) had to be replaced. This may well have represented the balance of forces within the peerage as a whole—at any rate it accords with some rather speculative calculations made by Danby and his friends. A list apparently dating from May 1687 shows eighty-five peers opposed to the government, nineteen doubtful and fifty-seven supporting it—but twenty-two of these were catholics.[2] Such peers and gentry as did follow the government needed heavy support from other classes. This was the point of appealing to the dissenters. The encouraging of addresses from them was an attempt to start a popular movement in the government's favour. It was natural to try and make use for this purpose of what was left of the whigs. Shaftesbury's methods in the desperate fight for exclusion were copied and electoral management was entrusted to a dubious crowd of Shaftesbury's former underlings.[3]

The government had increasingly to rely on the activities of these men, directed and financed from the centre, rather than on local initiatives. Originally it was the lord lieutenants who were told (in the instructions for the survey) to report on the corporate towns within their lieutenancies and say what persons willing to 'comply' with the King's wishes might win elections there, either through their own 'credit' or with the help of friends. But the government decided to keep the necessary purging of the corporations under its own control. On 14 November a commission of regulation was established for the task. A leading light in it was Sir Nicholas Butler, a catholic convert from the baptists. A committee of the privy council was set up to implement its recommendations. There seems already to have been a body of local 'regulators' to supply the information necessary for the work, supervised by a subcommittee under Robert Brent. This

[1] Kenyon, pp. 172–3.
[2] K. H. D. Haley, 'A List of the English Peers, c. May 1687', *English Historical Review*, vol. lxix (1954), pp. 302–6. But cf. the lists in A. Browning, *Thomas Osborne, Earl of Danby and Duke of Leeds, 1632–1712* (3 vols., Jackson, 1944, 1951), vol. iii, pp. 152–63, where lower opposition totals (49 or 38) are given.
[3] J. R. Jones, 'James II's whig collaborators', *Historical Journal*, vol. iii (1960), pp. 65–73.

mysterious individual was the main organizer of the electioneering. He is said to have been a 'popish attorney' and was related to Lord Carrington. Little more is known about him.[1] In the spring, his men were given the main responsibility for promoting candidatures. Reassuring speeches by the judges on circuit were to second their efforts. Travelling agents were to receive 10*l*. for the provision of a horse and be paid 20*s*. a day. They were to establish contacts in all the boroughs—two reliable men in each corporation if possible, as well as correspondents to distribute propaganda. When candidates emerged, they were to set a campaign on foot and they were to report to Brent or his deputy what further changes were needed in the corporations and what persons might usefully be rewarded with government jobs.[2]

The organization had many weak links. The whig element was unreliable. It included venal turncoats like Ralph Montagu and Sir William Williams, the former Speaker, and Sir Francis Winnington. James Vernon, who had formerly served Monmouth and was to serve William, was one of the race of administrators prepared to work under anyone. Others worked for James because their previous activities had led to conviction in his courts and this was the only way that they could escape fines or worse punishment. Lord Brandon escaped the scaffold in this way and served loyally as lord lieutenant of Lancashire.[3] Colonel Titus, who sat briefly in James's privy council, owed the government 8,000*l*. He subsequently made his peace with William. Two of James's leading collaborators among the dissenting clergy, Stephen Lobb (independent) and Vincent Alsop (presbyterian), had received royal pardons.[4] A humbler collaborator was Nathaniel Wade, ex-plotter who had turned king's evidence against his associates.[5]

Though there were nobles and gentlemen among them, the turncoat whigs were badly handicapped by their lack of social weight. Lord lieutenants reported that they could find nobody with estate and interest enough to be worth promoting as a parliamentary candidate and

[1] Kenyon, p. 167; sq. Jones, 'Whigs', p. 67.

[2] Duckett, vol. i, pp. 194–9. Kenyon, pp. 191–2.

[3] His father, the earl of Macclesfield, commanded William's bodyguard in 1688 but thought that his son could not betray James 'after having had his life given him so graciously'. Ailesbury, vol. i, p. 133.

[4] R. Thomas, 'The Seven Bishops and their Petition, 18 May 1688', *Journal of Ecclesiastical History*, vol. xii (1961), p. 57. Alsop's pardon was for his son.

[5] See generally Jones, 'Whigs', pp. 68–70.

members of corporations often avoided commitment when canvassed by saying that they could never expect to enter parliament. Mr Timothy Davison, merchant of Newcastle, for instance, considered himself a 'mean person' and 'never designed it. Looking on myself utterly unfit for acting in so high a station'.[1] Brent's agents were expected to win allies among the gentry, but they were warned to be careful in their approach 'to such gentlemen as you will have occasion to discourse, for you must expect to meet with discerning men and men of great parts'. It was advisable to have letters of introduction and also a suitable person actually to accompany and introduce the agent. This lack of social influence was not made up for automatically by great local popularity. It is revealing that Brent's agents were told to smear undesirable candidates by spreading word that they were working with the government.[2] Beaufort reported that in most of the boroughs in his lieutenancy, even a purge was unlikely to produce the right result:

the election, having been by prescription, could not be regulated by the new charters and placed in the magistrates, but continues still in the freemen, which are very numerous and not subject to be put in or out at the King's pleasure and generally averse to the taking away of the Test.[3]

The weakness of the government's position stimulated ever more arbitrary behaviour. Since suitable candidates often failed to emerge locally, over a hundred were nominated from the centre. Sixteen of them were army officers and there were plans for soldiers to vote and for men to be given votes in several boroughs and to be moved from place to place to cast them. A single purge of the boroughs was not enough to make them docile. Many were 'regulated' twice, some four times or even more. Reading corporation was regulated in December 1687 and again in January, February, May and August 1688. The mayor of Buckingham was changed three times. The administration began to break down under the weight of work involved in changing officials and amending charters. There were desperate plans for taking seats from obdurate boroughs and giving them to places that were more tractable. At Queensborough the people were even 'dragooned' by the soldiers, in the style of Louis XIV.[4]

Yet in spite of all these signs of unpopularity, the reports of Brent's

[1] Duckett, vol. i, p. 139.
[2] *ibid.*, vol. i, pp. 194–9. [3] *ibid.*, vol. i, p. 288.
[4] Kenyon, pp. 189–90. Jones, 'Whigs', p. 72.

agents were consistently and strongly optimistic. In April 1688 they said that the anglicans and presbyterians were 'moderate' and willing to accept some substitute for the laws which the King wished to have repealed. The remaining dissenters and the catholics were firmly on the government's side. Reports concerning 140 seats in seven counties suggested that the government would win 100 of them. Even as late as September, the same sort of thing was being said. Reports of this kind were very misleading and it could be argued that they were only wishful thinking. They seem in fact to have been not quite that: what the electioneers had mainly done was to estimate the strength of the whig and dissenting interest and assume that it would do the government's bidding.[1] Now the whigs had certainly won elections in the past and it is likely that they had always had less upper class support than the tories and that they had made up for it by greater popularity.[2] There was no reason why they should not do so again. At Honiton for instance the corporation was

> composed of country gentlemen perverse to Your Majesty. The town earnestly desire a regulation, otherwise their market is like to be ruined. The election is popular, consisting of about 300; only the last (without precedent) was by the body corporate. The majority of the town are dissenters and the whole town against their magistrates and unanimous to choose right men.[3]

As this case suggests, the government might hope to swing popular feeling in the whig direction by offering suitable favours and it did indeed put forward, as Shaftesbury had done, a programme of popular reforms:[4] a national land registry, abolition of imprisonment for debt, reform of the coinage and so forth. The great uncertainty was not whether the whiggish interest could win an election but whether it could be got to vote for the government's religious policy.

This was not altogether impossible. We have seen how relations between churchmen and dissenters had been deteriorating since about 1675, with a closing of ranks on both sides. Moderate churchmen continued to keep in touch with those outside the church who still hoped for comprehension and the advance of popery in the new reign

[1] Duckett, vol. i, pp. 222–4, 101–2.
[2] Above, p. 43. J. H. Plumb, *Growth of Political Stability in England* (Macmillan, 1967), pp. 41–2, notes that in disputes about the right to vote in particular boroughs the exclusionists favoured widening the franchise.
[3] Duckett, vol. ii, p. 232.
[4] Jones, 'Whigs, 'p. 69.

(particularly its triumphs in Ireland) gave new point to their efforts. The expulsion of the Huguenots from France and the flight of many of them to England in the winter of 1685–6 was likewise a portent which James found most embarrassing. At first he praised the efforts of Louis to spread the faith and he suppressed Claude's account of it because 'dogs defend each other when attacked; so do kings'. But French envoys found him increasingly unsympathetic on this question, and he told the Dutch ambassador that Louis's conduct had not been 'politic, much less christian'.[1] Perhaps this really was his opinion, but the same could not be said of the catholic extremists who followed him. 'They would do here,' Barrillon told Louis XIV, 'what is being done in France if they could hope for success'.[2] James tried to reassure his subjects by encouraging help for the Huguenot refugees, though keeping it as inconspicuous as possible. In the last phase of the reign, James's flirtation with radicalism was a further reason for moderate men not to follow him. Sensible dissenters (even Penn) disliked his patronage of rabble-rousing and the shadier type of whig.[3] Some whigs restored to office by James showed what they thought of his religious policy by taking the religious tests although they were no longer compulsory.

But the effect of the Declaration of Indulgence must not be under-rated. As in 1672, dissenters did not generally allow scruples about the law to deter them from taking advantage of the Indulgence. It was at this point and not in 1689 that they gained the religious freedom which they have enjoyed ever since. John Evelyn noted with dismay in his diary that on the Sunday after the issue of the Declaration 'there was a wonderful concourse at the dissenter's meeting house in this parish and the parish church left exceeding thin'.[4] The temptation was strong to join in the overthrow of the anglican monopoly while the opportunity lasted. Of course, this was uncongenial to those dissenters who had wanted comprehension rather than toleration and they continued to be champions of protestant unity, resistance to popery and respect for the laws. Foremost among them was the venerable Richard Baxter, whose mainly presbyterian circle also included George Griffiths, an important independent. John Howe and Daniel Williams

---

[1] M. Ashley, *The Glorious Revolution of 1688* (Hodder and Stoughton, 1966), pp. 62–4.
[2] Mazure, vol. ii, p. 127.   [3] Jones, 'Whigs', pp. 67, 70.
[4] 10 April 1687, quoted by Davies, 'Tory churchmen', p. 71.

were other members of the group: the former had lived in Holland and the latter had witnessed the decline of the protestants in Ireland. But Morrice, Baxter's chief assistant, admitted that the Declaration had reduced interest in an alliance with the anglicans against popery. Alsop and Baber, the King's chief agents among the presbyterians, induced some even of them to join in addresses of thanks, though many refused and some appear to have felt insulted by the attempt to associate them with quakers and papists. The only reservation which was at all common in the dissenters' attitude to the crown was that they tried to avoid pronouncements in favour of the dispensing power.[1]

It was essential for the opponents of James's policy to persuade the dissenters that they were 'to be hugged now, only that you may be the better squeezed at another time'. These were the words of Halifax, whose *Letter to a Dissenter* published in the summer of 1687 was the most famous attempt at persuasion. The catholics, he argued

> have ever made their first courtships to the church of England and, when they were rejected there, they made their application to you in the second place. . . .
> This alliance between liberty and infallibility is bringing together the two most contrary things that are in the world. The Church of Rome doth not only dislike the allowing liberty, but by its principles it cannot do it.

The papists' readiness to end their loudly proclaimed friendship with the churchmen, he later remarked, showed how little the dissenters could trust them. He insinuated that dissenting ministers had only been drawn into working with James by bribery or 'by incurring the want of a pardon'. The dissenters' addresses of thanks were not spontaneous: 'the first drafts are made by those who are not very proper to be secretaries to the protestant religion.' Whenever 'instead of silently receiving the benefit of this indulgence you set up for advocates to support it, you . . . look like counsel retained by the prerogative against your old friend Magna Charta'. Halifax argued that, now persecution had ceased, the dissenters should seek reconciliation with the churchmen in order to preserve the constitution. But how could they be sure that there would not be a revival of the traditional anglican policy of intolerance? The answer was that the anglicans had repented:

---

[1] Thomas, 'Bishops', p. 58; 'Comprehension', pp. 235–7. On refractory presbyterians, *Ellis Correspondence*, vol. i, pp. 252, 270, 274.

the common danger hath so laid open that mistake that all the former haughtiness towards you is for ever extinguished, and that it hath turned the spirit of persecution into a spirit of peace, charity and condescension.

The churchmen could recover the King's favour and again crush the dissenters if they would consent to work with the catholics, but in spite of the sufferings of the church, they had refused. Writing before the Queen's pregnancy, Halifax advised the dissenters to wait patiently for 'the next probable revolution'—the death of James, after which everything would be in their favour:

the Church of England convinced of its error in being severe to you, the parliament, whenever it meeteth, sure to be gentle to you, the next heir bred in the country which you have so often quoted for a pattern of indulgence, a general agreement of all thinking men that we must no more cut ourselves off from the protestants abroad. . . .

Meanwhile

let us be still, quiet and undivided, firm at the same time to our religion, our loyalty and our laws.

The official pamphleteers answered this case by trying to show that religious freedom was salutory: something has already been said of the arguments employed. In addition there was the idea of an 'equivalent', which when fully developed amounted to a constitutional guarantee for liberty of conscience. Penn had told William of Orange in 1686 that if the tests were abolished 'the King would secure the toleration by a solemn and unalterable law'. In 1688 he wrote of 'a new Great Charter for liberty of conscience'. 'Let that liberty be declared to be the natural right of all men', said another writer, 'and any violation therof be therefore accounted criminal'. Not only infringement of the law but even proposals to alter it should be severely punished. It was suggested that every man in the kingdom should take an oath to observe the law and that any transgressor should be hanged on a gallows made from the timbers of his own house. A more interesting suggestion was that the King might renounce a part at least of his dispensing power.[1] One 'expedient' actually agreed upon between Sunderland and Penn in January 1688 was the continued exclusion of catholics from parliament. Sunderland seems to have believed that none of the dissenters would be ready to allow catholics to sit in the

[1] See footnotes to Foxcroft, vol. ii, pp. 432, 437–9, 440–1; R. E. Boyer, *English Declarations of Indulgence 1687 and 1688* (Mouton, 1968), pp. 102–6.

commons, though some would support their admission to executive office and even to the lords.[1] Just before the Revolution, Halifax published *The Anatomy of an Equivalent*, in which he brilliantly attacked these ideas. An equivalent, he said, implied a bargain freely entered into by parties who were genuinely on an equal footing. The party giving something up would need to be convinced of the value of the equivalent and could only be expected to agree if its position was actually improved thereby. Since the royal prerogative was said to be inalienable and parliament could not bind its successors, nothing was to be gained by their promising not to tamper with the new law in the ways that had hitherto been allowed.

(III)

The crucial point in the struggle for the allegiance of the dissenters came with the republication of the Declaration of Indulgence on 3 May 1688. Its purpose was to provide an election platform for Brent's newly expanded corps of agents. The date for the elections was now given as not later than November—the continued postponement, unwelcome to the deluded catholic zealots, was a measure of Sunderland's difficulties. In March he had convinced the privy council of its necessity by arguing that the government must be absolutely sure of not losing. The anglicans had been alienated and anything that suggested that the dissenters too were estranged must be avoided.[2] But the reappearance of the Declaration started a train of events that had just that result. The republication was followed (next day) by a royal order that the Declaration be read in church on two successive Sundays (20 and 27 May in the London area; 3 and 10 June elsewhere). The bishops were required to see to it that copies were distributed and read accordingly. One purpose of this order was probably just to give full publicity to the Declaration. Announcements from the pulpit in those days of universal churchgoing were a regular way, and perhaps the only sure way, by which the government could communicate with the entire population. Charles II had used this method for diffusing the conciliatory manifesto which he issued after

[1] Kenyon, pp. 160–1. The government dared not use the dispensing power to admit catholics to parliament because it dreaded further parliamentary discussion of the subject.

[2] On Sunderland's tactics see Kenyon, pp. 167–94.

the dissolution of his last parliament in 1681.[1] It is to be noted that the 1688 proclamation was originally intended to be read in the dissenters' chapels as well as in the churches: Morrice managed to get this idea abandoned.[2] But it is probable that the main purpose was to damage the political position of the church. At the end of 1687 Sunderland had successfully opposed a Jesuit scheme to summon Convocation and threaten the clergy with the penalties of praemunire unless they acknowledged the legality of the dispensing power.[3] Making them all read the Declaration was a milder method of achieving the same result, calculated to demoralize all those trying to resist royal policy. Petre was supposed to have said that the anglicans would have to eat their own excrement.[4]

If the clergy refused to obey orders, that might serve the government's purpose just as well. It would tend to disprove Halifax's argument that adversity had taught the churchmen to be friendly towards the dissenters. Certainly the King's activities had led the clergy and their lay friends to regard him as a menace and not a protector: there was a growing realization that James was beginning to govern as Louis XIV did.[5] But it was not clear to everyone that an alliance with the dissenters against the papists was the way out of trouble. The anglicans feared both: when Monmouth was defeated, Dr Fell, the famous Bishop of Oxford, wrote 'we are free from the hazard of one sort of enthusiasts. God grant we may not be overrun by another.'[6] It was precisely the King's collusion with dissenters that looked so sinister: in London for instance, where 'all the jolly, genteel citizens are turned out and all sneaking fanatics put into their places'.[7] The Bishop of Peterborough was reported to have said that there was 'no danger at all of popery but only of the fanatics' and this was right in a way because the dissenters were a substantial party but the papists

---

[1] And the Exclusion Bill was intended to be read twice a year in church. Turner, p. 396 n: against his 'unpolitical' view he cites Ranke, vol. iv, p. 345.

[2] Thomas, 'Bishops', p. 57.

[3] Kenyon, p. 175.

[4] Citing 2 Kings xviii: 27. Boyer, p. 108. The bishops were not the usual channel for sending out papers for the clergy to read but it seems the government would have spared them: Thomas, p. 66 n. 1.

[5] Ailesbury, vol. i, pp. 174–5, comparison with Cromwell. *Ellis Correspondence*, vol. i, pp. 55–6: Dover like Louvois.

[6] Doreen J. Milne, 'Results of the Rye House Plot', *Transactions of the Royal Historical Society*, 5th ser. vol. i, p. 101.

[7] Ailesbury, vol. i, pp. 175–6, cited Davies 'Tory Churchmen', pp. 75–6.

were so few that they were helpless without allies. The Chancellor of York diocese advised clergy to go on enforcing the penal laws despite the Declaration. James tried to exploit the anglican state of mind by telling the dissenters that they could never trust the churchmen—just as Halifax was telling them that they could never trust the papists. The King told Stephen Lobb that the churchmen had offered him a bargain—to extend toleration to papists provided that it was denied to dissenters—but that he had refused.[1] Sunderland's agents in London reported that churchmen were deeply divided on the question of toleration[2] and calling on the clergy to read the Declaration was just the thing to bring their embarrassments into the open. Morrice duly found that 'the fiercer men' (*i.e.* the more intolerant) 'were rather more fervent for the refusal' (to read it) 'than the other sort'.[3] Penn and Lobb have been credited with advising the King to make this move. Van Citters, the Dutch ambassador, said that its purpose was generally believed to be

> to bring the clergy into disgrace with their community if they read it . . . or by not reading it, as has been the case, to estrange the nonconformists the more from the Church of England.[4]

The churchmen came near to being completely trapped.[5] Of their lay champions, Rochester advised obedience, Halifax was undecided, Nottingham was for disobedience only if they could be sure of near unanimity (which they could not) and only Clarendon was clearly for disobeying. A meeting of some influential clergy in London on 11 May decided that the bishops must take the lead. On the 12th Sancroft and some of his colleagues decided on disobedience and a petition to the King: bishops in the country who were expected to agree were urgently summoned to town. But it seems that the bishops were only prepared to act if they could have some assurance of support from the lower clergy. On the 13th two bishops met fifteen leading clergy at the Temple: the main question here seems to have been whether the more liberal clergy would join with the more intolerant in refusing to read the Declaration. At first there was a majority against refusal, both out of sympathy for the dissenters and because of the

---

[1] Thomas, 'Bishops', p. 66. Foxcroft, vol. i, p. 480 n. 4.
[2] Kenyon, p. 194. [3] Thomas, 'Bishops', p. 59 n. 1.
[4] *ibid.*, p. 57 n. 2. Barrillon also picked up this idea, Mazure, vol. ii, p. 446.
[5] What follows derives from Thomas, 'Bishops', pp. 59–70. Quotations are from Morrice's journal there cited.

'coldness and wavering' of the nobles. But those present who had been in touch with the moderate group among the dissenters had an answer to the first objection: 'the most considering persons' among the dissenters wanted refusal because they gave priority to political considerations, that is 'to keep out popery, and to unite the nation . . . to fall in with the King in all things consistent with the security of religion, liberty and property'. Edward Fowler, who was a friend of Morrice, further said that it would be against his conscience to read the Declaration. Eventually everyone present decided on refusal, though not all for the same reason.

The churchmen, with the aid of their dissenting friends, were finding a way out of the trap. They would refuse to read the Declaration but they would do so for political and not religious reasons and so, they hoped, check the King without offending the dissenters. Further hurried soundings among the dissenters appeared to confirm that they were at one with the churchmen in wishing to uphold the rule of law. Morrice, for instance, gave Fowler a paper which said among other things that 'it is most heinously criminal to publish the prince's private will and pleasure against his legal and incontrovertible will'. So on the 15th a further meeting of clergy adopted a suitable document and set on foot a canvass of all the clergy in London. Seventy signatures were collected in two days—almost all who could be found were willing to sign. The document and the names were passed to Sancroft and on the 18th he met the leaders of the clergy together with such bishops as he had been able to assemble. The document, slightly amended, was turned into a petition of Sancroft and six of his bishops to the King, asking to be excused from distributing and reading the Declaration; not, they said

> from any want of duty and obedience to Your Majesty . . . nor yet from any want of due tenderness to dissenters, in relation to whom they are willing to come to such a temper as shall be thought fit when that matter shall be considered and settled in parliament and convocation, but among many other considerations from this especially, because that declaration is founded upon such a dispensing power as hath often been declared illegal in parliament . . .

The bishops did not gain access to the King until nine in the evening. He received them graciously, but when he had read the petition his manner changed completely and he railed furiously at them, calling it a 'standard of rebellion' from which they inferred that tho' his majesty had notice they would come with a petition, yet he apprehended the tenor of it had been only against liberty of conscience and not against the dispensing power.

The strategy of exploiting the rift between church and dissent was not working properly.

The bishops' petition grew into a national gesture of resistance, as is well known. A garbled version of the petition instantly appeared in print: the text was actually that of the document which had been signed by the London clergy.[1] Nine more bishops speedily declared their agreement with the petitioners.[2] Both in London and the provinces the clergy mostly failed to read the Declaration when the appointed days arrived. On 23 May there was an important meeting of dissenters at which the supporters and the opponents of James confronted each other. James was eager for an address from the dissenters that would give convincing evidence that he had their backing. Two emissaries from court (Penn and Baber probably) came to the meeting and said that the King would not stir from his closet till he had their answer. The view hostile to James prevailed. Besides sympathy with the clergy, the reasons which led the meeting to refuse to promote an address were that the dissenters wanted 'liberty by law' and were 'utterly against letting papists into the government'; also (significantly) that 'none will offer it of condition or quality'. This seems a recognition that in the dissenting community as in the nation as a whole, the party against James included most of the socially influential people. On 1 June d'Adda reported to Rome

the whole church espouses the cause of the bishops. There is no reasonable expectation of a division among the anglicans and our hopes from the nonconformists are vanished.

When the petitioning bishops were arrested, ten dissenting leaders visited them in prison.[3]

The King and Sunderland had been trying to procure a docile parliament by a mixture of bullying and political manoeuvre. With the emergence of something like national unanimity against them, bullying alone was useless. There was no real attempt to use the high

[1] Thomas, 'Bishops', p. 67.

[2] Including Compton. There were twenty-two English and Welsh bishops alive at that point. Mackintosh, p. 251.

[3] Thomas, 'Bishops', p. 69. The quakers did present an address on their own.

commission to break the resistance of the church: the most it ever attempted was to make a list of the recalcitrant clergy. Though the subject is obscure, it seems that even Sunderland and Petre were against any attempt to punish the bishops and they were not arrested till 8 June. James was advised by his law officers that they were guilty of seditious libel: he intended to exercise clemency after their conviction.[1] But the trial only made things worse. Both the populace and the nobility turned out in force and, as already noted, the legal profession was enabled to make a demonstration of its own against what had been happening. The judges were evenly divided on whether the bishops had been guilty of seditious libel and one of them declared that the suspending power was a usurpation of the legislative authority: James had gone beyond the point where he could use the judges to legalize what he was doing. The bishops were acquitted amid general rejoicing; James was alarmed to find that the troops joined in this.

The first half of 1688 saw the decisive culmination of the religious struggles that had been going on for a quarter of a century. Two different policies of toleration had triumphed: one for the present, the other for the future. James had emancipated the catholics and the dissenters by the use of his prerogative. He had failed, however, to gain enough ascendancy over his people to enable him to change the laws and so it was likely that his achievements would die with him. This was because the moderate anglicans and moderate dissenters had made their views prevail within their respective groups. These men wanted to end the strife between the communions to which they belonged. Since they were well disposed towards their fellow protestants, they were not eager for royal protection against them and so were disinclined to acquiesce when the King overrode the law in the interests of popery. There was nothing inevitable about their triumph: sectarian spirit had often made anglicans and dissenters act as the docile tools of monarchy. But in 1688, when political life had been almost extinguished, they managed to make themselves the focus of all the national feeling against popery and in favour of the rule of law. In the religious field they were immediately rewarded by a restarting of the discussions to find a *modus vivendi* between church and dissent, with the bishops keenly interested. There could be little doubt that if James was removed, a new religious settlement would be adopted,

[1] Thus Kenyon. But see Turner, p. 401.

based on the peaceful co-existence of the protestant groups and the renewed repression of the catholics.

The situation was modified by the birth of James's son on 10 June, two days after the arrest of the bishops. This meant that the next sovereign might be a catholic and not a protestant and might there-fore continue James's policy. There was a general suspicion of a fraud. As early as 1682 the pregnancy of Mary Beatrice gave rise to the suggestion that if she did not produce a son, a male child would be found and passed off as hers.[1] The plans and behaviour of the catholic extremists since then had encouraged such suspicions. The unimagina-tive James failed to take the simple precaution of providing un-impeachable witnesses to the birth. The catholics must have seemed to many to have brought off a masterly coup just when the final triumph of their enemies had become almost certain.

This was the likeliest moment for an indigenous revolt against James II's government. Hoffmann, the Austrian ambassador, had reported in April that the birth of a prince was expected by many 'judicious' people to increase the unity of the protestants and make them try 'by every means' to prevent the succession of a catholic. He found that the trial of the bishops was expected to be 'the beginning of a revolution'.[2] Van Citters thought it surprising after the trial 'that in view of so great a concourse of people so very much affected for the bishops a general insurrection did not take place'.[3] An attempt has already been made to explain in general terms why there was no revolt. A more immediate and personal explanation can be found in the attitude of the protestant political leaders. On the whole it was only those who had been proscribed who were ready for resistance and they were in no position to start a revolt on their own and had to look to William of Orange. Those who had not been outlawed but only at the most disgraced were in a better position to rebel, but they did not attempt it, and they were reluctant even to encourage William positively to come over. The 'immortal seven' who were eventually induced to sign a formal invitation to him could not really claim to represent the leading elements in the nation. Devonshire had the best claim: he was a territorial magnate and had been one of the leaders of

---

[1] Dalrymple, vol. ii, bk. v, p. 185.
[2] La Marquise Campana de Cavelli, *Les Derniers Stuarts à Saint-Germain en Laye* (1871), vol. ii, pp. 181, 205.
[3] Ashley, p. 119.

the whigs. Henry Sidney and Edward Russell bore famous names but could not speak for their families, each of which was headed by an old man in retirement. Shrewsbury and Lumley were interesting as converts from catholicism but theirs were typical catholic families—that is to say, their wealth and influence were limited. Danby was a magnate and had been a powerful political leader. But his career had been totally ruined in the course of the exclusion crisis and he had spent several years in the Tower. He was a politician in eclipse making a last desperate attempt at recovery. Bishop Compton, who was a protégé of Danby, had distinguished himself in defence of the church, but he was not to be regarded as representative of his fellow bishops. Unlike most of them, he was of noble family and strongly protestant in his churchmanship.[1] An attempt to list comprehensively the probable leaders of the opposition for William's benefit, perhaps with a view to getting a more broadly based invitation, shows more men 'considerable' for 'parts' than for 'interest' and 'estate'.[2]

The bishops were in touch with William and seem to have hoped for his aid.[3] The laymen currently with most influence were also mostly in touch with him but tended to content themselves with waiting upon events. Sometimes this was due to religious convictions, sometimes to fear of the consequences and sometimes (on the contrary) to the belief that things would not get too bad. Rochester had started on a visit to William but had thought better of it. Clarendon joined in all measures of opposition that were clearly lawful, but he could not condone revolt and was horrified later when his heir, Lord Cornbury, deserted to William. 'Oh God, that my son should be a rebel!' he wrote, 'the Lord in his mercy look upon me and enable me to support myself under this most grievous calamity.'[4] His poverty had made him a timeserver in office. As lord lieutenant of Ireland, he objected less to the preferment of papists than to his loss of authority to Tyrconnel, sent over to catholicize the army. 'I could have done all that my Lord Tyrconnel is to do, full as well to the King's intent,' he told his brother, '. . . the King's pleasure is to be fulfilled: and so it has been and ever shall be by me, notwithstanding the mean opinion it begets in people towards me.' He told Tyrconnel that 'it was not

---

[1] On the 'seven' see J. P. Kenyon, *The Nobility in the English Revolution of 1688* (Hull University Publications, 1963), pp. 9, 10.

[2] Anonymous list in William's papers: see Browning, vol. iii, pp. 152–63.

[3] J. Carswell, *The Descent upon England* (Cresset Press, 1969), pp. 143–4.

[4] *Clarendon Correspondence*, vol. ii, p. 204.

material how many Roman Catholics were in the army if the King would have it so'. The nearest he came to resistance was an unsuccessful attempt to have a formal record made of the order to dispense with the oath of supremacy for judges. 'I would not be thought scrupulous and therefore I have done the business already,' he said, but 'though I do not expect any alteration in my time of public affairs, yet I would not be willing to be questioned for having obeyed the King.' Though he told Evelyn that he would only serve 'upon the English principle of the excellent church of England', he had carefully avoided giving offence.[1] His logical course in 1688 was to wait in hopes of renewed royal favour.

Nottingham and Halifax were men of greater integrity, but we have seen that they gave the bishops less encouragement than did Clarendon. Nottingham believed that William 'had a just cause' for invading England because a catholic conspiracy appeared to threaten his wife's rights to the succession. But he could not join in the invitation to William because it would be

> high treason, in violation of the laws (which are the rules of our conduct) and that allegiance which I owed to the sovereign and which I had confirmed by my solemn oath.

He consulted two clergymen who confirmed him in his objection. But he also wrote to William that he did not fear from the government's policies 'such ill consequences to our religion or the just interests of your highness that a little time will not effectually remedy, nor can I imagine that the papists are able to make any further considerable progress'.[2] This was always the opinion of Halifax, whose opposition to the government was active but confined to paper. In May 1687 he prophesied that they would not venture to summon parliament for the ratification of their religious plans, that the dissenters would be neither able nor willing to give them a parliamentary majority for laws damaging to the established church, and that the number of catholics could not be increased:

> the great design cannot be carried on without numbers, numbers cannot be had without converts, the old stock not being sufficient: converts will not venture till they have such a law to secure them as hath no exception to it.

[1] *Clarendon Correspondence*, vol. i, pp. 362, 459, 460, 514. Cf. vol. ii, p. 128.
[2] H. Horwitz, *Revolution Politicks, the Career of Daniel Finch, second Earl of Nottingham 1647–1730* (Cambridge University Press, 1968), pp. 52–4. Dalrymple, vol. ii, bk. v, p. 118.

He did not vary from this opinion. In September he noted that 'it is grown into a point of honour universally received by the nation not to change their opinion'. In April 1688 he thought that 'they have run so fast that they begin to be out of breath' and deprecated 'unseasonable stirrings' by the opposition which might halt the growth of splits within the government that he believed he could detect. The birth of James's son did not invalidate these arguments—especially if it is remembered that the Queen's other children had all died young. The new prince himself almost perished in the first weeks of his life. Beside such certainties as these, the prospects of rebellion even with William's help showed up rather badly. Halifax complained that all would depend on the winds and tides.[1] Danby was enthusiastic in March 1688, but in September he wanted the enterprise put off till the following spring.[2]

There was therefore something like an equilibrium in England in the summer of 1688. The King had flouted the law, but it was becoming apparent that he could not change it. The nation had not the means without foreign aid to bring the King to book. The birth of the King's son gave him some hope that the equilibrium would continue. If it had, the Stuarts would have held a position quite normal for what we commonly call absolute monarchs: they would have been powerful but not all-powerful. It was the advent of William that upset the equilibrium and put an end to this prospect.

[1] For the views of Halifax, Burnet, vol. ii, p. 397; Dalrymple, vol. ii, bk. v, pp. 69–71. Cf. pp. 82–4, 95–9 and Nottingham's similar view, pp. 77–80.

[2] Cf. Browning, vol. ii, p. 121 and N. Japikse, ed., *Correspondentie van Willem III en van Hans Willem Bentinck* (Nijhoff, 1927), part i, vol. i, p. 49.

8

The Advent of William of Orange

WILLIAM HENRY, Prince of Orange, was thirty-eight years old on the day before his forces landed in England. But his health was so bad that he was already an ageing man. He had no children, and it was a miracle that he survived long enough to accomplish his historic work in the British Isles. He was to outlive his uncle James II by only a few months. Like James, he was pious, a good financial manager and first and foremost a keen soldier, who valued courage and firmness of purpose above everything. Unlike him, he was highly intelligent, and though this failed to make him successful as a general, it did enable him to make himself a power in politics and diplomacy despite the lifelong precariousness of his personal position.

William's power derived from his offices of captain general for life of the forces of the Dutch republic and hereditary stadholder of its more important provinces. But thanks to his tiny territory of Orange, near Avignon—usually under occupation by Louis XIV—he had the status of a sovereign prince. This had enabled his ancestor William the Silent to levy war lawfully against Philip II of Spain and it enabled him to levy war lawfully against James II, without officially involving the Dutch republic whose forces served only as his auxiliaries. Rebellion in both cases was given respectability by being disguised as a war between legitimate princes. The theorists of sovereignty sometimes admitted this as an exception to the rule that government could not endure unless governments were invariably obeyed. Bodin said that the people might not rebel against an oppressive prince but that it was lawful for another prince to come to their rescue. Grotius said the same. The example of William the Silent must have prompted them and now there was to be another case of revolt compatible with the theories of absolute monarchy.

William's mother was Mary, eldest daughter of Charles I, and he was therefore in the line of succession to the British crowns. It is probable that he regarded himself as the rightful heir of his uncle James. By continental standards, the first marriage of James with a commoner, Anne Hyde, was morganatic and their daughters, Mary and Anne, could have no claim to the throne. When for dynastic and political reasons William married Mary in 1677 he considered it a terrible *mésalliance*—made worse by the smallness of the dowry. The marriage, however, was a success, and it made him James's heir in fact though he was not so in law. Mary, though ill-educated, was not only beautiful but pious and intelligent like her husband. William became devoted to her, though he does not seem to have been entirely faithful to her until she was dead. Mary was intelligent enough to see his greatness and she completely idolized him. At the end of 1688, she wrote that the news of her stepmother's pregnancy (of which she had doubts from the start) did not at first upset her, for she was not in the least ambitious. But

> apart from the interest of the church, the love which I have for the Prince leads me to wish for him all that he deserves. And though I am sorry to have only three crowns to bring him, it is not because I am blinded by love—no, I can see his faults—but I say this because I know his merits also.[1]

William's position in English politics was to be greatly strengthened by the impossibility of treating his wife's interest as separate from his own.

William had always to take account of the possibility that one day he, or at least his wife, might reign in England. It is natural to ask if he actively desired to do so and if his decisive intervention in English affairs was not prompted by greed for the crown. He was a man who kept his own counsel and it is hard to tell save by inference what his exact aims were: perhaps a skilful politician never formulates them exactly anyway. Mary naturally believed him as free as herself from evil motives in the Revolution. When she rejoined him in England after the invasion

> as soon as we were alone, we both shed tears of joy to meet, and of sorrow for meeting in England, both wishing it might have been in Holland, both bewailing the loss of the liberty we had left behind and were sensible we should never enjoy here . . .[2]

[1] Bentinck, pp. 62–3.
[2] R. Doebner, ed., *Memoirs of Mary Queen of England*, etc. (1886): p. 10. This volume

At the end of December 1688, when he provisionally assumed the government of the country until the meeting of a convention, he told the Prince of Waldeck, whom he had left in charge of the Dutch forces on the continent, that he was remaining 'passive', although he had been

> extremely plagued. And even if I had wanted to give the least encouragement, I am sure that they would have declared me king, which I have no ambition for, not having come here for that. What they will do at the meeting of the convention I do not know but I fear that they will want to make me accept a thing that I in no way ask for though I forsee well enough that the world will judge otherwise.[1]

This was in line with his public pronouncements and may have been written with an eye to the Dutch and German potentates with whom Waldeck had to work and who would have been quite unwilling to help William if they had thought him no more than an ambitious usurper. William probably saw by then that he would have to take the crown. But all the signs are that he disliked the pomp of the English court (familiar to him from visits) and his new capital (where he could not live without being ill) and had no desire to reign in England. It will be shown below that his invasion was a desperately dangerous enterprise. He may have been willing to undertake it because he was naturally oversanguine in military matters.[2] But even so, ambition alone could hardly have moved him to it unless it was unusually strong—and if it was, it has left surprisingly little trace.

William's interest in England is far more naturally explained by the needs of his position in Holland and of the Dutch position in Europe. This was the period of Louis XIV's greatness—the supreme manifestation of seventeenth-century state-strengthening of which we have been observing the much humbler forms in the British Isles. The growth of French power was to be seen not only in better internal organization and stronger armed forces but in the growing penetration of neighbouring countries by French money and influence—England

---

continues the series begun in Bentinck. Mary kept journals (see p. 39) and made occasional notes (see Bentinck) so her annual summaries are probably fairly authentic.
[1] P. L. Müller, *Wilhelm von Oranien und Georg Friedrich von Waldeck* (1873–80), vol. ii, p. 126. 24 December. He described even his temporary regency as a 'terrible burden', p. 127. Waldeck thought a regency better than transferring the crown, p. 130, but William later told him it was unavoidable, pp. 137, 139.
[2] Powley, pp. 95–6.

being a conspicuous example. The Dutch were the only people at all near France who put up effective resistance. Mainly for this reason, Louis XIV attacked them in 1672. He was repulsed and for some years thereafter the Republic was the centre of a not very successful coalition against France.

Louis XIV's quarrel with the Dutch became entangled with the party struggles within the Republic. William III was a posthumous child and during his minority the headless party of the house of Orange was excluded from power by their republican rivals, who objected to the quasi-monarchical position enjoyed by successive princes. Largely for this reason, the republicans did not want a powerful army and tried to keep on good terms with the French. The catastrophe of 1672 showed the unwisdom of these policies; the young William III could no longer be denied the authority vested in his ancestors and it was under his command that the strength of the army was restored and the French driven out. The rival parties were not bound to be divided on the question of France. The republicans had not denied the need to resist her. William would probably have regained his family's offices even if there had been no French menace. His family had had many ties with France (Turenne was his cousin), he admired French culture and was still trying in the early 1680s to get on better terms with Louis XIV. But the French chose to see him as their most deadly enemy and to snub him and confiscate his estates when they could, while seeking to restore good relations with the republic he served. As the immediacy of the French threat receded, the republican predilection for peace revived, but the Prince gradually became the implacable enemy of France. Thus the French managed to sow discord in the Republic and build up their influence there as in the other states of the west.

William therefore found himself competing with Louis XIV both on the domestic plane, for influence over Dutch foreign policy, and on the international plane, for alliances which would determine the balance of power between France and the other great European states. England was important in both connections. With its naval power, it could obviously have a decisive influence on any contest between France and the Dutch. But it could also have an influence on Dutch internal politics. Ever since the marriage of William's parents, the fortunes of the Stuart and Orange families had been strangely linked. The republicans had triumphed almost simultaneously in both countries, the execution of Charles I coming less than two years before the death of William's father. The English republicans had gone to war with the Dutch and in making peace, Cromwell had forced them to promise that the Orange family would never be restored to their traditional position, from which they might have aided the Stuarts. After the Restoration and the death (in the same year) of William's mother, Charles II tried rather ineffectually to protect his nephew and Orange partisans looked to England for help even when the two countries were at war. This was indeed a subsidiary cause of the wars of 1665 and 1672 between them. On the latter occasion, the English toyed with the idea of carving a puppet principality for William out of Dutch territory. William was not prepared to betray his country, but with that limitation he was prepared to use English influence to strengthen his position at home. In 1672 he tried to induce the English to abandon France but make sovereignty of the Netherlands for himself one of the conditions of a peace.[1]

But Charles and James were not eager to help William if it meant a breach with France. The Anglo-French attack on the Dutch petered out, but Stuart sympathy with France remained and, more important, there was now a really clear understanding that an English king could achieve independence of parliament only if he remained at peace. James told William in 1682 that 'to engage now into a war and to call a parliament would endanger the monarchy and be the absolute ruin of our family'.[2] Barrillon in December 1685 classed James as 'not so amenable or tractable as the late King his brother' and 'believed to be more stubborn about what is called the interest of England and the honour of the nation'. In 1686 the King told Van Citters with heat that he was no vassal of France, that 'I was born an Englishman and I want all the world to know it', that 'if parliament had wished, if it still wishes, I would have carried, I will still carry the monarchy to a degree of consideration which it never enjoyed under my predecessors'.[3] That autumn he told his privy council

[1] Baxter, *William III*, pp. 89, 90. Baxter, pp. 123–5, discusses William's attempt to become sovereign of Guelders in 1675, shows how this apparently selfish ambition alienated English, Dutch and European opinion but suggests that the real reason was to conserve his position as a sovereign prince, threatened by the loss of Orange. Even as a boy he always used the royal 'we'.

[2] Baxter, p. 184. After the Rye House Plot James told William 'we here must look to ourselves and not engage in any war beyond sea'. Dalrymple, vol. i, pt. i, p. 109.

[3] Turner, pp. 344–7.

that next year they should see as great a fleet abroad as England ever had, and everything in order to secure him from his enemies and to keep his neighbours from insolencies.[1]

But though he may have wished to assert himself abroad, he did not in fact venture to do so. In any case, his religion, combined with his interest in the navy and commerce, made it quite likely that if he took the offensive it would be against the Dutch, not against the French. William constantly wooed his uncles and in 1683, seeking Rochester's help for this purpose, he assured him that

> in everything that concerns the internal affairs of the kingdoms, I will blindly do everything they wish, without enquiring into anything, but I hope also that in future they will have a little more trust in me in the matter of foreign affairs because, being nearer the spot, we assuredly know more about them. And England and this country having the same interests, I can have no other intention than to serve the King and the duke well.[2]

But as he so often got nowhere in this way, he found himself obliged to bring pressure to bear on England by working with the opposition. His first venture was during the third Dutch war when a French refugee, Pierre du Moulin, established links on his behalf with various English radicals and adventurers and by this means collected political intelligence and distributed pro-Dutch and anti-French propaganda in England. The effect on parliament seems to have been considerable. It had been enthusiastic for the war at the outset, but at the end of 1673 it refused to supply more money for it and called on Charles to make peace. Charles had no alternative but to comply.[3] Once England had become a neutral, attempts were made through parliament to press Charles into joining the anti-French coalitions. The Austrian and Spanish envoys in London were as active in the work of propaganda as the Dutch. The well-known French intrigues with the parliamentary opposition were largely a counter-attack against this anti-French offensive: both continued even in the parliament of 1685.[4]

Various important men in England—Arlington around 1670, Danby in the later seventies, Sunderland around 1680, Monmouth in his last

[1] Kenyon, pp. 134–5.

[2] *Clarendon Correspondence*, vol. i, p. 89.

[3] See K. H. D. Haley, *William of Orange and the English Opposition, 1672–4* (Oxford University Press, 1953).

[4] Kenyon, p. 125. Turner, p. 297.

years—tried to use William's supposed influence to aid them in the struggle for power. Occasionally this brought results. In 1677 there was William's marriage and Charles's brief intervention at the end of William's first great war against France. In 1680, England nearly joined in a new anti-French coalition. But Charles's relations with his parliaments and William's relations with the Dutch republicans were so bad that neither could even appear to be an effective ally for the other, or for anyone else. By the end of 1680, William was obliged to associate himself with the decorous pressure of some courtiers for exclusion, as the only way to reconcile king and parliament and so restore English power. In 1681 he was even induced to visit England, though too late to influence the issue. William seems to have believed that an Exclusion Act would have been innocuous since, like the attempts to exclude himself from his ancestors' offices, it would never really take effect.[1] But Charles and James could not accept this view and Charles gave up the struggle for compromises, again took a French subsidy and crushed the opposition. William had been able to drive him from hostility to neutrality, but he could not drive him farther because the resultant concessions to parliament were bound to be more perilous than even a fight to the death with the whigs.

Yet after the accession of James II, William gradually recovered his ability to intervene in English affairs and pressing new reasons drove him to consider doing so more actively than ever before. Paradoxically, the first event in the new trend was a reconciliation between William and James. There had never been an open breach between them and in the first months of his reign, when he was facing a parliament and then Monmouth, James needed all the help he could get. William wished to capitalize upon the fact that Mary was now next in succession to the English thrones and might quite soon be a queen. He at once got rid of Monmouth, who had been staying with him, and sent over a submissive message by special envoy. When Monmouth landed in England, he hastened to send over the British regiments in the Dutch service and offered to come in person. Louis on the other hand failed to send the financial help which had been hoped for from him. In consequence James was ready to confirm the Anglo-Dutch alliance of 1678. He had earlier written a cordial letter which was privately shown to leading Dutch politicians. As a result

[1] Baxter, William III, p. 170. In general he spoke out against exclusion and in 1681 rebuked Laurence Hyde for reporting him in favour of it. Turner, pp. 207–8.

of this the anti-Orange party was weakened and William was able to get the military budget for the year passed on his own terms. But for James's help, William might not have had sufficient command of Dutch resources to be able later to attack him.[1]

The general European situation also began to move in William's favour. Louis XIV reached his apogee after 1680 just as Charles II did. The impotence of England and the Dutch and the Turkish menace to Austria left him almost unopposed in the west. He made leisurely territorial gains and saw them mostly accepted in the Twenty Years' Truce of 1684. But in the following year his decline began with the revocation of the Edict of Nantes. Not only did this deprive France of many useful citizens, who went to strengthen her enemies in resources and firmness of purpose, but it also completed the restoration of William's power in Holland. Dutch trade with France was very large and the persecution ruined it, striking down the business associates of the Dutch and also many Dutchmen who had, or who were thought to have, become French citizens. France for the time being had no supporters in the Republic, just as the English were given a new reason to fear the catholics. Nor did Louis win much thanks for his services to the catholic cause, for he had opposed papal authority both at home and in Rome. Pope Innocent XI sympathized with the enemies of France and was cool towards James II, who treated him tactlessly and was suspected of being a French instrument.

In 1686 the League of Augsburg was formed for the protection of Germany. It included only princes of the Empire and although Austria, Sweden and Spain joined in that capacity, it was rather ineffective. Much more important were the victories won against Turkey in 1687 by Austria, Russia and Venice, of which the outstanding feature was the Austrian victory at Mohacs in August. The Turks' threat to central Europe was ended for good and the recovery of south-eastern Europe from them had begun. The strength of Turkey had explained a good deal of Louis XIV's success and the way was now open for a more effective coalition against him.

The new situation made it more desirable than ever that England should be brought into the anti-French ranks and it also made it possible for William to contemplate strong measures for this purpose.

---

[1] Kenyon, pp. 118–19. Baxter, *William III*, pp. 201–4. Cf. Turner, pp. 261–4. William had to promise to do as James wished in English and Dutch affairs before he got the letter but he evaded a demand to renounce anti-French policies.

At the same time, Anglo-Dutch relations were deteriorating and William and the Dutch began to feel that developments in England threatened their interests and called for a bold response. James was becoming suspicious of William. He blamed him for the Dutch failure to prevent the sailing of Monmouth and Argyll in 1685 and their readiness, despite British protests, to shelter a growing number of British refugees. He virtually withdrew his protection of William early in 1686 when he ceased pressing Louis to restore the principality of Orange. That summer his catholicizing took an aggressive turn, with the setting up of the ecclesiastical commission and the appointment of catholics to the privy council, just at the time when his restoration of the fleet was attracting attention. Van Citters, the Dutch ambassador, reported that as in 1672 the religious innovations portended an Anglo-French attack on the Dutch. William caused an official warning to be given to the Dutch States General that there would be war in the spring of 1687. Van Citters also reported the catholic plots to alter the succession and William knew too of the scheme for putting a natural son of James on the throne of Ireland. A different danger, of which William's British contacts warned him, was that if he did not come to the rescue of the English people, they would desert the royal family altogether and fight for the establishment of a republic. Nothing in fact was more unlikely, but it so happened that some of those in touch with William believed it. James II for his part did not cease to assure William that 'the republican spirit increases every day amongst us here' and that 'that restless and rebellious party will never be quiet'.[1] This seems to have been one of the few points on which uncle and nephew were misguidedly agreed.

William therefore had increasing reason to believe that he must intervene more actively in England, both to protect his own country and to safeguard the rights of his wife, which gave so much strength to his own personal position. It is not at all clear when he began to think in terms of coercing his uncle. He was perfectly sincere in wanting the defeat of Monmouth—indeed he could no more desire a King Monmouth than he could wish for an English Commonwealth. His instructions to Bentinck, his representative in England during the rebellion, even suggest that he hoped for military help from James

---

[1] May 1686. Dalrymple, vol. ii, bks. ii/iv, p. 55. On republicanism, Baxter, *William III*, pp. 220, 230. On the succession and danger of war, Baxter, pp. 205, 216–18.

if his relations with his Dutch opponents reached a crisis.[1] He failed to prevent whig plotting on Dutch territory but his authority in the republic was probably insufficient for the task, however hard he tried. At the same time he could not abandon his links with the English opposition,[2] because this was his only means of putting pressure on James in time of need. In September 1686 Lord Mordaunt urged him to invade England (though not to depose James). Burnet says that he promised to try and 'put the affairs of Holland in so good a posture as to be ready to act when it should be necessary' and

> if the King should go about either to change the established religion or to wrong the Princess in her right or to raise forged plots to destroy his friends, that he would try what he could possibly do.[3]

James, however, did not resort to violence, but tried to win William's assent to his religious policy and to prove that it did not menace his interests. In November 1686 Van Citters reported that the building up of the British navy was not with a view to imminent war with Holland[4] and William Penn set off on his conciliatory mission. William responded with the special mission of Dijkvelt in February 1687 to make a tactful answer on the religious question and try to re-establish a good political understanding.[5] On colonial and other purely political matters James was accommodating, but we have seen that William refused to endorse his uncle's religious policy, though he professed himself willing to accept general toleration for all religious persuasions. He was even ready to give pardons, should he come to the throne, to catholics who had held office illegally.[6] William was entirely sincere in his profession of religious toleration: his own willingness to employ catholic troops in the Dutch service is especially noteworthy. If nevertheless he stood by the English Test Act it was because he continued to regard what James was doing as politically dangerous and dared not sever his ties with the English opposition. He began on the contrary to put himself in a position to become its leader, should this seem necessary.

[1] Japikse, Part I, vol. i, p. 21, no. 24 item 9; pp. 26–7, nos. 30–3.
[2] Turner, pp. 276–7.
[3] Cited Baxter, William III, p. 217. Cf. Turner, p. 353 n.
[4] Dispatch cited in Ashley, p. 79.
[5] This is Japikse's view adopted by Ashley, p. 81. But see chapter vi.
[6] See his letter in Dalrymple, vol. ii, pt. i, p. 55. Cf. Baxter, William III, p. 219. It seems that he would not even consent to repealing the penal laws but he made it abundantly clear later that he favoured toleration in England even for catholics.

William had remained in occasional contact with English politicians and Dijkvelt's mission had as its second purpose the making of contacts with such people, collecting information, advising them to stand firm and explaining just what the position of William and Mary in the religious issue was. Dijkvelt brought back with him a number of letters in which influential persons expressed in suitably vague terms their devotion to William. Perhaps the most important was Churchill's letter, for the future Marlborough already could and did give assurances on behalf of his wife's friend, Princess Anne. In the summer, the death of the Queen's mother provided William with an excuse to send another special envoy, his cousin Count Zuylestein, on a mission of condolence. He too conferred with leading English personalities and William also encouraged such people to visit him in Holland. The purge of the Irish army and the 'closetings' had further produced a body of unemployed courtiers and officers, many of whom entered Dutch service. These events mark the reconstitution of a party for the Prince of Orange. Burnet gives a list of leaders whom Dijkvelt met at Shrewsbury's house and says that they often met together at that place.[1] In January 1688 the party made its appeal to the people. James Stewart, a Scottish whig refugee in Holland who had rallied to King James, remained in contact with the Dutch authorities. He tried to induce the Grand Pensionary Fagel to use his influence with William in favour of the King's religious policy. Fagel responded in November 1687 with a full statement of the religious position of the prince and Princess.[2] It was this letter that was published in the new year as a pamphlet and widely disseminated in England.

The context of all this activity was James's campaign to prepare the ground for a parliament that would alter the laws in the way that he wished, and it seems likely that William's initial purpose was to counter his preparations with a view to turning any parliament that met against the crown, as he had so successfully done in 1673. But Anglo-Dutch relations got worse and the European situation grew more tense. The question of the British regiments in the Dutch service was the immediate cause of trouble between the two countries. By custom the English king had been allowed to nominate their

---

[1] Cited in Baxter, *William III*, p. 230.

[2] Including their desire to give toleration to the catholics, important in reassuring the catholic powers. Turner, p. 355.

commander. In March 1685 James dismissed from this post Henry Sidney, who was the brother of Algernon but also a friend of William. He asked for the removal of officers sympathetic to Monmouth. William complied but seems to have resented the power which the English ambassador could exercise over the army by traducing officers to James.[1] Not until October 1686 did James nominate a new commandant—the Earl of Carlingford, an Irish catholic. In some embarrassment, William refused to support the appointment because it would compromise him with the States General. In 1687 James wanted to strengthen himself by calling the regiments over (they were almost certainly more efficient than his own troops) but he could not afford it.[2] Then Sunderland produced the plan for the French to finance the operation. In January 1688 the King, angered by Fagel's letter,[3] asked the Dutch to send the regiments back. The Dutch decided that they were not obliged to do so, though they admitted the King's right to recall his subjects individually. In March James did this, with results highly disadvantageous to himself. As already explained, he got only a few extra troops by this move but the incident revived all the rumours in Holland that an Anglo-French attack was in prospect. The Dutch fleet was strengthened, and the Dutch domestic situation became very propitious for any plan of William's to invade England.

Louis XIV meanwhile had his hands so full that he could spare little thought for James. The strong French position on the Rhine was crumbling. In 1685 the Elector Palatine had died and was succeeded by the Emperor's father-in-law. Louis was trying to repair the damage by claiming part of the inheritance for the Duchess of Orleans, sister of the former elector. The death of the pro-French Archbishop-elector of Cologne, who was also Bishop of Liège, occurred at the end of May 1688, but had long been expected by reason of his age. In December 1687 the French had induced the chapter to elect the Bishop of Strasbourg, William von Fürstenberg, coadjutor of Cologne. On the archbishop's death, they voted in favour of Fürstenberg's succeeding him, but not by the necessary two-thirds majority. The Pope pronounced in favour of the rival candidate, a Bavarian backed by the Dutch and Austrians. The chapter of Liège elected a pro-Dutch candidate. James rather unwillingly supported the French in

---

[1] H. C. Foxcroft (ed.), *A Supplement to Burnet's 'History of My Own Time'* (Oxford University Press, 1902), p. 147.
[2] Turner, pp. 348–50.   [3] Kenyon, p. 179.

the affair of Cologne, thereby forfeiting the sympathy of the Emperor.[1] Louis was also preoccupied with a quarrel between Denmark and Sweden and in the spring of 1688 he unsuccessfully tried to get James to strengthen his fleet with a view to helping the Danes. Then in June 1688 he received a report—which turned out to be too pessimistic—that the ailing, childless Charles II of Spain was dying. The long-awaited opportunity to assert the claims of the house of Bourbon to the throne of Spain seemed to be at hand. The main French fleet, which had been fighting the pirates of Algiers, was retained in the Mediterranean and was not available to influence events farther north.

The first clear signs that William had begun to think of invading England seem to date from the end of 1687. About that time Fagel began to remark in the Dutch council of state that William would have to go to England in person if the magnates of the realm invited him, in order to end the confusion there. Fagel argued that it was the duty of the Dutch to support him in such an event. William may have been influenced by the failure of James to respond positively to Fagel's letter to Stewart.[2] As the religious strife in England reached its height, important Englishmen duly approached William in a more pressing way than before. They told him that he could expect very general support if he intervened at once; delay on the other hand would enable James to consolidate his position. In March 1688, Danby wrote to him that the Government's 'examination of the minds of the nobility and gentry has made such an union for the defence' of the protestant religion that 'I verily believe they begin to despair of supplanting it by violent means, and it is certain they can do it no other way.' Fagel's letter had added 'courage to that union ... there wants only an opportunity to the greatest part of the nation to show their zeal for your services'.[3] In April, William was visited by two of his go-betweens with England, the naval officers Edward Russell and Arthur Herbert. Speaking on behalf of 'many of great power and interest', Russell warned that the present moment was too good to miss. Even those indifferent in religion had no desire to turn papist but 'men of fortune, if they saw no visible prospect, would be governed by their present interest'. The army was as yet too protestant to be a really reliable

---

[1] Ogg, *James II and William III*, p. 207, n. 2, thinks Louis's motive in this affair was only to humiliate the Pope: action against the Papal States was another prospective task for the French fleet in the Mediterranean.

[2] O. Klopp, *Der Fall des Hauses Stuart* (1876), vol. iii, p. 429.

[3] Browning, vol. ii, p. 121.

instrument for James but this too might alter.[1] In the previous year some opponents of the government had rejoiced in the strength of the army because it was not expected to be loyal. Now the possibility that James might fill it with entirely dependable men was taken more seriously.[2] If the King had force on his side, he was expected in the end to succeed in convening a docile parliament to legitimize his actions—though he would have to give up even the pretence of free elections.[3] It was no doubt the English and the international situation combined that made William say to Dijkvelt that it was 'now or never'.[4] He told Russell that 'if he was invited by some men of the best interest and the most valued in the nation . . . he believed he could be ready by the end of September to come over'.[5] He seems to have tried at once to hire some troops from the elector of Saxony who was visiting him.[6]

The royal pregnancy and the doubts concerning it did much to clear the way for the invasion. The subversion of the law and of private rights seemed to have reached the point of disinheriting the very heirs to the throne. Even those who held that a subject must not resist his sovereign in such a case did not deny that another sovereign prince might do so. Burnet believed himself no longer bound by the duty of non-resistance once he was convinced, by all that followed the second Declaration of Indulgence, that James intended to overthrow the laws instead of merely abusing them. But he thought too that William 'was the only person that either could save them or had a right to it: since by all the laws in the world' a lawful heir may protect himself against disinheritance. He says that the English bishops likewise told William that he had a just cause to make war upon the King.[7] William of course was not the immediate heir, but fortunately for him first Anne and then Mary endorsed the growing suspicions respecting their father. Anne's letters to her sister painted the English catholic court in the blackest hues. She expected to be asked to change her religion and was resolved to 'undergo anything', even to 'live on alms', rather than comply. She advised the Prince and

[1] Burnet, vol. ii, p. 377.
[2] Klopp, vol. iii, p. 375. *Supplement to Burnet*, pp. 277–8.
[3] *ibid*. Cf. Japikse, Part II, vol. ii, pp. 15–21.
[4] Macaulay, vol. iii, p. 1048.
[5] Burnet, vol. ii, p. 377.
[6] Baxter, *William III*, p. 225.
[7] Burnet, vol. ii, p. 376. *Supplement to Burnet*, pp. 277–8.

Princess not to visit England because 'I should be frightened out of my wits for fear any harm should happen to either of you'. She found the Queen insufferably proud and fanatical, her influence making the King 'more violent'. She began voicing suspicions of the pregnancy in March 1688, 'the principles of that religion being such that they will stick at nothing'. She found Mary disappointingly slow to share her suspicions.[1] Mary, however, was uneasy. The birth was premature and so, earlier, had been the certainty of the King that a child was coming. She was unwilling to show hostility to an innocent child and therefore ordered public prayers for him, in which William supported her. But she also sent a detailed questionnaire to Anne about the circumstances of the birth to which Anne (who had been at Bath at the time) answered as well as she could. William for his part sent Zuylestein to England again, officially to congratulate the royal parents but really to plot. On his return, Mary became convinced that her father had been guilty of a crime so horrible that only his de-throning by her husband could save church and state.[2] There is no more poignant illustration of the protestant inability to trust catholics, however well known and loved.

William apparently shared the general suspicion regarding the royal baby,[3] but he told Russell that 'no private ambition or resentment' could induce him to take up arms against a near relation. This was his ostensible reason for demanding 'formal and direct invitations' from leading Englishmen[4]—he would only come if English national interests seemed to require it. In view of the need for secrecy, the plan was not really practicable. There were many messages from individuals, but only with great difficulty could a formal invitation from as many as seven suitable persons be brought into being, on 30 June. This maladroit procedure has led to the suspicion that William was only bent on collecting compromising letters from influential men. He certainly showed no continuing desire for popular participation in his enterprise. When it came to drawing up a public declaration of his intentions, he objected to making parliament the arbiter of England's future: 'though I fear it cannot be otherwise, yet to entrust one's destiny to them is no small risk.'[5] He naturally rejected a draft by the

[1] Dalrymple, vol. ii, bk. v, pp. 170–6.
[2] Bentinck, pp. 62, 72–6.
[3] L. Pinkham, *William III and the Respectable Revolution* (Harvard University Press, 1954), p. 141.
[4] Burnet, vol. ii, pp. 396–7.   [5] Japikse, Part I, vol. i, p. 49.

republican Wildman which would have condemned the tory régime of the earlier eighties.[1] His object was to preserve the monarchy and the dynasty in their traditional rights against subversion from whatever quarter. But paradoxically this widened instead of diminishing the circle of those willing to adhere to him: tories could feel that in constitutional matters he was one of them. Sensible whigs realized this and did not press him to espouse radical views; the extremists grumbled, but they were helpless without his patronage. In one respect William probably took an uncongenial line in order to please the tories, though diplomatic considerations were important here too. It is likely that he had decided that he could produce a stable settlement only by himself replacing James upon the throne. But this was not one of his professed objectives and even when he was physically able to seize the crown by force, he rejected whig pleas that he should do so.

(II)

William's physical capacity to intervene had been emerging since 1686. At that time the Dutch fleet was weak and William had no money. He could not even have given financial support to English rebels and he did not dare to join the League of Augsburg. But in that year William was able to get authorization to farm out the Dutch customs dues and by this means he raised a large loan which was used to pay for a build-up of the navy. The States General were got to vote forty ships for a war against the pirates of Algiers and William added twelve more on his own authority. In 1688 four million guilders were voted for fortifications on the southern frontier. This was a four-year programme, but William was able to borrow the full amount at once and divert it temporarily for his own purposes. Another fund of almost equal size was also diverted.[2] An important milestone in the preparations—it may even have helped to determine William to make the expedition—was the death of the old 'Great Elector' of Brandenburg, 29 April/9 May. He had latterly been unwilling to act against France but his son was not only a weaker and more impressionable man but he was first cousin and heir of the childless William. If William perished in England, he would inherit his estates and perhaps

[1] Burnet, vol. ii, pp. 415–17.
[2] Baxter, *William III*, pp. 232–3. Dalrymple, vol. ii, pt. i, bk. v, p. 25.

some of his power in Holland; on the other hand, William could disinherit him. William had great difficulty in winning him over: they met at Minden in September and William seems to have confided his whole plan to his cousin. Thereafter Brandenburg's forces were available for the support of the Dutch in Germany and Elector Frederick hopefully lingered at The Hague during the English adventure, ready to claim his inheritance should it prove fatal to William.[1] Other German princes were also induced to help, notably the Duke of Hanover and his brother the Duke of Celle. The availability of these troops made it possible to use part of the Dutch army against England.

The uncertainties of the European situation made it possible for William to collect forces for the invasion without attracting too much suspicion. The navy was busily recruiting seamen and getting ready to send out a strong squadron. But explanatory rumours were spread about: the squadron was going to fight the Danes or the Algerines—or the French, in the event of a continental war over Cologne. Large numbers of transports were hired, but they were not concentrated. Large quantities of supplies were procured, but the possibility of a continental war was the excuse. A camp was set up at Nijmegen apparently with a view to seizing Cologne. The stores were ostensibly sent there, but they were sent back again secretly to the coast.[2] Some of the English leaders passed over to Holland with a view to joining in the expedition and there was a fair amount of contact during the summer between William and his English friends—partly covered by Zuylestein's mission. But the English government seems not to have detected this correspondence.

The British and French governments were embarrassed in dealing with the situation not only by being kept in the dark but by the fact that if they did make preparations against the Dutch, this might draw upon them a Dutch attack not otherwise inevitable. Van Citters, the Dutch ambassador in London, was recalled in July and did not return until September. He may not have been in the secret. Before he left, he assured James of the peaceful intentions of the Dutch and said that they had not naval forces enough to attack England. On his return, he justified the naval armament in the ways indicated above. James had been worried by the Dutch naval preparations all through

---

[1] His letter of congratulation on William's accession (Dalrymple, vol. ii, bk. v, p. 131) implies that he was let into the secret.

[2] Dalrymple, vol. ii, pt. i, bk. v, pp. 27–8.

the year and in June Louis proposed to reinforce him with sixteen of his own ships. But James had wanted help by land (the subsidy to the ex-Dutch regiments) not by sea. He declined the offer and its only effect (since it became known) was to speed the Dutch armament.[1] The British took care to tell the Dutch ambassador that the French offer had been refused. In August the English ambassador at The Hague at last concluded that the preparations being made were directed against England and at the end of the month Bonrepos, a special envoy of Louis XIV, came over and told James that if he did not believe that the Prince of Orange was going to attack him, he was the only person in Europe of that opinion. James by now was making more active preparations, but he and Sunderland did not believe that the English would rebel, or that William would invade without assurance on this point, or that the States General would consent to the use of their forces in such an enterprise. They were sore at the French, who evaded a full alliance with them and seemed only to want to use them as catspaws in their own quarrels—notably that with the papacy which the English regarded as a disaster and which Sunderland had been trying for a year to compose. Sunderland started talks for a naval treaty, as an excuse for proposing a joint preventive attack on the Dutch. Nothing came of this and the treaty was signed (3/13 September) with the amount of help that the French were to give left blank. The French meanwhile had made a provocative gesture in lieu of practical aid. At the behest of Skelton, now English ambassador in Paris, they had officially warned the Dutch that they would assist England if she was attacked. The Dutch could only conclude that the English King was the tool of the French. The English government reacted by denying that it had any secret treaties with France, recalling Skelton and putting him in the Tower.

The French were surer than the English of what was coming, but they too had doubts. They felt that their own coasts might be the object of attack and anyway their fleet was far away. In September they comforted themselves with the quite sensible belief that it was now too late in the year for a naval campaign and the blow would fall in the spring, when the French fleet would be back in the north to meet it. The English were proving difficult people to help and even if William did attack at once he was unlikely to win a quick victory.

---

[1] Kenyon, pp. 202–14. Louis's subsidy in the spring to keep up the squadron in the Downs had a similar effect. For this page cf. Dalrymple, vol. ii, pts. i, v, pp. 31, 152–4.

The threat from Germany was much more immediate. By September Brandenburg troops had occupied the city of Cologne and on the 10th/20th the Pope declared in favour of the Austro-Bavarian candidate for the archbishopric. French troops were already in the electorate and on 15/25 September Louis resolved to attack the imperial fortress of Philippsburg in the Palatinate. By thus tying up his forces over 200 miles from the Dutch frontiers, he made it impossible even to demonstrate in William's rear. At long last James and Sunderland became completely convinced of their danger: a royal proclamation to warn the country was issued on 28 September/8 October.

It was at this stage that William avowed his plans and officially asked for support in quarters where hitherto he had canvassed only privately: the Dutch republic, the Spanish and Austrian courts and among the English people. On 17/27 September the news of Louis's military movements reached Holland and stocks rose 10%. On 19/29 September the States of Holland voted to support William. On 8 October NS. William addressed the foreign affairs committee of the States General. He argued that the Kings of England and France desired to subvert both the protestant religion and the Dutch republic. James could do nothing at present because of his domestic situation. Either he would surmount his difficulties or a republic would be set up—and the Dutch were likely to find an English republic a far more formidable foe than a monarchy, as the war of 1652 had shown. There was a good chance of success for an invasion now and the moment must not be missed. He would undertake the expedition in his own and his wife's name and only desired the Dutch to act as auxiliaries. He did not intend to dethrone James, but would secure the meeting of a free parliament that would firmly establish the protestant religion and the laws and liberties of the nation. James and his people would then live together in amity and be useful to the confederacy of powers to which the Dutch belonged. On the recommendation of the committee the States gave the Prince the help he asked.[1]

The Habsburg powers were at one with William and the Dutch in wishing to restrict French influence, but regarding England their views tended to diverge. Austrian and Spanish statesmen had no interest in quarrels that were simply between England and Holland and as

[1] Baxter, *William III*, pp. 235–6, citing *Kronijk van het Historisch Genootschap*, Veertiende Jaargang (1858), pp. 135–42.

catholics they were bound to wonder if James could be weaned from the French by supporting his religious designs. It was necessary to convince them that William's policy was not mere self-seeking but was needed to check French progress. A joint memorial from the Prince and the States to the Emperor in the spring of 1688 tried to show that an Anglo-French attack on the Dutch was in preparation as in 1672. This could not but be damaging to France's other neighbours. The only way to stop it was to promote a reconciliation between James and his people on the basis of respect for the existing laws. The English protestants were too numerous and fanatical to submit to James. If they were not helped, they would either get up a republic or themselves turn to France in order to gain protection.[1] On the eve of his expedition William told the Emperor that the 'misunderstand-ings' between James and his people had almost reached the point of 'formal rupture'. He was going over at the pressing invitation of many 'considerable persons' and would take a body of troops for his own protection. He had no desire to hurt the King or 'those who have a right to pretend to the succession', still less to take the crown himself. He hoped that the calling of a free parliament would lead to a reconciliation between King and people, who would then be 'able to contribute powerfully to the common good'. He promised to try and ensure liberty of conscience for the catholics, 'provided they exercise their religion without noise and with modesty'.[2]

On 30 September/10 October the Prince published a declaration that was to serve as his manifesto in England. He began by denouncing the 'evil counsellors' who had subjected the British realms 'in all things relating to their consciences, liberties and properties to arbitrary government' by the use of the dispensing power and a commission for ecclesiastical matters in which a papist (Sunderland) sat. Various acts of oppression were listed. Against all this William and Mary had respectfully protested. The calling of a parliament was the 'last and great remedy', but the evil counsellors had tried to neutralize its dangers for themselves by spreading dissension among protestants 'under the specious pretence of liberty of conscience' and by pressure in advance of the elections on all electors who were 'in any employ-ment' or 'in any considerable esteem'. To gain time, encourage their 'complices' and discourage 'good subjects', they had 'published that

---

[1] Klopp, vol. iii, pp. 453–4.
[2] Dalrymple, vol. ii, pt. i, bk. v, pp. 132–3.

the queen hath brought forth a son'. The truth of this 'not only we ourselves but all the good subjects of those kingdoms do vehemently suspect'. The Prince and Princess both had a right in the succession and they had always enjoyed the 'particular affection and esteem' of 'the English nation'. Therefore 'we cannot excuse ourselves' from 'contributing all that lies in us for the maintaining both of the protestant religion and of the laws and liberties of those kingdoms'. The Prince had been 'earnestly solicited by a great many lords both spiritual and temporal and by many gentlemen and other subjects of all ranks'. He was coming with a force for his own protection, his only object was 'to have a free and lawful parliament assembled as soon as possible', and he called on all ranks of the people to come and assist him.

William could only improvise a fairly modest force for his expedition and it had to sail at a time of year regarded as quite unsuitable for campaigning. He had achieved a degree of surprise and so his opponent had equally to rely on such forces as could be quickly got together. But the 12,000 horse and foot that he brought to England[1] faced an army of 40,000 men. James raised five new regiments of foot and five of horse, besides bringing in Scottish and Irish troops.[2] The prospect of invasion had a bad effect on trade and so on his financial position. He had to use his ready money for fitting out the fleet, the customs revenue was drying up and a London banker refused to lend anything. But here French aid was still available. Louis sent over 300,000 livres at James's request, which might have been quite important if James's resolution had not weakened.[3] (William was short of ready money too.[4]) William's associates in England appear to have despised James's army—or else to have thought highly of their own military prowess. In view of the English dislike of foreigners, they advised William to bring no more than 7,000 troops. They evidently expected the navy to serve James better than the army, urging William to bring as many ships as possible and to come before the English fleet had been fully manned. William was not confident that either the army or the people would desert James. He wanted to bring a force 'superior to anything the King could bring against him'

[1] The total was supposed to be 11,212 according to list in *Journal of Society for Army Historical Research*, vol. xliv (1966), pp. 152–3.

[2] Dalton, vol. ii, p. xviii. HMC *Dartmouth*, vol. v, p. 171 cited Carswell, p. 164.

[3] George, 'Financial Relations', pp. 409–12.

[4] Pinkham, p. 137 n. 9.

if the army remained loyal. He failed, however, to achieve even the strength of 15,000, which was the lowest he thought acceptable. To equip his English supporters he brought 20,000 stand of arms.[1] We must consider a little later whether he really desired English support.

At sea there was more equality between the opposing forces and William had strength enough for the vital first step of effecting a landing. At least 200 transports were required to carry his army. The size of the escorting fleet is not quite certain, but it seems to have included forty-nine warships with more than twenty guns—eight of them had sixty or more—and ten fireships.[2] If James had been able to mobilize all his ships he could have crushed this force with ease, but not only was he slow to take alarm, he was compelled to fight with peacetime revenues only. The original plan for 1688 envisaged only twenty-six ships, mainly small, in home waters. Early alarms brought a mild strengthening and in June the catholic Sir Roger Strickland had more than twenty 'nimble frigates' under his command in the Downs and various scouting expeditions were made. In mid-August Sir Roger still had only twenty-six ships but they included seventeen third and fourth rates (fifty guns and over). Thirty-five more ships were now ordered to be fitted out, including a score of the larger rates. A month later (23 and 24 September) two much more warlike measures were taken: a press of seamen was ordered and the supreme command was transferred to Lord Dartmouth, a protestant and a faithful personal adherent of James. It was high time, for when Dartmouth received his instructions on 1 October, the reinforcements ordered in August had still not reached the fleet. The instructions therefore required the initial concentration of the ships to take place at the Buoy of the Nore, where they were fairly safe from attack, but not in a position to shield the country. William, however, was unable to get under way before the English reinforcements began to arrive. On 24 October Dartmouth felt strong enough to take his force seaward to the station he had chosen for it—the Gunfleet, south of Harwich. With justifiable satisfaction, he reported to James that 'we are now at sea before the Dutch

---

[1] Burnet, vol. ii, pp. 412–13. *Supplement to Burnet*, pp. 284–5, 292. The quotation is from Burnet's original account in the *Supplement*. The revised text which appears in the History makes William want an army as big as James's: surely this was a slip in revision, the aim being impossibly high. William no doubt hoped to equal James's main field army: this in fact amounted to about half the English strength (Carswell, p. 196), the rest being in garrisons.

[2] Powley, pp. 35–6. The ensuing account of events at sea follows Powley.

after all their boasting'. His fleet never reached its planned strength and when the Dutch finally came in sight he seems to have had thirty-two fighting ships and thirteen fireships. But the fighting ships were almost all third and fourth rates and so bigger than most of the Dutch vessels. After a slow start, and amid great difficulties in collecting men and materials, Pepys and his men had done quite creditably and the Dutch and English took the sea in roughly equal strength, as they commonly did.

The political circumstances governing the military operations dictated not only that the forces on both sides should be improvised but that the tactics of the invaders should be unorthodox and highly dangerous to themselves. William hoped if at all possible to avoid a naval battle: even if he won it, the moral effect of a combat with the traditional foe would be bad in England. He appointed an Englishman, Herbert, to command his fleet therefore and he told him 'this is not the time to display your courage or fight if it can be avoided'. Herbert's instructions, dated 17/27 October, required the fleet to 'convey', 'protect and defend' the Prince and his land forces. 'When an enemy fleet shows itself, the war fleet shall place itself between the enemy and the transport ships.' Transporting an army by sea in the face of an unsubdued enemy fleet is one of the most hazardous operations conceivable. The operation, moreover, was being attempted at the wrong time of the year, and for this William's armada soon began to be punished. It sailed from Helvoetsluys on 19/29 October, getting out before the English fleet had been able to reach its cruising station. Before his departure, William told the Princess that if he perished it would be necessary for her to marry again.

> 'It is not necessary', he continued, 'for me to tell you that it should not be to a papist.' He could not himself speak these words without shedding tears. . . . He protested to me that only the anxiety which he had for our religion made him speak thus.

Mary replied that she could never love any one but him or wish to bear another's child if she could not bear his.[1] No sooner was the fleet under way than a gale scattered the ships and they had to creep back into port. None was lost, but more than a thousand horses perished and had to be replaced.

This was how it came about that Dartmouth could boast that he

[1] Bentinck, pp. 80–1.

had beaten the Dutch after all. But the situation was really just as awkward for the English. A close blockade of an enemy coast was an operation never then attempted and the bad weather made any such offensive action as dangerous for the English as the invasion was for the Dutch. Dartmouth on 12 October wrote that it would be best 'if the weather be anything reasonable, to show myself upon their coast as near as conveniently I can in the daytime, still standing off to get good sea room every night. . .'. His 'ablest men and pilots' all agreed 'that there is no attempting anything in their ports at this time of year'. James replied to this cautious suggestion with 'I think you ought to consider well of it before you do it' and Dartmouth promised not to make the experiment without 'settled fair weather'.[1] After the initial Dutch fiasco, James through Pepys tentatively suggested a move towards the Dutch coast, but Dartmouth pointed to the experience of the Dutch themselves as showing that it was not safe. He consulted his subordinates, who confirmed him in his opinion: no doubt their political sympathies weighed with them. He now relied on going to sea and looking for the Dutch as soon as the wind became favourable to their sailing: he thought that he could not miss so large a force. He was no doubt encouraged to adopt this course by the belief which James and he mostly held to that the Dutch would not venture to land without fighting him first. On 24 October he had further committed himself to the view that

> I cannot see much sense in their attempt with the hazard of such a fleet and army at the latter end of October . . . Your statesmen may take a nap and recover, the women sleep in their beds and the cattle, I think, need not be drove from the shore.[2]

This was to ignore the precariousness of the English position in face of an enemy prepared to brave the storm. The English had been comforted through the earlier part of October by the prevalence of westerly winds that kept their foes in port. Once the wind turned east and allowed their enemies to come over, it was the English that were in danger of being hamstrung. Two points of vantage were considered where the English fleet might await the Dutch: the Gunfleet and between the Kentish Knock and the North Sand Head (*i.e.*, northeast of the North Foreland). In either position, the English were likely to find themselves immobilized if the Dutch approached during an east

---

[1] Powley, pp. 60, 63.
[2] Ashley, p. 149, citing HMC *Dartmouth*, vol. xi, pp. 5, 158.

wind and flood tide. From neither could they initiate an attack against a Dutch fleet passing to the north of them, to attack the east coast. If the Dutch skirted round them and went through the Straits of Dover, the English could follow them if they were at the Kentish Knock, but not if they were at the Gunfleet. On the other hand, it would take so long for scouting vessels to report to a fleet at the Kentish Knock position that unless the Dutch came past it, there was no chance of catching them at all. This seems to have been why the Gunfleet position was chosen.

The Dutch were able to sail for the second time on 1/11 November. Their initial course was northerly, but after noon on the 2nd they turned to the southwest. The wind was boisterous, but not a storm. On the morning of Saturday, 3 November, they could see the English coast and were themselves sighted by the English fleet. The English weighed anchor but they were just too late to catch the Dutch: the ebb tide was almost spent. The combined effect of the flood tide and the east wind made it impossible for them to get round the sandbanks on the south side of the Thames estuary. They did not do so until next morning, the 4th. The Dutch had reached the Straits of Dover by noon on the 3rd and their passage through it was an imposing demonstration. The transports in convoy reached to within a league of the shore on either side. Guns saluted both Calais and Dover. Military music was played on the ships for three hours. The Prince led the van: his flag was the English colours with the motto 'the Protestant Religion and the Liberties of England' and underneath, the motto of his family, 'Je maintiendrai'. A French refugee aboard the fleet wrote 'France trembled at the sight and England, seeing her deliverer coming in full sail to her aid, trembled with joy.' This was certainly the effect aimed at. The fleet now made for Torbay and its most dangerous moment came when it overshot the mark and seemed condemned to sail into Plymouth—a hopelessly remote point even if the commander proved friendly. But the wind miraculously changed and blew it back. The landing began on Monday, 5/15 November. The English fleet got into the Channel on the 4th but it was not at full strength, and the flag officers and captains unanimously advised Dartmouth not to engage if the possibility of hindering a landing had passed.[1] The fleet hung about in the Downs collecting reinforcements

---

[1] Powley, p. 84. The officers' opinions were taken separately so it would seem that professional opinion concided with the politics of the disaffected.

and only on the 16th did it sail for Torbay in search of the Dutch. Storms prevented it making contact and it returned to Portsmouth considerably damaged on the 22nd. Thereafter it did nothing. Its officers had done a little to hinder its coming into contact with the Dutch, but nature had done much more, and there is no evidence beyond contemporary conjecture for the view that it would not have fought. Well might the calvinist William landing at Torbay ask Burnet what he thought of Predestination now.

William's unavoidably reckless tactics brought success at sea but made his task when he got ashore harder than ever. He had followed a course that carried him away from the English fleet but also away from his most useful English supporters. It was in the north that an organized rebellion was being prepared. In the west there were plenty of whigs, but they had shot their bolt in Monmouth's rebellion and the savagery with which this was repressed had cowed the whole area. At first nobody of importance joined William. Men of property said 'if this thing do miscarry, we are all undone'.[1] It has been suggested that William deliberately went to the west because he expected it to be passive; more generally, that he was determined to succeed by his own efforts and to owe nothing to rebels.[2] There can be no doubt that he wished to remain in control of events and that the relative passivity of the English during his expedition helped him to do so. It is less certain that this was the result of clever planning in advance. William had begun by considering whether to land in one or several places, including perhaps Scotland. 'Act according to circumstances', was his decision.[3] The effective choice was between the west and the north. An agent in England reported in the autumn against any landing nearer to London than Yorkshire or Devonshire. James had concentrated his forces round the capital and the invaders could not hope themselves to raise men there.[4] The advice of the 'immortal seven' was to land in the north, where the gentry were loyal, supplies plentiful and the roads good. They explained that the west was friendly but intimidated. There were suspicions, however, that these views derived from

[1] Baxter, *William III*, p 238.
[2] This seems to be the main point of disagreement in recent writing on the subject. Broadly speaking, Pinkham and Carswell argue that William was not eager for rebel support while Ashley and Baxter attribute the paucity of it to circumstances and not to his design.
[3] Memo. by William, Browning, vol. i, p. 388.
[4] Japikse, part i, vol. ii, pp. 618–19.

the personal ambitions of Danby, whose influence lay in the north and who was eager to play a leading role.[1] Approaching the subject from a naval standpoint, Arthur Herbert tended to favour the west against the north. He thought that there should be landings in both quarters—one the main attack and the other a diversion. The western coast he considered less dangerous for the fleet and for landings than the northern. If the fleet went west through the Channel, it could, moreover, interrupt James's communications with France and Ireland, affording cover incidentally to a northern diversionary attack. If the main attack was in the north, James would remain able to communicate with his friends and in collaboration they could easily destroy any force sent westward as a diversion. Herbert thought that west country roads were better than those in the north and that James's harsh measures in the west would actually mean more support for William. But he conceded that the west was farther away and that the decision must largely depend on the wind, which if favourable would neutralize that disadvantage.[2]

Burnet says that William rejected a division of his forces as too risky and that he favoured a landing in the north.[3] The instructions to Herbert as commander of the fleet certainly envisage such a landing: after the troops had got ashore, the fleet's orders were to go first to Scotland and then to the west of England in order to make diversions.[4] Current rumours[5] and the initial northerly course of the fleet suggest an initial attempt to carry out this plan and William does not seem to have been pleased at having to go to the west instead. After the landing he wrote home to Waldeck

> it is a nuisance that we have been obliged by the wind to set foot on this west coast because it has removed us so far from communication with Holland, so that here we are as if on another planet (*hors du monde*), knowing nothing except what happens roundabout.[6]

When the Dutch fleet turned south on 2 November the official reason was that the wind was 'so strong and full in the east'. It is tempting to ask if the Dutch had not then discovered that the English were at the Gunfleet and seized the chance this presented of getting past into the Channel without a fight, sacrificing a possibility of contact with

[1] Burnet, vol. ii, pp. 412–13.   [2] Japikse, pt. i, vol. ii, pp. 610–13.
[3] Burnet, vol. ii, p. 413.   [4] Powley, p. 44.
[5] Ashley, pp. 142, 144.   [6] Müller, vol. ii, p. 118.

English rebels.[1] This lack of contact noticeably delayed the opening of a land campaign against James: it is hard to see that as anything but an accident. William's northern friends could not begin their risings until 15 November. William himself made Exeter his head-quarters and did not advance further until 21 November. James's army, concentrated round London till it was known where William was going, was sent to Salisbury to contain him. It was the defection or passivity of James's own subordinates that broke the impasse in the west and facilitated rebellion in the north. This suited William's interests well in the end: there was no civil war, William avoided making enemies or becoming too dependent on his rebel friends; bloodshed and subsequent bitterness were kept to a minimum. But probably as much was due to the fortunes of war as to William's superior wisdom.

(III)

The men who tipped the scale in the conflict were the protestants still in office and the former servants of James who had broken with him on the religious issue. They were mostly, but not all, tories just as the rebels who plotted with William were mostly, but not all, out-lawed whigs. They had not dared and were not able to organize a rising on their own account, but the leading men had been in touch with William and some were willing to organize conspiracies on his behalf in the forces. Their positive achievement in this direction was small, but the moral effect of apathy and still more of desertion among the erstwhile loyalists was enormous. James was completely unnerved by it and decided to capitulate to William almost without firing a shot. This was the signal for men of all parties to rally to William. There was no longer any moral objection to it and it seemed the only sensible thing to do.

James's more intelligent ministers had realized that his only hope lay in reconciliation with the men who had served him so loyally at the start of his reign and they had tried to bring it about. Leading tories and moderates in opposition had also tried to make the king see reason. But James made no really wholehearted concessions until the desertions came and the futile haggling with him served only to encourage desertion. The attempts to reconcile King and loyalists had

[1] Powley, p. 80.

begun at the time of the bishops' trial. Jeffreys, who had long been uneasy, confided to Clarendon that 'he was much troubled at their prosecution, and made many professions of service for them, which he desired me to let them know. . . . Some men would hurry the King to his destruction'. He hoped to have a 'correspondence' with Sancroft through Clarendon 'which it was yet too soon for him to have openly' and believed that the King might be induced to be more moderate when parliament met. He thought that 'honest men, both lords and others (though the king had used them hardly), should appear often at court; I am sure it would do good'. For good measure he added that the judges were 'most of them rogues'.[1] Sunderland had broken with Jeffreys and his first move was to restore his tottering position at court by at last declaring himself a catholic. But his continuing intense activity in preparation for the elections took a distinctly protestant turn. On 6 July the privy council was attended by the two most eminent dissenters supporting the government, Henry Vane and Silas Titus, and Sunderland made a speech urging James to retain for the time being the Test Act of 1673. During the August scare he induced the King to accept this (Jeffreys opposing) and on the 24th it was announced that parliament would meet on 27 November. Lady Sunderland told Sidney that her husband was sure 'the King will make such offers that the Church of England men must accept'. The leading protestant courtiers (Dartmouth, Godolphin, Feversham and Churchill) would support the new policy.

When the possibility of invasion became a certainty, the government guardedly avowed a shift of policy. On 21 September the privy council approved a Declaration which Jeffreys said was drafted by himself with the concurrence of Sunderland, Middleton, Dartmouth and Godolphin. It reaffirmed that parliament would meet in November, but promised the preservation of the church of England and the Acts of Uniformity as well as universal liberty of conscience, and explained that the King was willing that catholics should remain excluded from the house of commons. On the 22nd the writs went out and also orders to reinstate the county magistrates ousted in preparation for the elections.[2] Jeffreys was authorized to restore the aldermen of the City of London who had been turned out in 1687 and he thought that James intended to restore the whole state of things

[1] *Clarendon Correspondence*, vol. ii, pp. 177, 179, 180, 185.
[2] For the foregoing, Kenyon, pp. 197–202, 214, 217, 218.

existing at his accession. The King saw Clarendon and told him that there was certain to be an invasion. ' "And now, my lord," said he, "I shall see what the church of England men will do." I answered, "And Your Majesty will see they will behave themselves like honest men; though they have been somewhat severely used of late." ' The King subsequently saw Sancroft and a number of the bishops. The States General meanwhile were told that the King was not allied with France and was willing to discuss measures for the preservation of the peace of 1678 and the truce of 1684. This message had no effect except to show that James was isolated and to increase his isolation by making Louis more cautious in sending money to his aid.

But the King had not surrendered to the protestants. Jeffreys' Declaration had suffered amendments in council and on 27 September he told Clarendon that 'some rogues had changed the King's mind; that he would yield in nothing to the bishops; that the Virgin Mary was to do all'. The bishops got nothing but fair words and the promise that Compton would be restored.[1] James had no intention either of negotiating with William or of meeting parliament till his attack had been repelled. The proclamation of 28 September respecting the coming invasion called for unflinching resistance and put off the meeting of parliament because of the national danger. The King told his people that 'although some false pretences relating to liberty, property and religion, contrived or worded with art and subtlety, may be given out', it was clear that the object of the attack was 'an absolute conquest of our kingdoms and the utter subduing and subjecting us and our people to a foreign power'. The project was 'promoted' by certain wicked subjects for their own selfish ends: oblivious of

former intestine distractions, the memory and misery whereof should endear and put a value upon that peace and happiness which hath long been enjoyed; nor being moved by our reiterated acts of grace and mercy, wherein we have studied and delighted to abound towards our subjects, and even towards those who were once our avowed and open enemies . . .

James declared that he had 'declined any foreign succours' and would 'rely upon the true and ancient courage, faith and allegiance of our own people'. He besought them to unite, ordered the lord lieutenants and their deputies to resist all attacks and forbade anyone to have any

[1] *Clarendon Correspondence*, vol. ii, pp. 188–92. *Ellis Correspondence*, vol. ii, pp. 206–28. For the foreign aspect, Kenyon, pp. 217–18; Turner, pp. 415–17, 426 n. 7.

contact with the invaders 'upon pain of high treason'. The militia was ordered to make ready and instructions were given for removing horses and cattle from the invaders' reach.[1] In effect the restored tory magistrates were being asked to help in repelling the invasion, but had no guarantee that there would be a free parliament and the redress of grievances once the King was safe.

The government continued to woo the church and its friends but not with sufficient ardour. The bishops met the King again on 3 October, after word had come from Godolphin that the court expected an approach by them and might 'by degrees' grant what 'was fit to be asked'. He thought that their duty to the King required them to 'be plain' and propose whatever they 'thought necessary for the public security'. They were allowed to present a paper of advice to the King. It asked him to dissolve the ecclesiastical commission, restore the corporations and universities, abandon the dispensing power and bestow office only on those legally qualified, and finally to call a free parliament.[2] James also saw the restored City aldermen and decided to restore the City charter. The ecclesiastical commission was abolished and on 8 October Magdalen College was restored to the care of its visitor, the Bishop of Winchester. But on 4 October, James had held a meeting of the catholic courtiers and promised that he would make no concessions to their disadvantage. He 'seemed displeased' at the bishops' paper and after further meetings with him, they resolved to go home. Princess Anne told her uncle Clarendon that it was 'plain they can do no good' and would only 'expose themselves' by remaining in town. The King likewise rejected Sunderland's advice to make a potent political gesture by restoring all the displaced members of corporations en bloc. Only if this was done could a free parliament such as William demanded be guaranteed. Instead, James sent instructions to the lord lieutenants to reform the corporations in their localities, and when he went further it was to cancel all charters granted since 1679 and displace all those holding office under them. This created confusion and annoyed the tories.[3] Calculated to benefit the whigs, it was really a harking back to the policy of alliance with

[1] Ashley, pp. 155, 205–6.
[2] *Clarendon Correspondence*, vol. ii, pp. 492–3; cf. p. 192. The paper: Ogg, *James II and William III*, p. 210.
[3] Kenyon, p. 219. For Sunderland's fall, pp. 219–23. For the Bishops, *Clarendon Correspondence*, vol. ii. pp. 193–4. Confusion resulted especially when there had been a formal surrender of the old charter. It could not then be revived.

the dissenting interest which the government had adopted in its fight with the church. Sunderland's influence henceforth steadily waned because he was losing his nerve. At the end of the month he was dismissed. James had little chance after this of successfully implementing a popular new policy. He was working mainly through protestant courtiers and officials not personally objectionable to his subjects but he had no able political adviser.

The initiative at court passed to what might be called the 'loyal opposition': Sunderland's old enemies the Hydes, another group including Halifax and Nottingham, and lastly the bishops. All had felt the government's displeasure, but none (save Compton) had pledged themselves to William and they do not seem to have wished for the overthrow of James. They failed to fill the gap that Sunderland had left partly because of their own divisions. There was no love lost between the Hydes and their associates on the one hand and Halifax, Nottingham and theirs on the other. Their rivalry continued right down to the fall of James and they neutralized each other. Princess Anne, moreover, refused Clarendon's repeated requests to help by using influence with the King: whether because she was afraid or because she did not wish to is not very clear. James in any case was not much inclined to listen and only the progress of events made him at all tractable. He held a meeting of all the peers in town on 22 October, but this was for the ludicrous purpose of publishing an attested account of his son's birth, to prove him legitimate. When a deputation waited on Princess Anne with the proof, she made the very fair and damning reply that the King's 'word must be more to me than these depositions'. The meeting spurred the more active politicians to consult and Nottingham and Clarendon together told the King that they could not return to the privy council if Petre remained a member. James would not remove him but promised he should be absent.[1]

James also tried to reassemble the bishops and induce them to issue a manifesto abhoring the intended invasion. He became especially eager for this when he obtained a copy of the Prince's declaration and found that William claimed to have been invited over by some of the spiritual and temporal peers. The bishops eventually refused to issue a disavowal of the invitation—largely at the prompting of Compton, who was hard put to it to avoid untruths when personally questioned by the King. Compton argued that if there was to be any public

[1] *Clarendon Correspondence*, vol. ii, pp. 195–6, 199,

statement it should be by the temporal as well as the spiritual peers, since the invitation mentioned both. This led him to say that the right place to take any notice of the offending document was in parliament. The bishops adopted these arguments and communicated them to the King when they met him on 6 November to tell him of their unwillingness to issue a statement. To the royal expostulations they made some telling replies. Nobody believed that the declaration was genuine, they said, and in any case affairs of state were not their concern. Sancroft pointed out that some of them had

> presented your majesty a petition of the most innocent nature, and in the most humble manner imaginable, yet we were so violently prosecuted, as it would have ended in our ruin, if God's goodness had not preserved us

and the case against them was

> that the honestest paper relating to matters of civil government might be a seditious libel, when presented by persons who had nothing to do with such matters.

He went on to complain of the libellous remarks about the bishops made by the justices on assize, apparently by official order. The bishops suggested that the King should simply publish the fact that they had denied any complicity in the invitation. The King was reduced to the last indignity of saying 'if I should publish it, the people would not believe me'. They then proposed that at least they should be allowed to consult with some temporal peers appointed by him, instead of having to act on their own. At length the King said he would

> urge you no further. If you will not assist me as I desire, I must stand upon my own legs and trust to myself and my own arms.

The bishops said that as bishops they would pray for him;

> as peers, we entreated we might serve him in conjunction with the rest of the peers, either by His Majesty's speedy calling a parliament or, if that should be thought too long, by assembling together with us as many of the temporal peers as were about the town.[1]

On this same day the news of William's landing reached London and soon some of the bishops and temporal peers were pressing the King to call parliament as a means towards making peace with him.

---

[1] *Clarendon Correspondence*, vol. ii, pp. 493–504; cf. pp. 199, 200. Cartwright and Watson were excluded from their confidence by the other bishops. Leading temporal peers were also asked to repudiate the invitation.

On the 8th Rochester and Clarendon met White of Peterborough and Lloyd of St. Asaph and it was agreed that the two bishops should suggest to Sancroft an address by spiritual and temporal lords for the calling of a parliament 'to prevent the shedding of blood'. Sancroft approved and White went on to visit Halifax, who turned out to be starting a similar move on his own account. On the 12th a petition was drafted by White and Lloyd in conjunction with Halifax, Nottingham and Weymouth. But these lords persuaded the bishops that the address should be signed 'only by such lords and bishops as had not made themselves obnoxious by any late miscarriages'. They believed that otherwise it would not be taken seriously by William and so would not lead to an accommodation. The bishops were sent off to collect signatures, but on approaching Clarendon they were met by a request for a meeting of all the peers in town, so that the petition could be discussed and if need be amended. Clarendon met the authors of the petition and Halifax, after some evasiveness, avowed that he would not act with anyone who had sat in the ecclesiastical commission (meaning Rochester). Even Nottingham recognized that this might be put down to personal rivalry. But Halifax and his associates were now inclined anyway to think that any petition at all would be welcome to the court rather than otherwise and they decided to go no further. In the end, Clarendon and some bishops met at Lambeth and agreed on a petition, in the light of soundings that the bishops had made. Rochester and some other peers met at Sprat's house with the bishops and discussed this draft. Eventually this group presented a petition to the King on 17 November. He 'seemed not pleased' and told them shortly that he would call a parliament but not 'whilst the invasion and rebellion lasted'. That evening he set off for his army at Salisbury still determined to fight William.[1]

The King had failed to reassure even his leading subjects and in consequence there had been no resurgence of loyalty in face of the invaders. National feeling was blunted by religious sentiment: it was possible to believe that this was a religious war, as indeed to some extent it was. Reresby wrote that 'neither the gentry nor the common people seemed much afeard ... saying, the Prince comes only to maintain the protestant religion; he will do England no harm'.[2] This

---

[1] Horwitz, pp. 56–8. *Clarendon Correspondence*, vol. ii, pp. 201–5.
[2] Reresby, p. 522.

feeling was reflected in the state of the militia, reactivated under the command of its traditional leaders now restored to local office. On 6 November Lord Bath reported from Plymouth to Secretary Middleton that

> the common people are so prejudiced with the late regulations and so much corrupted that there can be no dependence at present on the militia but only upon his majesty's standing forces.[1]

Another report said that no preparations had been made in Devonshire to resist the Prince when he arrived. There were no beacons and the militia were so out of order by long disuse that they could not easily be restored. The Earl of Huntingdon, going to take command at Plymouth, told his wife that the militia was not up in any of the counties he passed through in the days immediately following the landing. On arriving he found that the militia 'are of least use' and 'cannot be confided in either for resolution or fidelity'. They could only take over outlying garrisons like Pendennis from standing companies which were then concentrated at Plymouth. In the Isle of Wight the militia was mutinous and the governor thought he could use them to defend Yarmouth and Hurst only if he had a troop of regulars to keep them in awe.[2] At Dover the mayor was reluctant to send his trained bands into the castle to guard prisoners: it was against the rights of portsmen to be called out of their liberties. He was told 'they shall be dismissed as soon as possible'.[3] In Derbyshire, where Secretary Preston was lord lieutenant, there were only two legally qualified deputies. On 1 November they wrote and told him that if he sent a certificate of being himself legally qualified by having taken oaths, gave commissions to those who had been purged and reinforced this with a royal letter commanding them on their allegiance to do so, they hoped to get the militia organization functioning again.[4] Perhaps the most depressing report was from the Duke of Norfolk, who told Secretary Middleton that it would be unwise to light beacons in the event of invasion since they 'might as well guide them where we would not have them go, as shew them where they should'.[5]

[1] Baxter, *William III*, p. 431 n. 1.
[2] HMC *Hastings*, vol. ii, pp. 188–9, 191–2; 7th rep., p. 416; *Dartmouth*, vol. i, p. 185.
[3] HMC 7th rep., p. 414.
[4] *ibid.*, p. 412.
[5] Baxter, *William III*, p. 239 and p. 431 n. 26.

After a period of apathy came the desertions and risings in the Prince's favour. The attempts by whigs within reach of his army to rally to his support were rather a fiasco—only a few notables got through and their action had no effect. Lord Lovelace tried to lead a body of followers westward, but he was intercepted by the Gloucestershire militia and captured. It was the tory desertions that really had an effect and enabled William to advance. The Earl of Abingdon was the first peer to join William. On 14 November Lord Cornbury reached him: he had, although only a colonel, been left in temporary command at Salisbury and he tried without success to bring over three regiments. Macaulay suspected that he had been put up to this by Churchill, the leading spirit not only in the army but in the household of Cornbury's cousin, the Princess Anne. Even if it was not a symptom of plotting in the innermost court circle, the desertion of this young member of a leading cavalier family—grandson of the great Clarendon, nephew both of the King and of Rochester—was a thunderclap. If it was his own idea, it may have owed something to his recent personal experience of what full-fledged absolutism could be like. In 1687 he had accompanied Princess Anne's Danish husband on a visit to his home country. Denmark had become an absolute monarchy by a coup d'état in 1660 and Cornbury told Evelyn that he had not liked what he had seen:

> The miserable tyranny under which that nation lives, he related to us: the king keeping them under by an army of above 40,000 men, all Germans, not daring to trust his own subjects: notwithstanding which, that the Danes are exceedingly proud. The whole country very poor and miserable etc.[1]

The next notable deserter was Sir Edward Seymour, who came to Exeter on 17 November. By that time a number of western notables were coming in and the climax came locally when the Earl of Bath betrayed the important citadel of Plymouth—again the leader of one of the foremost cavalier and tory families. William's rear was at last secure and so on 21 November he began his march towards London.

Meanwhile, the northern insurrection had begun, helped by the apathy, incompetence and betrayals of local officials and by the concentration of the royal forces in the south. The first rising, in Cheshire, showed very clearly how the King had not managed to escape trouble by simply restoring authority to the traditional local

[1] Evelyn's Diary, 15 August 1687, vol. iv, p. 559.

leaders. On 15 October he received and 'caressed' the Earl of Derby and gave back to him the lieutenancies of Lancashire and Cheshire. Derby spoke strongly of the loyalty of his family, but he took care to consult friends who were involved in the Prince's plans. Their advice to him was to work with the government so as not to lose his commission and at the same time so to organize the militia as to make it completely loyal to himself. The plotters hoped in this way to be sure of an area which contained many papists and was the likeliest point of ingress for the Irish. When the time came, Derby was to raise his two counties and those to the north: meantime he was to consult with Delamere, the chief plotter in his area. A meeting took place on 1 November and Delamere seemed highly satisfied with the outcome. It was agreed that Delamere was to rise as soon as the Prince landed, but Derby was to do nothing until he marched away. When the militia was raised, Derby was to send some to protect Delamere's house. The scheme did not work perfectly. Derby's activity was hampered by delay in sending him his commission and a general mobilization of the Lancashire militia was not ordered until 21 November. Both in Lancashire and in the city of Chester, the militia was active in restraining and trying to disband bodies of riotous popish soldiers, but Derby does not seem to have achieved a general mobilization of the Cheshire militia and there were recriminations when Delamere accused him of failing to defend his house. The truth is that Derby's influence in Cheshire was inferior to Delamere's and after the Revolution Delamere secured the lieutenancy of Cheshire for himself. But his benevolent neutrality gave Delamere safety in the rear—just as Bath gave it to William. On 15 November Delamere raised his tenants in Warrington, Manchester and Ashton and from them formed a force which he led off towards the south. He only took those able to provide themselves with a tolerable horse and he promised that if any men were killed, their families should continue on their farms. He was able to encourage them by disclosing that Derby was on their side.[1] So the whig rebelled while the loyal monarchist looked the other way.

Delamere took with him some 250 horse, consisting of gentlemen and tradesmen of good class, able to equip themselves at their own expense. He politely rebuffed the many poorer men who were willing

---

[1] See a memo. in Bentinck's papers, British Museum MSS Egerton 1755, f. 7. Also HMC *Kenyon*, pp. 198–202; HMC *Ormonde*, NS. vol. viii, pp. 10–11; HMC *Le Fleming*, pp. 213, 221–4, 229.

to go as infantry by telling them that the Prince had foot enough but was in need of horse.[1] He marched to Derby, where the Earl of Devonshire had risen and was at the head of 400 horse. Nottingham was the final point of concentration of this groups of rebels.[2] From there they put out on 22 November a resounding whig declaration, setting forth the 'innumerable grievances' by which they had been 'made sensible that the very fundamentals of our liberty, religion and properties are about to be rooted out by our late jesuitical privy council' and calling on 'all good protestants and subjects' not to be 'bugbeared with the opprobrious term of rebels' but to join them in helping the Prince of Orange. The concessions which the King had lately made were dismissed as 'given as plums are to children, but to still the people by deceiving them for a while', and the manifesto ended by dilating on 'the papists' old rule—that faith is not to be kept with heretics'.[3]

But not all the rebels were whigs. In Yorkshire there was a tory rebellion. Again it was aided by the authorities—this time by their sheer myopia and inability, no doubt, to believe that a tory could be a rebel. The plotters were able to use the proclamation of 28 September as an excuse to take up arms themselves![4] Under Danby's inspiration, the Yorkshire gentry asked the King to remove catholics from command in the county. In consequence the Duke of Newcastle was appointed lord lieutenant of all three ridings and all catholics were dismissed from the lieutenancies. Danby assembled horses and retainers at Ribston Hall, which belonged to an important follower, Sir Henry Goodricke. He concerted plans for the tory rising with Devonshire and his whig friends, just as Derby and Delamere concerted their action further west.[5] The Duke of Newcastle expected the invasion to take place in Northumberland and wanted Lumley to be arrested. At the end of October he began to call out the Yorkshire militia, but soon retired to his seat at Welbeck in Nottinghamshire. On hearing that William had landed in the west, he decided that it was only necessary to keep up a foot regiment and two troops of horse out of the militia, for police work round York. He even proposed to resign his colonelcy of the city militia regiment: as a result, Reresby,

---

[1] *ibid.*, p. 222.
[2] HMC *Hastings*, vol. ii, p. 211.
[3] *Ellis Correspondence*, vol. ii, pp. 314–19.
[4] HMC *Lindsey*, pp. 447, 449.
[5] Browning, vol. i, pp. 389–94.

the salaried governor of York, felt obliged to resign the lieutenant-colonelcy and effective command, which he had found a valuable means to 'know opinions'. As it had not prevented him from believing that the city and county continued loyal, he did not perhaps lose much with it. With similar improvidence, Langdale, the governor of Hull, gave up a plan to garrison it with the East Riding militia.

On 13 November greater energy was shown when a meeting of all three lieutenancies at York ordered the assembly of all the militia cavalry. But this was a blind for the next move of the plotters: a further meeting was summoned for the 22nd at which all gentlemen and freeholders were invited to take 'engagements and concurrence' for the defence of the realm. It chanced that a new commission of the peace for the West Riding arrived that day, from which the names of some important men at the meeting were omitted. Reresby thought this a mistake and was fearful of the effect it might have on a score or so of the gentry: it may rather, perhaps, indicate a greater understanding at court of what was afoot. The Duke of Newcastle was sent an invitation to the meeting and in consequence returned to Yorkshire. He showed some understanding of what was going on, for on his arrival at York he told the new sheriff, Sir Richard Graham, that he believed that the object of the meeting was to petition for the calling of parliament. He called his deputy lieutenants together on the 19th to find out their purpose and some of them avowed that a petition was intended. The Duke and Graham both said that they could not join in it, but the only countermove the Duke could think of was to leave York on the evening before the meeting in order to show his disapproval. Reresby could do no better: he merely did not attend.

The meeting took place in the Common Hall at York, with four troops of militia outside to keep the peace. While the petition was being adopted, Mr Tankard (one of the prominent men left out of the West Riding peace commission) ran in and said that the papists had shot at the militia. Everyone ran out and those who were in the know appeared with horses and arms which they had ready. A body of horse under Danby's command (and including Lumley, who had been in hiding) rode up to the militia, who instantly joined them, their captains having been warned the night before. Reresby was placed under arrest, after refusing to join the rising. The company of regulars in the town was captured, as were two more companies on the march from Tynemouth, the magazine was seized and the papists were disarmed. In due course Scarborough Castle was taken and Hull was betrayed by a conspiracy of its protestant officers. At home in Nottinghamshire, the Duke of Newcastle was disarmed by Devonshire's followers, but he managed to issue an order to the militia there to disobey the rebels' instructions to assemble.[1]

James went to his army as the desertions and revolts were gathering momentum. They reached a climax while he was there and effectively broke his will to resist. His demoralization seems to have begun with the defection of his nephew Cornbury. He wrote afterwards that

> it broke the King's measures, dishearten (sic) the other troops and created such a jealousy that each man suspected his neighbour, and in effect rendered the army useless. It also gave encouragement to the country gentlemen to go in to the Prince of Orange, who hitherto had been diffident, especially on what happened to my Lord Lovelace . . . but now not only the discontented party but the trimmers and even many that wished well to the King went in, merely for apprehension; which gave mighty courage to the enemy, who till then were in a despairing way, and hindered many of them from coming over to the king, who otherwise were upon the point of doing it.

James's biographer says that the news surprised the King just as he was going to dinner, and that in consequence he took only a piece of bread and a glass of wine and at once began to consider what to do. Several decisions resulted from this. First, James delayed his departure for the army two or three days in order to 'see peoples' minds settled a little' in London. Next, he called the senior officers in town together, told them 'he had ordered a parliament to meet as soon as things were a little pacified' and 'that he was now resolved to content them in all things relating to their liberties, privileges and religion'. Any who were not 'free and willing to serve him' might resign their commissions and 'go whereever they pleased'

> . . . he looked upon them as men of too much honour to follow my Lord Cornbury's example and was therefore willing to spare them (if they desired it) the discredit of so base a desertion.

They all swore that they would serve him faithfully: Churchill and Grafton in particular.[2]

James's third decision was to send his son to Portsmouth when he

---

[1] HMC 7th report, pp. 412–20. HMC *Lindsey*, pp. 449–50. British Museum Add. MSS. 28053, ff. 353–4, 375. See too Reresby's memoirs and Browning, vol. i, pp. 394–405.

[2] *Life of James II*, vol. ii, pp. 217–19.

left town and to place Lord Dover in command there 'to have him there in order to send away the Prince of Wales for France, if he found things went worse'.[1] Even in September there had been plans for strengthening Portsmouth and placing the Queen and her son there with a large Irish guard in the event of invasion, while the King took command of the army. The moral effect of the Queen and Prince leaving the capital for the coast was likely to be bad: it would look like desertion. Nevertheless, on 11 October the Abbé Rizzini managed to persuade the Queen that it would be the right thing to do. When James took the field, he accordingly began to prepare as well for flight to France. This was calculated to speed his own demoralization. When things got worse, Rizzini played an important part in inducing the King to send his family away and then to follow himself. An agent of the Queen's brother, the Duke of Modena, he also served Louis XIV. Though wishing James to win, Louis would wish him to flee if he could not do so, rather than surrender to the opposition. French policy was always to keep the English King and people divided.[2] Catholics less French-oriented did not agree with Rizzini and the panicky priests who were in accord with him. Terriesi, the Tuscan envoy, thought that the acceptance of asylum in France would be fatal to the dynasty. Ronquillo, the Spanish ambassador, vainly suggested a retreat to his master's territory, as less provocative to English feeling.[3]

James was personally half-beaten by the time that he put himself at the head of his army and his short stay with it was a nightmare. When he reached Salisbury on 19 November, he found it impossible to implement his initial plan of advancing to Axminster, Chard and Lamport, bottling up the Prince in the southwest and using the narrow lanes and 'exceeding great' hedges and ditches to establish a strong defensive position: 'the late treachery had made this impracticable',[4] he says, and of course his initial delay in going down had not made it easier. He could not sleep and for two days was afflicted with nose-

---

[1] *ibid.*, pp. 220, 229. James here dates Dover's appointment from when he went to Salisbury, but the sealed instructions he mentions seem to have been later. Cf. below p. 285.

[2] Mazure, vol. iii, p. 76. Campana de Cavelli, vol. ii, pp. 272, 291. Klopp, vol. iv, pp. 175–6; cf. for Rizzini's later activities, pp. 247–8, 269. From Mazure, vol. iii, pp. 218 sq. it would seem that Barrillon had relatively little knowledge of the royal plans for flight.

[3] Klopp, vol. iv, pp. 236, 252–3, 260–1.

[4] *Life*, vol. ii, p. 222.

bleeding. He had no accurate intelligence of the Prince's movements.[1] On the 22nd he called a council of war at which Feversham argued for a retreat towards London and Churchill for standing firm. James already felt that he had missed the best moment for making a stand and his suspicions of his officers were increasing. He decided on retreat. That night, Churchill and Grafton absconded, and from now on there was a steady trickle of officers across the lines, although few men followed them. The retreat began on the 24th and the army was now falling into increasing disorder.

> Everybody in this hurly-burly was thinking of himself and nobody minded the King who came up to Dr. Radcliffe and asked him what was good for the bleeding of his nose.[2]

James paused for the night at Andover and here Prince George of Denmark and the young Duke of Ormonde, having supped with him, deserted. So too did Lord Drumlanrig, son and heir of the Duke of Queensberry: Scottish tories were evidently behaving in the same way as English. Resignedly James sent the Prince's servants and equipage after him. He posted his army along the Thames, to defend the approaches to the capital from the southwest. On the 26th he reached London, to find that Princess Anne and Lady Churchill had fled. 'God help me,' he cried, 'my own children have forsaken me.'[3]

After this, James ceased to think in terms of resistance to William. Belatedly he adopted the suggestion which the 'loyal opposition' had made to him before he joined his army: to call parliament and come to terms with the invader. Apparently the army officers who remained loyal also demanded a parliament, partly because they did not wish their support of James to be regarded as the reason why parliament was not called.[4] James therefore

> ordered all the lords spiritual and temporal to wait on him at Whitehall in nature of a Great Council, as had been usually practised in such disorderly times, and tho' it was generally observed it scarce ever did any good, however, to take away all objections (and that the lords might not say, had they been called upon by the King, they would have done wonders for him) he assembled them accordingly

[1] Turner, pp. 431–2, brings this out well.
[2] Turner, pp. 430–2.
[3] *Life*, vol. ii, pp. 222–5.
[4] Campana de Cavelli, vol. ii, p. 344.

to the number of nine bishops and thirty or forty peers,[1] on the 27th. He told them that the 'occasion' of the meeting was the petition delivered to him before his departure, which he had not had time to answer. 'He had observed in his journey the general desire of the countries through which he passed was for a parliament.' He had therefore called them together to ask their advice. He noted that not all of them had signed the petition, 'so that he perceived it was not by the general assent of all the peers'. This was indeed the meeting of the petitioners and the rival group around Halifax that Clarendon had tried in vain to bring about. Clarendon and Rochester were in an awkward position. Though they had been disgraced, they were compromised by their former association with the government and they had not made their peace with William. Unless they could win the initiative now, they were threatened with eclipse or worse. But the King had neither listened to them nor proved able to defend his authority: their loyalty had been strained in every possible way. The leading non-petitioners had been in touch with William and this group had nothing to fear from his advance. They could watch the anguish of the petitioners unmoved and safely reinsure themselves by currying favour with the King. The Earl of Oxford, who was the first to speak, said that the petitioners were probably the 'most ready to offer their advice'; he had refused to sign the petition because he knew it would displease the King. Rochester thereupon spoke in favour of calling a parliament and apparently also in favour of negotiating with the Prince of Orange: Jeffreys and Godolphin among others supported him. Clarendon, according to James, 'flew out into an indiscreet and seditious railing, declaiming against popery, exaggerating fears and jealousies, and blaming the King's conduct'. He particularly complained of the raising of a regiment of papists under Lord Stafford and is supposed to have said 'that the King can do no wrong, but his ministers may, and be called to an account for it too' and 'people do now say that the King is run away with his army—we are left defenceless and must therefore side with the prevailing party'. He too wanted a parliament and a treaty with William.

In contrast Halifax and Nottingham 'spoke', James wrote, 'with great respect and seeming concern'. Halifax said he would not petition because he knew it would displease the King and he thought the meeting of parliament 'very impracticable'—though at the same time

[1] *Life*, vol. ii, pp. 238–9.

he would never advise against the meeting of parliament! They gave in effect the same advice as the others, and it was also suggested that preliminary concessions ought to be made, such as a general pardon and the dismissal of all the papists. The King at the end said that he had decided to call a parliament but that he would 'take one night's time' to consider the other proposals. Next day writs were ordered for a parliament on 15 January and a proclamation soon came out which promised free elections and immunity for all peers and members of the commons and to this end granted a general pardon. On the 30th the *Gazette* announced that Halifax, Nottingham and Godolphin were to treat with William on the King's behalf. Sir Edward Hales was replaced as Governor of the Tower by his protestant prisoner, Bevil Skelton.[1] This was James's nearest approach to a general dismissal of papists.

William advanced methodically and put off seeing the royal commissioners until he was at Hungerford in Berkshire: he arrived there on 7 December. By the time that he did see them, James's authority in the country had been reduced to something mainly honorific. In effect he had capitulated to William and by so doing he legitimized the rebellion. Since King and Prince were to be friends again, there was no reason why loyal men should not rally to the Prince. By giving up the fight (and hinting that he intended to flee), James further speeded the process of desertion which he had encouraged by his earlier failure to heed loyal counsellors. Clarendon took the calling of parliament and the intended proclamation to mean that it was no longer treasonable to resort to the Prince of Orange: especially as the Prince was then passing through Wiltshire, the very county where Clarendon needed to go in order to promote his son's election to parliament. He rushed off to make his peace, getting in ahead of Halifax who had refused to join the embassy to William unless Rochester was excluded.[2] 'We could devise no means to prevent that utter ruin of his majesty but our applying to his highness', wrote Bishop Turner of the Hydes and their frenids.[3]

Right across England there was something like a dissolution of government, though not of ordered society since the lead of the

[1] *Clarendon Correspondence*, vol. ii, pp. 208–12. *Life of James II*, vol. ii, pp. 238–40.
[2] Ashley, p. 169.
[3] R. A. Beddard, 'The loyalist opposition in the Interregnum: a letter of Dr Francis Turner, Bishop of Ely, on the Revolution of 1688', *Bulletin of the Institute of Historical Research*, vol. xl (1967), p. 106.

propertied class was unquestioned. The Revolution was to this extent in the spirit of Locke. Bristol, reported by the lord-lieutenant to be overwhelmingly hostile to the royal authorities, rallied to William as James was retiring east.[1] Princess Anne, escorted by Bishop Compton, joined the rebels at Nottingham. By William's advice they marched to Oxford, arriving on 15 December. The midlands rose to join them—in some places the rebels called out the militia. Eventually there was a little army 1,500 strong and including fifteen noblemen, though by its leaders' confession its military value was slight. Many had joined it only to protect the Princess and refused to have anything to do with rebellion.[2] Lumley meanwhile secured the county of Durham,[3] and Sir John Lowther and his friends established a strict watch in Cumberland and Westmorland and adopted a petition for the meeting of parliament.[4] In Norfolk there were great meetings at Norwich and King's Lynn at which the lieutenancy, militia officers and corporation likewise called for a free parliament.[5]

The Revolution had been accomplished by William invading, the whigs rebelling and the tories deserting. All had joined the movement in the end, though for different reasons; there was no civil war. William had made a revolution without having to commit himself to the revolutionary party or revolutionary ideology. Should he eventually be given control of the government, there was a fair chance now that it would be done within the existing constitutional framework and by incontestably legal means; likewise that he would have the support of the royalist party, not to speak of the possibility of playing off the parties against each other. The Revolution might have ended the career of James, but it had not made a strong monarchy impossible.

[1] Baxter, *William III*, pp. 239 and 431 n. 27.
[2] *e.g.* Lord Chesterfield. There may have been 5,000 at the end. Carpenter, pp. 132–9. HMC 2nd report, p. 16; 3rd report, p. 259. HMC *Leeds*, p. 27. HMC *Le Fleming*, pp. 224, 229. HMC *Various*, vol. viii, pp. 67–8. *Hatton Correspondence* (Camden Society, 1878), vol. ii, pp. 115–17, 120–1.
[3] Browning, vol. i, p. 416.
[4] HMC *Le Fleming*, pp. 223 *et seq.*
[5] HMC *Lothian* (*Blickling*), pp. 133–5.

9

The Quest for a Lawful Ruler

EVEN when he had avowed his inability to fight William, James was by no means finished. His deposition had not figured among the professed objects of the invasion and certainly was not contemplated by a good many of those who rallied to the Prince. Churchill, after joining him, rather absurdly told Clarendon 'that he would never be ungrateful to the King; that he would venture his life in defence of his person; and that he had never left him but that he saw our religion and country were in danger of being destroyed'.[1] Danby late in life confessed that he had been

> but a rebel, and if King James had taken me, I merited losing my head. I acted not then out of principle but as I thought as *se defendendo*, imagining all at stake.[2]

Claiming no right for the subject to depose his rulers, he seems at first to have hoped to hold a balance between the King and William. In the exclusion debates at the start of the decade the whigs had failed to dispose of the tory argument that if a lawful ruler was set aside, confusion was bound to follow. Even in the Convention of 1689 they proposed the removal of James only in the most circumspect way. If James had possessed his brother's capacity for waiting on events, the difficulty of doing without him might well have afforded means for his preservation. But James chose to exploit his position in a more impetuous way. He had always believed more firmly than anyone else that the alternative to monarchy was chaos. He therefore fled, expecting that anarchy

---

[1] *Clarendon Correspondence*, vol. ii, p. 214. For the confusion in men's minds, cf. Oxford who told Clarendon 'he did not think of making this journey, when we were together with the King'. 5 December, p. 216.
[2] Ailesbury, vol. ii, p. 621.

would result and that his subjects would soon call him back on their knees. This was an absurd caricature of the perfectly rational monarchist philosophy. James's flight completed his ruin and made possible a modest triumph for whig principles. Support for the legitimate ruler ceased to seem the surest way to preserve society—James had behaved too outrageously to be credible as a restorer of order and the general wish was that he should never return. The ruling class looked for preservation to their own efforts and to William. The Prince and not the King was the indispensable man and that was why the Convention's continuing doubts about deposing James were overcome. William had at first restrained the whigs, but after the flight of James he helped them. He was convinced that he needed to be king if stability was to be restored and his influence was decisive with the Convention. The whigs were able to give effect to their belief that in extreme cases a king might be deposed, but they were able to do so thanks only to princely patronage. They were junior partners to William in 1689 just as some of them had been to Sunderland in 1687-8. The gains of William in 1689 were decidedly more solid than theirs.

(I)

James's behaviour after his capitulation must not be seen as entirely rational—panic is more in evidence than guile. His wife and son seem to have been his first concern. The compiler of his *Life* says that after Anne's desertion he 'turned his whole attention' to how to 'save' them with 'most security and secrecy' and that when it was clear that the whole country was in revolt, he decided to send his son abroad.[1] It was on 25 November at Andover that he gave Lord Dover verbal orders to take command at Portsmouth in the absence of Berwick and a letter, to be used if the occasion arose, directing Dartmouth to follow his directions concerning the baby prince. Orders to Dartmouth on the 29th (confirmed on 1 December) required him to help Dover send the child to France. ''Tis my son they aim at, and 'tis my son I must endeavour to preserve,' he said, 'whatsoever become of me.'

The execution of these orders was frustrated by the fact that the fleet had as good as deserted to William. Churchill's brother took his ship over and the plotters who remained sent Lieut. Byng to the

---

[1] *Life*, vol. ii, pp. 229, 233. As to the moment of decision, p. 229 notes, the King cried out like David 'O if my enemies only had cursed me, I could have borne it.'

Prince. Byng met him in Dorset at the end of November and came back with a letter to be delivered in due season to Dartmouth. That officer did not dare to order a pursuit of Churchill and on 28 November he wrote to James that there had been 'a great alteration in most people's faces' because 'the daily impressions they receive make them stand amazed. For God's sake, Sir, call your great council and see which way a parliament may best be called', he went on, promising that 'you will soon have the thanks and approbation of your whole fleet, with assurances of standing by Your Majesty in it'. The letter was not sent until after the news had arrived that parliament was to be called. On 1 December a council of war was told of it and sent up an address of thanks to the King. Dartmouth reported on the same day 'it is no small endeavour I am put to make them in good humour' and for the present they were in no state to fight the Dutch. Nor were Dartmouth and his officers in the least prepared to allow the spiriting away of James's son. In a most interesting letter to the King he gave four reasons against it that by implication make up a whole political programme. First, it would be 'treason to your Majesty and the known laws of the Kingdom'. Second, it would play into the hands of those who had challenged the child's legitimacy. Third, it would show such distrust of his subjects that they would probably 'throw off their bounden allegiance to you' whereas 'I do not despair', but that otherwise they 'will yet stand by you, in the defence and right of your lawful successor'. Lastly, sending the Prince of Wales out of the country, which 'without the consent of the nation, is at no time advisable', would be terrible if he was sent to France for it would give that country a perpetual temptation to invade England. The letter emphasized the loyalty of Church of England men and said that it should be 'the prayer of every honest loyal subject' that the young prince be brought up in that faith. Dartmouth suited action to these remarkable words, and when the conspirators under his command reported that the child was to be secretly removed, he ordered—by their own account they 'obliged' him to—a close watch to prevent it. James replied noncommittally to Dartmouth's protest and the baby was brought back to London.[1] In the small hours of 10 December the Queen crept off with him, embarking at Gravesend. She made good her escape to France, where Louis at once ordered her to be taken under his protection and came out to St Germains to meet her.

[1] Dalrymple, vol. ii, pt. i, bk. vi, pp. 231–4, 243–8. Powley, pp. 122–41.

As soon as he came up to the Prince of Wales, taking him in his arms he made him a short speech, wherein he promised him both protection and succour, and then going on to the Queen, he left nothing unsaid which might mollify her present sufferings and encourage the hopes of a speedy redress.[1]

James himself set out very early on 11 December on much the same route as his wife and son. He was intercepted and obliged to return, but it was soon deemed more prudent to allow him to set off again. He fled partly because he was afraid for his own safety. He told the meeting of lords on 27 November

> that it would appear that the Prince of Orange came for the crown, whatever he pretended; but that he would not see himself deposed; that he had read the story of King Richard II.[2]

On the day of the Queen's departure he was notified by the commissioners sent to negotiate with William of the terms on which the Prince would end hostilities: they did not go much beyond what he had offered and in no way made him William's prisoner. Nor did they, as Halifax had warned him they might, seek to limit his prerogative of dissolution.[3] But, he later wrote,

> seeing no security where he was and well remembering how the King his father and several of his predecessors had been used on like occasions, he was resolved never to consent to those mean things which would have been imposed upon him, and saw plainly by the Prince of Orange's answer which he received that night that nothing but the crown would satisfy his ambitious nephew and son-in-law.[4]

After being captured on his flight he declared in scriptural vein that he might fall a sacrifice, 'for I repent that I gave my daughter unto him, for he sought to slay me'.[5] Just before his second flight he told Ailesbury 'if I do not retire, I shall certainly be sent to the Tower, and no king ever went out of that place but to his grave'.[6] He had appealed both to the City and to the bishops to guarantee his personal safety, but without result.[7] Other notable reasons for his flight were the wishes of the Queen[8] and the collapse of his limited mental powers in face of a situation too unusual for them to cope with. He did not

[1] *Life of James II*, vol. ii, p. 248.
[2] *Clarendon Correspondence*, vol. ii, p. 211.
[3] Turner, pp. 441–2. Cf. below p. 292.   [4] *Life*, vol. ii, p. 249.
[5] Baxter, *William III*, p. 242 and p. 431 nn. 31, 32.
[6] Ailesbury, vol. i, p. 224.   [7] *Life*, vol. ii, pp. 271–2.
[8] The *Life*, vol. ii, pp. 244–5, defends her and says that her only wish was that they might not be separated.

know whom to trust or how to inspire loyalty. As he said to Ailesbury before his first departure

> My daughter hath deserted me, my army also, and him that I raised from nothing the same, on whom I heaped all favours [Churchill]; and if such betrays me, what can I expect from those I have done so little for? I know not who to speak to or who to trust.[1]

The crass materialism of this religious man, deriving from stupidity, is nowhere better brought out.

Nevertheless, there was a definite political strategy working in his mind. Immediately after his decision to summon parliament, he told Barrillon that it would give him a breathing space of seven weeks to make himself safe: he only promised to do nothing against the interests of Louis, but a day or two later he said that the negotiation with William was only to gain time to place his wife and son in safety. When that was done, he would take refuge in Ireland, Scotland—or France. The extreme catholics such as Melfort urged him to flee: they could not safely stay themselves and early in December they surreptitiously departed to avoid protestant vengeance. It was they who argued that a government established by William would be weak and quoted historical precedents for English kings who went into exile but returned in triumph. Hamilton and Tyrconnel offered him refuge in Scotland and Ireland respectively—the former told him to bring no catholics. Protestant courtiers and officials like Middleton, Preston, Halifax and Godolphin, with the moderate catholic Belasyse, wanted him to trust himself to the parliament that he was calling and believed that he was in no personal danger.[2]

Before he left, James tried to make it impossible for government to continue lawfully, in his name, when he had gone. Some days in advance he made the lord chancellor come and reside in the palace, so that he could always lay his hands on the Great Seal. When the moment came, he burned all the writs that had not been sent out for the summoning of parliament, annulled formally those which had, and dropped the Seal in the Thames. On 10 December likewise he wrote to his military and naval commanders, telling them that he had sent away his wife and son for their safety and was withdrawing himself, since by the admission of both of them, their forces were no longer to be relied on. 'If I could have relied upon all my troops,' he told

---

[1] Ailesbury, vol. i, p. 195.   [2] Turner, pp. 435–6, 440–1.

Feversham, 'I might not have been put to this extremity I am in, and would at least have had one blow for it.' To Dartmouth he declared that though 'resolved to venture all rather than consent to anything in the least prejudicial to the crown or my conscience', he found it wisest 'to withdraw till this violent storm is over'. 'This I must say,' he ended, 'never any prince took more care of his sea and land men as I have done, and been so very ill repaid by them.' Dartmouth's orders were that any units of the fleet still 'free' to serve him should go to Ireland and put themselves under the orders of Tyrconnel. Rather in contrast he thanked Feversham 'and all those officers and soldiers who have stuck to me and been truly loyal'. He hoped they would remain so and while not exposing 'yourselves by resisting a foreign army and poisoned nation' yet keep 'free from associations and such pernicious things'. Dartmouth had already taken another course by the time the letter to him arrived, but Feversham interpreted the one to him, apparently correctly, as an invitation to disband his force, which he did. This was not only a threat to public order but it was also calculated to deprive William of troops that he might hope to use in his continental schemes. William was very angry and when Feversham came within his reach, he had him arrested—one of his few lapses from tact.[1] When James was brought back to London after this initial attempt at flight he boasted to Barrillon that

> The Prince of Orange . . . will find himself very much embarrassed what form of government to establish. The meeting of a parliament cannot be authorized without writs under the great seal . . . the great seal is *missing* . . . All this will create difficulties and incidents, which afford me occasion to take suitable measures.[2]

The flight of James did eventually win him a little support, but it was the whigs who were really helped by it. Before he left, the whigs, especially the outlaws who had come over with William, were pressing for radical and even arbitrary measures to set up a new government but only to be rebuffed by the tories and by William too. Soon after he joined the Prince, Clarendon was told by Abingdon that

> he feared we should be disappointed in our expectations, for he did not like things at all; that he was resolved to keep to his principles, and not join with what, he saw, was aiming at. He said, he did not like Wildman's and

---

[1] For the above see *Life*, vol. ii, pp. 249–51; Baxter, *William III*, pp. 241–2, 431 n. 30.

[2] Mazure, vol. iii, p. 264. James said all England was in arms and a fisherman had taken possession of Dover Castle like Massaniello in Naples.

Ferguson's being in the Prince's train; nor several other persons, who, he found, were of their principles, whatever they pretended.

Clarendon found that Burnet would not pray for the King in church and denied that there could be a treaty between King and Prince: 'the sword is drawn: there is a supposititious child which must be inquired into'.[1] Sir John Hotham and William Harbord opposed 'the meeting of the parliament which was summoned' since because of their absence abroad 'they could not expect to be chosen if they had not time to go down into their countries; as if it could not be a good parliament in case those gentlemen were not in it'. Harbord 'said, he had drawn his sword against the King; that he had no need of his pardon; but they would bring the King to ask pardon of them for the wrongs he had done'. This talk Clarendon called 'seditious': it was clearly different in his mind from what he himself was doing. But it was nothing compared to what he heard on his return to London from Pollexfen, who had been counsel for the seven bishops and was soon to be a judge. This was after the King's first attempt at flight and Pollexfen said that

he had made a cession and forfeited his right; that his being now at Faversham, though he should come back to London, signified not a rush; that the Prince of Orange had nothing to do but in the head of his army to declare himself King and presently to issue out writs for the calling a parliament according to Cromwell's model; which, he said, was a far more equal way of election than the old constitution.[2]

Respecting the proposed agreement between James and William, Sir Robert Howard told Halifax that no 'accommodation' would be endured, for there was no room left for trust, and everything must be built upon new foundations. He wrote to William 'by the advice of some considerable persons here, whose interest in the city and parliament will be very great' to warn him that any delay in his advance would depress his sympathizers who

only fix upon hopes of remedy by the total change of persons; judging it the greatest folly to graft anything upon the old stock; taught by too sad experience that the difference of religion makes it irreconcilable to trust though but the name of power with it; for all limitations of power are but notions that may be raised to interupt or hinder that blessing to us all, which nothing but mistakes of such a nature can now prevent.[3]

[1] *Clarendon Correspondence*, vol. ii, pp. 216–18.
[2] *Clarendon Correspondence*, vol. ii, pp. 219, 225–6.
[3] Dalrymple, vol. ii, bk. v/vi, pp. 254–6. Cf. Foxcroft, vol. ii, p. 20 n. 3.

Sir Robert Howard was to take a leading part in the debates of the Convention and in drumming up support for William within and outside it. The motley personality of this whig parliamentary leader deserves a moment's attention. Son of the Earl of Berkshire, he had fought bravely for the King in the civil wars. Though Dryden was his brother-in-law, his attempts to win fame as a poet and dramatist had been unsuccessful. Since 1673 he had been auditor of the receipt in the exchequer, doing little work and blackmailing clerks who misused the balances in their hands instead of bringing them to justice. His profits had enabled him to build a fine country house. The most whiggish thing about him was perhaps the hatred felt for him by Danby.[1]

William would have nothing to do with plans to set up government by force or to claim the crown by right of conquest ratified afterwards by parliament. A memorandum by Burnet apparently dating from this time may well have appealed to him if he saw it. Burnet thought that the only choice was between 'suspension' and 'deposition' of James, William becoming regent in the one case and King in the other. He tried to weigh objectively the relative merits of each course and argued that William would have a more solid legal position if he was made King. But deposition would give more offence and 'may seem to subject the crown too much to the people'.[2] William sided with those who wished to avoid such a break in the continuity of government. At Hungerford, where he treated with the royal commissioners, there assembled not merely the notables who had accompanied or joined him but also some of the northern leaders as well: Macaulay may be right in suggesting that he chose this place because the leaders of all those who had rallied to his cause could get to it. He asked the commissioners to put what they had been told to say to him in writing and referred the resulting paper to the lords and gentlemen with him, who were to advise him as to the answer. A great meeting was held with Lord Oxford in the chair. The commissioners' instructions were to arrange an armistice with William that would allow the free and unhindered assembling of the parliament that James had called. The whigs at the meeting, however, demanded that the writs for the calling of parliament should be superseded—in effect, that James's proposal of an armistice should be rejected. Tories and moderates like

---

[1] *Dictionary of National Biography*. Baxter, *Treasury*, pp. 127, 153–4, 164–6, 181–2.
[2] R. W. Blencowe, ed., *Diary of . . . Henry Sidney* (1843), vol. ii, pp. 288–91. Undated, but Burnet speaks of the flight of James as a possibility.

Shrewsbury opposed this but it was carried by a majority. A delegation representing both points of view carried the draft reply to the
Prince and argued the case before him. He sided against the majority
and referred the draft back to the meeting. To Sir Henry Capel who
had put the whig view, he said 'we may drive away the King; but,
perhaps, we may not know how easily to come by a parliament'. Next
day, 9 December, the meeting reconvened and reaffirmed its decision.
Again the issue was debated before the Prince by a deputation and
this time he flatly overruled the meeting.[1] It is evident that he wanted
an undoubtedly lawful parliament, the measures of which would
have a lasting authority which revolutionary acts would not possess.
The terms which the commissioners carried back to James were that
the rival armies should keep at least forty miles distant from the
capital where parliament was to meet; that the Tower and Tilbury fort
should be entrusted to the City and Portsmouth to a commander
acceptable to both Prince and King; that all persons holding office
without legal qualification should be dismissed; that no French troops
should be brought in and that William's army should be paid for by
England.[2] James had empowed the commissioners to agree to the
removal of troops from the capital and so on the face of it uncle and
nephew were very near agreement on how to end hostilities.

By running away, however, James more or less forced William and
the tory leaders to fall in with the whig policy and a new government
forthwith began to be set up. William saw at once that authority might
pass to him by default. This was a simple solution to the problem of
making a viable political settlement and he was pleased. He was at
Abingdon when the news reached him and he at once abandoned the
intention of going to Oxford, the main rallying point of the rebels,
and turned towards London. Clarendon noted that 'he was very cheerful, and could not conceal his satisfaction at the King's being gone'.[3]
In London Rochester and Turner, Bishop of Ely, had persuaded Sancroft a few days earlier to convene a meeting of peers at the Guildhall
in the event of James's flight, to 'take upon them the government for the
preservation of the kingdom and this great City'. This assumption of

---

[1] *Clarendon Correspondence*, vol. ii, pp. 219–23.
[2] *Life of James II*, vol. ii, pp. 240–1. Additional instructions had allowed the commissioners to concede the removal of the army from the capital, save for guards, Ashley,
p. 170. The reply conceded the guards and asked for the disarming of catholics and the
ending of measures against William's supporters.
[3] *Clarendon Correspondence*, vol. ii, p. 224.

power duly took place, for 'we had otherwise been a state of banditti'. The originators of the scheme took the lead in drafting an address from the meeting to William. They tried to avoid giving a revolutionary objective to their proceedings. The Prince was to be asked to secure the meeting of a free parliament to enact 'effectual securities for our religion and laws' so that the King might be called back 'with honour and safety'. But the draft was sharply criticized by some of the peers at the meeting, notably by old Lord Wharton who had been a parliamentary leader during the civil wars. Expressions of loyalty in it were cut out.[1] The City produced addresses of their own and went further than the lords by actually inviting William to town. When the addresses reached William, 'he seemed much pleased with those that came from the City, but not at all with that from the lords'. Meanwhile, the armed forces, deserted by their sovereign, placed themselves under William's orders. The army officers in London met and agreed to submit to him and to keep their troops together for the preservation of order. The plotters in the fleet decided that the moment had come to give Dartmouth the Prince's letter (written on 29 November) inviting his adhesion and Dartmouth at once wrote to him (on the 12th) putting the fleet at his disposal and promising to remove all papists from command and to do his best to resist any French forces that appeared. He declared himself confident that the Prince would show the

> utmost regard and tenderness to the person and safety of the King my master, whose just commands all his majesty's subjects (but men of honour especially, under his commission and pay) are bound to execute; and among that number, I held myself very particularly obliged, but to my great amazement (which I cannot but tell your highness, with great confusion and grief of heart) I understand just this moment that his majesty hath sent away the Queen and Prince of Wales (contrary not only to my advices, but earnest endeavours to prevent) and is resolved to withdraw himself, which (on a firm belief of your highness's just duty and care of him) I cannot apprehend his majesty can have any reason to do, otherwise than that he is not willing to be a witness of, or consent to, what the laws and a free parliament (which myself and the fleet addressed for 11 or 12 days ago) shall inflict on his evil advisers . . .[2]

[1] See Beddard, 'Loyalist opposition', pp. 101–9 and his articles on 'The Guildhall declaration of 11 December 1688 and the counter revolution of the loyalists', *Historical Jol.*, vol. xi (1968), pp. 403–20; 'The violent party—the Guildhall revolutionaries and the growth of opposition to James II', *Guildhall Miscellany*, vol. iii (1969–70), pp. 120–36.

[2] Powley, pp. 143–5. Dartmouth wrote to James and explained frankly what he had done and why. He was especially pained that James had not at least taken refuge on

The lords in London sent instructions to the fleet, replaced Skelton by Lucas in control of the Tower, and did their best to preserve quiet. But effective control was steadily passing to William. On the 14th he reached Windsor. Churchill and Grafton set about bringing the disintegrating English army under his control. On the 16th he sent Dartmouth orders to bring the fleet round to the Nore[1] and this was eventually done. On the 12th he had told Danby that the situation had so improved that he could dismiss most of his force: the gentry would be better employed in preparing to stand for parliament, 'keeping their inclinations for me'.[2] This was the end of Danby's attempt to make himself an independent power, but William surely wrote as he did not to bring this about but because he now felt confident that there was no longer any rival to his influence.

The only thing that James gained at this stage by promoting anarchy was that his own flight was stopped by it. He fell into the hands of, in effect, a mob. In a moment of shrewdness he said afterwards 'the Prince of Orange would much rather that I had gone away'.[3] Loyalists could no longer justify their rallying to William by saying that their lawful ruler was not to be found. Burnet said, 'it was foolishly done of those who stopped him at Faversham; and that his coming back to Whitehall would very much disturb things'.[4] Sancroft ceased to attend the meeting of lords as soon as he heard that James had not left the country and, on hearing from James, the lords felt obliged to have him escorted back to town. James returned to his capital on the evening of 16 December and received a tremendous reception as he passed through the City. This showed that there was indeed much in the idea that the nation felt it could not do without him: it was the sort of return, 'liker a day of triumph than humiliation', as he wrote,[5] that he had probably counted on gaining in the end by his retirement. He hastened to prove his value by calling the privy council together and giving instructions for the restoration of order.[6] He was very angry indeed with the lords who, by undertaking this task in his absence,

his fleet: 'this looks like so great mistrust of me that many can witness it hath almost broke my heart.' 'I hope all will end in Your Majesty's happy re-establishment.' Dalrymple, vol. ii, pt. i, bk. vi, pp. 248–9.
[1] Powley, 152, and generally chs. vi and vii.
[2] Browning, *Danby*, vol. ii, p. 152, n. 1.
[3] Mazure, vol. iii, p. 264.
[4] *Clarendon Correspondence*, vol. ii, p. 227.   [5] *Life*, vol. ii, p. 262.
[6] Turner, pp. 449–50.

had given credence to the idea that kings could be done without. 'You were all kings when I left London' was his irritated greeting to Ailesbury when, after 'great dangers' he had reached him at Faversham.[1]

Embarrassing though James's return was, the effects of his flight could not be undone. Even the loyalists could not simply return to their allegiance after such outrageous behaviour—nor was James helped by foolish way in which the catholics came out of hiding on his return and thronged to court. Sir Henry Sheres, surveyor of the ordnance and a later Jacobite, wrote to Dartmouth 'I cannot say but that I now wish the King had not come back.'[2] Many were converted to the view that the King's departure amounted to a cession of the crown which could not be undone. Clarendon was shocked to find that Lloyd, Bishop of St Asaph, was such a convert.[3] But the unconverted were hardly preaching orthodox royalism. Lloyd, endeavouring to win over his brother Turner of Ely found

> that now he believed his majesty was willing to do all that could be required of him, and even to be reduced to the state of a Duke of Venice, committing all the power of war and peace and of making all officers ecclessiastical and civil to the Prince for his lifetime; or that he would consent to bills in parliament for that purpose and to all other bills that should be offered for the security of religion and civil rights.[4]

Almost all the prominent people who had not already rallied to William did so on James's return. Notably this was the case with Halifax, who had come back from his mission to Hungerford to find the King gone and had thereupon joined the provisional council of peers. He considered that he had been duped by James and wanted nothing more to do with him. A sceptical theoretician in politics who preferred the weighing of arguments to action and decision and who always played safe, the Trimmer had opposed exclusion and held aloof from the making of the Revolution. But in 1689 he was to side firmly with the whigs in the debate on the future of the monarchy, to offer the crown to William and Mary on behalf of the Convention and to be William's counsellor and leading minister. His political evolu-

---

[1] Ailesbury, vol. i, p. 202. But Bishop Turner claimed on the contrary that James approved of what had been done. Beddard, 'Loyalist opposition', p. 107.
[2] Baxter, *William III*, pp. 245, 431 n. 2.
[3] *Clarendon Correspondence*, vol. ii, p. 228.
[4] Dalrymple, vol. ii, pt. i, bk. vi, pp. 252–4.

tion is the clearest sign that the watchword for the prudent man was now limited revolution not loyalty at any price.

William thus retained and consolidated his new position of leadership on James's return. He took it upon himself to refer both the future of James and the future of the country to the consideration of the notables who had adhered to him. When they gave him whiggish advice, he did not reject it as he had at Hungerford. It came from more widely representative gatherings and was more likely to command general assent. It is evident that William hoped to keep James out of the picture. While on his way back to London, James sent Feversham to William to invite him to the capital. William arrested Feversham and sent a message back asking James not to go to London but stay where he was, at Rochester. James, however, had already set out again when the message arrived. On 17 December William summoned a meeting of all the peers at Windsor to advise him as to what should be done about the King's return. Delamere, Macclesfield and Stamford were for putting him in the Tower and Delamere later said 'he did not look upon him as his King'. This was rejected (and William afterwards said that Mary would never have stood for it). But all were opposed to his going to one of his own houses and 'would not do anything that might look like treating him as a friend'. Clarendon, who came late, objected to this, but it is striking that he 'said it would bear a debate whether the King should be left at liberty', He is said to have wanted him sent to Breda: he wanted a hostage for his friends the Irish protestants. The final decision was that James should go to Ham, the large luxury residence that Lauderdale had built on the Thames. The Prince accepted this decision. He had not been present at the meeting and he made three of the lords carry its verdict to the King, but he gave orders himself for some of his troops to go and take over the guard at Whitehall. James was awakened in the middle of the night by the deputation: he asked to go to Rochester instead of to Ham and this was referred to William, who agreed.[1] In this the motive of uncle and nephew alike was to allow a second flight by James and he duly set off for France on the 23rd. William entered London on the 18th, the day that James left it. On the 20th he summoned all the peers in town to meet him next day, when he asked them 'to advise

---

[1] Dorothy H. Somerville, *The King of Hearts: Charles Talbot, Duke of Shrewsbury* (Allen and Unwin, 1952), pp. 50–1. *Clarendon Correspondence*, vol. ii, pp. 228–30, 286–7. *Life of James II*, vol. ii, pp. 265–7.

the best manner how to pursue the ends of my declaration in calling a free parliament'.[1] The peers agreed to meet next day in the house of lords with lawyers to advise them. The Prince also invited all who had sat in the commons in Charles II's reign, together with a deputation from the City, to meet him on the 26th. Both gatherings invited him to assume charge of the civil administration and summon a convention—in effect, a parliament, but not so called because not summoned by royal command. On the 28th he agreed and so the government passed into his keeping.

But James, having helped William by his original desertion, managed by his second flight to make it harder for William to establish himself firmly. The original flight had looked like a wilful attempt to cause confusion, but the second flight appeared to have been forced upon him and motivated by fear—as to some extent it was. James was in such a state of collapse by this time that it is impossible to know what he would have done had he been left alone. Probably he would have fled again anyway. His friendly reception in London does not seem to have altered his feeling that he was unpopular and in danger and he said that he would have taken William's advice not to return there if it had reached him in time.[2] The fact remained that his capital had been seized by foreign troops and he had been peremptorily ordered to leave. In his last letter home, Barrillon reported that the Prince commanded in London as in a camp and the English troops murmured at their supercession. On 19 December Clarendon wrote:

> It is not to be imagined what a damp there was upon all sorts of men throughout the town. The treatment the King had met with from the Prince of Orange and the manner of his being driven, as it were, from Whitehall, with such circumstances, moved compassion even in those who were not very fond of him. Several of the English army, both officers and soldiers, began to murmur.[3]

Burnet's view was not very different. James was able in his memoirs to record a considerable number of defections from the army[4] though most of the civil and military servants of the government hung on. One noted on the 29th how

[1] Horwitz, p. 66.
[2] *Life of James II*, vol. ii, pp. 261–3, 265. *Clarendon Correspondence*, vol. ii, p. 229. Mazure, vol. iii, p. 288.
[3] *Clarendon Correspondence*, vol. ii, p. 231; cf. p. 234 n. 3.
[4] *Life*, vol. ii, p. 268.

The Prince is very unwilling to break any one regiment; so that he must have farther work ere long for them. I know not what will be my lot but I am vain enough to think, in a general bustle I shall shift for one . . . [1]

Leading men of tory views had a chance before James's final departure to beg him to behave responsibly and stay. Bishop Turner sent Dr Brady, whom we have met before, to try and persuade him. Clarendon had the good idea of sending an 'honest Roman catholic' for this purpose and a Mr Belson was dispatched. The answers which James made to such entreaties were calculated very much to embarrass tories who hoped to work with William. Secretary Middleton went down by arrangement on the 19th to describe the Prince's arrival and told him that he was sure

that if his majesty went out of the kingdom, the door would immediately-be shut upon him; however in conclusion owned, there could be no safety for him to stay, and that no reasonable and thinking man could advise him to venture it. [2]

'I call God to witness I had no design of retiring.' James told Ailesbury just before his departure. 'I declare to you that I retire for the security of my person, and I shall always be in a readiness to return when my subjects' eyes may be opened.' When the Convention met, Ailesbury made use of this remark, as was intended, to canvass for James among the lords and for some it seems to have been decisive. [3] Others had drawn their conclusions already; Sancroft was persuaded on the 22nd by the Hydes, Turner and White that he should attend the emergency assembly of peers, but when the King fled he changed his mind. [4]

At his departure James left behind a paper for Middleton that was to be his manifesto. 'The world cannot wonder,' he said, at his withdrawing a second time, after his ambassador Feversham had been arrested contrary to the law of nations, his palace surrounded by foreign guards and he himself bidden to be gone from it by an order given him past midnight when he was in bed. What protection could he expect from a man guilty of 'the greatest aspersion upon me that malice could invent' (concerning his son), who had caused 'so general

[1] *Ellis Correspondence*, vol. ii, p. 376.
[2] *Life of James II*, vol. ii, pp. 270–1. *Clarendon Correspondence*, vol. ii, pp. 232–3.
[3] Ailesbury, vol. i, pp. 224, 229, 232–3.
[4] *Clarendon Correspondence*, vol. ii, pp. 233–4.

a defection in my army as well as in the nation' by making 'me appear as black as Hell to my own people as well as to all the world besides?'

I was born free and desire to continue so; and tho' I have ventured my life very frankly on several occasions for the good and honour of my country, and am as free to do it again (and which I hope I shall yet do, as old as I am, to redeem it from the slavery it is like to fall under) yet I think it not convenient to expose myself to be secured so as not to be at liberty to effect it, and for that reason do withdraw, but so as to be within call when the nation's eyes shall be opened so as to see how they have been abused and imposed upon by the specious pretences of Religion and property. I hope it will please God to touch their hearts out of his infinite mercy and to make them sensible of the ill condition they are in and bring them to such a temper that a legal parliament may be called, and that amongst other things which may be necessary to be done, they will agree to a liberty of conscience for all protestant dissenters; and that those of my own persuasion may be so far considered and have such a share of it, as they may live peaceable and quietly, as Englishmen and Christians ought to do, and not be obliged to transplant themselves, which would be very grievous, especially to such as love their country; and I appeal to all who are considering men and have had experience whether anything can make this nation so great and flourishing as liberty of conscience, some of our neighbours dread it . . .[1]

When the lords met the day after James left, Godolphin prevented the reading of this declaration by saying that 'it would give them no satisfaction'. 'Most men,' continued Clarendon, 'believed that lord true to the King's interest (which I confess I did not) and therefore acquiesced in what he said.' On the 29th the paper appeared in print and Clarendon studied it with Lloyd and Turner. Clarendon and Turner were 'moved', but Lloyd said 'it was a jesuitical masterpiece'.[2] Either way James had managed to put the future of the provisional government a little in doubt—it could not hope for unanimous acceptance.

(II)

James, by the cumulative effect of his journeyings, had removed himself from the scene, but not in such a way that he could incontrovertibly be said to have abdicated. It was therefore clear there must be a new government but unclear and contentious how far James's rights might be disregarded in setting one up. James had managed to

---

[1] *Life*, vol. ii, pp. 273–5.
[2] *Clarendon Correspondence*, vol. ii, pp. 235, 237.

that extent to undo the consensus created by his first flight. As at the time of the exclusion controversy, there were differences, especially but not solely between whigs and tories, as to the extent to which he might be set aside. Each group believed its own view to be the most conservative, the most likely to promote stability. The debate was already beginning when the peers met on 22 December to advise the Prince how to come by a free parliament. How could there be a lawful parliament which every one would accept unless it was called by the King? The fiercer whigs raised anew the cry for an arbitrary solution: convening a parliament under the provisions of the repealed triennial act of 1641 or having William claim the crown by right of conquest. But the peers were split down the middle even by the suggestion that they should sign the Association in defence of the Prince originally set going by the tory Sir Edward Seymour at Exeter. Nottingham explained at length that he believed it to be inconsistent with his oath of allegiance to James. The lords next met on the 24th after James had fled, and various expedients were suggested that might provide the country with a lawful sovereign or a lawful parliament or both. Clarendon proposed the reading of the Prince's declaration and an enquiry into the birth of the Prince of Wales, which moved Lord Wharton to say that he 'did not expect, at this time of day, to hear anybody mention that child'. Lord Paget moved that the flight of the King was a 'demise in law' and that Mary was now Queen. This was to be the thesis of some dissident tories of whom the most important was Danby. North and Compton supported it on this occasion along with leading whigs, but Bishop Turner and Pembroke opposed it, and it was the latter who recommended the expedient finally adopted of a convention on the model of 1660. Clarendon suggested instead the electing of the 184 members who could be returned on the writs that had already gone out and who would then order new elections. Nottingham said that the kingdom 'cannot come to have a parliament but by the king' and so he 'would treat with the King'. His plan was for the King to return and call a free parliament for the redress of grievances. William was to be in effect regent; the lords and commons should take the oath of allegiance 'upon this express condition to be declared by the King: in case of non-performance of his part' they should be absolved from it; and there were to be statutory guarantees for the annual meeting of parliament.[1]

[1] Horwitz, pp. 66–70. *Clarendon Correspondence*, vol. ii, pp. 233–7.

As in the last stages of the exclusion crisis, the main body of the tories plumped for a regency, that is, the simplest form of 'limitation' of the lawful ruler's power, as the best solution to the problem presented by James. To some extent this was a matter of conscience. They had acknowledged James to be their lawful ruler and, in most cases, taken an oath of fidelity to him. They would be foresworn if they ceased to acknowledge him as their King—which even those that had rebelled against him had hitherto done. Some believed that the death of James absolved them from this obligation and were prepared after that to swear allegiance to the government that had supplanted him.[1] But more important was the argument from expediency. If it were once conceded that the lawful ruler might be removed, no subsequent ruler would be immune from the same fate and there would be a standing threat of disorder. The tories hoped to make the view prevail in the convention to which the country's future had been referred. The bishops continued to consult together and tried once more to give a political lead. A paper by Sancroft pointed out that 'it is referred to the convention to consider how to restore the ancient government, and to settle it legally'. It was inappropriate therefore to argue that the government had ceased to exist or had been supplanted by a conqueror. 'By the common law of England,' moreover, 'the mutual ties of protection and subjection cannot be separated or dissolved by any human mean whatsoever.' For 'if once the style of the government be altered, how just a claim have any strong combinations to refuse obedience, or, if they can, even to assume the governing power?'[2] Some of the advocates of a regency regarded it as a step towards the return of James but most did not.[3] Their central concern was to preserve the existing constitution and so have a government that was indisputably legal and therefore sure of general obedience. For some, at least, the preservation of royal power or even of hereditary right was secondary. Nottingham wrote (respecting the exclusion crisis) that he did not believe 'that the right of succession was an indelible character that even the legislative power could not abrogate, or that the oath to the King, his heirs and successors precluded a parliament from doing it'.[4] But, as his brother said, 'that which comprehends most will be most secure'.[5]

---

[1] Ailesbury, vol. ii, p. 531. [2] Feiling, pp. 250–1.
[3] Horwitz, pp. 70–3. [4] *ibid.* p. 22.
[5] Feiling, p. 251.

William, however, had decided, whatever his earlier hesitations, that he must have the crown and the whigs were equally determined that James should not retain it. A regency was open to all the objections to 'limitations' that they had made ten years before. Setting up a new king, moreover, gave the subject a certain security against punishment should James ever be restored. Since the Wars of the Roses allegiance to a king *de facto* had not been accounted treason to the rightful but dispossessed king. But after the Restoration the royal judges held that this did not apply to allegiance to a republican government. It was not clear that it would necessarily apply to adherence to the proposed regent. William for his part had several reasons for deciding that he needed to be king. If he were made regent for James, his position might be called in question if James died before him. The same might happen if Mary were deemed to have become queen and he ruled as her consort—Mary did in fact die first. William was also influenced by his erroneous belief in the great strength of the 'commonwealth' party. He thought it essential both to win its support and to put himself in a position to keep it in check. To Halifax at the end of December he

said that the Commonwealth party was the strongest in England;
he had then that impression given.
They made haste to give him that opinion.
Note: he and the Commonwealth party seemed to play *au plus fin.*
Said that at the best they would have a Duke of Venice; in that
perhaps he was not so much mistaken.
Said he did not come over to establish a commonwealth.
Said he was sure of one thing; he would not stay in England if
K. James came again.
He said with the strongest asseverations that he would go if
they went about to make him regent.[1]

William continued to fear the machinations of the 'commonwealth' party after he had secured the crown. Halifax records that in July he 'said he now discovered plainly there was a design for a Commonwealth'. He pointed particularly to the abolition of the hearth tax and the raising of a regiment of volunteers in the City by Lord Mordaunt as intended to forward this design.[2] Yet he felt obliged to conciliate the extreme whigs. For instance, he made Lord Delamere lord lieutenant of Cheshire 'though with great repugnance. That lord said,

[1] Foxcroft, vol. ii, pp. 203–4. 30 December.
[2] Foxcroft, vol. ii, pp. 226; cf. 222, 224, 225.

he would not value all the king could give him, except he might have that'. He even gave Titus Oates a pension, 'though it went hard with him'.[1] Assuming the crown made him better able to hold his own. As regent he would have been a bit too like a doge for comfort. We have seen that 'limitations' was commonly regarded as a step towards a commonwealth. At the same time the whigs themselves wanted him to be king and by seeking the crown he bound them to him. The extremists would have liked him to rule alone, by right of conquest or election. This solution had the merit of simplicity and may have had the support of the radical and rational Halifax.[2] But its flouting of the hereditary principle and cruel injury to Mary and Anne made it generally obnoxious. So the joint sovereignty of William and Mary became the aim of William and the whigs.

By deciding that he must have the crown, William had set himself a difficult task—it was by no means certain that the whiggish element in the country was powerful enough to give it to him. If the Revolution had been at all democratic in character, there would probably have been little difficulty. Almost all the evidence suggests that popular feeling was against James and in favour of William. From the time of his landing there was a mounting tide of anti-catholic riots. The departure of James from London on 11 December was followed by a night of uproar and the sacking of catholic chapels and several foreign embassies. The next night was 'Irish night', a tumultuous panic which gripped not only the capital but large parts of the country. It was caused by rumours that disbanded Irish troops were on the rampage. Many years later a whig, Hugh Speke, claimed the dubious honour of having started it by distributing a forged proclamation in which William was supposed to have ordered the disbanding and crushing of the Irish.[3] It seems rather to have been spontaneous, like the *'grand peur'* which briefly gripped France in 1789.

There was pretty general agreement among the political leaders that popular frenzy of this kind must be kept out of politics and not allowed to intimidate the nation's traditional ruling class working through its traditional institutions. 'We represent,' said the eminent whig lawyer Sir George Treby to the convention, 'the valuable part, and those that

[1] *ibid.*, pp. 209, 236, 238.
[2] *ibid.*, p. 54 n. 4. William's own hereditary claims were not mentioned: Pinkham, pp. 222–3.
[3] W. L. Sachse, 'The Mob and the Revolution of 1688', *Journal of British Studies*, vol. iv (1964–5), pp. 23–40.

deserve a share in the government.' On 1 and 2 February, 1689, there were noisy popular demonstrations outside the two houses caused by the delay in bestowing the crown on William. They were countenanced by Lovelace at least, among the extremer whigs, but the politicians as a body would have nothing to do with them. 'If your debates are not free,' said Sir Edward Seymour,

> there is an end of all your proceedings. You are to sit sure here, else there is no other way than to go home into the country. What comes from you is the result of reason and no other cause . . . which cannot be, unless some care be taken to preserve you from the Mob.[1]

On 9 March the commons decided that even their votes should not be published. (It was another century before they gave up trying to stop publication of the actual debates.) Sir William Williams said that votes published without the antecedent debates were liable to mis-construction. He was moved to compare England and Holland: 'they are a commonwealth and we under a monarchy. There every man has a share in the government, but here not.' Sir Richard Temple hoped 'we shall not imitate Holland, to go to our principals for instructions'. Admittedly other speakers thought that publication of the votes would have a good effect on public opinion.[2] The commons reversed their decision in the autumn, but they continued to repudiate very firmly anything that savoured of republicanism. Treby protested that

> rather than have a hand in any thing of a republic, I would have lost my hand. Where there is a great territory and a warlike people, as the English are, monarchy is a government fit for that part of the world; the experiment of a commonwealth will be impracticable.[3]

When the veteran regicide Edmund Ludlow returned from exile in Switzerland in November 1689, the commons without a division asked for his arrest and he had to go back.

Republicanism in any case had little to do with democracy in those days. Nor were the masses capable of bringing much pressure to bear upon the upper class—they could not organize without a lead from above. This can be well seen in the experiences of Ailesbury as he journeyed through Kent in December 1688 to rescue the fugitive King from his captors. He found the people in abject terror of the approach of imaginary Irishmen and by his noble presence he calmed them and

---

[1] Grey, vol. ix, pp. 13, 45.
[2] Grey, vol. ix, pp. 142–6.
[3] Grey, vol. ix, p. 238.

restored order. At Rochester he persuaded the mayor to go to bed and apparently prevented the destruction of the bridge. He got the town clerk to read an order issued by the lords in London and assure the town that all was safe. At Chatham and Sittingbourne, the women were standing at their doors crying, and he and Colonel Graham went down the street reassuring them. At Chatham dockyard he dispersed a mob.[1] As the only political ideas which the people were allowed by their betters to have were anti-popery and xenophobia, it was no doubt as well that the Revolution was no more democratic that it was.

The whigs, then, had to work within the existing political institutions and here they were not as strong as William seems to have supposed. He had some good reasons for attaching importance to the supposed 'commonwealth men'. The whig exiles who had returned with him might well be expected to be his loyalest supporters. He used them as his agents in taking over the English government and no doubt they were valuable in keeping watch over an organization still manned by the nominees of James. The City of London too gave him vital help. Early in January it organized a loan of 200,000*l*., which came in the nick of time as his own funds ran out. With the restoration of the old charter, it was fair to look on the City as once more a whig stronghold.[2] All the same he greatly exaggerated the influence of the extremists—a royal failing which he shared not only with James but with his sister-in-law. Anne told Clarendon that 'the commonwealth party was very busy'.[3] They needed to be, if they were to undo the effects of repression in the mid eighties: in the elections to the convention the whigs were far from repeating the electoral triumphs of Shaftesbury's day. The provisional government did not interfere in the elections—indeed it was too confused to do so effectively. The attempts of the previous government to control elections had a certain after effect even though it did not survive until the poll, but it is hard to tell how great that effect was, especially since the former rulers had supported different people at different times. Forty-five of the over 100 candidates recommended by Sunderland in 1688

[1] Ailesbury, vol. i, pp. 204–6.
[2] The London aldermen removed in 1683 were put back at the end of 1688 and a common council elected. R. R. Sharpe, *London and the Kingdom*, vol. ii, pp. 530–1. Halifax said William at first thought Harbord, one of his whig helpers, was an able man of business but changed his mind, Foxcroft, vol. ii, pp. 226; cf. 225, 242.
[3] *Clarendon Correspondence*, vol. ii, p. 248.

were elected in 1689. But in 1688 the government often found itself supporting whigs, who were unlikely to stay loyal to James after his fall, and opposing tories, who might do so. In Yorkshire six candidates were returned whom James's agents had considered reliable and seven more whom they considered doubtful, but only one was eventually to vote against declaring the throne vacant. In Suffolk on the other hand only two candidates were elected whom James's agents had wanted, but eleven members from the county voted that the throne was not vacant. With government influence absent or erratic, it was the traditional influence of the leading local families that dominated the elections. The suppression of political activity by the late government probably accentuated this, for there was little discussion of the great constitutional issues at stake. Religious issues figured a bit in the election contests and some of them were fought on party lines, but others were purely personal. It is not surprising under these circumstances that there was no sweeping victory for any political viewpoint. Whigs and tories were both returned in large numbers. One hundred and ninety-two of the members had sat in the last 'exclusion' parliament (1681), but 196 had sat in the ultra loyal parliament of 1685. (One hundred and eighty-three of the members were new to parliament.) The number of strong partisans on either side is shown by the votes on declaring the throne vacant (5 February 1689) and on disfranchising those who had co-operated in the surrender of the borough charters (Sacheverell clause, January 1690). One hundred and fifty-one voted against the former (strong tories) and 174 in favour of the latter (strong whigs).[1] As a rule the whig view prevailed in the commons, but the tories still had a majority in the lords.

The even balance of forces in the convention was reflected in the caution with which even the whigs approached the problem of who should be king and in spite of that caution an impasse was soon reached. When the convention assembled on 22 January the whigs at first did well. Their candidate, Henry Powle, was elected speaker by the commons without opposition and in the absence of the lord chancellor, Halifax was chosen to preside in the lords. Knowing that they were stronger in the lords than in the commons, the tories tried to get the great question debated in the lords first. Clarges induced the commons to put off debate until the 28th because not all the members

---

[1] J. H. Plumb, 'The Elections to the Convention Parliament of 1689', *Cambridge Hist. Jol.* vol. v (1935–7), pp. 235–54.

had arrived. But Halifax told him that 'the lords should not proceed upon any public business till they saw what the commons did', and sure enough when Nottingham and others tried to make them begin on the 25th the only result was an adjournment until the 29th.[1] However, when the sense of the commons reached them on that day, it proved to be a very confused and negative resolution:

> that King James the Second, having endeavoured to subvert the constitution of the kingdom by breaking the original contract between king and people, and by the advice of Jesuits and other wicked persons having violated the fundamental laws and having withdrawn himself out of this kingdom, has abdicated the government and that the throne is thereby become vacant.

In the debate on the 28th of which it was the outcome,[2] the commons had shown themselves pretty well united in wanting to keep out James, but they had maintained unity only by avoiding the problem of how to replace him without shaking the old framework of government. Whig and tory views ran closely parallel, especially in the case of the lawyers. Sir George Treby declared 'that king that cannot, or will not, administer the government, is no longer king' and recalled that James I had told parliament in 1607 'that when a king breaks in upon his laws, he ceases to be a king'. Sir Robert Sawyer thought that there had been 'an abdication' and that 'his intention was to govern without law'. Finch and Somers both thought that the flight of James to France made things worse. Somers said that 'the King's going to a foreign power and casting himself into his hands absolves the people from their allegiance'. Revolutionary implications in such statements were disclaimed—especially by whigs. Finch said 'the question now is of vacancy in the government; that of the right and title to fill it up comes too late after the other question'. Harbord warned that 'if the question be, whether you have power to depose the King, that may tend to calling him back again and then we are all ruined'. 'We have found the crown vacant,' said Treby, 'and are to supply that defect. We found it so, we have not made it so.'

Once attention shifted from the past to the future, the conservatism of the commons led them to an impasse. Even a motion 'that the throne is void' led Clarges to object that this implied 'we have power to fill it, and make it from a successive monarchy to an elective'.

---

[1] Nottingham went hunting on the 24th, and so was not available for action. Horwitz, pp. 73–4.
[2] Grey, vol. ix, pp. 7–25. Dolben, p. 8, said the flight of James was 'without duress'.

Finch made the traditional tory connection between hereditary monarchy and the rights of property:

> If we were in the state of nature, we should have little title to any of our estates—that the King has lost his title to the crown and lost his inheritance, is farther than any gentleman, I believe, has or will explain himself.

Sir Robert Howard perhaps intended to reply to this when he gave the house a rather muddled exposition of advanced whig theory. 'I have heard "that the king has his crown by divine right" and we (the people) have divine rights too,' he explained. Government was 'grounded upon pact and covenant with the people' and by abdication 'it is devolved into the people, who are here in civil society and constitution to save them'. Sawyer retorted that 'the vacancy of the throne makes no dissolution of the government, neither in our law, nor any other'. If it did, power would revert directly to the people, not to a parliament in which less than a quarter of them were represented. But in fact their task was to restore the 'rights of the kingdom', 'by what free parliament we can, in such a form and frame and constitution as the government will admit'. The whigs really felt the same way. 'Should you go to the beginning of government,' Sir William Williams had said, 'we should be much in the dark.' As a result of this feeling, little was said in the commons about how the government was to be reconstituted, though Finch tentatively suggested a regency. They could not get beyond registering the removal of James.

The debates of the next few days show the commons just as conservative and still unsure how to take the next step. On 29 January they resolved that it was 'inconsistent with the safety and welfare of this protestant kingdom, to be governed by a popish prince' and that they should 'secure our religion, laws and liberties' before going on to 'fill the throne'. A committee was set up 'to bring in general heads of such things as are absolutely necessary' for this purpose.[1] These might seem to be proposals that the whigs would relish. But they were a means of evading for the moment the central question of 'filling the throne' and this some whigs did not like. William had been able to undertake his English enterprise because Louis XIV was occupied elsewhere and whig leaders realized that it was essential to complete the revolution before the international situation became more dangerous. As soon as it had been resolved not to have a popish

---

[1] CJ vol. x, p. 15.

prince, Wharton called on the lawyers to find a way to put William and Mary on the throne. Pollexfen warned that

> If but a noise of this goes beyond sea, that you are making laws to bind your prince, it will tend to confusion . . . To stand talking and making laws, and in the mean time have no government at all! They hope better things from our actions abroad, and a better foundation of the protestant interest.

It was a tory, Henry Seymour, who asked 'will you establish the crown and not secure yourselves? What care I for what is done abroad if we must be slaves in England, in this or that man's power?' Birch by contrast thought that repealing the hearth tax would be a sufficient redress of grievances for the moment and Harbord put his trust in parliament's control of the revenue to restrain the government.[1] A familiar later pattern was emerging: tories were suspicious of the throne once it was not filled by a ruler congenial to them, while whigs showed their 'revolutionary' zeal by upholding the strength of the monarchy.

Meanwhile, the lords were considering the commons' original rather negative resolution and showing themselves more negative still. On 29 January they considered it in committee under the chairmanship of Danby. Bishop Turner pointed out its inconsistencies, likening it to an 'accumulative' charge of treason, made by adding together lesser charges that were not connected. Nottingham attacked the constitutional ideas behind the resolution with a trenchancy that tory speakers in the commons had not shown. James could not have 'forfeited' the crown because this had the revolutionary implication that parliament could judge him. He had not 'ceded' it because his withdrawal was due to fear. In any case, did the supposed 'cession' cover Scotland? There had been talk in the commons of a 'demise' of the crown, but Nottingham pointed out inconveniences in this idea. Not only was James still alive, but to assume a demise meant the expiry of the revenue granted to him for life: the convention, not being a parliament, could not regrant it. There would also have to be an embarrassing enquiry into the legitimacy of his son. Halifax retorted that the opponents of the resolution ought 'to show either that there is no danger or to shew a remedy'. Rochester thereupon proposed a regency, and when Halifax objected that it would arouse expectations of James's return he proposed that it be for James's life. Defending

[1] Grey, vol. ix, pp. 29, 34–6.

this as the right solution against the criticisms of Halifax and Danby, Nottingham stressed that his concern was 'not for the monarch but the monarchy'. The plan was defeated by three votes, Danby and the other partisans of Mary voting with the whigs.[1]

The lords readily accepted the commons' vote against having a popish prince and on the 30th the greater part of the main resolution was carried, though with a division on the reference to an original contract. In the absence of a reputable bench of judges, the lords had appointed a group of distinguished lawyers to advise them and they were consulted about several of the key terms in the various resolutions before the house. To the question 'what the original contract is, and whether there be any such or not', they tended to give positive answers. Atkyns pointed out that even James I had believed there was a 'paction between prince and people'. Levinz thought that 'you may call it an original contract, though you know not when it began, because there are oaths on both sides, king and people, one to govern, the other to obey'. Nevill said that even a government founded by conquest 'in a little time becomes an original contract'. Petyt, the whig historical expert, explained that 'the original of government came from Germany' and found traces of a contract in every age.[2] The weight of legal opinion and the many authorities quoted may have carried the day. Though Clarendon continued to complain at the use of the contract idea,[3] it is doubtful if its adoption was really a concession to whig views. The contract in question was supposed to be between king and people. For writers like Locke on the other hand, the king was not a party to the contract but an official set up under it: the contract was supposed to have been entered into by the people to constitute the state, before there was a king. Only this extreme version of the contract theory had the revolutionary implication that the people were sovereign and could 'cashier' the king.

On the 30th the lords decided that James had 'deserted' rather than 'abdicated' the government, and on the 31st they concluded their debate by considering whether the throne was 'vacant'. The outcome suggests that both strong whigs and strong tories were more numerous or at any rate more confident in the lords than in the commons.

[1] Horwitz, pp. 75–7.
[2] HMC *House of Lords MSS 1689–90*, pp. 15–6. On this and on these debates in general see G. L. Cherry, 'The legal and philosophical position of the Jacobites, 1688–9', *Journal of Modern History*, vol. xxii (1950), pp. 309–21.
[3] W. Cobbett, ed., *The Parliamentary History of England* (1806–20), vol. v, p. 76.

Two amendments were considered. One, to have no vacancy but simply declare William and Mary King and Queen, was lost by 52 votes to 47. The other, simply to omit the reference to a vacancy, was carried by 55 votes to 41.[1] The houses were thus agreed on the removal of James, but both had failed to point out what should be done next. Instead of turning to this question, however, the houses continued to wrangle over the working of the resolution respecting James's removal. The commons decided on 2 February to stand by their original wording and the lords decided on the 4th to stand by theirs. There were conferences between the houses on the 4th, 5th and 6th. The commons needed to satisfy the lords that even if the crown was taken from James, the subject would continue to be absolutely bound to obey the sovereign and preserve the existing constitution. Much of the argument concerned historical precedents, or the meaning of words such as 'abdicate' and 'desert', but abstract political and constitutional doctrines were also involved. At the conference on the 4th the message from the commons recalled the radical thinkers of the Interregnum for whom obedience was simply due in return for protection.

> It is from those who are upon the throne of *England*, when there are any such, from whom the people of *England* ought to receive protection, and to whom (for that cause) they owe allegiance; but there being none now from whom they can expect regal protection and to whom (therefore) they owe the allegiance of subjects, the commons conceive the throne is vacant.[2]

The lords replied on the 5th that while 'willing to secure the nation against the return' of James, they could not accept 'such a vacancy in the throne as that the crown was thereby become elective'. The crown was hereditary, 'no act of the king alone can bar or destroy the right of his heirs' and so even if James was no longer King, 'allegiance is due to such person as the right of succession does belong to'.[3] Whether intentionally or not, this stimulated Clarges to say in the commons that the next protestant heir should succeed (*i.e.* Mary). James he held to have abdicated and 'the pretended Prince of Wales' was in French hands. He thought that a regular parliament could actually have altered the succession—but they were not a

---

[1] LJ vol. xiv, p. 112.

[2] LJ vol. xiv, pp. 115–6.

[3] *ibid.*, p. 117. It seems unclear whether this was intended to be a plea for Mary, see Horwitz, p. 79 and n. 1.

regular parliament.[1] The impatience of the whigs was mounting.[2] Harbord pointed out that 'the Dutch have sent their best troops to our assistance and the King of France is to rendezvous his army the 10th of March, and we are under unfortunate delays here of settling the government'. This led to some revolutionary talk. Birch, annoyed at the lawyers' slowness, claimed 'that the power of disposing of the crown is in the lords and commons; and', he added, 'by virtue of that power fill the vacancy'. Wharton exclaimed, 'I own driving King *James* out and I would do it again. Let everyone make his best of it.' Others were careful to emphasize the normal whig view that any uncustomary assertion of parliamentary authority was strictly for emergency use.[3] 'Where a divided inheritance is the case,' said Sir Robert Howard, 'all things are not so clear as we could wish; but let us preserve ourselves, which must be our supreme law.' 'No man,' said Boscawen, 'does say the crown is elective; but in an intricate case, the parliament must say where is the most right.' The commons on the 5th did not go beyond a reaffirmation that there was a vacancy—this time the tories even forced a division and were beaten by 282 votes to 151.

On the 6th the commons' representatives in conference[4] with the lords repeatedly protested that declaring the throne vacant was the way to save the constitution, not to alter it. Howard argued that the two houses had power 'to supply the vacancy that now is'. There was no 'intention' or 'likelihood of altering the course of the government so as to make it elective' but 'give us leave to remember "salus populi est suprema lex" '. Sir Thomas Lee asked 'whether upon the original contract there were not a power preserved in the nation to provide for itself in such exigencies'. Maynard thought that 'if we look but into the law of nature (that is above all human laws) we have enough to justify us in what we are now a doing to provide for ourselves and the public weal in such an exigency as this'. It was only in connection with the removal of James that whig speakers put forward views that really suggested that the king was inferior to the people. Holt said that 'the government and magistracy is under a trust, and any acting contrary to that trust is a renouncing of the trust'. Somers thought that 'by avowing to govern by a despotic power, unknown to the constitution and inconsistent with it', James

---

[1] Grey, vol. ix, pp. 54–5.
[3] *ibid.*, pp. 62–3.
[2] *ibid.*, pp. 54, 59–60, 64.
[4] Cobbett, vol. v, pp. 66–108.

hath renounced to be a king according to the law, such a king as he swore to be at his coronation, such a king to whom the allegiance of an English subject is due.

But when it came to laying down the character of the constitution there was a curious similarity between the view of Bishop Turner, who became a Jacobite, and Treby the whig lawyer. Turner held that the hereditary succession to the crown was a law which formed part of the 'original contract' and could only be altered by a new law. The line of succession had, it is true, been broken seven times since the conquest, but more recently the oath of allegiance had been modified by statue so that it extended not merely to the existing ruler but to his heirs and successors. Treby expounded the same doctrine.

> That this kingdom is hereditary, we are not to prove by precedent ... The laws made are certainly part of the original contract; and by the laws made, which establish the oath of allegiance and supremacy, we are tied up to keep in the hereditary line, being sworn to be true and faithful to the king, his heirs and successors; whereas the old oath was, only to bear true allegiance to the king. There (I take it) lies the reason why we cannot (of ourselves), without breaking that contract, break the succession, which is settled by law and cannot be altered but by another, which we ourselves cannot make.[1]

Basically the whigs had a better chance than during the exclusion controversy of demonstrating that their policy was the truly conservative one. The continued exile of James was thought necessary by almost everyone. Risks were involved, but to allow him to remain king in name would not diminish them but on the contrary would create uncertainties and make things worse. 'If the throne were full, what do we here,' said Sir Richard Temple, 'nay, how came we hither?' 'If the right of kingship be still ... due to him,' said Pollexfen, 'we cannot in justice agree to keep him from it.' A regency would be 'a strange and unpracticable thing'; 'it would be setting up a commonwealth instead of our ancient regulated government by a limited monarchy'. It would not help to pretend that the crown had passed to James's heir. Not only was there an old legal maxim that a living man could not have an heir, but also there was no certainty as to who the heir was. Nottingham would not accept such arguments because

> if the head be taken away and the throne vacant, by what laws or constitutions is it that we retain lords and commons? For they are knit together in their common head; and if one part of the government be dissolved, I see not any reason but all must be dissolved.

[1] Cobbett, vol. v, pp. 75; cf. 102–3.

This rather than any predilection for strong monarchy is the characteristic tory note in the debates of 1689. In reply to it, Foley

> put the case the whole royal line should fail (as they are all mortal, as well as we ourselves are), should we in that case have no government at all? And who then should we have but the lords and commons?

At length Nottingham conceded that 'any government is better than none; but', he added, 'I earnestly desire we may enjoy our ancient constitution' and he reported to the lords that 'when we desired what method it should be upon our successors that they should not elect, we had no reply'.[1] Here was the difficulty that the whigs could not overcome. They could not devise a lawful way of implementing their policy. Could there now have been an Exclusion Bill even the tories might have accepted it—this was what James had made impossible by burning the election writs and absconding. What the whigs were evidently trying to do by declaring the throne vacant was to initiate quasi-judicial proceedings in which lords and commons took it upon themselves to determine who as things stood had the best right to occupy it but avoided any claim to dispose of it as they pleased. But this fiction was too transparent to convince the sceptics.

There was therefore an impasse just as there had been in 1681, and William found himself obliged to solve it in the whig sense as Charles had resolved the earlier one in favour of the tories. Though William was still but a Prince, he was the man whom whigs and tories alike thought it necessary to have—by some title or other—as their ruler. It was he therefore and not James who could to some extent oblige the nation to accept him on his own terms for fear of the anarchy that would otherwise follow. He had not concealed his wishes from such influential politicians as Halifax, and Burnet had published 'by authority' a statement of the case that the throne was vacant, while a proclamation against 'scandalous and seditious books' discouraged any really intransigent opposition.[2] Hints having proved insufficient, William, probably on February 3, sent for some leading peers and told them that he was unwilling to be either regent or king consort.[3] Unless he was made king regnant he would go home. Meanwhile, Mary had written to Danby a strong disclaimer of any wish to reign alone; Burnet was also aware of her views and saw to it that they be-

---

[1] Lords' MSS., p. 18.   [2] Feiling, pp. 246–7.
[3] Horwitz, p. 79, citing Pinkham, pp. 233–4.

came known. It was further thought essential that Anne should waive her claim to succeed at once if Mary died before William. The Prince negotiated with her for a long time through the Churchills and during the conference between the houses on the 6th it became known that she had agreed.

James II contributed as well as William to end the immobility of the lords. On 4 February a truculent letter from him came into their hands (he was getting ready to invade Ireland) and was laid aside unread when it was found to be countersigned by the detested Melfort.[1] Further delay would clearly be dangerous, and after the conference on the 6th the lords voted by a majority of at least 15 to agree with the commons that the throne was vacant. Various lords who had not appeared before had been drummed up and others absented themselves so that the whigs and their supporters might win: Nottingham encouraged this 'for fear of a civil war if they had lost it'[2]. Clarendon tried to get the defeated party to secede from the convention but in vain. Pembroke told him that 'the government must be supported, or else we should be all ruined', Nottingham said the same, another earl feared losing his estate and others would not expose themselves to 'severities' from those now in power. William's cause was clearly seen as the cause of order, which all conservatives must support. Even the secession, apparently, was only expected to 'have discomposed our undertakers and [to] have put the Prince of Orange upon new counsels'—*i.e.* it was directed against his advisers rather than his own authority.[3]

The lords had been defeated in their attempt to avoid a break in constitutional continuity. But they now took the initiative in seeking to minimize the break and at first the commons followed their lead. It was in the lords that the whigs (still on the 6th) took the positive step of moving that William and Mary be declared King and Queen and this was carried without a division. Then the tories reasserted themselves. Nottingham said that he had opposed

the Prince his accession to the crown, not believing it legal, but that since he was there and that he must now owe and expect his protection from him as King *de facto*, he thought it just and lawful to swear allegiance to him.[4]

---

[1] A. Simpson, 'Notes of a Noble Lord', *English Historical Review*, vol. lii (1937), p. 93.

[2] Horwitz, pp. 81–2.

[3] Simpson, pp. 97–8.   [4] Horwitz, p. 82.

But he pointed out that many people could not conscientiously take oaths to the new rulers in the existing forms, which implied that they were the rightful and lawful sovereigns. Danby seconded his call for reworded oaths of allegiance and supremacy: 'they had resolved to make them King and Queen upon this crisis of affairs, yet no man would affirm that they were rightfully so by the constitution.'[1] Halifax 'said it would be to ridicule their title' and sharp words passed between him and Danby,[2] but the house agreed. On the 7th the lords sent new forms of oaths to the commons together with their vote respecting William and Mary. The new oath of supremacy expressed, more trenchantly than the old, a faith common to whigs and tories.

> I do swear that I do from my heart abhor, detest and abjure as impious and heretical this damnable doctrine and position, that princes excommunicated or deprived by the Pope or any authority of the see of Rome may be deposed or murdered by their subjects or any other whatsoever. And I do declare that no foreign prince . . . hath or ought to have any jurisdiction . . . within this realm.

But the new oath of allegiance simply said 'I do sincerely promise and swear that I will be faithful and bear true allegiance to their majesties King William and Queen Mary, so help me God.'[3] It registered the tory belief that the new régime was provisional, rather as a regency would have been: a violation of the constitution to be tolerated by reason of exceptional circumstances until better times returned.

When the lords' various votes reached the commons on 7th, the hope of the whig Lord Wiltshire was that 'you will proceed to fill the throne'. He stressed once more that their object was 'to preserve the ancient government', not to make the monarchy elective. The old republican Wildman added that 'to prevent anarchy, nothing can be better', but another member wanted first to hear the report of the committee that had been drawing up the 'preliminary heads' of the subjects' rights.[4] This appeared in the afternoon, and on the 8th the commons approved a draft of what became the Declaration of Rights, in which were combined part of the 'heads', the new 'tory' oaths and a resolution that William and Mary 'be and be declared

---

[1] Feiling, pp. 262–3.

[2] Foxcroft, vol. ii, p. 55.

[3] The oath is supposed to have been the work of White, Bishop of Peterborough (who would not take it). Horwitz, p. 82 n. 4 cites Ailesbury.

[4] Grey, vol. ix, pp. 70–1. Wiltshire's father the Marquis of Winchester had proposed the lords' motion to make William and Mary King and Queen.

King and Queen'. It was stipulated that if they had no children, Anne and her descendants would take the crown when they were both dead. If that line failed, and if William had survived Mary, remarried and had issue, the succession was to go to them. The lords accepted the Declaration with little change, Mary reached England on the 12th and next day the two houses waited on the Prince and Princess to 'pray' them (as the document says) to 'accept' the crown. 'We thankfully accept what you have offered to us,' replied William. The forms used in these proceedings seem designed to sustain the impression that the lords and commons were recognizing, not choosing the new king and queen.

In the later proceedings of the convention the whigs scored some ideological points at the expense of the tories which served to give the Revolution a more whiggish appearance than it had at the outset. But these did not amount to much. Once they had a king able to pronounce the royal assent, the convention could pass an act by which they declared themselves to be a lawful parliament. This seems to have been done so that money could be speedily voted for the impending wars. The tories opposed it and called for new elections. Not only did they hope to win more seats but the thought that a royal summons (if only by a king *de facto*) was essential to constitute a parliament: for an assembly not so convened to claim to be one was revolutionary. The new parliament passed an act which imposed the new 'tory' oaths of allegiance and supremacy on the nation but also abolished the 'non-resisting' oath imposed after the Restoration and restored to the subject whatever right he may previously be supposed to have had to rebel. To oblige the new sovereign[1] to govern according to law, a new coronation oath was introduced and the Declaration which had placed William and Mary on the throne was turned into the Bill of Rights. But we shall see that these measures did little to restrict royal power. The really whiggish feature of the Bill was its tampering with the hereditary principle. As eventually enacted, it not only reiterated the order of succession agreed on in February but laid down that no one could come to the throne who was or ever had been or had married a papist, the subjects being absolved of their allegiance if such a person should succeed. On coming to the throne future sovereigns were to make the declaration against transubstantiation in the Test

---

[1] At first the sole exercise of regal power was vested in William, but this restriction on Mary was not needed and was later removed.

Act of 1678, either at their coronation or before the house of lords.[1]

Some tories were upset by the way in which the succession was being settled and a quarrel arose between the two houses about it which delayed the enactment of the Bill of Rights until the autumn of 1689. On 8 May Charles Godolphin called in the commons for a proviso that nothing in the measure be allowed to 'prejudice the right of any protestant prince or princess' to the succession. This was so 'that the monarchy might be looked upon as hereditary and not elective'. 'Those,' said Garroway, 'who expect a commonwealth in England by failure of those you have named, I would disappoint them all.' But Treby explained that the Bill would leave the further 'descent of the succession to the common law' and another member feared that the proviso would 'comprehend the Prince of Wales if he turn protestant'. It was rejected. 'Make your succession so founded on grace,' said Somers, 'that none but protestants succeed.'[2] The lords, however, decided that the Bill ought to name the next protestant heirs after William, Mary, Anne and their descendants: the house of Hanover. The commons responded that 'a further limitation of the crown may be dangerous and of ill consequence'[3] and there the matter rested through the summer. The birth of a son to Anne in July made the matter more academic and the lords gave way. It cannot be said that the commons had attacked the hereditary principle, but the doubts remaining about the succession left them with a weapon against the crown.

(III)

The setting up of new sovereigns in 1689 was a makeshift arrangement which did not properly square with either whig or tory beliefs and was thought by some and felt by all to be provisional. It was accepted by different people for different reasons, some of them recalling Hobbes or Filmer more than Locke. William and Mary disliked their revolutionary role. Mary believed that she was obeying God, who had 'decided between the daughter and the wife and shewed me, when religion was at stake, I should know no man after the flesh'. But she nevertheless regarded what had been done as sinful.

---

[1] These amendments were the work of the lords: LJ, vol. xiv, pp. 345–6.
[2] Grey, vol. ix, pp. 237–42.   [3] CJ vol. x, p. 213.

When Anne's new baby had convulsions in the summer of 1689, she looked on it as 'a continuance of the righteous judgment of God upon our unhappy family and these sinful nations'. She saw the hand of God in her serious quarrel with Anne in 1692

> and look on our disagreeing as a punishment upon us for the irregularity by us committed upon the revolution. My husband did his duty and the nation did theirs and we were to suffer it and rejoice that it pleased God to do what he did. But as to our persons, it is not as it ought to be, tho' it was unavoidable, and no doubt that it is a just judgment of God, but I trust the church and nation shall not suffer but that we in our private concerns and persons may bear the punishment as in this we do.[1]

She was concerned for her father's safety as well as her husband's and the 'dreadfullest prospect in the world' was that they might meet in battle. Her worst moment was when it became apparent in 1692 that James had connived at a plot to murder William. 'I was ashamed to look anybody in the face. I fancied I should be pointed at as the daughter of one who was capable of such things, and the people would believe I might by nature have as ill inclinations.'[2]

William had done his best to bring a stable government into being, but felt nevertheless that his personal position was weak and doubted his ability to maintain it. The day after he had been offered the crown, he told Halifax 'he fancied he was like a king in a play'. He also said, 'I am a young King' and needed help. By June he was complaining

> that a King of England who will govern by law, as he must do if he hath conscience, is the worst figure in Christendom. He hath power to destroy the nation and not to protect it.

He began to speak wistfully of leaving the country.[3] The political situation in 1689 did not allow him to go campaigning or visit Holland as he was usually to do, but he did not mix readily with his people. His English was imperfect, his habits not convivial and the London climate almost killed him in the spring of 1689, forcing him into the isolation first of Hampton Court and then of Kensington. He tried to make up for this by a visit to Newmarket but sadly told Dijkvelt, 'I see that I am not made for this people, nor they for me.'[4] Far from

[1] R. Doebner (ed.) *Memoirs of Mary*, pp. 3, 15, 45–6.
[2] *ibid.*, pp. 5, 48, 54; cf. 16, 32.
[3] Foxcroft, vol. ii, pp. 204, 221, 222.
[4] Baxter, *William III*, pp. 248–9, 255. Mary likewise felt no desire to rule or fitness for it, but it was not intended that she should. Doebner, pp. 11, 19, 23.

revelling in possession of the throne, he was already thinking of the diplomatic advantage to be won by promising the ultimate succession to another prince. He would have liked parliament to make this promise to the house of Hanover in 1689 and was disappointed when they failed to do so.[1] It is true that Sir John Lowther seems to have won his affection by expressing a preference for 'his own family' over the Hanoverians, but as Halifax says, 'personal compliments must prevail if they are dextrously applied and not daubed'.[2]

The basic tory attitude to the new administration was that it had to be maintained in order to prevent social collapse. Many even of those who hoped to bring back James on the first opportunity were ready to take advantage of the new oaths and associate themselves with the *de facto* government without renouncing their principles. 'I took the oath,' said Lord Ailesbury

> which I termed before like to a garrison one, for it was my opinion that he being declared king (although I did in parliament do all that lay in my power to obstruct it) he was to protect the kingdom, and that those that desired protection ought to take some oath.

To show his firmness to principle he did not attend the coronation, but he afterwards carried the sword of state before the new King and Queen at Hampton Court—and indignantly denies a slanderous suggestion that he had thought of using the opportunity to kill the King.[3] Many of those who regarded the new régime as perfectly lawful and did not think that James was still the true King were nevertheless at one with the true tories in regarding the settlement as only provisional. Halifax told his friend, Sir John Reresby, on 1 February 'that the King having relinquished the government, it was not for that to be let fall . . . *salus populi* was *suprema lex*'. But through Reresby, who took the new oaths himself but had Jacobite friends, he tried to keep in touch with the exiled court. He is supposed to have told a Jacobite lady on 9 February that 'there were no great hopes of a lasting peace from this settlement. However, it was the best that could be made at this time of the day'. He asked both this lady and Reresby to help him keep in good repute among the Jacobites. 'Come, Sir John,' he said, 'we have wives and children and we must consider them and not

---

[1] Baxter, *William III*, p. 251.
[2] Foxcroft, vol. ii, p. 225.
[3] Ailesbury, vol. i, pp. 237, 254–5.

venture too far.' For this reason 'he took no great nor additional places, no honours, or blue ribbons'.[1]

Danby, who certainly was not prepared to pass by an opportunity of feathering his nest, covered himself in another way. He got himself made Governor of Hull and so secured 'a place of retreat and whereby to make his terms'[2] in case of counter-revolution. This is a strange attitude for men who had become the leading ministers on William's accession. It reflected the belief which Halifax shared with the tories and which was more basic in tory thinking even than religious faith—namely, that only a legitimate government could be strong and stable. It is fair to add that Halifax did his best to strengthen the new order; also that he eventually concluded that if William did not fall a victim to illness or assassination during the summer, the government would 'scarce be shaken' by his death thereafter.[3]

Some pamphleteers took the opportunity which the revolution afforded to put forward schemes for making the government more republican or carrying out reforms beneficial to ordinary people. In order to encourage loyalty to the new settlement certain popular measures were passed, such as the repeal of the hearth tax and the abolition of the Court of the Welsh Marches, against which there was a substantial popular agitation in the form of petitions to parliament.[4] But the promoters of the revolution were so conservative that they could do little to make their work popular in this way. Other methods had to be adopted to persuade everyone that it was expedient, and indeed a moral duty, to accept the new order. It was a hard task: even a zealous whig and clergyman like Thomas Tenison could only say

there had been irregularities in our settlement; that it was to be wished things had been otherwise; but we were now to make the best of it and to join in support of this government as it was for fear of worse.[5]

This sort of attitude harked back, as already noticed, to the view current in the Cromwellian period that obedience was due to whoever had power enough to maintain order and afford protection. It is inter-

---

[1] Foxcroft, vol. ii, pp. 52, 56, 68–9. The lady is supposed to have been Lady Oglethorpe.

[2] So Reresby and Halifax thought, Foxcroft, vol. ii, p. 211 n. 5.

[3] *ibid.*, vol. ii, p. 68.

[4] Lords' MSS. no. 80. This was the last of the prerogative courts and the complaint was that litigation in it was expensive.

[5] *Clarendon Correspondence*, vol. ii, p. 300.

esting that a notable production of that time, Anthony Ascham's *Confusions and Revolutions of Government*, was republished in 1689 under the title of *A Seasonable Discourse*. Whig writers were happy to use this argument and went on doing so right into the eighteenth century. It was attractive to radical thinkers because it was an appeal to utility or 'interest' rather than traditional moral ideas. John Shute, arguing that 'allegiance is only due for the sake of protection', said that to deny this would be 'inconsistent with the happiness of mankind'.[1] But traditionalists could also use it: the ideas of a government being established by conquest and achieving thereby a legal title to obedience was a familiar one to lawyers and hence had commended itself to some of William's adherents.

These ideas were unpalatable to moderate opinion as they stood, but an attempt was made to season them by ascribing the Revolution to divine intervention. It seemed quite natural to account for remarkable political happenings in this way—especially when tory churchmen preached on the anniversary of the Restoration or the Gunpowder Plot. Preaching before the commons in 1701, Atterbury said that nowadays God's chief 'extraordinary indications of his power and providence' are 'such signs of the times, such wonders of government' as achieve 'political justice'. The application of this idea to the Revolution is particularly associated with William Sherlock, a leading London clergymen who at first refused the oaths to the new government and was deprived of his living.[2] He later recanted and was rewarded with the deanery of St Paul's. Unkind critics blamed his change of heart on his wordly wife or said that having prayed 'that heaven would instruct him in the right way', he had prudently taken the Battle of the Boyne as a sign. His conversion owed much to the publication by Sancroft of a treatise on political matters written by John Overall, Bishop of Exeter, in the reign of James I, which had been sanctioned by convocation. The 'convocation book' had been expected to help the Jacobite cause, but in fact it said that any government which was 'thoroughly settled' was to be 'reverenced and obeyed'. Sherlock wrote a pamphlet on the *Allegiance due to Sovereign Powers* in which he argued that God made and unmade kings and if God set

[1] Q. Skinner, 'History and Ideology in the English Revolution', *Historical Journal*, vol. viii (1965), pp. 171–5 and nn. 133, 154.
[2] G. Straka, 'The final phase of divine right theory in England, 1688–1702', *English Historical Review*, vol. lxxvii (1962), pp. 641–6. But this is a theory of 'providence' (divine intervention) not 'divine right' (the order God establishes).

up a king he was to be obeyed.[1] The lawful king was to be supported for as long as possible but, as Sherlock said in a later pamphlet, a prince who 'can no longer govern' must be abandoned lest 'society dissolve into a mob, or Mr. Hobbes's state of nature'.[2] The argument was carried further by Bishop William Lloyd who in 1691 expounded *God's Ways of Disposing of Kingdoms*. Kings had to rule according to laws and God punishes bad kings. He 'administereth judgment and justice . . . particularly when he decrees a conquest of any king or kingdom'.

The Revolution particularly lent itself to this sort of interpretation: its success owed so much to good fortune in the diplomatic field, in the development of a particular state of mind in England—and in the way the winds blew. 'Opinion,' Lloyd thought,

governs the unthinking sort of men, which are far the greatest part of the body of a nation. And when all these go together, they are like the atoms of air, which though taken apart they are too light to be felt, yet being gathered into a wind, they are too strong to be withstood. But he that brings the winds out of his treasures, he also governs these and turns them which way he pleases. It is the same great God that rules the roaring waves of the sea, and the multitude of the people.

Burnet likewise observed that

in the revolutions of states and empires . . . both the course of natural agents, the winds and seasons, and the tempers of men's minds seem to have been managed by such a direction . . . that those who observe them with due attention are forced on many occasions to cry out 'this is the finger of God, this is the Lord's doing'.[3]

Actual leaders of rebellion could speak like this during the Revolution itself. The manifesto issued by the whigs at Nottingham said

we own it rebellion to resist our king that governs by law; but he was always accounted a tyrant that made his will the law. To resist such an one, we justly esteem it no rebellion but a necessary defence; and in this confidence we doubt not of all honest Englishmen's assistance; and humbly hope for and implore the great God's protection, that turneth the hearts of his people as pleaseth him best; it having been observed that people can

[1] C. F. A. Mullett, 'A case of allegiance: William Sherlock and the Revolution of 1688', *Huntington Library Quarterly*, vol. x, pp. 85–8.

[2] Skinner, 'Ideological context of Hobbes political thought, *Historical Journal*, vol. ix (1966), pp. 298–9.

[3] Straka, pp. 648–56. For an instance of the 'voice of the people' theme, see p. 657 n. 2.

never be of one mind without his inspiration, which hath in all ages confirmed that observation—*vox populi, vox dei*.[1]

The whigs wished to strengthen the moral position of the new
order by forcing those who did not like it to acknowledge that it was
lawful. They scored an early success when it was enacted that the
new oaths should be imposed on the clergy as well as on the servants
of the state. The clergy were rightly regarded as the focus of opposition to the equivocation which had allowed the tories to adhere to the
new government: a number of them refused the oaths, whereas few
laymen did so. In the new parliament of 1690 the whigs turned against
equivocators too, and bills were brought in to require office holders,
and indeed anyone who came under suspicion, explicitly to abjure
King James. But the tories were in greater strength in the new parliament and the bills were defeated. There were signs of scepticism
regarding this sort of test, which had been imposed by each of the
successive governments that had ruled England since 1640 and had
not been the means of preserving any of them. The old parliamentarian,
Lord Wharton, told the upper house that he had taken many oaths in
his time and had not kept them all, for which he hoped to be pardoned.
The old royalist, Lord Macclesfield, said that his case was much the
same. In spite of this the whigs went on trying. In 1696 the frustration
of a plot to assassinate the King enabled them to bring forward their
old scheme of an association for the protection of the royal person
and get it sanctioned by parliament. Office holders and members of
the two houses were required to declare that William was the 'rightful and lawful' King[2] and to promise to join together in his defence.
The penalties of praemunire were decreed against anyone who denied
that he was the rightful King. A few Jacobites were removed from
political activity for a while by this means but there was no great upheaval. Probably most of the ruling class remained equivocal in their
attitude to the new order for a long time: the readiness with which
politicians corresponded with the exiled dynasty is a sign of this.
Because the Revolution did not mark the triumph of a particular
party or point of view, it was followed by a long period of uncertainty.
Because the moral basis of the new order was so fragile, only the pas-

[1] *Ellis Correspondence*, vol. ii, pp. 314–19.
[2] In 1702, after Louis XIV had espoused the cause of the Old Pretender, an oath in
this sense and an abjuration of the Pretender were much more widely imposed. G.
Holmes, ed., *Britain after the Glorious Revolution, 1689–1714* (Macmillan, 1969), p. 41.

sage of time could make it appear, and so become, permanent. To this extent James had scored and William had reason to be uneasy. But the situation had its advantages for William. The reluctance to undermine the monarchy and the fact that only with his own backing could radical measures be carried meant that the Revolution left the powers of the crown substantially intact. If he could keep the crown, he might hope to rule with a strong hand.

10

Crown, Parliament and Religion after the Revolution

THE respect for the constitution as it stood which was fundamental to the Revolution meant that the change of ruler was not exploited as a pretext for lessening the powers of the crown. Of course whigs and tories agreed in believing that the rights of the subject were as much a part of the constitution as the monarch's rights. William's declaration before he set sail had placed the maintenance of the country's laws and liberties among the objects of his expedition, and we have seen that the commons had resolved to 'secure' those laws and liberties before 'filling' the throne. But what they mainly envisaged was the assertion of the subject's rights under the existing laws which James had failed to respect. When the select committee, to which the matter had been referred, produced a summary of the nation's grievances under 28 'heads', the commons decided 'to distinguish such of the general heads as are introductory of new laws from those that are declaratory of ancient rights'. Sir Henry Capel said

> we have been branded often with alteration of the government. 'Tis our right to assert our freedom. 'Tis likely whoever you shall inthrone will thank you for giving light into the miscarriages of the last government. And we only assert our rights and liberties, pursuant to the Prince's declaration.[1]

A document was therefore prepared which first expounded the 'heads' that were supposed to be 'declaratory', and then said that it was 'proposed and advised' that 'there be provision by new laws' for the redress of grievances which could not otherwise be remedied. The Declaration of Rights which the commons eventually sent up to the lords was exactly that—the proposals for new laws were omitted

---

[1] CJ, vol. x, p. 19. Grey, vol. ix, pp. 51–2.

altogether. Sacheverell said that he did 'not suppose this Instrument of Government to be a new limitation of the crown but what of right is ours by law'.[1]

This procedure meant that few grievances were remedied at the time that the throne was filled. It was piously believed in the seventeenth century that the sufferings of the subject were almost all due to the failure of the government to abide by the law. This was nonsense. Of the twenty-eight different species of grievance which made up the commons' 'heads', no less than twenty-two required legislation for their redress. (Admittedly eleven of the 'heads' were declaratory, but in five of these cases legislation was needed as well.)[2] The Declaration disappointed some. Sir Richard Temple had 'thought it your intention when you filled the throne to do these things which will be too late afterwards'. Earlier he had wanted 'the coronation oath to be taken upon entrance into the government; and as we arc sworn to our kings, so they be sworn to protect us'.[3] But tories certainly, and even strong whigs like Sacheverell, probably would have held that the Declaration was the most that could be achieved. A new sovereign could plausibly be asked to promise to observe the law as it stood— this was already done at coronations. But the only lawful way of placing further limitations on him was by statute. Only parliament could pass statutes and there could be no parliament without a sovereign. William could not with any semblance of legality be made to assent to any changes in the law as a condition of being offered the crown. Once he was King and the lords and commons were sitting as a parliament, bills could be offered to him for the subject's relief and he could assent to them—if he felt like it.

When the crown was tendered to the Prince and Princess by the two houses, William promised to 'support' the nation's laws and liberties, to 'concur in anything that shall be for the good of the kingdom; and to do all that is in my power to advance the welfare and glory of the nation'.[4] But this was only a declaration of intent such as James II had also made in his day. For the coronation a new oath was instituted, as projected in the 'heads', but only in religious

[1] *ibid.*, p. 74. CJ, vol. x, pp. 20–2.
[2] *ibid.*
[3] Grey, vol. ix, pp. 31, 74.
[4] CJ vol. x, p. 30. Macaulay (p. 1303 and n. 2) on the authority of Van Citters makes William promise to recur constantly to the advice of the two houses. But the record in CJ must be considered official: the Speaker had asked for the King's words in writing.

matters was a real new restriction placed on the King. On the secular side he promised little more than his predecessors. He undertook to govern 'according to the statutes in parliament agreed on, and the respective laws and customs' of his dominions. But Charles II had confirmed by his oath the 'laws and customs' granted by his predecessors and had undertaken to 'hold and keep the laws and rightful customs which the commonalty of this your kingdom have'. The sovereign was not legally obliged to be crowned and sworn. The declaration against transubstantiation incorporated in the Bill of Rights had by contrast to be taken at the coronation or at the new sovereign's first meeting with parliament, whichever came first.

The conditions imposed upon William at his accession were thus few and vague. It is important to emphasize in particular that nothing had been done to compromise the sovereign's independence—his right to carry on the government as he thought fit, restrained only by his promise to respect the law and his concern for his people's welfare. It is a commonplace among historians that nothing could have been more monarchical than William's government and that nobody could have been less like what he called 'a Duke of Venice'. He had an almost military idea of how a government should be run and on a number of points his views coincided strikingly with those of his uncle James. He did not care for argument among his servants. 'He hath naturally an aversion to talk with many together; his practice in Holland otherwise. Loveth single conversation.' Believing mistakenly that the government was to 'reside' in the privy council, he was anxious to keep down its numbers. He wanted only one secretary of state in Scotland, not wishing 'to have one advise him one thing and the other another'. 'His nature', is Halifax's comment. He also 'said there were two places which should ever be in commission, viz. admiralty and treasury'[1]—in other words he would have no overmighty ministers. His authoritarian bent was strengthened by his contempt for the leading English politicians. In his conversations with Halifax, nearly everyone figures as 'mad', 'a blockhead', 'weak' (in the head) or unhelpful in some lesser way. Devonshire, of whom he 'said he never heard him give a reason for any one thing',[2] was one of the least blamed. Even the mild Mary spoke scathingly of the men appointed to help her govern while William was reconquering

---

[1] Foxcroft, vol. ii, pp. 202, 204, 218, 221.
[2] ibid., p. 236.

Ireland. Devonshire was 'weak and obstinate', Dorset 'lazy', Pembroke 'as mad as most of his family tho' very good natured', Monmouth 'is mad; and his wife who is madder governs him', Marlborough 'can never deserve either trust or esteem', Lowther 'very honest but weak', and so on.[1] The King and Queen both felt that the religious life of their leading subjects left much to be desired and this gave a sombre reinforcement to the poor impression which their personalities made. 'We seem only prepared for vengeance', Mary thought.[2] More immediately significant for William was the ignorance of his advisers in his chosen field of international affairs.

Not only did William expect those who served him to be docile instruments but he was not eager to shape his policy according to the advice of his leading subjects. He did not often follow Charles II's custom of attending debates in the lords incognito. He did not enjoy debates and he mistakenly thought the lords of little account compared to the commons.[3] He was disinclined to align himself with either whigs or tories, though at different times he found himself tending to march in step with the one or the other. He several times paid Halifax the compliment in conversation of describing himself as a Trimmer.[4] He was 'cruelly galled' by parliament's proceedings, Halifax noted. He 'said the commons used him like a dog' and in July 1689 'he said he was so weary of them, he could not bear them; there must be a recess'.[5] It was natural that he should react by taking up an aloof posture of superior wisdom. He 'said he would think no more of doing things popular, but doing what was right'.[6] His determination therefore to maintain the prerogatives of the crown did not falter. 'He had no mind to confirm' the articles of the Declaration of Rights by a statute 'but the condition of his affairs overruled his inclinations in it'.[7]

The government which he set up on his accession really consisted of politicians for show and administrators for the work, policy being decided by himself. Whigs and tories were both given jobs and so there was no natural cohesion in the ministry. Halifax and Danby, the chief ministers, were old enemies. Halifax was too much the intellectual to be a good minister and Danby would do little work

---

[1] Doebner, p. 30. Some of this echoes William's views.
[2] Doebner, cf. pp. 59, 76. [3] Foxcroft, vol. ii, pp. 208, 218, 244.
[4] *ibid.*, pp. 206–7, 242, 252. [5] Foxcroft, vol. ii, pp. 207, 224.
[6] *ibid.*, p. 219. [7] *ibid.*, p. 217.

because he found that he was to have no real power. His main gain at this time indeed was a step in the peerage and henceforth he was Marquis of Carmarthen. Shrewsbury, who became a secretary of state, was potentially a powerful figure because he was liked and respected both by the King and in parliament. But he was young, inexperienced and in bad health. Foreign and military affairs were directed by the King himself and there was nobody so well qualified to do it. He also, like James, took an active part in managing the finances and striving for frugality. It was natural that he should turn quite readily to the administrators who had served James as the people most suitable to execute his will. He regarded some with distaste—paymaster Ranelagh for instance.[1] But from the first he wanted to employ Godolphin,[2] who stayed at the treasury board and sat there with useless politicians as he had in the previous reign—remaining, with one short intermission, until 1696. Army administration remained the province of Blathwayt, and he was one of several essentially non-political figures who did the duties of secretary of state during the reign.[3] Naval affairs William did not profess to understand, and the Revolution ended the career of Pepys, though men whom he had trained stayed on in subordinate positions. Much influence in this field was exercised by two rather politically-minded admirals, Arthur Herbert (tory) and Edward Russell (whig): the King also placed increasing reliance here on Nottingham, whom he had made secretary of state. Nottingham had once been on the admiralty board, but he did not distinguish himself in this field. It was the King's Dutch associates who received the leading court offices and therefore saw most of him and had the best chance of influencing him. As the reign advanced, William paid increasing attention also to the views of Sunderland, who crept home from Holland when it appeared safe. This is perhaps the most astonishing point of similarity between William and James.

(II)

For all their respect for the rights of the crown, the Convention had wished to protect the subject against the abuse of its powers, both by a

---

[1] *ibid.*, p. 216. [2] *ibid.*, p. 205.
[3] Administrators like Southwell, Trumbull or Vernon, or the king's friend, Henry Sidney, essentially a courtier.

clear statement of the existing law and by changes in the law. Many changes were deemed necessary and William, at least in theory, did not need to assent to any of them. Progress was therefore slow and the embarrassment of the crown was kept within bounds. A convenient standard against which progress can be measured is provided by the commons' 'heads' of February 1689. They were as follows:[1]

1. The pretended power of dispensing or suspending of laws, or the execution of laws, by regal prerogative without consent of parliament is illegal.

2. The commission for erecting the late court of commissioners for ecclesiastical causes and all other commissions and courts of like nature are illegal and pernicious.

3. Levying of money for or to the use of the crown by pretence of prerogative without grant of parliament, for longer time or in other manner than the same shall be so granted, is illegal.

4. It is the right of the subjects to petition the king: and all commitments and prosecutions for such petitioning are illegal.

5. The acts concerning the militia are grievous to the subject.

6. The raising or keeping a standing army within this kingdom in time of peace, unless it be with the consent of parliament, is against law.

7. It is necessary for the public safety that the subjects which are protestants should provide and keep arms for their common defence: and that the arms which have been seized and taken from them be restored.

8. The right and freedom of electing members of the house of commons; and the rights and privileges of parliament and members of parliament, as well in the intervals of parliament as during their sitting, to be preserved.

9. That parliaments ought to sit frequently, and that their frequent sitting be secured.

10. No interrupting of any session of parliament till the affairs that are necessary to be dispatched at that time are determined.

11. That the too long continuance of the same parliament be prevented.

12. No pardon to be pleadable to an impeachment in parliament.

13. Cities, universities and towns corporate and boroughs and

---

[1] See CJ, vol. x, pp. 15, 17.

plantations to be secured against quo warrantos and surrenders and mandates; and restored to their ancient rights.

14. None of the royal family to marry a papist.

15. Every king and queen of this realm, at the time of their entering into the exercise of their regal authority, to take an oath for maintaining the protestant religion and the laws and liberties of this nation; and that the coronation oath be reviewed.

16. Effectual provision to be made for the liberty of protestants in the exercise of their religion, and for uniting all protestants in the matter of publick worship as far as may be.

17. Constructions upon the Statutes of Treason, and trials and proceedings and writs of error in cases of treason, to be regulated.

18. Judges' commissions to be made *quamdiu se bene gesserint*; and their salaries to be ascertained and established, to be paid out of the public revenue only; and not to be removed nor suspended from the execution of their office but by due course of law.

19. The requiring excessive bail of persons committed in criminal cases, and imposing excessive fines and illegal punishments, to be prevented.

20. Abuses in the appointing of sheriffs and in the execution of their office, to be reformed.

21. Jurors to be duly impanelled and returned and corrupt and false verdicts prevented.

22. Informations in the court of king's bench to be taken away.

23. The chancery and other courts of justice and the fees of offices, to be regulated.

The commons agreed to these items proposed by its committee and added five 'additional' heads:

24. That the buying and selling of offices, may be effectually provided against.

25. That upon return of writs of Habeas Corpus and mandamus the subject may have liberty to traverse such returns.

26. That all grants of fines and forfeitures are illegal and void; and that all such persons as procure them be liable to punishment.

27. That the abuses and oppressions in levying and collecting the hearth-money be effectually redressed.

28. That the abuses and oppressions in levying and collecting the excise be effectually redressed.

This in effect was the political programme of the revolution. Like the Peoples' Charter in the nineteenth century, it took many years, centuries in some cases, to carry out. The first gains came from making the crown observe the law as it stood and taking away all power to set it aside. The Declaration of Rights incorporated 'heads' 1 to 4, 6 to 9, 19, 21 and 26 (though in the case of the last five of these heads it was thought that 'new laws' would be required as well[1]). The turning of the Declaration into a statute, besides giving it extra force, was the vehicle for an outright abolition of the dispensing power. The lords had refused in February to concur with the commons in declaring it illegal. They knew that it had a perfectly respectable place in the history of the law. So it was declared to be illegal only 'as it hath been assumed and exercised of late'. Further discussion between the houses during the year ended in agreement in a clause which abolished dispensations save as provided for in special legislation to be forthwith passed. But it proved impossible to do this, though the lords several times instructed the judges to prepare a bill: Dolben reported that they had found it 'marvellous difficult'.[2] An attempt was made to add head 12 (no pardon pleadable to an impeachment) to the Bill of Rights.[3] This would have made it much harder for the King to indemnify ministers who had broken the law. The whigs believed such pardons to be unlawful because an impeachment 'is at the suit of the subject'.[4] It was believed that the King could pardon an offence against himself but not one against a third party.[5] On this occasion, however, the proposal was made for the factious purpose of attacking Danby, who had been given a pardon to preserve him from impeachment in 1679, and it did not succeed. Heads 14 to 16, dealing with religion and the crown's relation to it, were all made the basis of legislation in 1689 but are discussed elsewhere.

A very important theme of the 'heads' was the reform of the legal system to make its abuse for political purposes impossible: the suffer-

---

[1] CJ, vol. x pp. 20–2. The houses agreed that the final document should be enrolled in chancery 'to remain to Perpetuity', pp. 27–8.

[2] The Lords would have liked to confine all condemnation of abuses to James's reign but the commons would not agree, *ibid.*, p. 25–7. On dispensation, further, pp. 126, 214, 277, 280; LJ, vol. xiv, pp. 214, 349–50; Lords' MSS., pp. 29, 346–9, 361.

[3] Lords' MSS., p. 345. LJ, vol. xiv, p. 351. The commons had decided in February to drop this head, CJ, vol. x, p. 22.

[4] Sir William Williams, Grey, vol. ix, pp. 285–6.

[5] Cf. p. 16.

ings of the whigs directly inspired some items in the list and nine of the 'heads' (17 to 23, 25, 26) concern the ordinary administration of justice. William went a long way towards compliance with one head (18) when he decided to appoint judges during good behaviour instead of during pleasure. But we have seen that Charles II had done this at first, but had later changed his mind and even got rid of a judge so appointed. Attempts in 1692–3 to make the new policy obligatory by statute failed, partly because supporters of the court did not wish to see the royal power diminished. In 1692 the King vetoed a Bill which would have fixed the judge's salaries and made them financially independent of the crown—but his reason was probably that he would have had to pay these substantial and unalterable salaries out of his overburdened ordinary revenue.[1]

The 'heads' incorporated in the Bill of Rights did something to improve the fairness of trials by stopping the giving away of fines and forfeitures: the crown could no longer give anyone a blatant incentive to help in getting a particular wealthy offender convicted, though rewards to informers continued, of course, and were provided for in many statutes. It was also laid down that jurymen in cases of high treason must be freeholders.[2] The head which called for a general reform of trials for treason found an instant response in the lords. When parliament was not sitting, peers accused of treason or felony were tried by the Lord High Steward's court—in effect, a body of some two dozen peers nominated specially for each occasion by the crown. The opportunity for packing such a court was glaring (in spite of which, it had failed to convict Delamere of complicity with Monmouth in 1685). There had already been six attempts to reform it since the Restoration. The lords' Bill of 1689 sought to ensure that a large number of peers should be summoned to each trial and allowed the accused to 'challenge' up to twenty of them, *i.e.* require that they should not take part. Provisions were added to the Bill which would make it useful to the commons as well. In all cases of treason there were to be two witnesses to each act and the prisoner was to be allowed counsel for his defence. In all capital cases the accused was to have a copy of the indictment five days before he was

---

[1] D. Rubini, *Court and Country, 1688–1702* (Rupert Hart-Davis, 1967), pp. 119–21. Rubini rejects the financial explanation of the veto offered by Macaulay but ignores the draft bill which Macaulay discovered and cites as his evidence.
[2] Cf. heads, 19, 21, 26.

charged and a copy of the list from which the jury was to be chosen to try him two days before the trial began. In all criminal cases witnesses called for the defence were to testify on oath.[1]

The Bill was lost, owing to disagreement between the two houses. The commons would not allow the peers the specially favourable form of trial which they sought. The whigs did not want a law that would have made it easier for Jacobite plotters to escape. Whig lawyers, like Atkyns and Hawles, had formerly championed reform, but the convention parliament suspended the Habeas Corpus Act and loyalty oaths and wider definitions of treason were in the air. It was a tory lawyer, Sir Bartholomew Shower, who emerged in the ensuing years as the most conspicuous champion of reform, though in the days of tory ascendancy he had written in defence of the law as it stood. In five successive sessions treason-trial Bills were proposed, only to be attacked as a danger to national security and sabotaged in the lords by the insertion of a provision relating to the trial of peers which the commons could be counted on to reject. Once at least the King attended a debate in the lords in order to discourage support for such a Bill. At length in 1696 a compromise was reached. The commons conceded that for trials in the Lord Steward's court all the peers should be summoned to attend. The reforms in procedure so long projected were to be introduced for treason trials, but they were not to apply in impeachments, nor in trials for any offence other than treason. A month after the Act was passed came the discovery of the great assassination plot against the King: no doubt the reform would have been further postponed had this come a little earlier. The first trial under the new procedure soon followed: that of Ambrose Rockwood with Shower appearing for the defence. The most obvious change was that the arguments of defending counsel made the trial longer. It lasted from 7 a.m. to 3 p.m. without a break, and the court was only able to try two prisoners that day, instead of three as had been planned.

The legal reforms resulting from the Revolution were important but limited. The judges henceforth were more independent, but they continued to work closely with the politicians and to regard themselves very much as servants of the crown, with a special responsibility for encouraging loyalty and tracking down disaffection. Trials for treason were 'regulated'—except when this was too inconvenient for

[1] Lords' MSS., item 18,

the authorities. Fenwick, the most important conspirator of 1696, was condemned by attainder because only one witness could be produced against him.[1] Lord Winton, a rebel of 1715, was impeached in order to deny him the benefit of the new procedure; his trial was a noisy farce. In 1708 further privileges were given to the prisoner in a treason trial, but the act was only to come into force at the death of the Old Pretender! Only in 1748 was the new procedure applied to impeachments for treason. The feeling in 1689 that changes were also needed in respect of lesser offences did not entirely die. In 1703 the swearing of witnessses for the defence was sanctioned for all cases of felony and not merely treason, thus increasing the credibility of the evidence in the accused's favour. But only in 1837 were defendants in such cases given a statutory right to have counsel.[2] As for the general reform of the legal system pointed to by head 23 in 1689, that was to be the task of the nineteenth century, and indeed of our own.[3]

Perhaps it was because so little had been done to dismantle the legal machinery which the crown could use against opposition that the censorship of the press was allowed to expire in 1695. The freedom of the press is conspicuous by its absence from the 'heads' of 1689 and there is no reason to suppose that thinking men in general believed it to be desirable. But the censorship had not been a very efficient arm of the government and its reputation was not improved by the censors successively employed by the secretaries of state after the Revolution to watch political writings. The whig Fraser, and the tory Bohun, gave offence in turn—not because of what they banned but because each failed to ban a work especially annoying to their political opponents. The Censorship Act expired at the time of Bohun's disgrace and was renewed for only two years. Its further renewal was prevented by disagreement between lords and commons. Charles Blount, a disreputable publicist who procured the fall of Bohun by writing a 'spoof' tory pamphlet which he failed to censor, also helped the cause of freedom with pamphlets cribbed from Milton's *Areopagitica*. But the commons, in declining to agree with

[1] But the whigs had a good excuse: Fenwick's friends had spirited away one of their witnesses. Fenwick was given what amounted to a trial and was allowed counsel.

[2] For most of the above see S. Rezneck, 'The statute of 1696: a pioneer measure in the reform of judicial procedure in England', *Journal of Modern History*, vol. ii (1930), pp. 5–26. Cf. Rubini, pp. 122–6.

[3] Fees were enquired into in 1689, Lords' MSS. item 160.

the lords in renewal of the censorship, only complained of the monopoly of the Stationers' Company and the vexatious activities of licensers and customs officials. It was as a hindrance to commercial enterprise that the censorship was disliked. Freedom of expression remained suspect, but plenty of ways were left, and new ones were devised,[1] to limit it.

The Revolution did not put an end to the expansion of the army which James had undertaken in order to increase his power. Disarmament was scarcely possible in view of the threat of counter-revolution in Scotland and Ireland, supported by France. Control of the forces remained with the crown. William was just as much a professional soldier as James, and he used the same methods to try and ensure that the army would be a thoroughly reliable instrument. Untrustworthy officers were removed and when a regiment contained too many of them it was broken: the rank and file were encouraged to enlist in other units.[2] New regiments were raised from groups especially likely to be loyal. Just as James had recruited papists, so William looked to whigs and especially to those who had sought refuge with him in Holland. Even before the end of 1688 he had ordered the raising of two new regiments of cavalry and four of infantry. In March 1689 he set about raising fourteen more English regiments of foot. The English who came with him from Holland were among the first to enter these units and their colonels included well-known whigs like Mordaunt, Cavendish, Delamere, Lovelace and Winchester. One regiment was even commanded by an ancient Cromwellian colonel, Sir Henry Ingoldsby, and the lieutenant colonel was related to the Protector.[3] While James had dreamed of regiments trained in France, William in April 1689 ordered the creation of three Huguenot infantry regiments, again formed in the first instance from refugees who had accompanied his expedition. That summer Schomberg raised a further Huguenot regiment, of cavalry. Scotland and Ireland also produced their own brands of particularly loyal troops.

William did not greatly trust his English troops, new or old. There were too many political and social notabilities in both. It was not easy to maintain subordination and efficiency, in which English

---

[1] *E.g.* taxes on periodicals. On the end of the censorship see Siebert, pp. 260–5; Macaulay, vol. v, pp. 2299–2309, 2540–8.

[2] Foxcroft, vol. ii, p. 203.

[3] Dalton, vol. iii, p. 78. See in general this vol. sub 1689, especially the regimental list at the beginning.

standards had long been lower than continental. At the end of March William told Halifax that he would raise more regiments but not put lords in command of them. 'The humour and character of a peer of England,' noted Halifax, 'do not agree very well with the discipline to which a colonel must be subject.'[1] William was delighted when Sir John Guise resigned the command of his regiment in September 1689, though Guise and his men had served him during the invasion. But Guise was now giving trouble in the commons and had quarrelled with his lieutenant colonel, whom William considered to be in the right.[2] Schomberg's reports from Ireland that autumn show the English troops there to have been in a lamentable state of inefficiency.[3] To cure this was the work of time, but the more immediate problem was the disaffection still lingering in the army. To neutralize it, William, like James, tended to isolate his troops by stationing them at a distance from the places where they had been raised. British troops were sent to fight in Flanders and Ireland, Dutch troops replaced them in England and the native units who remained in England all had specially reliable commanders. On 1 April 1689 there were almost 11,000 British troops on the continent and 9,000 in Ireland, leaving less than 11,000 in England where they were outnumbered by 14,000 men of the Dutch army.[4] The colonels of the native regiments left in England had mostly either accompanied William in the invasion or taken the lead in subverting James's army.

William gained more confidence in the loyalty of his English troops—and of the country as a whole—as time went on. In February 1690, when he was preparing to go in person to subdue Ireland, he told Halifax that he did not intend to bring any foreign troops into England and that he did not think it necessary to leave more than 4,000 or 5,000 men there, besides garrisons.[5] In March 1689 'unwary speeches' had led to the dismissal of the Duke of Grafton from a colonelcy of guards and Halifax thought that 'the jealousy the king then had of the English troops made the King so much more dissatisfied with' him, 'but as that wore off by time, so did his dislike to the Duke', who was eventually given command of a warship. (William

[1] Foxcroft, vol. ii, pp. 205–6.
[2] Foxcroft, vol. ii, p. 232.
[3] Dalton, vol. iii, pp. 106–23. Cf. Foxcroft, p. 239.
[4] But of course these were not necessarily Dutchmen. Dalton, pp. 10–11. British papist-soldiers were sent to fight on the continent,
[5] Foxcroft, vol. ii, p. 248,

also 'said he did not apprehend the Duke of Grafton so much as he did once; for he lived in a bawdy house and minded nothing else'.[1])

William, like James, followed a military policy that was contrary to traditional English sentiment and had usually been unpopular in parliament. The whigs in particular had inveighed against standing armies and opposed the disarming of the people and the total concentration of force in the hands of the crown. In 1689 the whigs tried to restore to the people some of their lost military power, while giving the crown strength enough to defend the Revolution. They cannot really be said to have succeeded in altering the system. The sixth of the 'heads' which condemned standing armies was included in the Declaration of Rights, but it was too vague to be useful. William was able to keep troops in his other kingdoms or in the navy when parliament would no longer tolerate them. At a pinch the crown could legalize its army by declaring war on someone. The seventh head also appeared in the Declaration, but amendments in the lords had emasculated it. The original wording implied that everyone had a duty to be ready to appear in arms whenever the state was threatened. The revised wording suggested only that it was lawful to keep a blunderbuss to repel burglars: 'Subjects which are protestants may have arms for their defence suitable to their conditions and as allowed by law.'[2] A more practical way of rearming the people would have been to revive the militia and this the convention parliament attempted. The fifth head condemned the existing militia laws and in June 1689 a Militia Bill intended to replace them was introduced in the commons. It sought to make the force more efficient and at the same time to prevent its resuming its traditional role as an instrument of repression. Equipment was to be modernized, a more efficient recruiting system introduced and a little more training done. But central control was to be diminished: nobody was to be lord lieutenant of more than two counties and the King lost the power to appoint officers and deputy lieutenants without reference to the lord lieutenant. Above all, the militia was to lose the general power of searching for and confiscating the arms of persons suspect to the government—for, as the Convention was told, the militia act

[1] Foxcroft, pp. 208, 212, 235.
[2] CJ, vol. x, p. 25. The lords thought that the two houses ought to legalize the existing army by a resolution, but the commons do not seem to have concurred in the one they passed.

had been used to disarm all England. The Bill passed the commons but stuck in the lords and perished with the Convention. The tories had not been loath to use the militia against opponents of the crown. The parliament of 1690, in which they were stronger, left the militia as it was, apart from passing minor measures to make it easier for the crown to call it out.[1]

Practical as well as legislative measures could be taken to restrict the crown's monopoly of armed force. In the appointment of lord lieutenants and justices at the start of his reign, William took the advice of the existing lord lieutenants and of the M.P.s for each county.[2] This arrangement was calculated to give all parties a share in the control of the militia and to keep it out of the hands of mere tools of the government. It marked the return of control in county government to those with local influence. Some of the whigs went further and tried to equip themselves with a measure of local armed support. To augment the militia with bodies of volunteers was a well-established custom. Loyalists had done it after 1660 and in 1685.[3] But whig efforts in this direction aroused a good deal of suspicion. The King's fears of Mordaunt's City regiment have already been mentioned: he was clearly relieved at their eventual 'small appearance'.[4] In Lancashire and Cheshire the whigs were in the ascendant. Delamere had supplanted Derby as lord lieutenant of Cheshire and Derby was so disgusted that he resigned Lancashire also, giving place to Lord Brandon who had previously served James. Delamere was active in training the militia, which he put under the command of his own followers, and he was accused of disarming his political opponents. On 3 June 1689 he held a huge rally of armed men near his home, on Bowdon Downs. To a partisan of the other side reporting to Lord Derby it seemed alarming in the extreme. Two halberdiers (one an old Cromwellian soldier) went through Manchester with drums beating, calling on the people to appear in arms. Constables were threatening to report men who did not go as disaffected. It was 'indecency in a settled government'. Estimates of numbers at the meeting varied from 5,000 to 40,000 and they were

---

[1] Western, pp. 85–9. An amendment offered to the first of these measures would have allowed all who had taken the oaths of allegiance and supremacy to arm themselves in time of invasion or rebellion.

[2] Western, p. 59.

[3] Western, pp. 25–6.

[4] Foxcroft, vol. ii, pp. 222, 224, 233.

said to have come from places up to two or three days' march away.[1]
In Lancashire, Brandon reported that he had some officers and
gentlemen to oblige and wanted to raise six troops of horse, mounting
them on horses confiscated from papists. He hoped to arm 10,000
men to defend the coast and said that he could raise 20,000 at short
notice. But the government rejected his plans.[2]

Perhaps the whigs would have been able to produce a substantial
effect if there had been more willingness in the nation to undertake
military activity. We have seen that William felt obliged to work with
them, whatever his misgivings, and that he used them to augment his
army. He seems also to have wished to have the militia restored to
efficiency. In June 1689 he told the Convention that he was anxious
for an adjournment so that (among other things) the members could
go and help reorganize the militia in their several counties. In 1690
he was trying to get the militia properly armed.[3] But the disarming of
the country had gone too far to be reversed. Even the standing army
was rather unmilitary and serious discipline and training were absent
entirely from the irregular forces. Militia and volunteers turned out
momentarily when a French landing seemed likely and desultory
police work by the militia continued. But increasingly both defence
and police came by default to be the responsibility of the regular
forces.

The most important military measure of the Revolution did not
limit the royal power but increased it, and helped to consolidate the
new regular army. William's purge of the English army and the post-
ing of much of it overseas out of harm's way led to one spectacular
mutiny. In March 1689 the Royal Regiment of Foot, at Ipswich en
route for Holland, declared for King James. It set off for its native
country, Scotland, but was pursued by Dutch troops and surrendered
at Sleaford in Lincolnshire.[4] As a result, parliament passed a short
'Act for punishing officers and soldiers who shall mutiny or desert
Their Majesties' Service'. The crown was empowered to have these
offences tried by courts-martial, which might inflict any punishment,
even death. Soldiers were in no way exempted from the ordinary

[1] HMC *Finch*, vol. ii, pp. 210–11. HMC *Kenyon*, pp. 222–3.

[2] CSPD 1689–90, pp. 166, 171.

[3] Western, pp. 29, 85.

[4] Reasons not already mentioned for the mutiny of this regiment were that a foreigner
(Schomberg) had been appointed to command them and that the Scottish estates had not
yet declared James deposed.

process of law, but the gravest military offences could now be punished without recourse to the civil courts. The first mutiny act expired after only six months but it was succeeded by others, which were valid for about a year and which covered some additional offences, such as false musters and abuses in the payment of billets. To this extent these acts protected the taxpayer and the ordinary subject. But their main purpose was to give the king more power over his troops. The immediate gains were to royal authority and military efficiency. Parliament and the people gained indirectly, and as long as the king used his extra power wisely. It cannot even be said that the need for a mutiny act gave parliament a new hold over the crown. After the conclusion of 'King William's war' in 1697, no more mutiny acts were passed for the remainder of the reign.[1] But the army was perfectly able to exist without them, just as it had for many years before 1689. Military discipline could still be maintained, if with greater difficulty. If discipline did deteriorate, the people would probably suffer more than the King.[2]

(III)

The Revolution deprived the King of his power to alter the law by suspension or dispensation, but it left his executive, judicial and military power largely intact. A great deal therefore depended on whether parliament could be made securely independent of the King and whether the financial arrangements between them would be such as to make the King dependent on parliament. The Declaration of Rights contained platonic statements that 'parliaments ought to be held frequently' and that elections to them ought to be 'free'. There was also the more useful provision that 'proceedings in parliament ought not to be impeached or questioned in any sort or place out of parliament'.[3] When considering the Bill of Rights in November, the lords decided that they ought to revive the triennial act of 1641 which had required elections and the meeting of parliament to take place even if the King failed to order them. Nothing was

---

[1] Except at the very end when war with France was beginning anew. 13 and 14 W. III, c. 2.
[2] Walton, pp. 539–42. See the apposite remarks in J. W. Fortescue, *History of the British Army*, vol. i (Macmillan, 1910), pp. 337–8.
[3] Cf. heads 8–10.

achieved before the dissolution,[1] and Triennial Bills failed in 1692 and 1693 because respectively of a royal veto and a disagreement between the houses. The Triennial Act of 1694 provided that parliament should meet at least every three years and also that no parliament should last longer than three years.[2] But as after the Restoration, parliament did not persist with plans to make its own meeting independent of the royal command: it trusted in the readiness of the King to obey the law.

It is not surprising that whiggish plans for arming the people, and the automatic assembly of parliament, did not get far: they were too close to giving the subject a right to rebel. But measures to safeguard the freedom of elections were not open to this objection and were badly needed to counteract the well-established tradition of pressure on the electors. The commons showed their awareness of this in February 1689 by including among their objectives not merely free elections (head no. 8) but the protection of the rights of corporations (head 13). Unfortunately the achievement of this key objective was impeded by legal difficulties and at length frustrated by party animosity. Tories and whigs did not really differ about the need for a free parliament or the danger of a standing army. Even the radical Triennial Bill of 1689 was partly drafted by Nottingham.[3] But the purges of the municipal corporations under Charles II had been detrimental to the whigs but welcome to the tories, who looked on them as removing social upstarts and enemies of the church. The Revolution was made by harmonizing whig and tory points of view, but no harmony was possible here. The King therefore was not deprived of his power to garble corporations and the rising animosity between the parties gave him the option of once again trying to pack parliaments.

The commons took up the question of the boroughs on 25 February 1689 when they decided not to have a special committee on the subject but gave leave for the presentation of a bill to repeal the Corporation Act—a measure that soon succumbed to anglican hostility.[4] The

---

[1] See Lords' MSS., pp. 342–4; LJ vol. xiv, pp. 345–6, 353, 362, 364–5 for the antecedents of the Bill. Lords' MSS., pp. 364–78, LJ vol. xiv, pp. 374, 421 for the Bill itself.
[2] Cf. head 11.
[3] As n. 1.
[4] For what follows see in general R. H. George, 'A note on the Bill of Rights—municipal liberties and the freedom of parliamentary elections,' *American Historical Review*, vol. xlii (1936–7), pp. 670–9.

subject was referred to the general Committee of Grievances that was set up, and on 5 March the commons accepted its report that the rigged election of sheriffs in London in 1682, the quo warranto proceedings, the various commissions and instructions for purging corporations and managing elections, and the canvassing of 'votes to take off the Penal Laws and Tests' were all grievances.[1] A Bill was duly introduced in the autumn to restore the rights of corporations as they had existed in 1675. It covered not only municipalities but also colonies and plantations—New England was specifically mentioned. Surrenders and forfeitures since that date were annulled and corporations were as far as possible to revert to the condition they had been in six months before the initial purge. The religious test in the Corporation Act was abolished and royal powers to appoint and displace municipal officers were disallowed.[2]

Whatever chances this Bill for undoing the purges intrinsically had were spoiled by the determination of the whigs to conduct a new purge on their own account. A belief that the government that was overthrown had many times broken the law was common to all who supported the Revolution. But since many of them (including even whigs) had supported that government, the wisdom of punishing those responsible for illegal acts was questionable. King William naturally was against it: he wanted harmony among his subjects and he wanted to employ the former servants of King James. On 25 March he asked parliament to pass an act of indemnity with only such exceptions as were necessary for the 'vindication of public justice' and the safety of the state. But on 5 March the commons, on the recommendation of the Committee of Grievances, had set up a committee to find out who were responsible for the misdeeds on which it had reported—not only the attack on the corporations but also the illegal levying of money, the disarming of protestants and the quartering of soldiers.[3] When a Bill of Indemnity did appear, twelve categories of offences were excepted from it and the commons began to consider what persons should be regarded as having thereby been denied pardon. This task was still far from completed when the convention parliament was dissolved, and so the quick burial of the past

[1] CJ, vol. x, pp. 41–2.
[2] Lords' MSS. item 208. A separate bill was to have secured the rights of the universities (see CJ, vol. x, pp. 300–1, 343) and there were to have been other bills for London and Nottingham.
[3] CJ, vol. x, p. 42.

that was the object of the indemnity was not achieved. Present servants of the government were in no way exempt from this enquiry into past misdeeds and Halifax, for instance, was tormented by scrutiny of his conduct as a minister of Charles II. In part the whigs wanted to avenge and rehabilitate their martyrs—a rather ill-assorted body ranging from Algernon Sidney to Titus Oates.[1] But punishment of past offences was also seen as an essential supplement to constitutional safeguards, which had not been unduly increased by the Revolution and which never bound the crown very tightly. On 15 June, for instance, Ettericke put the tory view that it had been the prospect of a catholic king that had 'put men upon a compliance with arbitrary government, and to close with popery' and the removal of that incentive made harsh measures unnecessary. Lowther for his part 'would punish for the future, and pardon all that is past'. But Harbord wanted to hang two of James's judges at Westminster Hall, and Hawles thought that 'if you do not punish the *bene placito* men, you will confirm those of *quamdiu etc.* to do as those before them'.[2] The commons were spurred on by rage at the ill success of the war in Ireland, which they put down to Jacobites in the government. 'I find stones thrown at my back, and I know not who does it,' said Jack Howe, 'but if I find persons in the crowd that are my enemies, I believe they did it.'[3]

It was in this spirit that the commons reached the committee stage of the Corporation Bill in January 1690 and the whigs decided to write into it a new purge. The Bill already provided that freemen brought in after a corporation had been 'regulated' should have no parliamentary vote if they would not previously have been qualified to be freemen. A clause was now inserted which barred from a corporation for seven years those who had formerly taken a part in the surrender of its charter without the consent of the majority of the members of the corporation. The 'regulators' of corporations and municipal officials, who had obtained their posts by royal warrant, were also barred. The clause declared it

> necessary, for the sake of public justice and securing the government for the future, that such open attempts upon the constitution and so notorious violations of oaths and trusts should not go wholly unpunished, lest hereafter ill

[1] Measures to annul their punishment and enquiries into the proceedings against them went on alongside the Indemnity Bill.
[2] Grey, vol. ix, pp. 314, 316–9.   [3] *ibid.*, p. 276.

men might be encouraged to the like guilt, in hopes to come off with impunity, though they should fail, of success.[1]

The reasoning behind this was illuminated when the Bill reached the lords a little later and the judges were there asked their opinion of the words in it which said that the surrenders of charters 'were and are illegal and void'. The judges could not agree whether a corporation could surrender its charter, but Atkyns and Lechmere were positive that it should not if it had the privilege of returning members to parliament. In such cases the charters were not so much the property of the corporations as of the kingdom. 'Out at this leak may run all the government of England. As a peer cannot surrender, so a corporation cannot surrender.'[2]

Be that as it may, the 'Sacheverell' clause would have cleared from the corporations a great many of the local tory wirepullers and could not be tolerable to them. It seems to have been carried in a thin house when many members were still away celebrating Christmas[3] and a week later a fuller house took the almost unprecedented step of ordering it to be torn out of the Bill on the third reading. 'If those surrenders stand,' protested Maynard, 'they may make what parliament they will at court.' 'If these men be put out of the Bill,' retorted Finch, 'you put out the men of estates, and the ancient corporations are put into the hands of men of little or no fortune, and some call them the Mobile.'[4] The Whigs consoled themselves by inaugurating a persecution of the tories. The commons decided to add a Bill of Pains and Penalties to the Bill of Indemnity and it expelled Sir Robert Sawyer for his share in the judicial murder of a whig plotter, Sir Thomas Armstrong, in 1684.

The attempt to make parliament more independent of the King cannot be further discussed without considering the parallel issue of finance: that is, the degree to which the King was to be allowed independence of parliament. For the time being his financial independence was at an end. War had broken out and in wartime the sovereign traditionally did not 'live of his own' but looked to parliament for succour. The next chapter will show how crucial this was to the out-

[1] CJ, vol. x, p. 322.   [2] Lords' MSS., pp. 429–33.
[3] Feiling, p. 270. It was carried 133 to 68, on report, 2 January. It is unclear why the third reading was delayed till the 10th: royal displeasure is one suggestion.
[4] Grey, vol. ix, pp. 514, 519. The whigs moved recommittal and were beaten by 182 votes to 171: CJ, vol. x, p. 329.

come of the Revolution. But the transformation wrought by the war cannot be fully appreciated without prior study of the attempts made after the Revolution to set up a new system for meeting the regular (as distinct from the wartime) needs of the crown. It is not clear that the Revolution alone, unaided by a lengthy war, would have ended the crown's financial independence.

It was well understood that parliament might make up for any lack of constitutional safeguards by keeping the King short of money. Arguing against those who wanted more elaborate safeguards before the crown was bestowed, Harbord told the commons on 29 January 1689

> You have an infallible security for the administration of the government: all the revenue is in your own hands which fell with the late king, and you may keep that back.[1]

But the commons, even the whigs, showed themselves decidedly uneasy about acting in this way. For one thing there was a feeling that the sovereign was in effect the proprietor of the ordinary peacetime revenue—in part hereditary proprietor and in part proprietor for life by virtue of a parliamentary grant. Hence the strange doctrine that the revenues granted to James did not cease with his departure from the throne and technically still belonged to him. It was the tories who originally raised this point when arguing against declaring the convention a parliament: it was not necessary, they said, in order to continue the revenue.[2] But when on 26 February the commons came to consider how the revenue should be settled, whig and tory lawyers seemed to agree that it was still in being and that William might appropriate it. 'If a man enters into religion,' said Sawyer (*i.e.* if he becomes a monk), 'it does not determine the estate but the heir shall enter.' 'If King James be alive,' said Holt, 'the revenue continues; and who must take it? The King [sc. William] takes it in his political capacity, which is not dead but remains.'[3] The commons decided that there ought to be a new grant and Jack Howe hoped 'Westminster Hall shall never decide our purses, what we are to give'.[4] But the main consideration here seems to have been the avoid-

[1] Grey, vol. ix, p. 36.
[2] Grey, vol. ix, pp. 88–9, 96, 109.
[3] Grey, vol. ix, pp. 115–16. See the whole debate, pp. 112–28. For what follows see W. A. Shaw's introduction to CTB vols. ix and x (in vol. ix, pt. i).
[4] Grey, vol. ix, pp. 117–18.

ance of any doubt, to say nothing of the sudden ceasing of the revenue for life when James eventually died. The convention was in no hurry to make a new grant. They had authorized William to collect the revenue during the Interregnum. On 8 March he asked them that it be 'so settled as that it may be collected without dispute'.[1] A temporary Act was thereupon passed continuing the existing revenue to 24 June and indemnifying those who had been collecting it. There was still no permanent settlement of the question in sight when the act expired, but it was only in December that another temporary act was passed, extending the old revenue for a year. Unparliamentary taxation had been condemned in the Declaration of Rights and parliament was keen to enquire into James's irregular levy of 1685.[2] But they not so much allowed as obliged William to do the same thing. The hereditary part of the revenue in the end was not to be re-granted at all.

The old-fashioned attitude of the commons towards the ordinary revenue was further seen when the King announced on March 1 that he was ready to give up the hearth tax. This took care of one of the specific financial grievances in the commons' 'heads': the other, relating to the more valuable excise, apparently went unredressed.[3] Sir Thomas Littleton welcomed it as a 'gracious condescension of his majesty; perhaps the most grateful and the greatest grace that has been done by any king formerly'.[4] It was thus described because it was felt to be a voluntary surrender by the King of his own property.

Respect for the King's rights, however, was tempered by the realization that it was the large ordinary revenue granted to James II which had made him so formidable. Whigs and tories alike were determined that this should not happen again. The debates of 26 and 27 February included several demands that the revenue be granted for three years only. Colonel Birch believed that 'our greatest misery was our giving' the revenue 'to King James for life'.[5] By a three-year grant, said Clarges, 'you will be secure of a parliament'. At the same time there was a disinclination to reduce the ordinary revenue unduly for fear that it would weaken the government and cause dissension between it and the people. Whigs, as warm supporters of the Revolution, may well have felt this more strongly than tories. But Clarges

---

[1] CJ, vol. x, p 45.   [2] Cf. head 3.
[3] Cf. heads 27 and 28.   [4] Grey, vol. ix, p. 129.
[5] For the debates on 26–27 February see Grey, vol. ix, pp. 112–28. For those on 11 and 20 March see *ibid.*, pp. 148–50, 153–8, 176–80.

'would have the monarch and the people in mutual confidence, or else there is no safety to either'. Sir John Lowther referred to the danger from France and asked 'whether it is not necessary that there should be confidence in the King. I doubt not but that the King will call parliaments often.' Sir Francis Drake said 'the same reasons for not giving formerly make me for it now, for our Prince to support the honour of the nation'. A judicious balance between the royal and the popular interest was called for from both the whig and the tory side. Sir Edward Seymour said:

> What you settle on the crown I would have so well done as to support the crown and not carry it to excess. We may date our misery from our bounty here.

Sir Robert Howard said:

> When a popish king has received such testimony of kindness from the parliament as to have the revenue for life, if a prince come in to save your religion and laws should not have the same confidence, it will be thought a great coldness . . . It may give encouragement to your enemies . . . You yourselves, when you shall see the condition of the revenue, may more easily settle your thoughts, what you will do for three years or longer.

Eventually the commons decided that William and Mary should have less than James but ought to be as well provided for as Charles. Restoration experience is particularly apparent in the key suggestions of Colonel John Birch, auditor of the excise, a civil war veteran who had already been in parliament in 1660. On 11 March the whig Papillon moved for a bill to 'give and grant the revenue' to the King and he received some support from Pollexfen and Lowther. Sacheverell, declaring his belief that 'the revenue ceases', said that 'you may declare such a part hereditary; but I shall be against a great revenue, as in former time'. Birch suggested temporary continuation of the revenue while the question was studied (as in 1660) and this was duly voted. On the 20th, detailed figures of revenue and expenditure under James were before the house. Williams pointed out that 'if you give the crown too little, you may add at any time; if once you give too much, you will never have it back again. Therefore I would declare the constant charge of the crown.' Sacheverell was against regarding peacetime expenditure on the armed forces as a 'constant charge'. He thought that it should be an 'extraordinary charge', which parliament should review and provide for from time to time as it saw fit. Birch wanted to show more confidence in the crown and give it greater independence than that. It was hard to tell what would be the appropriate amount in the hypothetical future when peace had returned so he again fell back on Restoration precedent.

> I never was so puzzled in a question in my life as in this. We are establishing a revenue as in time of peace; pray God we may see it! . . . I really would vote 1,200,000*l.* and I would have the world know that the King has such a revenue.

The house approved this amount but tried to reach a more accurate figure by appointing a committee to consider what should be the peacetime expenditure on the forces.[1] It proposed a figure of 718,680*l.*, keeping naval expenditure roughly where it had been under James, but halving his army expenditure and bringing it to the level it had reached under Charles.[2] On 25 April the commons resolved that civil expenditure should be 600,000*l.*, making a grand total a little above what they had originally voted.

The commons had fixed a figure for the revenue that was not entirely hopeless from the King's point of view—though it probably would not have paid for as much as they expected it to.[3] But they failed to make progress in the admittedly tricky task of fixing the ways and means to supply it. We can almost certainly regard this as the point at which the fiscal impact of the war began to mar the crown's longer term financial prospects. Considerable extraordinary revenues had already been voted to pay for the war. Since the King's ordinary revenue was felt to be in some way his property, there was a feeling that he ought, as it were, to be taxed as the subject was when there was extraordinary expenditure. The royal message of 8 March asking for the ordinary revenue to be settled had also asked for money for the war in Ireland and for repaying the Dutch the money they had spent on the invasion. On the 11th, Clarges called for the applying of the 'redundancy of the crown revenue' to these purposes, and Garroway said that he would oppose a grant that was not for 'aid and supply' as well as 'revenue'. On the 20th he hoped that 'the king will contribute to the war as well as we; it is for his safety'. In June Mus-

---

[1] For what follows, though not the way it is put, see Shaw, pp. xxxvii–viii, xlv–xlix.

[2] Detailed figures were: navy 496,080*l.*, army 200,000*l.*, ordnance 22,600*l.* Cf. CTB 1685–9, pp. xciii–iv for previous reigns.

[3] I deduce this from Shaw's calculation, p. xxxviii, that Howard's report underestimated James's expenditure.

grave was saying that the war in Ireland meant that the English were now bearing heavier burdens than the Dutch.[1] Desire not to pay more than their share, and the growing uncertainty about the yield of different taxes as taxation increased, retarded further action by the commons towards settling the ordinary revenue.

William became increasingly restive at the lack of support from the commons, especially in financial matters. He understood the inescapable weakness of his position, telling Halifax in July that 'whilst there was war he should want a parliament and so long, they would never be in good humour'.[2] But he was beginning to feel that the whigs in the commons were making things worse than they might be. He complained that the privy councillors in the house 'obstructed his revenue' and would not move the voting of the money to repay the Dutch. He sent stiff messages to parliament about this and about the settlement of his revenue and eventually decided in disgust on a recess.[3] He 'said if the parliament did not repay the Dutch, he verily believed the States would make a peace next year'. He imagined that there was a 'commonwealth' plot, an early move in which had been the advice to him to give up the hearth tax. He told Halifax that

> he saw the design in the managing the business of his revenue in the house. That they would not have it for the Queen's life, but he would have it for both.
> Said the presbyterians now delayed it for some days, that they might have the honour of it themselves.

Halifax commented that 'about this time there seemed to be the first turn in the King's mind in relation to the dissenters'. He 'said, the revenue once settled, he would take his measures' and Halifax 'supposed the parliament was apprehensive of it'. In September he 'said he heard the commons intended to be as mad as ever' when they met again but 'in case the parliament should do amiss, he said he would never want money for forty days'.[4] Presumably he was beginning to think of calling a new parliament which would treat him better.

William, however, could only achieve this if he could win support among the tories and use them against the more obstreperous whigs,

---

[1] Grey, vol. ix, pp. 148, 150, 178, 376–7.
[2] Foxcroft, vol. ii, p. 223. Halifax noted 'a prosperous war might put them in better humour'.
[3] *ibid.*, pp. 221, 224, 228. Shaw, pp. li, lvi.
[4] Foxcroft, vol. ii, pp. 224–8, 237.

and for the time being he did not trust the tories either. If he imagined a whig plot, he also 'heard something was doing against him by the church party'; that there was a 'design' to 'return to a regency'. He began to consider 'whether he might rely upon the church party', but said that Sir John Trevor, one of the instruments of the alliance when it came, 'was such a knave, that it would be objected if he was employed'.[1] He continued to think 'there was nothing to be done, but to form a party between the two extremes'.[2] Even in January 1690 he 'said it was dangerous to trust the High Tories' and was afraid that a new parliament might question the validity of everything the convention had done, including his own elevation to the throne.[3]

The commons, however, went from bad to worse. They voted the money for the Dutch in great haste before the recess[4] and in the autumn they voted two millions for the war. But after imposing a land tax to cover part of this, they became dilatory in supplying the remainder. They became increasingly eager to drive out of office the leading non-whigs—who were in fact the leading members of the government if the great activity of the king be ignored. In December there was a campaign against Nottingham, Halifax and Godolphin, who could be linked together because they had been James's envoys to negotiate with William a year before and so could be charged with having tried to frustrate the revolution. Halifax by this time was bent on retiring. William told him that after a short Christmas recess 'he should see if they would give money enough to make up the Two Millions, if not there was nothing to be done with them'. After the recess came the Sacheverell amendment. The King 'would not have the Bill of Corporation pass' and 'seemed to be weary of the parliament'. Some of the whigs 'had sent him word, that if he interposed or meddled in it, they would not finish the money Bills'.[5] The tories meanwhile were getting ready for battle. Nottingham, afraid of what the Corporation Bill might do to the church interest in parliament, had been mustering all the votes he could against it and apparently

[1] *ibid.*, pp. 218–9, 227–9. 'King of another opinion since', notes Halifax.

[2] *ibid.*, pp. 229, 230, 232. He was equally dissatisfied with the Scots parliament and ready to dissolve it. He 'could lose nothing' for they 'would give him no money', pp. 223, 236–7.

[3] *ibid.*, pp. 243, 246.

[4] 600,000*l.* (CJ, vol. x, pp. 258–9) which Baxter, p. 250, says was 13% less than they spent.   [5] Foxcroft, vol. ii, pp. 241–3.

had the makings of a majority to beat it in the lords.[1] But the King seems only to have been forced into action when the whigs tried to meddle with the real executive power in the country, namely himself. Despairing of his power to influence events in England, he wished to exert himself where he could make more impact. He considered going to the continent,[2] but eventually decided to take personal charge of the war in Ireland and strengthen his government by defeating its most immediate external enemy, the resurgent power of James. The whigs did not want him to go. He had to prorogue parliament in order to avoid addresses of protest and eventually decided on a dissolution because he did not dare to meet that parliament again.

The general election of 1690 was a turning point in William's reign, though he viewed it with foreboding and initially gained little from it. He told Halifax 'he wished he could trim a little longer but things pressed so, he could not'. He had to call another parliament at once for want of money, but he expected so little from them that he talked vainly of delaying their meeting and also of adjourning them if they did not 'presently supply him'.[3] The new parliament gave him in fact only a little more room to breathe. The government wooed the tories by giving them a slightly larger share of offices at the expense of the whigs. The tories gained ground in the elections sufficiently to be able to carry the election of Trevor as Speaker of the new house, displacing the whig Powle. The new parliament abandoned the persecution of ministers and officials. It at once passed an Act of Grace which pardoned almost all the offences supposed to have been committed before the revolution.[4] This was the end, for the time being, of whig attempts to proscribe the tories. It was a measure of national reconciliation, but it also protected the King's right to the service of all his subjects, allowing him to choose his servants freely from any party.[5] More money was at once voted for the war, though not as much as had been asked.[6] Tories also came to the government's aid

---

[1] Horwitz, pp. 104–6.

[2] Macaulay thought he intended to abdicate, but Baxter, p. 257, believes that he merely wished to take charge of the continental war.

[3] Foxcroft, vol. ii, pp. 247, 249.

[4] A few supposed offenders were excepted but nothing was done to them.

[5] The whig proscriptions would in effect have extended the restrictions imposed by the Test Act and kindred measures on the King's choice of his servants. Any king, William as well as James, was almost bound to resist attempts to deprive him of his subjects' service.

[6] Horwitz, p. 112.

with loans, while impecunious whigs were removed from the treasury board in order to make room for 'such as would advance money'[1]— an interesting sign of how primitive the financial system still was. But William must have felt himself deceived by those who had told him that 'a new parliament would immediately settle a revenue upon him which would give him credit'.[2] They did so, but not in a durable or satisfactory way.

The plan seems to have been that the King would induce parliament to vote him a regular income and to give his Irish campaign a good financial send-off by yielding to the feeling that he ought to contribute something to the war out of his 'own' money. His contribution was to be relatively painless—he would sanction the temporary pledging of his income as security for war loans. When he asked the new parliament for the settlement of the revenue, he declared himself willing 'to have it made such a fund of credit as may be useful to yourselves as well as me', supposing 'no quicker or more convenient way can be found for the raising of ready money'. He was sure that they would 'provide for the taking off all such anticipations'.[3] The commons rose to the bait, but hesitantly: the prevailing attitude in their two-day debate (27–28 March 1690) was the same as in the previous year, namely that the King should have enough for comfort but not so much that they could not be sure of frequent meetings of parliament.[4] Sir John Lowther, now head of the treasury board, proposed the voting of a revenue for life. Sir Edmund Jennings 'would save religion and property: therefore settle the revenue upon this King as upon King James'. Ettericke protested against any idea of keeping the King 'as it were at board wages'. But Hutchinson warned that

> if you gave this revenue to a bad prince, you cannot now decently take it away; if you give it to a good prince, he may be thrifty and may have a bank and may presume upon it to destroy our liberties.

The spectacle of the Dutch guards had evidently made an impact on Sir John Thompson, who said that 'the revenue will keep 30,000 men. I should be loth to see so many foreigners in England in time of

---

[1] Horwitz, p. 110.
[2] Foxcroft, vol. ii, p. 247.
[3] Shaw, p. lxv.
[4] See notably Sir Joseph Williamson's speech, Grey, vol. x, p. 11. The debates occupy pp. 8–22.

peace'. Many therefore wanted a grant for a short term of years only. They had a technical point in their favour also: such a grant was more specific and certain in amount than a grant for life (especially such a poor 'life' as William's, who was about to risk death in battle) and so would be a better security for loans. But members who argued in this way really do not seem to have wished to destroy the King's freedom of action. Maynard proposed a grant for three years, but he said that 'if all were quiet I would have it for life, that the King may be a freeholder as well as we'. Colonel Austen was against a grant for life 'for the King and Queen's sake . . . Granting it for life will prevent any ill ministers from being called in question'. But he hoped the King would be 'as rich'. Sir Joseph Williamson held that 'it will certainly be for the King's service, that people may see themselves out of fear of not meeting the King frequently in parliament'.

The outcome was a compromise between the wish to make adequate provision for the King and the need to grant funds in such a way that they would afford good security. The hereditary part of the revenue (mainly excise) was to continue and a Bill was brought in to effect this which charged it with the repayment of loans but also required grants paid from it to cease at the King's death. William did not like this provision and thought the Bill 'would bring him no credit'. He evaded passing it by bringing the session to an end, but continued to enjoy the hereditary revenue unchallenged.[1] The rest of the excise was granted to him for life, but the customs were voted for four years. Both were to be used for the repayment of substantial loans. The revenues granted to James for a term of years were mostly continued for a further term before they expired.[2] The commons in 1689 had decided that the King should have a peacetime revenue of 1,200,000*l*., but their votes of 1690 halved the hereditary and lifelong component of the revenue and left it at barely 700,000*l*.[3] This was to prove an unhappy precedent for the King. The longer the war lasted, the heavier became the burden of debt placed upon the regular revenues.[4] The commons showed no eagerness to make alternative provision for servicing the loans with which they were charged. When at length they did so, after the war, it was only to the extent

[1] Shaw, pp. lxxi–ii, lxxx–lxxxii.
[2] 2 W. and M. sess. 2 c. 5.
[3] If we accept the calculations presented to the commons in 1689, CJ, vol. x, pp. 37–8.
[4] On the consumption of the revenue by the loans, see further CTB 1695–1702 (vols. xi–xvii), introduction, p. viii.

necessary to give the King an income of 700,000*l*. This is not to say, however, that the commons in 1690 were already regretting the relative generosity of 1689. On the contrary, they showed themselves sympathetic to William, voted revenue enough to make good their former pledge and made a temporary settlement of some of it, above all because of the needs of the war. If William's financial position never improved it was largely because his wars lasted so long and cost so much.

The events of 1690 were only a beginning, but they were enough to show that the sovereign had a good chance of recovering full freedom of action. The government had resumed its manipulation of elections and local administration and by exploiting the heightened antagonism of whigs and tories it might hope to recover much of the ascendancy in local affairs and in parliament which it had had around 1685. The elections of 1690 were accompanied by changes in the composition of the local lieutenancies (especially in the City) to the benefit of the tories.[1] Sir John Trevor, back in the Speaker's chair which he had occupied during the servile parliament of 1685, was given the job of making government influence effective once more in the chamber itself: he distributed the rewards in the gift of the crown to members whose support could in this way be won. The attempt to safeguard the independence of parliament by legislation petered out. No general act was passed to regulate corporations, nor did anything come of the interest apparent after the Revolution in wider measures against electoral malpractices. An act of 1690 restored the Corporation of London to its condition before forfeiture and another annulled the claim of the Lord Warden of the Cinque Ports to nominate one of the members for each town, because 'the elections of members to serve in parliament ought to be free'.[2] But future governmental interference in the towns was not ruled out, and the confusion caused by all the 'regulating' in the eighties was not cleared up so that plenty of scope was left for sharp practice. Curiously, though the 'heads' of February 1689 mentioned the sale of offices as a grievance, they said nothing of the already well-known practice of bestowing offices so as to win parliamentary votes.

---

[1] I imagine this came too late to have any immediate result on the elections. The suspension of the Habeas Corpus Act in the previous year was justified by the local magistracy not yet being in working order again. See Grey, vol. ix, pp. 262–76.

[2] George, 'Bill of Rights', pp. 678–9.

What the whigs and tories were ready to promise to do for the King in order to win his support against each other is strikingly apparent in the rival bids that were made for his favour in the last weeks of the convention's life. Trevor wrote him a long letter in which he detailed the misdeeds of the Convention. 'I am afraid,' he said, 'that the opinion remains still with some people that they are not safe in their power and greatness unless Your Majesty depend upon them.' He advised William how he might best hope to get more money from the existing parliament. But if that failed, 'unless you will absolutely throw yourself and your crown upon the dissenters', there should be new elections and

> proclamations, removals [sc. of whig officials] and other wise methods whereby the church party may be so encouraged and yet the dissenters be assured of their indulgence and your favour.[1]

Promises of tory support for the vote of supply were endorsed by a meeting of 150 members of the outgoing parliament at the Devil Tavern on 5 January.[2]

It seems appropriate for tories to be helping the King to recover his independence, but was the whig attitude any different? A prominent whig wrote to William on Christmas Day 1689—he is thought to have been Thomas Wharton, later a marquess and the great electoral manager of the whig 'junto'. The letter is, as might be expected, mainly an insolent rebuke to the King for having so far forgotten himself as to employ tories and keep James's troops on foot. 'There is scarce one word against King James in your declarations [sc. before the invasion]: The evil ministers are alone complained of, yet King James alone is punished.' 'We have made you King . . . and if you intend to govern like an honest man, what occasion can you have for knaves to serve you?' Because of enemies at home and wars abroad, 'you will always want to be supported by parliaments, therefore it is necessary that you do what you can to satisfy your people'. But amid this insolence it is striking to see how much this whig was prepared to concede to the King in the way of money and executive power. Of the existing ministers he said

> The pretence of their being experienced is very weak. Their experience was only in doing ill; and our laws having sufficiently chalked out the functions of all civil ministers at home, plain honest men of good understanding and

[1] Dalrymple, vol. ii, pt. ii, appendix to bk. iv, pp. 182–6. CSPD 1689–90, p. 441.
[2] Horwitz, p. 107.

principles, suitable to the ends you declared you came hither for, might have
performed these duties, especially since your majesty's great wisdom can well
supply their defects in foreign affairs.

In other words, if the whigs got the jobs they would be quite happy to
accept the menial position that William assigned to his ministers.
The tories on the other hand were accused of having wished to deny
William effective control of the country: their resistance to his being
made King was interpreted in this light and Nottingham was virtually
accused of republicanism. As for money, it was only because the
ministers were 'a medley of men who can never act heartily together'
that 'your friends could not serve you'. Putting this right 'will make
the parliament give you all the money you can want or desire'.[1]

Neither party was able entirely to fulfil their financial promises to
William because in this matter there was still something like a
national consensus, limiting what it was thought proper that the
King should have. But it was largely the needs of the war that frustrated William's efforts in that direction and it was to feed the war
that William chose to use the political influence which he had in his
kingdoms. Inclining now to the whigs and now to the tories, he
managed to get parliament to vote the great sums needed to maintain
the war and yet keep control of it in his own hands: in this achievement he showed himself a stronger king than his Stuart predecessors
and relatives—as he also did in being more ready than they to use his
veto against bills which threatened his authority. Like Charles II
and James II, however, William had to face a great upsurge of
opposition in the latter part of his reign. When the war ended, there
was a general movement of protest against the way in which he had
ruled which to some extent transcended party differences. Just as the
Bill of Rights and the other measures of 1689 were inspired by the
misdeeds of James and attempted to prevent their repetition, so the
Act of Settlement (1701) and other measures of William's last years
were an attempt to stop the misdeeds of William. Laying down conditions to be observed when the throne passed to the house of
Hanover, the Act of Settlement secured two of the objectives of 1689:
judges were to have fixed salaries and not be removable save by parliament and a royal pardon was not to be a bar to impeachment. But
its other provisions related primarily to what William had done.
Future sovereigns must 'join in communion' with the Church of

[1] The letter is in Dalrymple *loc. cit.*, pp. 187–200. Cf. CSPD 1689–90, p. 367.

England and without the consent of parliament were not to leave the British dominions nor involve the country in war for the defence of any foreign territory. No foreigner was to hold any office or receive any grant of crown property or be a member of the privy council or either house of parliament. No one receiving official emoluments or a pension from the crown was to be a member of the house of commons. All matters 'properly cognizable in the privy council' were to be 'transacted' there, and the resulting 'resolutions' were to be signed by the councillors who advised them. (In other words, the country was to be governed by the men who were supposed to be ministers, not by the king and his personal associates.)[1]

The sovereign did not lose his independence at the Revolution. Such ground as he did lose he might hope to regain through the continuance of his local and parliamentary influence. It can plausibly be argued that royal independence ceased at the end of William's reign, not at the beginning. If this was so, it was not because of the laws that were passed then. The Bill of Rights had not shackled William because it looked backward—it restated what was conceived to be the existing law and condemned the infringements of it made by a particular sovereign. The Act of Settlement did the same (and its provisions were impracticable anyway). But just as William did not repeat the misdeeds of James, so future sovereigns would not exactly repeat the misdeeds of William. As in the past, the imposition of new curbs on the crown meant only that the crown revived by developing in a new direction. Only a more direct attack on the institution of monarchy could interrupt this process. Some of the hostility for William and his successors did take the form of seeking to reduce royal authority in local affairs and even to place certain sections of the central government under parliamentary control. But the monarchical viewpoint usually prevailed in the end.

If nevertheless William was gradually losing his independence, it was not because of deliberate efforts to restrict it, but because his lengthy involvement in war was altering the character of government and the balance of political forces in the state. How the changes which began in his reign led to the final domestication of the monarchy is a story stretching far beyond the confines of this book. One

---

[1] See Rubini, Appendix C, pp. 282–3, for interesting comments which show that, perhaps unintentionally, parts of the Act were so drafted that they should have come into force at once. Aliens were excluded from office even if naturalized.

aspect of the subject, though, is of very pressing relevance here: to what extent was the war a necessary consequence of the revolution? What exactly was the connection between the two? The final chapter very briefly considers the war and its consequences. But first the religious side of the revolution must be examined and something said of the illuminating contrast between English and Scottish experience in 1689.

(IV)

In the religious no less than in the political debates which followed the Revolution there was a rehash of old quarrels which led to no definitive result. William took the radical side in the argument, as his predecessors had done in the religious question and as he did himself in the question of disposing of the crown. He was no more able than Charles and James had been to overcome the widespread aversion to a really generous religious settlement. But much had been done in the religious question before the Revolution, both by and against the crown. The dissenters had been allowed freedom of worship. It was inconceivable that they could again be deprived of it, especially as some degree of protestant unity had come to seem essential for national well-being. The convention parliament had an inescapable duty to regularize the position created by past action. As their task was so clear, they achieved more in the settlement of religious quarrels than in the resolving of secular issues. But religious issues, too, of the first importance, remained intractable.

The 'heads' of February 1689 proposed the outlawing of the ecclesiastical commission and provision for the 'liberty of protestants'.[1] The former was achieved by the Declaration of Rights and to achieve the latter there was virtually a revival of the proposals made in 1680. The general religious situation in the two years was much the same. The dissenters and their whig friends were in a relatively strong position and so were inclined to disdain measures to make it easier for them to join the established church and to dream of outright emancipation, which would give them in particular the right to hold public office. The anglicans, on the defensive, hoped to weaken the dissenters by a Comprehension Bill which would bring most of them into

---

[1] Heads 2 and 16.

the church and to give the remainder nothing more than toleration. In 1689, however, the dissenters were better, and the churchmen were worse, placed than in 1680. The new King was not an anglican, though the Queen was. Not only had persecution of the dissenters ceased but punitive action was threatened against some of the anglicans. The demand was being made that the clergy should take an oath of loyalty to the new rulers, but many bishops and clergy were such strict legitimists that they would clearly refuse to do so. In this situation even the presbyterians, who wanted to reinvigorate the church rather than destroy religious uniformity, adopted a stiffer attitude towards the anglicans. In January 1689 Baxter, Bates and Howe wanted a remodelling of the church which would have required bishops to exercise their functions in conjunction with presbyters. Bates told the new King and Queen that the proper basis of comprehension was 'the terms of union wherein all the reformed churches agree'.[1] The church had escaped the perils of King James's reign only to face new perils under King William.

Churchmen had come to agree that in face of either class of peril, conciliation of the dissenters was essential. This was accepted by high churchmen as well as by latitudinarians. Sancroft told Clarendon and Tenison on 3 January 1689 that he was sure that all the bishops were ready to make good the assurance to the dissenters which had been included in the bishops' famous petition to James. Already after his trial in 1688, he had issued articles to his bishops in which the clergy were called on to 'have a very tender regard to our brethren, the protestant dissenters' and to encourage joint prayer 'for an universal blessed union of all reformed churches, both at home and abroad, against our common enemies'—a remarkable pronouncement for a high churchman. According to John Kettlewell, a later nonjuror, 'consults' at Lambeth produced the heads of a plan, which was sent to dissenting leaders, 'for the better securing and strengthening of the protestant interest and religion and for making the Church of England the head of that interest'.[2] On 14 January 1689 the subject was considered at a meeting at St Paul's deanery to which Bishop Lloyd of St Asaph came, bringing the Primate's approval. Stillingfleet, Tillotson, Sharp, Patrick and Tenison were there and they

---

[1] Thomas, 'Comprehension and Indulgence', p. 244.
[2] N. Sykes, *From Sheldon to Secker*, pp. 83–6. G. Every, *The High Church Party 1688–1715* (S.P.C.K., 1956), pp. 22–5. But the dates of what was done are conjectural.

prepared the outline of a Comprehension Bill, to be proposed in parliament by the bishops. It was Nottingham, however, who, after six meetings with bishops and clergy, introduced the Bill. Few of the bishops were prepared to come to parliament once they had to take the new oaths. But until forced to withdraw, they spoke in favour of comprehension.[1]

Nottingham introduced two Bills in the lords—one for Toleration on 28 February and one for Comprehension on 11 March. The former was almost the same as that of 1680 and little further needs to be said about it. The latter mentioned the Worcester House scheme of 1660 and resembled it in envisaging not merely concessions on contentious points but some more general reshaping of the church. The Comprehension Bill of 1680 had consisted merely of concessions: these mostly reappeared. Recognition was not this time offered to those who had received presbyterian ordination during the Inter-regnum, but presbyterian ministers wishing to enter the church could be ordained according to the formula proposed in 1668, which did not cast doubt on the validity of their previous ordination. The really ambitious feature of the Bill was a royal commission of twenty clergy, including the two archbishops, to prepare improvements in the liturgy and canons and in ecclesiastical justice and discipline. In particular, they were to try and ensure 'due preparation and solemnity' in confirmation and 'strict care' in examining candidates for ordination. The emphasis on discipline had been characteristic of the presbyterians and of the effort to compromise with them in 1660.[2] But it was also a characteristic of the more militant anglicans, who still hankered after the system of Laud. They were nearer to the presbyterians on this point than the 'latitude men', who were more ready for compromise on ordination and points of doctrine. Henry Dodwell, who was to be a leading high church extremist, had corresponded with Baxter on the question of discipline. His friend William Lloyd, on becoming Bishop of St Asaph (1680), conferred with John Howe, who told him that enabling ministers to promote 'parochial reformation' was the way to heal the schism. Lloyd agreed on the importance of this. He tried, as bishop, to reserve the power of excommunication to himself, denying it to his (lay) chancellor

[1] Sykes, pp. 86–7. Horwitz, p. 87. Feiling, p. 264. Bishops White and Turner were allowed to speak in committees though they had not taken the oaths: Every, p. 33.
[2] Thomas, pp. 245–6, for comparison with 1660, 1668. Every, p. 32. Horwitz, p. 87.

for whom it was merely a procedural device in the largely secular business of the ecclesiastical courts.[1]

When therefore the stricter anglicans at last became more interested in comprehension in 1688, the issue of discipline naturally came to the forefront. The plan emerging from the Lambeth 'consults', if it really dates from this time, shows this clearly. It envisaged not only stricter catechising, greater care in examining ordinands, a new book of canons and the reform of church courts, but also an end of pluralism, the relief of clerical poverty, a 'more effectual way' to remove 'scandalous ministers', the building of more churches in the metropolis and above all the redivision of dioceses[2] so that 'none be larger than one man can take care of'. A paper in Sancroft's hand which has survived covers much the same ground: excommunication, pluralism, scandalous ministers.[3]

It is doubtful if the Comprehension Bill ever stood much of a chance. Morrice complained at once that it was less generous than the bill of 1680.[4] On the other side, as early as the perilous days of September 1688, Bishop Turner of Ely had protested to Sancroft against offering up 'all our ceremonies in sacrifice to the dissenters', whom the anglicans outnumbered anyway.[5] But any chance the Bill might have had was swept away by the onslaught on the anglican monopoly now made by its more radical critics. In face of this the anglican instinct was to close ranks, concede toleration to the dissenters because it was unavoidable, and fight hard against conceding more. The greatest onslaught on the church was in Scotland, where the presbyterians were seizing ecclesiastical power by force just as conciliatory proposals were being brought forward in England. It had an increasing impact on anglican opinion as the year went on, especially when the English presbyterians began once more to ordain ministers. Apparently even the most moderate of the dissenters must be counted as enemies. Writing to Simon Patrick from York in October 1689, Dr Comber admitted that some presbyterians were moderate and friendly, but said that their 'late successes' in Scotland

---

[1] Every, pp. 10–13. But Lloyd was a friend of Wilkins too. Dodwell's view tended to be very odd.

[2] Every, pp. 22–3, 41–2 (note discussion of date). The diocese article precedes the others. Ordinations were to be limited to prevent 'over-stocking'. Simony and clandestine marriages were to be hindered.

[3] Sykes, pp. 188–92.

[4] Horwitz, p. 88.   [5] Every, p. 25.

'and the opinion of their number and interest here hath lately advanced their pretences to liberty of conscience into hopes of legal establishment and dominion over all others'. This did not so much mean that comprehension must be given up as that it must be deferred until the church was not actually under attack.[1]

In England the attack began with a Bill in the commons respecting the new oaths of allegiance and supremacy which would have made them obligatory for the clergy as well as the lay servants of the crown. A Bill introduced at the same time in the lords would have left it to the King to decide whether to enforce the oaths on the clergy.[2] Then on 15 March, when Nottingham's Bills reached the committee stage in the lords, Winchester moved for a select committee to devise an alternative to the system whereby officeholders were obliged to take the sacrament according to the rites of the church. This proposal was carried with difficulty. Next day the King addressed the two houses from the throne. 'I hope,' he said, 'you will leave room for the admission of all protestants that are willing and able to serve.' He let it be known that if the anglican monopoly of office were thus abolished, he would be ready to allow the clergy not to take the new oaths. This rather crude attempt at political pressure appears to have been suggested by the whig leader Richard Hampden (son of John).[3] It was followed in the commons by a proposal to bring in a Bill to repeal the Corporation Act. On 1 April the friends of the church managed to get the committee stage of the Bill postponed, but they had to accept the appointment of another committee led by Hampden's son (another John) which was to draw up a fresh Comprehension Bill.[4] This measure appeared on 8 April and proved very different to the lords' bill. Ordination in any reformed church was to be accepted as qualifying a man to enter the anglican ministry and the clergy in the established church were no longer to be obliged to read from the book of common prayer. The first provision was Elizabethan and the whole measure, like Nottingham's, was rooted in the bill of 1680 and the antecedent discussions. But it was now far too

---

[1] Every, pp. 37–41. Howe and Bates were wisely unwilling to ordain and there were no presbyterian ordinations in London till 1694.

[2] Feiling, p. 264.

[3] Feiling, p. 264. Every, p. 33. Horwitz, p. 88, who suggests Lord Wharton was working with Hampden. The King expressed his confidence that they would 'sufficiently provide against papists'.

[4] Macaulay, vol. ii, p. 1407. Horwitz, p. 91.

radical to commend itself to churchmen. A newsletter not unfairly said that it 'made the Church of England more dissenters and not dissenters Church of Englandmen'. This measure, too, was adjourned by the commons—one member wanted it adjourned till Doomsday.[1]

The King's remarks had been followed at once by a strong rallying of the friends of the church, whose power can be seen in the checks its assailants received even in the commons. On the very day of the King's speech a meeting of militant anglican M.P.s at the Devil Tavern in Fleet Street had resolved to oppose his plan. Two days later they frustrated an attempt in the commons to dispose of the sacramental test and they saw to it that the new coronation oath bound the sovereign to preserve the church 'as by law established'.[2] In the upper house the proposals to get rid of the sacramental test were finally rejected on 21 and 23 March. Nottingham said that even in Holland office was confined to adherents of the strict form of calvinism officially established. Not only Danby but Devonshire took the church side, and when the committee stage of the Comprehension Bill was reached, Devonshire secured the removal of the clause which made kneeling at communion optional. It was later restored, but the clause allowing a special form of ordination for those already in presbyterian orders was completely cut out.[3]

It is evident that the friends of the church included whigs as well as tories and that they were not prepared, as one said, 'to barter and break the church to save a few churchmen'.[4] On the contrary, they opened a counter-attack. Churchmen in the commons insisted that 'no man, from the bishops downward, is against any comprehension or ease to tender consciences'.[5] But Nottingham's Bills were amended in the lords not merely to limit the gains of the dissenters from them but to give the church a chance to make gains of its own. An important church grievance against the Comprehension Bill was 'that a parliament should reform our liturgy, expunge creeds, tell us what we must not believe and what we must, without advising with a convocation'.[6] Since it had lost its taxing powers in 1664, convocation

---

[1] Horwitz, p. 92. Thomas, pp. 249–50.

[2] Feiling, p. 265. Horwitz, p. 91. Sawyer, Finch, Clarges, Musgrave and Sir J. Tredenham were leading men at the Devil meeting.

[3] Horwitz, pp. 88–90. Every, p. 34.

[4] Feiling, pp. 264–5. [5] Every, pp. 34–5. Thomas, p. 249.

[6] Strictly speaking there were two convocations, of Canterbury and York, but the fact was often forgotten. For what follows see nn. 4, 5 above.

had met when parliament did but had not been allowed to do business. In the irregular circumstances of the calling of the Convention, it had not been summoned at all. Now, it seems, the spineless old Lamplugh, archbishop of York, was put up to argue that this was irregular and that parliament should not 'meddle in matters spiritual or ecclesiastical before they are first handled by the clergy in their convocation'. The lords accordingly amended the Comprehension Bill to require the proposed royal commission to report to convocation as well as to parliament. The church was taking advantage of the Revolution to demand a say in its own affairs, such as the laity were hoping to gain through parliament.

Another provision which the lords added to their Bill was directed against occasional conformity: the practice of receiving the sacrament in an anglican church in order to qualify for office while continuing normally to worship at a dissenting chapel. Some dissenters who sympathized with the church sometimes attended her services for genuine religious reasons, but this was clearly a means by which dissenters could infiltrate their way into office and power. The clause now adopted came from a complete Bill which Nottingham had drafted on the subject—the first in a notable series.[1] A change of comparable importance, which likewise opened a whole campaign, was made by the lords in the Toleration Bill: they deleted the clause exempting dissenting schoolmasters from prosecution.[2] This change expressed an important feature of the militant anglican approach to toleration: they thought of it as a temporary expedient for avoiding violence while they wore down the dissenters by non-violent means. The ending of nonconformity remained their goal, but their methods were to be milder: comprehension perhaps, and above all a monopoly of education. As Sacheverell said in 1709, the Toleration Act

> was intended for the ease of those whose minds through the unhappy prejudices of education were already estranged from the church; not, as he humbly conceived, to indulge men in the most effective methods to propagate and perpetuate their schism.[3]

This had been the philosophy behind the Edict of Nantes in France—and its revocation. The extinction of dissent by attrition, along with a strict anglican monopoly of secular offices and greater autonomy for

[1] Horwitz, pp. 89–91.
[2] Horwitz, p. 93. Thomas, p. 251.
[3] Not to be confused with the whig Sacheverell. Sykes, p. 95.

the church, was to be the programme of the 'high church' party for the next generation. The party acquired its name soon after the Revolution[1] and the form it took may fairly be regarded as a crystallizing of militant anglican sentiment in response to the emergencies and particular circumstances of 1688–9.

The lords' Comprehension Bill reached the commons on 9 April, just after the whig Bills introduced in that house had been adjourned. It had become apparent to some observers that 'the Church of England has a majority in both houses',[2] but pressure against it was still strong. It is pretty clear from the ensuing events that the leaders on both sides agreed on a compromise. On 9 April the whig Harbord asked the commons to draw up an address to the King thanking him for his coronation promise to defend the church and asking him to summon convocation. Harbord reassured those who had 'jealousies of the King in that point' that he 'was altogether of the judgment of the Church of England'. He suggested that they should further tell the King that there would be no delay in enacting toleration. A committee was at once appointed to draw up the address and it included both tories (Musgrave, Finch, Clarges) and whigs (Somers, Treby). That evening a meeting of 160 'Church of Englandmen' at the Devil Tavern agreed to support the address to the King which, it was said, 'is done with his own consent, I suppose at the motion of the Earl of Nottingham'. The address that was drawn up warned the King that the best way of 'securing the hearts' of his subjects was to protect the church. The lords were asked to concur in it and it was presented to the King as a joint address on 19 April. William promised to summon convocation, both Comprehension Bills were dropped and there were no more attacks on the sacramental test. In May the Toleration Bill became law, after Clarges in the commons had tried to have its life limited to seven years. He was fulsomely reassured: 'if they make an ill use of it,' said one member, 'there will be always enough in this house to take it away.' 'The Committee,' said Littleton, 'though they were for indulgence, were for no toleration.'[3] But indulgence by law instead of by royal edict was a victory

---

[1] Every, pp. 1, 2. The meeting of convocation in 1689 seems to have been the point at which the two sides in the church clearly appeared as parties.

[2] A letter of 21 March often cited, *e.g.* Horwitz, p. 91.

[3] The address was amended in the lords. Horwitz, pp. 92–3. Feiling, pp. 265–6. Grey, vol. ix, pp. 261–2.

for dissent and so in a way was the check to comprehension. As John Hampden said,

> The design of some who drove it was only to destroy obliquely and by a side wind what has been gained at a favourable time in the act of toleration, which they durst not directly attempt to overthrow.[1]

But the summoning of convocation and the strict limits to toleration were victories for the church.

The question of the oaths to be taken by the clergy was not included in the compromise. The King[2] supported the lords' plan of leaving the matter to the discretion of the government, but the commons insisted that all should be sworn and their view prevailed.[3] They were willing to allow the king to make financial provision for twelve clergy unwilling to take the oaths. Bishops and incumbents had to do this by 1 August. If they did not, they were to be suspended until 1 February 1690 and then deprived if they remained recalcitrant. Sancroft and five bishops suffered deprivation, together with about 400 clergy.[4] As in 1662, the commons protected the church, but insisted on a purge of the clergy. No doubt in both cases it was the supposed political danger that they represented which was decisive in enabling the commons to have their way.

The measures of the spring of 1689 represent the religious settlement of the Revolution, but it was not apparent at the time that this was so. As after the Restoration, the situation appeared fluid, with clerical activity for the reform of the church and negotiations between the different clerical parties, including the men about to be proscribed. Most of this activity proved abortive in both cases but each time it might have been otherwise. Comprehension was adjourned rather than given up in the spring of 1689 and the question was given a wider and greater importance by parliament's decision regarding the oaths. It was no longer just a matter of coaxing nonconformists into the church—the stricter anglicans must be soothed and nothing further done which might tempt them to leave it. The oaths, coupled with the dire Scottish situation, led to passionate pleas for the preservation of the church from lay control. This involved more empha-

---

[1] Feiling, p. 266 n. 1.   [2] Every, p. 36.
[3] Horwitz, p. 94.
[4] Every, pp. 61–2. Three more bishops had died, including Cartwright, who fled with James.

sis on the claim that the apostolic succession gave the anglican clergy an authority which owed nothing to the state and which set them apart from almost all protestant communions. This claim was really a seventeenth-century formulation and we have seen that only since 1662 had episcopal ordination been required for anglican priests. Now Henry Dodwell was writing that bishops could never be deposed and he and others were saying that the acts of a convocation from which the primate was excluded might be invalid. Especially perilous would be the admission of persons to the ministry whose ordination was dubious. Dodwell told Tillotson, who was the royal choice to succeed Sancroft, that 'the lay pretended law' was not 'sufficient to discharge you in conscience from your promised canonical obedience'. This would be 'heretical' and 'puts it into a King James's power to ruin our church by an act of state'.[1] There was a danger that nonjurors would seriously disrupt the church by seeking to form an independent, more truly 'apostolic' one of their own. Therefore while Burnet, now Bishop of Salisbury, and Lloyd of St Asaph negotiated with leading dissenters, Nottingham twice visited Sancroft on the King's behalf.

Nottingham gained steadily in influence with William during the later months of 1689 and deserves some of the credit for the King's beginning to favour the tories. His continuing efforts to strengthen the church by promoting comprehension were complementary to this, but the tory revival was so virulent in the ecclesiastical sector that he could accomplish nothing. It was impossible to call convocation until the date for taking the oaths had passed and the position had became clearer.[2] Early in September some of Nottingham's moderate clerical friends were promoted and a commission of ten bishops and twenty other clergy was appointed to pave the way for convocation as envisaged in Nottingham's abortive Bill. But stricter anglicans regarded it as another piece of lay interference: ten members of the commission failed to attend and four more soon gave up.[3] All that the commission managed to achieve was a revision of the Prayer Book, based it seems on the work inspired by Sancroft in the previous year. The changes were verbal rather than doctrinal. Stillingfleet said that

[1] Every, pp. 39, 41, 66.
[2] Every, p. 43.
[3] Horwitz, pp. 99, 100: not all the absentees were high churchmen.

they sat there to make such alterations as were fit, which would be fit to make were there no dissenters and which would be for the improvement of the services.[1]

Concessions that Nottingham had offered to dissenters in his Comprehension Bill reappeared—over ordination, baptism, kneeling at communion—but in a carefully circumscribed form.[2] Convocation met on 21 November and the elections for the lower house (representing the ordinary clergy) were almost a dress rehearsal for the tory successes in the ensuing parliamentary elections. Burnet says that the 'great canvassings' which took place—Clarendon was involved in them at Oxford—were not usual. The lower house at once showed its temper by electing a high-church Prolocutor (Speaker), Dr William Jane, Regius Professor of Divinity at Oxford, in preference to Tillotson, the future archbishop. They showed no desire to do anything but put and score debating points. Compton, who presided over convocation in the absence of the primate, was nominally in favour of comprehension. But Jane had once been his chaplain and Tillotson attributed Janes's election in part to Compton's jealousy of his own coming advancement. Nottingham was able to address convocation briefly when he brought them a message from the King. The lower house quarrelled with the bishops even about the terms of the reply to the royal message, questioning words which implied close assimilation of the Church of England to protestant churches elsewhere. They considered means for the suppression of a supposedly heretical pamphlet. There was a speech in favour of admitting the nonjuring bishops to the assembly. No progress had been made by the Christmas recess after which the dissolution of parliament automatically brought that of convocation.[3] Things were so obviously hopeless that convocation was not again allowed to do business until 1701. Instead there was another fruitless attempt at the end of December, apparently inspired by Nottingham, to negotiate with the nonjuring bishops.[4]

This was really the end of comprehension but many have thought (with Burnet) that it also meant that the danger of a grave new schism was removed. Traditional anglican worship was preserved unimpaired

[1] Carpenter, *The Protestant Bishop*, p. 159.
[2] Every, pp. 47–56.
[3] Every, pp. 57–60. Carpenter, pp. 162–8. Ironically Jane was a predestinarian and Tillotson an arminian: Every, p. 44.
[4] Horwitz, p. 101.

and so there was no pressing reason for strictly anglican laymen to desert their parish churches. Nonjuring remained a mainly clerical movement. Some of the credit for this, however, must go to the non-jurors themselves: they were not eager to break up the church. Ken and Frampton among the bishops continued their episcopal work for as long as they could, while refraining from conflict with the new authorities in church and state. Frampton would have eased the position by resigning if he had been allowed to. Sancroft, while he continued to be recognized as archbishop, issued commissions to others to institute new bishops. Though they looked on the church-men who took the oaths as being in schism, the nonjurors did not deny that their bishops were true bishops. They were reluctant to perpetuate a hierarchy of their own. Eventually two suffragan bishops were consecrated but their existence was kept secret for many years. When the old bishops were all dead, some nonjurors returned to the church. Politically only one of the deprived bishops was at all active as a Jacobite—Turner of Ely.[1] It seems fair to regard nonjurors as anglicans often regarded moderate puritans: they were in schism because their consciences were over scrupulous and they wished the church no harm.

The religious outcome of the Revolution was rather surprising and satisfactory to no one. There was a strong church still in a highly privileged position but also a strong body of dissenters now free to organize. Uniformity had ended but religious liberty had not properly been established. The prosperity of dissent is attested by the growing number of places registered for dissenting worship: 796 temporary and 143 permanent (plus 239 for the quakers) appeared in the first year and by 1700 thirty-two permanent and 1,247 tem-porary places had been added.[2] Not only did many people change from church to chapel—many gave up religion altogether. Humphrey Prideaux, Archdeacon of Norwich, wrote in 1692 of the Toleration Act that

> unless there be some regulation made in it, in a short time it will turn half the nation into downright atheism. I do not find . . . that conventicles have gained anything at all thereby, but rather they have lost. But the mis-chief is, a liberty now being granted, more lay hold of it to separate from all

[1] Every, pp. 61–74.
[2] E. D. Bebb, *Nonconformity and Social and Economic Life, 1660–1800* (Epworth Press, 1935), app. i, p. 17, cited *e.g.* Sykes, p. 91.

manner of worship to perfect irreligion than goes to them; and although the act allows no such liberty, the people will understand it so.[1]

In 1715 William Wake, then Bishop of Lincoln, said that

> if any persons be admonished to come to the Holy Communion, or threatened for that or any other neglect, they presently cry they will go to the meetings to avoid discipline.

It was necessary, he urged, that 'the canons should be revised and fitted better to the toleration, if that must be continued'.[2] The legal machinery for obliging people to go to church seems to have worked fairly well until the Declarations of Indulgence, but toleration fatally impaired it. This was the price which both high churchmen and presbyterians paid for the failure of comprehension.

An important step having thus been taken towards the secularization of society, religious leaders began to adopt new and more 'modern' methods of maintaining their influence. Voluntary activity and appeals to the civil power began to take the place of discipline exercised through ecclesiastical courts and ecclesiastical censures. The different denominations co-operated to some extent against the common foe of godlessness. Bishop Compton, advising his clergy how they 'ought to behave themselves under a toleration', wanted to 'render charity triumphant over division'. Clergy and dissenters should not only respect each other's legal rights but they should co-operate in pressing the civil magistrates to enforce the penalty on not attending church. This joint venture would encourage 'familiar and friendly conversation'.[3] Missionary societies, religious societies and societies for the reformation of manners were an important feature of the post-Revolution era. This was a move towards the system of Penn, for whom general toleration was to pave the way for union against vice and its suppression by christian magistrates. It also meant encouragement for those who wished to simplify religious beliefs, for this would facilitate both missionary activity[4] and Christian unity. John Locke drew up about the time of the Revolution rules for a 'society of pacific Christians' whose leading principle was to be 'love and charity in the diversity of contrary opinions'. Their meetings, 'laying aside all controversy and speculative ques-

---

[1] *Letters of Humphrey Prideaux* (Camden Soc., 1875), cited *e.g.* Every, p. 67.
[2] Sykes, p. 91.
[3] Carpenter, pp. 168–9.
[4] For foreign missions, interesting examples in Sykes, pp. 162–3.

tions', were only to 'instruct and encourage one another in the duties of a good life'. They would 'propagate the doctrine and practice of universal good-will and obedience' and 'withdraw' themselves from 'every brother' that 'walketh disorderly'.[1] In 1689 Locke's views on toleration were published in England for the first time, in the form of a translation of a Latin epistle written in 1685. He now maintained that churches ought to be democratic and entirely voluntary societies. He continued to deny toleration to 'opinions contrary to human society', to atheists, papists and, significantly, to those who were themselves intolerant.[2]

But modern methods did not triumph through the Revolution— they were often adopted, if at all, only as a temporary second best. Many, perhaps most, churchmen would have fallen under Locke's ban on 'those who attribute unto the faithful, religious and orthodox —that is, in plain terms, unto themselves—any peculiar privilege or power above other mortals in civil concernments'. Locke told his Dutch friend Limborch, to whom the epistle had been written, that the new toleration was not as broad as 'true men like you, free from Christian arrogance and hatred, would desire; but 'tis something to get anything'. He hoped 'the church of Christ can be built up' on these 'foundations' and thought that the dissenters used their liberty 'much more peaceably and modestly than I should have expected'. But he predicted 'constant strife and war until the right of everyone to perfect liberty in these matters is conceded'[3] and in this he was right. Determined efforts continued to restore the dominance of orthodoxy by such means as the law still afforded. The Toleration Act as passed did not protect dissenting schools and the church authorities sometimes harassed the teachers.[4] The Act specifically refused protection to those who denied the doctrine of the trinity and most of the thinkers who made themselves unpopular in strict church circles after the Revolution either did this or could be accused of it (as Locke himself eventually was). Convocation had shown the way in December 1689 by its attack on a pamphlet sponsored by a unitarian merchant, Thomas Firmin. (Another such merchant,

[1] Fox Bourne, vol. ii, pp. 185–7.
[2] *ibid.*, pp. 34–41. On who was not to be tolerated, pp. 40–1.
[3] *ibid.*, pp. 155, 158–9.
[4] Sykes, pp. 92–4. For an excellent account of the ecclesiastical situation in the generation after the Revolution see G. V. Bennett, 'Conflict in the Church', in Holmes, *Britain after the Glorious Revolution, 1689–1714*, pp. 155–75.

William Popple, was the translator of Locke's epistle and both were friends of Locke.) In 1690 Arthur Bury was deprived of the Rectorship of Exeter College, Oxford, for (among other things) heresy and his book *The Naked Gospel* (one of the attempts to simplify Christian belief) was condemned by the university. The Queen tried to protect him (just as James or Charles might have done) but without success.

The hubbub increased until in 1695 the King (again following precedent) issued directions to the hierarchy requiring preachers and writers to 'avoid all new terms, and confine themselves to such ways of explication, as have been commonly used in the church', avoiding 'bitter invectives and scurrilous language'. Enforcement of the law was promised against all who caused 'scandal, discord and disturbance in our church and kingdom'. Luckily for the unorthodox, there was no real consensus even among loyal churchmen as to the true doctrine of the Trinity. The expiry of the censorship law also hindered repression—a Blasphemy Act passed in 1697 was ineffective. But the churchmen, though baffled, were full of fight. The campaign against William and all his works that ended in the Act of Settlement had its ecclesiastical counterpart in a new clamour for the calling of convocation. Francis Atterbury, in his *Letter to a Convocation Man* (1697), complained of 'open looseness in men's principles and practices', 'contempt of religion and the priesthood' and 'demand for a universal, unlimited toleration'. Convocation must be allowed to sit to devise remedies and even well-meaning dissenters should be glad to see orthodoxy 'asserted against heresies and innovations by a synod of English divines'.[1] William eventually had to allow the sitting of convocation just as he had to accept the Act of Settlement and Anne's reign saw efforts to implement the high church programme that came very near to success. Toleration cannot have seemed very secure for a considerable time. It is not surprising that Locke was keen to conceal the authorship of his religious writings.[2]

Papists, like unitarians, were denied the benefits of the Toleration Act and in view of their complicity with the exiled King they were in danger of active persecution. The mutiny of the Royal Regiment of Foot led to talk of a popish plot. Harbord told the commons that a papist at Norwich had been seen to go into a house which then caught

---

[1] For the foregoing see in particular, Every, pp. 75–84.
[2] Fox Bourne, vol. ii, pp. 205–8, 291–3.

fire 'and he got to a place to have the prospect of it'.[1] Acts were passed requiring papists to leave London[2] and there were plans to raise money for the war by confiscating their estates[3] and levying fines for the infringement of the Test Act.[4] A Bill which was killed by the adjournment of August 1689 and subsequent prorogation would have empowered any two justices to summon suspected persons (not just papists) before them and tender to them the oaths of allegiance and supremacy and the declaration against transubstantiation. Those who would not take them (unless they were quakers or foreigners) were to be imprisoned.

But the 'no popery' bark tended to be worse than the bite. During the March scare, Maynard said that the papists should stay at home—unless the justices allowed them to leave—and surrender their arms—'unless for the necessary defence of their houses'. He continued

> I would not imitate their cruelty; I am far from it. I would let them have their religion in their private houses but no harbouring priests and *jesuits*.[5]

The English gentry might hate Rome, but in practice were very unwilling to enforce even such laws as there were against the ordinary catholics who were their neighbours.[6] King William, who had always to consider the susceptibilities of his catholic allies, was likewise for toleration in this case as in others.[7] A Bill introduced in the lords in December 1689 tried to reconcile the two points of view. It would have given the benefits of the Toleration Act (except the right to worship publicly) to papists who took the oath of allegiance and an oath repudiating the belief that the pope could sanction the deposition and murder of kings. But papists not taking these oaths were to be adjudged 'recusant convicts'.[8] and there were fresh provisions for removing papists from London. The Bill failed, for it seems to have satisfied neither the tolerant nor the severe. The King disliked it and the toleration clause is scored through in the draft.[9] Laws went on being

---

[1] Grey, vol. ix, p. 165.

[2] LJ, vol. xiv, pp. 191, 209. And for seizing their arms and horses, Grey, vol. ix, pp. 347–51; CJ, vol. x, p. 130.

[3] *ibid.*, pp. 136, 144.   [4] Grey, vol. ix, pp. 400–2.

[5] *ibid.*, p. 169.   [6] See Western, pp. 69–71, already cited.

[7] Foxcroft, vol. ii, p. 243.

[8] Legal proof that a man was a papist was difficult. Also tackled in the disarming act, n. 2.

[9] Lords' MSS. item 194. LJ, vol. xiv, pp. 365, 370, 375, 398–9. Cf. n. 7 above. Papists were not to be asked to say that belief in the pope's deposing power was 'impious and heretical'.

passed against the catholics from time to time but they were seldom enforced: the papists were too few to be dangerous. In Ireland, of course, it was a different matter.[1]

Religious like political freedom was eventually established in England after the Revolution of 1688. But neither was safely established immediately after it and in neither case should too much credit be given to the Revolution itself. It was rather that conditions developed after the Revolution in such a way that political and religious freedom were eventually promoted.

(V)

The unrevolutionary character of the Revolution in England comes out very clearly when comparison is made with events in Scotland. The greater bitterness of party divisions there, which made a strong king stronger still, was very dangerous to the crown if once its position was shaken. Scotland had been even more incapable than England of making a revolution on its own. Not only was the system of government more authoritarian but the inclination to resist it was waning. The episcopalians needed royal support to maintain their power and so the Scottish bishops remained loyal to James and failed to provide a focus of opposition, unlike their English brethren. The presbyterians likewise, having been persecuted with extreme severity, were less inclined than those in England to oppose James's policy of 'indulgence' on constitutional grounds. When James removed the Scottish army to help in the defence of England, the Scottish government collapsed because it had rested on acquiescence rather than positive loyalty. William took over the administration of Scotland at the request of a large delegation of magnates and ordered the assembling of a convention, which met on 14 March 1689. The Scottish convention seems at first to have been broadly representative of all points of view, like its English equivalent. It pronounced in favour of William and against James largely on the strength of the letters—the one tactful, the other outrageous—which the two princes characteristically wrote to it. But the decision was not the outcome of a consensus, as it was at least superficially in England. The Scottish Jacobites, unlike the English tories, seceded from the conven-

[1] See the report of the Portuguese ambassador in 1710, pub. W. L. Sachse, *Catholic Historical Review*, vol. xlix (1963–4), pp. 20–46.

tion and started a civil war. Already the presbyterians had begun to eject episcopalian ministers and the proportion of the clergy refusing to pray for the new sovereigns was considerable. These developments made William heavily dependent on the whigs, who were left in control of the convention. He sent only a few troops to Scotland and cannot have wished to send more—for him, even the reconquest of Ireland represented an unwelcome diversion of military resources from continental campaigning. He relied on his Scottish partisans to crush his enemies there and he had therefore to make important political concession to them. In England this was less necessary because there was a general desire to avoid civil war and a general agreement to defer to William as a means of avoiding it.

The first and clearest indication that the Revolution was to be more revolutionary in Scotland than in England came in the enactments by which the crown was transferred to William and Mary. The Scottish convention claimed in them something that the English Declaration of Rights carefully refrained from claiming—that it had the right to dispose of the crown and reshape the constitution. James was roundly declared (4 April) to have 'forfaulted' the crown by his misgovernment. A few days later the convention approved statements of the subjects' grievances, distinguishing as in England between those resulting from violation of the law and those where the law itself required amendment. But whereas the English had expected William only to promise to respect the existing law, the Scots tried to obtain from him a further promise respecting future legislation. The three commissioners whom the convention sent to London to offer the crown to William and Mary carried with them not only a Claim of Right on English lines but also Articles of Grievances which were demands for changes in the law. The royal pair were expected to accept both documents and to take a rather vague oath. To the whigs in the convention this represented the conclusion of a contract, the assembly bestowing the crown on terms which the new sovereigns promised to observe. Foremost among the grievances to be removed by legislation were the Lords of the Articles and the Act of Supremacy of 1669. The ultra-royalist statutes of 1685 were also condemned. One grievance was thought so important that it was not made an Article but put in the Claim of Right: episcopacy. The Scottish whigs were bent on great changes in the church, even more than in the state.

In Scotland as in England, William had no wish to adopt whig measures or be dictated to by whig politicians. In both countries he entrusted the administration mainly to servants of the former government and his Scottish advisers encouraged him not to feel bound to assent to the legislation which emerged from the Convention Parliament. But the Scottish whigs were not only well placed but well organized. In Sir James Montgomery they had a leader who resembled Shaftesbury in his unbalanced opportunism and skill in party management. A caucus was established, known as the Club, which seems to have been followed by about 70 of the little parliament's 125 members. At its headquarters in Penstoun's tavern, Edinburgh, plans for organizing parliamentary business were worked out and members coming up from the country were received and indoctrinated. The Club's policy was to make William carry out the promises which they believed he had made and to exclude from office by law all those who 'had behaved ill in the last government or had been opposed to this revolution or had not concurred in the present measures'. William and his advisers would not agree and in the summer of 1689 there was a parliamentary impasse: taxes were not voted and the law courts could not function for want of necessary legislation. An act abolishing episcopacy was passed, but the Club did not press at this stage for the restoring of the presbyterian system. Presbyterian suspicion of the government was useful to them and so they were not eager for the extinction of religious grievances.

Eventually William ended the parliamentary session and during the winter of 1689–90 he tried to build up support for the government. Hamilton, the royal commissioner in Scotland, was replaced by Melville, who was on good terms with the presbyterians. Montgomery and his friends were firmly snubbed, whereupon they tried to make an alliance with the Jacobites. This was no more than many presbyterians had done when they accepted the protection of James II 1687–8, but it does not seem to have been acceptable to most of the Club's supporters. But Melville, though he did much by the skilful bestowing of bribes and jobs, had eventually to adopt most of the whig programme in order to make parliament tractable. When it met again in 1690, the Lords of the Articles were abolished, the Act of Supremacy of 1669 was repealed and presbyterianism was re-established. Private patronage in appointments to church livings was done away with—a remarkable attack on upper-class influence and property rights. A political purge was avoided but an ecclesiastical one was not. Only the convinced presbyterians among the clergy were allowed to attend the general assembly of the Kirk, revived in 1690, and they set about expelling such episcopalian clergy as remained from the parishes and universities.

The revolutionary implications of these Scottish events must not be exaggerated. Scotland had been moving towards absolutism faster than England. Radical reform in Scotland coupled with very modest reform in England meant that the two countries were now much more in line. But Scotland had ceased to provide an extra source of strength for the English monarchy. With its bitter feuds and increasingly uncontrollable parliament, it was once more a source of weakness. William possibly showed some understanding of this when he revived in 1689 the plan of a legislative union between the two kingdoms. His suggestion found some favour with the Scots, but it was unacceptable to the English. The achievement of union was delayed until the next reign, but it was the Revolution that above all made it necessary.[1]

NOTE

New England, like Scotland, had a little revolution of its own in 1689, made possible by the absence of any strong forces controlled by either James or William. At the end of James's reign representatives of Massachusetts were trying to get its charter restored and made some impression on attorney-general Powys. Increase Mather, who was one of these informal agents of the colony, lobbied the Convention Parliament and managed to get the abortive bill for restoring corporations extended to include the plantations. William on the advice of the privy council decided early in 1689 to maintain the Dominion of New England that James had established, while giving greater political rights to the inhabitants. But in April Boston rose against the government of Andros and imprisoned him. A provisional government was established in Massachusetts on the lines of its forfeited charter. The other colonies making up the Dominion mostly followed this example. The new governments were not very effective but apparently they managed to persuade William that they would be capable of defending the area against the French in Canada. No attempt was therefore made to restore the Dominion. Rhode Island and Connecticut recovered their charters, which provided for an entirely elective system of government. Massachusetts received a new charter in 1691 which reserved the appoint-

[1] For the Revolution in Scotland see W. Ferguson, *Scotland 1689 to the Present* (Oliver and Boyd, 1968), pp. 1–15; J. Halliday, 'The Club and the Revolution in Scotland, 1689–90', *Scottish Historical Review*, vol. xlv (1966), pp. 143–59.

ment of the governor to the crown and established an elective two-chamber legislature, the General Court.[1] This was the nearest thing to a victory for democracy that results from the Revolution of 1689 and it was an important one: the political system of New England thus restored and strengthened was to be in due course a cornerstone of the American Revolution.

[1] V. F. Barnes, *The Dominion of New England—a Study in British Colonial Policy* (Yale University Press, 1923), pp. 234–77.

11

King William's War

WHEN William took charge of the government after the flight of
James, one of his very first acts was the expulsion of the French
ambassador. His very first message to the Convention urged them to
hasten the constitutional settlement in view of 'the dangerous condition of the protestant interest in Ireland' and 'the present state of
things abroad'. The Dutch had denuded themselves to help England
and now required help against 'a powerful enemy'. William pointed
out that 'England is by treaty already engaged to help them'.[1] He
promised English help to the Dutch as an inducement to declare war
on France and make an alliance with Austria. The Dutch did declare
war, the Emperor was eager for an alliance and it was concluded in
May.[2] The English at first did nothing, but it was different when
James returned to Ireland with French help. William, as Halifax
noted

> said he had a mind to propose a war against France upon the assistance given
> by that K. to K. James. Note: this was a good while before the war was
> declared. His eagerness that way never ceased: it may be a question, whether
> that thought was not the greatest inducement to his undertaking [sc. coming
> to England] perhaps the declaring it sooner had been more adviseable.
> The P—It might probably have checked at it, if offered unseasonably.

> . . . . .

> Said he had thought as much as he could think and that there must bee a war
> with France.
> The Confederates abroad expected it, their owning him [sc. recognising him
> as King] depended upon it. It was probably his engagement before he under-
> took the expedition;

[1] CJ, vol. x, p. 9.   [2] Baxter, *William III*, pp. 251–2.

France did in effect begin by sending into Ireland. It was a necessary consequence of what he had done and above all *he ever had a great mind to it*.[1]

The commons resolved on 16 April to support the King in a war and war was declared on 5 May. For the English the main purpose of this was the reconquest of Ireland, but William was already bent on attacking France and strengthening the coalition. In June he said that there was only one reason for making Milford Haven one of the rendezvous for the forces assembling to attack Ireland

> . . . and that was not to be told; viz. more convenient to go from thence into France.
> He hath such a mind to France that it would incline one to think he took England only in his way.
>
> .   .   .   .   .
>
> Said he had a great mind to land in France and that it was the best way to save Ireland.
> Note: still this ran in his mind.
>
> .   .   .   .   .
>
> If he could bring people to it, going into France was the only thing to be done—Nota.
> Note: a thought that was not new etc.[2]

He seems to have regarded the accession of England as essential to keep the coalition together. We have seen that he feared the Dutch would make peace if they were not repaid the cost of his invasion from the English revenues. He hoped to end the Irish war by winter and then

> there was nothing to be done but making a descent in France to give a diversion or else the Confederates would make peace, even Holland itself.

Halifax warned him that 'it must not be talked of beforehand'.[3]

For William the Revolution was above all a means of furthering his wider European aims. But did his new subjects share those aims? Were they ready to identify themselves with the policy of anti-French alliances which he adopted for England when he became King? To

---

[1] Foxcroft, *Halifax*, vol. ii, pp. 210, 212.
[2] *ibid.*, pp. 219, 220, 222, cf. 218.
[3] Foxcroft, vol. ii, pp. 228, 235.

some extent they were. The growth of French power had stimulated anti-French feeling in England. The combination of popery and great military strength under despotic control was alarming. French economic growth and Colbert's high tariffs were unwelcome to the mercantile community—though the damage to English exports seems to have been temporary and the talk of a huge payments deficit with France mere fable. The great City merchants who led London into the whig camp also clamoured in the 1670s for diplomatic action against Colbert's policies.[1] Dutch and Habsburg agents in England fanned anti-French sentiment. As early as 1667 the Austrian diplomat Lisola had published an anti-French pamphlet, *The Buckler of State and Justice*, which appeared in English, French and German. He tried to show that the French were bent on establishing a catholic and universal monarchy, destroying the political, commercial and religious freedom of other peoples. These ideas took root: by the time of the exclusion crisis, phrases like 'the protestant religion and the liberties of Europe' figured among the common slogans of the whigs. Leading non-whigs like Halifax and Danby shared these ideas. William of Orange, of course, came to be seen as the great defender of 'Europe', and when Burnet preached before him on his arrival in London in 1688, this idea figured prominently. On 19 April 1689 the commons formally condemned the French plan 'for the subversion of the liberties of Europe'. The idea was taking root that there should be a 'balance of power' and that England ought to preserve it.[2]

But in practice the English thought of the French menace in a far more localized way than did William and there was no real agreement about how it should be met. The immediate English fear, once there was a possibility of James being deprived of the throne, was that he would organize a counter-revolution based on Scotland and Ireland with French help.[3] This danger was foreseen during the exclusion crisis and duly materialized in 1689. Irish developments especially alarmed the English because they were not just a counter-revolution but the revolt of a subject people against English rule, accompanied

---

[1] Margaret Priestley, 'Anglo-French trade and the "unfavourable balance" controversy, 1660–85', *Economic History Review*, 2nd ser., vol. iv (1951–2), pp. 37–52. For the merchants signing the important memorandum of 1674 see p. 39 n. 4.

[2] H. D. Schmidt, 'The establishment of "Europe" as a political expression', *Historical Journal*, vol. ix (1966), pp. 172–8. 'Europe' was a word which masked the religious division between France's enemies. The French (and the Stuarts) spoke of 'Christendom'.

[3] Cf. pp. 40–41.

by the flight of English protestant settlers to England. William, however, did not give the impression of taking Ireland equally seriously. His first message to parliament after accepting the throne asked for financial help in meeting dangers overseas but mentioned Ireland only after Holland and his other allies. 'I believe it an inadvertancy', commented a tory in the commons. 'Ireland goes nearest us, and is of the greatest consideration.' When William asked for a large sum to support the war on the reassembly of parliament in the autumn of 1689 he failed to mention Ireland at all.[1] To anyone with a continental viewpoint Ireland was bound to seem something of a sideshow. When William found at the end of 1689 that Ireland was still unsubdued, he decided that he would have to go there himself but expected his allies to 'dislike his going' and, noted Halifax, 'this stuck most with him'.[2] It would be unfair to imply that William had done nothing in the matter until then. He had seen to it that forces were sent over to undertake the reconquest. The immediate reason for his not doing more was that he doubted the loyalty of his British forces and the security of his own position and dared not over-extend himself. But he seems to have been a little slow to realize fully the importance of Ireland, and he may in consequence have missed a chance to throw the opposition there out of gear before James and the French arrived. Tyrconnel remained in control of the country until then, but much of his army had been captured in England, he was ageing and not eager for a fight. He said once that he was weary of the sword, but 'there is no one to receive it'. William made one abortive attempt to negotiate with him but rejected Danby's suggestion that he should send a naval squadron, remarking that 'the business of Ireland was in a fair way to be settled'. Clarendon, who as a former viceroy tried to make himself the spokesman of the refugee colonists, found William not interested.[3] Understandably, William responded less promptly to Irish stimuli than did English politicians and this made some Englishmen extremely suspicious of him.

There was some understanding in England of the military and commercial perils that would result from a French acquisition of the

---

[1] G. Davies, 'The control of British foreign policy by William III', *Essays on the Later Stuarts*, pp. 95–6.

[2] Foxcroft, vol. ii, pp. 244–5.

[3] Among recent writers Baxter, pp. 253–5, defends William on this issue and Simms, pp. 48–52, is critical. William, of course, was almost bound to snub Clarendon, who opposed his becoming King.

southern Netherlands. When the French had seemed close to achieving this (in 1667–8 and 1677–8), England had drawn closer to the Dutch in order to hinder it. A Dutch alliance had been concluded on the second occasion which still existed in 1689. Though made in part so that Charles II could ask a higher price from Louis XIV for becoming friends with him again, it was also a response to anti-French feeling in parliament which Charles felt obliged to placate.[1] It could fairly be said therefore that English opinion favoured an alliance with the Dutch against France. But the alliance was one of strictly limited liability. Each country was to come to the aid of the other if it was attacked, but the treaty prescribed the strength of the force which each was obliged to send—it envisaged further negotiations if more help was required. If England was attacked, the Dutch had to supply twenty ships and 6,000 troops (their British troops of course were particularly envisaged). If the Dutch were attacked, the British were to supply twenty ships and 10,000 troops.

In 1689, with both countries in effect under attack, William instigated fresh negotiations between the English and Dutch with a view to extending and consolidating the alliance. These were fairly successful, but the English commissioners showed themselves unwilling to abandon the principle of limited liability. They were willing to assume the major responsibility in the war at sea: it was necessary and congenial to build up British power there. They undertook to provide fifty capital ships, not twenty. The two powers agreed not to trade with France and to try and prevent any other country doing so. This policy of close blockade (which was to prove impracticable) was in line with English protectionism. Parliament had prohibited certain French imports in the crisis of 1678 and prohibited trade with France altogether in 1689. The Dutch tradition on the other hand was to protect the trading rights of neutrals in wartime and even to trade with the enemy themselves. In the interests of stronger action against the French, William imposed English views on the Dutch.

When it came to the continental war he would no doubt have liked to do the reverse and make the English acknowledge that they ought to increase the contingent of troops which they were obliged to send to the Netherlands. This was duly proposed but the English commis-

---

[1] For making of the alliance see K. H. D. Haley, 'The Anglo-Dutch rapprochement of 1677', *English Historical Review*, vol. lxxiii (1958), pp. 614–48; C. L. Grose, 'The Anglo-Dutch alliance of 1678', *ibid.*, vol. xxxix (1924), pp. 349–72, 526–51.

sioners refused to have it written into a treaty.[1] When the commons debated supply for the war in the autumn, they too seemed inclined to think that England should not take much part in the continental fighting. Clarges thought that in view of the campaign in Ireland it was unreasonable to expect England to send to the continent even as many troops as were stipulated by the treaty of 1678. Seymour did not want England formally to join the general coalition of states that was being formed against France. Garroway wanted money spent on the fleet in preference to the army. He thought that the power of France had been exaggerated and that what really accounted for the coalition against France was the prospect of a struggle for the succession to the Spanish throne. These views were challenged. Against the objection to becoming 'principals' in the war with France, Wildman pointed out that 'against King *James* we are principals'. He thought there was a danger that France might buy off the Dutch if they were not supported. Treby 'would suppress so great a neighbour' as France. If the Emperor 'opposes France', he added, 'he helps to reduce Ireland.'[2] But William tacitly conceded that the country would not accept this argument. He never asked parliament to endorse his membership of the anti-French coalition. The 'grand alliance' began in May 1689 with the treaty between the Dutch and the Emperor. Bavaria and Denmark were drawn in more or less by bribery and Spain and Savoy followed in 1690. One feature of the alliance was indeed a promise of the Spanish succession to the Austrian branch of the Habsburgs. William acceded to it as King of England on 9 September 1689, but no Englishman participated in this act and the treaty seems only once to have been seen by an English official. It was never revealed to parliament, even though the Emperor desired that it should be. The Austrians realized that unless the English accepted it, the extent to which it bound them was in doubt.[3]

England did in fact participate fully in the war against France and did not confine herself, as many Englishmen would have wished, to those sectors of it that were immediately profitable to her. It was

---

[1] For the Anglo-Dutch negotiations see G. N. Clark, *The Dutch Alliance and the War against French Trade, 1688–97* (Manchester University Press, 1923), pp. 28–43. Even in 1678 there was a plan to give England a bigger naval and smaller land quota.

[2] Grey, vol. ix, pp. 388–94.

[3] Baxter, *William III*, pp. 251–2. Davies, pp. 96–102. Lord Villiers signed the renewal of the treaty. William eventually achieved peace by abandoning the Emperor and bargaining with France: the secrecy of the alliance no doubt helped him.

William who brought this about, by the untrammelled use of his prerogative. Though it is far from clear that parliament approved, he considered them morally bound to defer to his judgment because they had endorsed (by voting funds) his initial decision to go to war. In the spring of 1689 he told the commons that he had declared war on France 'encouraged thereunto by the assurance this house hath given him of their assistance'. 'Till I know your intentions,' he told parliament in the autumn, 'I shall not only be uncertain of myself what resolutions to take; but our allies will be under the same doubts.' Having taken the first step and voted some money, parliament was expected to go all the way. In 1695 he told them that the war had been begun by their advice and so he hoped that they would vote supplies to continue it. 'William,' it has been well said, 'did not hesitate to ask parliament for advice and assistance, but it was because he required assistance, not because he desired advice.' In all this he was following traditional Stuart methods. Charles II, for instance, had told parliament that he had entered the Dutch war of 1665 'by your advice and encouragement' and he was happy to solicit this when it helped him. But advice that limited his freedom of action he rejected—such as an address of 1677 because

> it is more liable to be understood to be by your leave, than your request, that I should make such other alliances as I please with other of the confederates. Should I suffer this fundamental power of making peace and war to be so far invaded . . . no prince or state would any longer believe that the sovereignty of England rests in the crown.[1]

This was really still the position in William's time and the important thing is that parliament acquiesced in it. They grumbled, they asked for more information and sometimes got it, but they never used their financial power to force the King to give them more say in strategic and diplomatic policy-making.[2] This is the strongest indication that England after the Revolution was still a real monarchy and not in any way a 'crowned republic'.

The justification, then and since, for giving William a free hand, was that he had expert knowledge and understood English interests better

---

[1] For this paragraph see E. R. Turner, 'Parliament and foreign affairs, 1603–1760', *English Historical Review*, vol. xxxiv (1919), pp. 177–82. The opinion quoted is his.

[2] See, *e.g.*, the end of the debate quoted on p. 386. Of course they liberally criticized the mismanagement of particular operations and, *e.g.*, the first Poll Tax of 1689 was specifically for the Irish war: CTB 1689–92, p. clxxvii.

than the English did.[1] It is worth considering whether the all-out war against France which he preferred really was consonant with English interests and a necessary outcome of the Revolution. Appropriately enough, the strongest reasons for saying that it was are ideological. The European monarchs naturally regarded the dethroning of James with horror and such public opinion as existed in their states seems to have supported them. (Since even British opinion was not really 'revolutionary', this is hardly surprising.) In order to commend the war (which was unpopular) to his subjects, Louis XIV emphasized in his propaganda the need to defend the rights of James. This was not the main point of the war for Louis but his hostility to the Revolution was real and obstinate. As the prospects of restoring James faded, he continued to hope for some compromise, such as the accession of the young Prince of Wales on the deaths of William and Mary. His refusal to recognize William as King delayed the eventual peace negotiations and even at the peace conference the French representatives were instructed not to recognize the English delegation. After private negotiations, Louis allowed a guarded recognition of William to be incorporated in the peace treaty of Ryswick (1697), however, he not only continued to honour James but also recognized his son as James III when the old man died in 1701. William's catholic allies, the Austrian and Spanish monarchs, were not much better. Their consciences did not allow them to support rebels and heretics cheerfully. From Austria, still at war with the Turks, came a curious plan for a compromise peace which would both promise the English succession to the Prince of Wales and lead to a European coalition for the purpose of putting his father on the throne of Egypt or Algeria.[2] It could be argued that the Revolution was so unpopular internationally that merely to repel French attacks on the British and Dutch would not make it secure. It needed the wider protection that William could afford it as head of a great and successful coalition. To give him this strong European position, much more extensive action against the French was necessary. The English commissioners who negotiated

[1] Cf. M. A. Thomson, 'Parliament and foreign policy', *William III and Louis XIV, Essays 1680–1720*, ed. R. Hatton and J. S. Bromley (Liverpool University Press, 1968), p. 131.
[2] This paragraph follows M. A. Thomson, 'Louis XIV and William III, 1689–97', *William III and Louis XIV*, pp. 24–48. He notes that there is no reason to believe, as many have, that William would have been willing for the Prince of Wales to succeed him. The French also had a plan to make James King of Poland.

with the Dutch in 1689 seem to have had some inkling of this: they made the Dutch bind themselves not to conclude a separate peace.[1]

But if feelings and threats are disregarded and only concrete dangers to English safety are considered, the picture changes. Louis had begun the war in order to bolster his influence in Germany and Italy and forestall the growth of Austrian power that might be expected to result from the defeat of the Turks. He always regarded England as a lightweight among the powers and his interest in what happened there was limited. Among his closer advisers, Seignelay (the son and successor of Colbert), was keen to increase the maritime power of France in opposition to the English and Dutch. But the plan of the war reflected rather the ideas of Louvois, who was in charge of the army. The French naval effort suffered by the death of Seignelay in 1690 for his successor knew nothing about the navy. The war as a whole began to languish after the death of the bellicose Louvois in 1691. Men like Pomponne, who believed that conciliation would preserve French influence more effectively than threats, henceforth had more weight in the government.

The French thus circumstanced were only a limited threat to English security and it was English unpreparedness which initially made the situation alarming. The English army consisted mainly of inexperienced new levies and the Revolution had disorganized it. The additions made by William were even greener that the troops raised by James. The navy was much better, but it was mainly based on the east coast, for fighting the Dutch. Only with difficulty could it be brought round to oppose the French forces based on Brest. The supply services for both army and navy were badly organized and this diminished their mobility. The English fleet engaged the French in Bantry Bay on 1 May 1689, but they were unable to interrupt French communications with Ireland. In August an English army under Schomberg landed near Belfast, but was unable to do more than recover the mainly protestant north. In 1690 the King had to go over to undertake the reconquest and in his absence the French fleet came out and defeated an inferior Anglo-Dutch force at Beachy Head on 10 July. The Queen and her advisers who had been left in charge of England began hastily to prepare to meet an invasion.

But the French never mounted a major offensive on the maritime front. When James reached Ireland in March 1689 he brought money

[1] Clark, pp. 41–2.

and arms and a small French contingent, which may have numbered 3,000 men, followed him. Six thousand more troops were sent in the following year. But the French did not provide resources enough to equip and maintain the large Irish army that was speedily raised, and in return for the troops they sent they demanded an equivalent number of Irish soldiers to fight for France on the continent. Over 5,000 Irish went to France in 1690, anticipating the fate of the Irish troops who capitulated at the end of William's reconquest, and the French tried to secure the pick of the Irish army.[1] James regarded Ireland only as a stepping-stone and was eager to push on into Britain, but here the French gave him even less help. They did not even use their naval ascendancy to interrupt communications between Britain and the English expeditionary force in Ireland. There was no serious attempt to destroy the English fleet and invasion attempts in 1690 were limited to the burning of Teignmouth in Devon. Tyrconnel proposed that James should land in England, but this was turned down.[2] A more serious possibility was action in Scotland. Many of the highlanders took up arms against the new government there in 1689, less from love of James than to take advantage of the general confusion to achieve local ambitions. James was anxious to send substantial forces thither but again the French did not help much and very little got through.[3] William on the other hand, as early as March 1689, sent up parts of the three Scottish regiments he had brought from Holland and thereby stiffened the scratch forces that were raised by his Scottish supporters.[4] The highlanders were contained in 1689 and thereafter lapsed into inactivity.

From 1690 the superior resources which the English were able and, of course, willing to devote to the maritime theatre of war began slowly to tell. William managed to hire 7,000 Danish troops for the Irish war and they arrived in March 1690. Dutch, German and Huguenot contingents also stiffened the inexperienced English.[5] The battle of the Boyne on 1 July 1690 gave William Dublin and led to the return of James to France. It was not strategically decisive for the Irish remained securely in possession of the western part of the island. William's campaign against Limerick in August was a failure, though

---

[1] Simms, pp. 58–73, for the arrival of James and the initial French help; pp. 72, 138–40, 203 and elsewhere for later help and the sending of Irish to France.
[2] Simms, pp. 137, 141.   [3] Simms, pp. 65, 69.
[4] Baxter, *William III*, pp. 252–4.   [5] Simms, pp. 122, 136.

Marlborough took Cork and Kinsale by sea attack in the autumn But the French, discouraged, withdrew their troops[1] and William was able to leave the command to a subordinate, the Dutch Baron Ginkel. The Battle of Aughrim on 12 July 1691 was hard fought, but ended in a decisive victory for Ginkel. The Treaty of Limerick in September ended resistance: the Irish troops were allowed to go and take service with the French and it is estimated that about 12,000 did so.[2]

The Irish had had a revolution in 1689, just as did the English and Scots. They took advantage of the situation to throw off English control and protestant ascendancy.[3] The military history of this revolt and its suppression has been touched on because it was vital to the success of the English Revolution. A full account of Irish development would take us too far afield. But it is worth dwelling a little on the comparison between the English and Irish Revolutions. Neither nation was in a position to overthrow its government unless it received help from beyond its borders. Both were lucky in the emergence of a patron before the complete consolidation of the existing government made resistance unthinkable. But the English were the more lucky because at the crucial moment William, their patron, obtained both Dutch backing and a favourable international situation for his English enterprise. James on the other hand, patron of the catholic Irish, not only lost his English throne but was unlucky thereafter in receiving only modest support from the French. The international situation was not such that they could make his interests their first concern. The Irish Revolution therefore failed—as the English Revolution might have, with a little less luck. The state of Ireland in the eighteenth century may well be an indication of what England would have been like had the Revolution failed there. Parliament continued to function, but it was subservient and could not seriously restrain the government, though it might obstruct it. Guarantees of the subject's rights which the Revolution established in England were lacking in Ireland. A large army was quartered upon the country to keep it in awe. Whether the English catholic minority would ever have lorded it in a Jacobite England as the protestant ascendancy lorded it in Ireland it perhaps to be doubted. The Irish

---

[1] Simms, pp. 172–3.   [2] Simms, p. 260.
[3] James did not wish Ireland to escape from English tutelage but he could not prevent the revolt in his support having this character.

protestants were kept in the saddle by English power. James and his family could similarly look for help to France but could not expect it to be on a massive scale. They would have needed protestant support.

After the reconquest of Ireland there remained only a slight external threat to England and her new government. In 1692 the English tried to take the offensive. At the behest of William, they made ready for the 'descent' on France which he had long aimed at.[1] Their plans were interrupted by the French who, far too late in the day, decided that signs of increasing Jacobite activity justified an attempt to land in England. They failed to collect superior naval force and their fleet was beaten at Barfleur and suffered serious losses in the ensuing pursuit. The idea of invasion was dropped, though it reappeared briefly in 1696. The French navy was by no means ruined and throughout the war serious damage was done to English trade at sea. But the threat of a Stuart counter-revolution based on Ireland and Scotland and supported by France had disappeared (or been shown not to exist). Only a new revolution in England itself would have provoked an invasion. As for the southern Netherlands, the other focus of British anxiety, the French occupied a threatening position there for most of the war but were never anywhere near to overrunning them: they had to fight in Germany and Italy as well. On land as on sea the war was mainly one of attrition and no state was fighting for its very existence.

It cannot be said that the fighting after 1692 did much to enhance English security. Both William and Louis seem to have decided, some time in 1691 or 1692, that they could not expect striking gains from the war. Henceforth there were negotiations each year to try and end it. The purpose of the remaining campaigns was largely to speed the bargaining by putting pressure on the enemy. Louis had a special reason for shortening the war: if the King of Spain died before the peace, the Emperor would receive the help of his allies in claiming the succession for his family. In 1696 Louis managed to buy off Savoy and the Emperor partially retired from the war by agreeing to a truce in Italy. England was deep in a financial crisis and William resolved to make peace whether his allies liked it or not. The terms eventually agreed upon in 1697 involved further concessions by the French, who

---

[1] A. N. Ryan, 'William III and the Brest Fleet in the Nine Years War', *William III and Louis XIV*, pp. 56–7. For the naval war in general see J. Ehrman, *The Navy in the War of William III 1689–1697* (Cambridge University Press, 1953).

gave up most of the gains made on their north-eastern borders during their period of triumph after 1678. But though Louis had latterly done rather badly in the fighting, he made concessions not because he had to but because he believed that a return to peace would be rewarding. Nor did his concessions give extra security to his opponents. He evaded a renunciation of the Stuart cause. The barrier of fortresses which he allowed the Dutch to establish against him in the southern Netherlands was useless if the Spanish rulers of the surrounding territory became hostile—which was to be the case. More valuable for England and Holland was the emergence of an *entente* between Louis and William. It was a bargain between them which restored peace and they went on to make further bargains for the peaceful settlement of the Spanish succession question, by means of a partition of the Spanish empire. The indecisive fighting after 1692 contributed to the growth of this *entente* by making it seem that nothing else would work. It is hard to believe that so much campaigning was necessary to produce this result.

It would not be right to leave the subject without pointing out that there is a considerable contrast between the latter part of King William's war and the opening of the next conflict with France at the very end of William's reign. This resulted from a fresh and serious threat to English interests which had to be warded off. Louis had violated his *entente* with William by accepting the Spanish throne for his grandson when at length it was vacated. England and Holland were willing all the same to accept the new Spanish king, but their attitude changed when the French set about curtailing their trade with the Spanish empire and turned the Dutch out of the barrier fortresses. The southern Netherlands were under French control at last and a general offensive was in prospect against England's whole commercial and colonial position. William believed that renewed resistance to France was essential and the situation enabled him to carry England with him. But this time he did not simply ask parliament to support him and assume that a hasty decision would oblige it to go on doing so until he or his successor chose to make peace. Wisely (especially since his days were numbered) he chose to surrender some of his control over foreign policy in order to make it more national, more binding on parliament. More information was therefore given to the lords and commons than in the past and in return they pledged their support more fully and specifically. Public opinion was also worked on and, above all, leading English statesmen were taken into the King's confidence. This time the Grand Alliance which linked Austria and the maritime powers against France was not only communicated to parliament but concluded on England's behalf by one of her leading men—Marlborough.

But though the War of the Spanish Succession was a truly national one for England, at least to start with, the old personal antagonism between William and Louis was an important factor in starting it. Louis had several reasons for his provocative action against the English and Dutch, but an important one was his belief that William remained an implacable foe who would make war if opportunity offered if only because it meant more power for him in his own dominions. Louis therefore felt that nothing was to be gained from conciliating him. Unfortunately too, England's performance in the previous war had not disabused Louis of the idea that she was a lightweight power. He seems to have given recognition to 'James III' because it was likely to win him the alliance of the Pope and this he believed to be of greater practical importance than English reactions.[1]

England was in process of becoming an opponent of France in the later seventeenth century and the Revolution both allowed this enmity to find expression and drew down French hostility upon England. War between the two countries was bound to come. But it is hard not to believe that placing William on the English throne made the fighting longer and more serious. William and Louis had come to see each other as inevitable foes. It was hard for them to make and keep peace, even when they believed it was the right thing to do. The conservatism of the English revolution meant that even though a king was deposed, the rights of the dynasty and the prerogatives of the crown were respected. William and no other had to be King and he was allowed to control foreign policy. The result was that Louis's attitude to England was determined by his attitude to William. His continuing disdain for his island neighbour expressed itself in hostility rather than indifference. It was because of its conservatism as well as because it was a revolution that the English upheaval of 1688 intensified conflict with France.

---

[1] Recognition came too late to affect English policy but it strengthened anti-French feeling. I here follow M. A. Thomson, 'Louis XIV and the origins of the War of the Spanish Succession', *William III and Louis XIV*, pp. 140–161; cf. 'Parliament and Foreign Policy', pp. 133–6; Davies, pp. 113–22.

(II)

William's control of foreign policy was the most striking evidence that he was a real and not a sham king. Yet paradoxically his commitment to a long war, and eventually to the renewal of war, was the thing that proved fatal in the end to the independence of the monarchy. It meant financial burdens which made the sovereign permanently dependent on parliament and permanently on rather bad terms with the crown's most natural supporters, the country gentry who were the backbone of toryism. Godolphin[1] wrote a most interesting letter to the King in 1693 to show him that he was at the parting of the ways. Finding that it was 'generally discoursed as if your Majesty had a peace in prospect', he urged 'how much it will contribute to your future happiness if it should, if possible, be perfected before the meeting either of this or any other parliament'. Godolphin saw the problems facing William as

> how to manage the parties so as to maintain yourself against your enemies abroad, and at the same time so to preserve your authority at home that the necessity of doing the one may not bring you to such circumstances that it will be impossible for you to keep the other; and this task is more difficult because the tories, who are friends to prerogative, are so mingled with jacobites that they are not to be confided in during the war; and the whigs, who are, for that reason, of necessity to be employed to support your cause against the common enemy, will at the same time endeavour all they can to make use of that opportunity to lessen your just power.

The hereditary revenue was already heavily burdened with war debts and if the war went on the customs would have to be 'pawned for five years at least'. Therefore

> it is more your interest, with relation to your affairs at home, to have a peace this summer, than ever it was since you sat upon the throne of England; and that if you have it not, as things have been managed, the next year's expenses will so anticipate those branches of the revenue that ever have been kept hitherto for the ordinary support of the government, that it will be scarce possible that your Majesty should ever see an easy day, though it should please God hereafter to give you such a peace as yourself could wish.

[1] The letter is unsigned and undated. It is clear from the contents that it was written in 1693. Dalrymple, who printed it, found it in a bundle of letters attributed to Godolphin; all save one were unsigned. Dalrymple noted that the other ministers commonly signed their letters. Dalrymple, vol. ii, pt. ii, appendix to bk. i, pp. 5–11.

It could never be possible 'for any king of England to be the least happy, who must depend upon a parliament every year to give him a million of money for his common and necessary support'. But after reviewing the likely ways of paying for the war through 1694 and 1695, Godolphin concluded that this would be William's position if the war lasted so long. The annual peacetime expenditure of the government could be taken as 1,400,000*l*. and the ordinary revenue left to meet it and not swallowed up in servicing war debts would be about 400,000*l*.

Godolphin argued that with a peace, parliament would become more manageable and the parties more docile. New elections would not help if the war continued: 'let what sort of men soever be chosen', the majority would always be 'much rather for mortgaging the revenue of the crown than their own land'. A general election might produce a great majority for the whigs, who would bully the King, or for the tories, who would hearken to the Jacobites;

> Whereas, as the house is now constituted, the whigs are not strong enough to make use of the necessities of your government as much as they are inclined to do; neither are the tories numerous enough to resent Your Majesty's favouring the whigs.

So the existing parliament should be kept until the peace

> And if it pleased God to grant your Majesty an honourable peace and you would then be pleased to set up for a party of your own, and let all people see that if they expected your favour they must depend upon you for it, and not let any one hope for promotion for being true to a faction, but by serving of you; I presume to say that the war being ended, a new parliament called and such measures pursued, your Majesty would quickly find that the jacobites would turn moderate churchmen and loyal subjects, and the whigs much more obsequious courtiers and easier servants than now they are.

The interesting thing about this prophecy of Godolphin's is that it was to be fulfilled in quite large measure when lasting peace really did return—that is, in the era of Walpole. But by that time it was too late to think of restoring the independence of the monarchy.

William did not follow the advice of Godolphin and the example of his royal uncles: he did not seek peace at any price in order to bolster his authority at home. This is the ultimate reason for dismissing the idea that his object in engineering the Revolution was to secure the throne for himself. The way he used his power showed that this was a means, not an end. He was childless and, for much of his reign, in physical decline. Personal grandeur interested him less than the European cause with which he had become identified. He clung to his powers as far as he could, but in the last resort sacrificed them to wider objectives. We have seen that at the end of his reign he gave up some of his control over foreign policy. He gave his assent to some statutes disadvantageous to the crown in order to win support. The Triennial Act was accepted in order to make parliament more willing to support the war. The constitutional clauses in the Act of Settlement helped to ensure parliamentary backing for the making of fresh alliances against Louis XIV. (The Act furthermore was the means of winning an ally: made necessary by the death of Anne's only surviving child, it carried through William's long-standing plan of tying the influential house of Hanover to English interests by writing them into the succession.)

More fatal than William's deliberate sacrifices of authority was the financial undermining of the crown by the war. As Godolphin had foretold, when the customs were regranted in 1694 they were pawned: in 1697 they were made entirely applicable, for the time being, to the repayment of debt. The remains of the ordinary revenue were not enough to pay for ordinary civil expenditure and by the end of 1695 there was a debt of over a million under these heads. The King several times complained of his poverty and in November 1695 told parliament 'that it will not be possible for me to subsist unless that matter be taken into your care'. After the war had ended in 1697 he reported himself 'wholly destitute of means to support the Civil List'. Parliament relieved him grudgingly. In 1694–5 they called for detailed accounts of the ordinary revenue and civil expenditure and debts and laid down in detail what they considered proper items of civil expenditure.[1] In 1697 they decided that the King should have 'not exceeding' 700,000*l.* a year for the support of himself and the civil administration. Special provision was made for paying off part of the debt which encumbered the ordinary revenue and by the end of the reign William was receiving from it roughly the sum that had been decided on. The

---

[1] Shaw in introd. CTB vols. ix, x, pp. lxxxiv, cxliii–iv, cxlviii–cl for the transactions of 1694–5. Civil list expenditure at this time was just under 700,000*l.* a year: p. cxciv. For later events see his introd. CTB vols. xi–xvii (1695–1702), pp. viii–xli; vol. xviii (1703), p. vi, etc. 3,700*l.* a week was taken from the excise from 1701. The Civil List debt at William's death was over 800,000*l.*

same amount was voted for Anne. Galled by the heavy burden of war costs, parliament was no longer willing to allow the sovereign any larger sum without annual scrutiny. At the end of William's reign they appropriated part of the excise (now the backbone of the ordinary revenue) to repaying war debts. They did not fully relieve William of his debts in respect of civil expenses and much of these remained unpaid long after his death. William does not seem to have suffered personally from these transactions: he spent a lot on building new residences during his reign.[1] But parliament had in effect laid down what only the hardier spirits had proposed in 1689: that the sovereign's permanent income should be only enough for his civil expenses and that if he wanted to maintain any armed forces in peacetime he would have to ask parliament specially for the money.

The financial burdens of the war were deleterious to the independence of the crown in wider ways that can only be sketchily indicated here. Like the ordinary revenue, the special taxes raised to pay for the war were 'pawned'. The statutes which imposed them also authorized borrowing and appropriated the produce of the taxes to the repayment of the lenders. At first only short-term borrowing was envisaged, the object being to make available rather more speedily the amount that it was hoped that the taxes would yield. But in 1692 parliament sanctioned a new departure—a long-term loan, to be serviced by taxes voted for ninety-nine years. The object now was to obtain a large sum in ready money at the cost of a modest but long-continued annual payment. Long-term loans played only a modest part in William III's finances and were raised on onerous terms. They provided under 7 millions of a total government expenditure of over 72 millions during the reign.[2] But the importance of this expedient steadily grew. The taxes voted for the war were not sufficient to discharge the mass of short-term debt that built up and in 1697 much of this had to be converted into longer-term debt, quick repayment being impossible. In Queen Anne's war much more use was made from the start of long-term loans, but again short-term debts built up and had to be converted into long-term debt at the end of the war. In 1714 there was long-term debt of over 40 millions and the annual cost of servicing it was $2\frac{1}{2}$ millions—more than the total annual expenditure

[1] Baxter, *William III*, pp. 302, 358.
[2] Dickson, *The Financial Revolution in England*, p. 47. This paragraph is mainly derived from this book.

under James II.[1] King William's war had naturally brought an increase in expenditure, from James's 2 millions up to five or six. The new system of borrowing meant that even in peacetime the tax burden might have to be something like double what it was before 1689.

To some extent all this was helpful to the crown. Wars might make the sovereign dependent on parliament but in practice parliament was rather docile in voting money for war and gave the sovereign quite a free hand in spending it. Royal patronage grew enormously and, potentially at least, this meant more votes for the crown in parliament and greater social weight in the country for those enriched by its expenditure. Godolphin, in the letter cited a little earlier, remarked that the house of commons elected in 1690 had served the King well, not least because he had given

> all employments to members of the house, which though it has not signified much in any party business, yet in the grand affair of carrying on the war, they have been of mighty service.

Halifax complained after his retirement from office

> Of what use are parliaments if when there is a war everything that is asked is to be given . . . So that a prince hath by consequence the power of money when he will, because he hath war when he will . . . Here hath been too much pains taken lately only for the name of liberty. If all is given whilst there is war there is nothing left when there is peace.
>
> The Jure Divino principle is nothing to this, that is a speculative notion, controverted too etc; here is a practical expedient that effectually doth the business.[2]

This increasingly was to be the standard line of everyone in opposition to the government, reflected of course in the many attempts to bar placemen from the house of commons. There was much truth in it. The executive with its extensive patronage and its standing armed forces was a formidable force in the eighteenth century and it might be debated whether parliament controlled or merely supported it.

But though the executive remained strong and definitely royal in character, the sovereign in the eighteenth century was not independent in the way that a seventeenth-century ruler could hope to be. To some

---

[1] Dickson, p. 80. For William's annual expenditure, p. 46. Of course, the debt was gradually reduced after 1714 and the national wealth was increasing, so the long-term burden must not be exaggerated.

[2] Notes for a speech in the lords, apparently: it does not appear when or whether it was delivered. Foxcroft, vol. ii, pp. 137–40.

extent this was simply because the state was beginning to become more impersonal. The government's power at home and abroad was henceforth based on the growth of a highly organized money market. Good budgetary management and parliamentary guarantees of the public debt were essential to make the system work. On pain of national ruin everyone—sovereign, ministers and parliament, too— had to play the game according to the rules. There was less room for individual caprice. Then, too, the wars and financing of wars enriched some sections of the wealthier classes but impoverished and disgusted other sections, perhaps less wealthy but probably stronger in numbers. The wars brought with them taxes on land, the bane of the country squires. This was only customary: what was new was that the land tax did not cease with the war. It was the indirect taxes which were voted for a long term of years and mortgaged in order to raise long-term loans. They could not therefore bear the whole burden of peacetime expenditure, which had been the philosophy of the squires and the government in the days of Charles and James. Each year the commons had to vote a land tax to keep the government going. This may well have been enough to keep the landed parliaments of those days suspicious of the executive and to have ruled out the sort of close collaboration between them that had momentarily existed in 1685.

Another difference between the two eras was that the money voted by the squires was not necessarily spent on them: they provided some of the servants and creditors of the government but as a class they did not recover what they had to pay. Henry St. John thought in 1709 that whereas 'the whole burthen' of two decades of war

> has lain upon the landed interest . . . The men of estates have, generally speaking, neither served in the fleets nor armies, nor meddled in the public funds and management of the Treasure. A new interest has been created out of their fortunes, and a sort of property which was not known twenty years ago, is now increased to be almost equal to the terra firma of our island.

It was in the main the big capitalists who lent the government money and the complaint was raised that capital was used in this way that might otherwise have financed trading activity or been invested in land (thereby keeping up the value of landed estates). The commons were told in 1702 that

> Our trading is now dead. There is a damp upon all manufactories, and well it may, for a merchant finds a better return between the exchequer and the

exchange than he makes by running a hazard to the Indies . . . our home
commodities and nation's produce lie dead, and that money which should
carry on trade and buy up our country growth is turned another way.

The speaker denounced the ostentatious wealth of the war profiteers

rich coaches, fine liveries, splendid equipages, luxurious tables, numerous
attendants . . . And yet I am certain that some of these gentlemen, not
many years ago were scarce able to keep a pad nag and a drab coat, and now
a gentlemen of 5000*l*. p.ann. is not a fit companion for their greatness.[1]

We do not really know how much substance there was in this sort of
complaint, though as the higher taxes coincided with some bouts of
agricultural depression, the landed classes certainly did have something to grumble about. At all events, the repercussions of war included a rift in the upper classes of the nation and an estrangement
between the government and those on one side of the rift. The government of James II had been financially tolerable to the squires and so
it had been possible to envisage a near absolutism enjoying their
acquiescence. The costlier governments which followed could buy
more support but they also attracted more hostility. The political
equivalent to this was not royal supremacy but a balance of power,
the crown checked by parliament, the monarchy by no means a mere
symbol but at the same time definitely 'limited' and not independent.
Such was the constitution in the eighteenth century.

The Revolution of 1688 could not have happened without the support of a foreign prince. The result was that it was relatively ineffective in curbing the sovereign's power and much more effective in
leading the country into foreign entanglements. But these entanglements did what the Revolution had not done. They made necessary
a great increase in the resources of the state, but in becoming more
powerful the executive also became less independent and more subject to parliamentary restraint. This was the paradox at the root of
eighteenth-century politics. Because English 'liberties' had been
established in such a devious way, many people found it hard to
believe that they had been established at all. What now seem rather
infantile fears of the executive flourished and inspired sterile political

[1] The quotations are in W. A. Speck, 'Social Status in late Stuart England', *Past and
Present*, no. 34, pp. 128–9. See also his 'Conflict in Society', Holmes, pp. 135–54;
Dickson, chap. 2; Habbakuk, 'English Landownership 1680–1740' already cited;
J. H. Plumb, *The Growth of Political Stability in England, 1675–1725* (Macmillan, 1967),
chaps. 4, 5.

debates for the better part of a hundred years. Eventually the solidity of the system came to be recognized and that, in a way, was when modern British politics began. In the seventeenth century, English politicians had tried to get the sort of government that they wanted by means of written enactments—mostly declaratory of what they believed to have been their legal rights, wrongfully invaded by the crown. The Bill of Rights and the Act of Settlement were late specimens of these enactments. All were a failure. In the eighteenth century the sovereign and parliament were forced by circumstances into mutual dependence and the desired result of a 'limited monarchy' was ineluctably achieved by the way in which the system actually worked, not by any set of rules prescribing how it should work. From this experience there sprang the 'empirical' attitude which has guided Britain's subsequent political steps from aristocratic monarchy to democratic 'crowned republic'. It is customary to say that this approach has been more fruitful than that of the 'doctrinaires' and in this there is much truth. But it must always be remembered that it was only circumstances that gave the system its initial impetus. It was not the deliberate choice of their wisdom; it did not correspond to what any of them deliberately set out to achieve, and it emerged out of their failure to control events. Nor was there anything ineluctable about the circumstances in question which guaranteed that English politics would develop in the way that they did. Conditions in the formative decades after 1680 might easily have been quite different, especially in the field of international affairs. Modern British liberties originated in a lucky accident. Good fortune—a favourable environment—has counted for much in their preservation and enlargement. Their capacity to survive under harsher conditions has yet to be determined.

An Extra Reading List

Sources of information on each of the topics dealt with in this book have been indicated in the footnotes. Some of the books and records that have been cited range over many topics and illuminate the period as a whole. A selection of these—and one or two extra items—is listed here for the convenience of readers for whom England in the 1680s is a totally new subject.

Despite its age and blemishes, Macaulay's *History of England* has still to be superseded by a full-scale modern history of the period. (How insufficient Macaulay seemed even before 1914 can be seen in C. H. Firth's *Commentary on Macaulay's History of England*, published by Macmillan in 1938 but written much earlier.) David Ogg provides the best modern account in *England in the Reign of Charles II* and *England in the Reigns of James II and William III*. He has great knowledge and insight, does much to suggest the character of the period and is fair to all parties. All the same he cannot help regarding departures from modern liberal standards as unnatural. Three other books may be mentioned which are rather more wholehearted in portraying English politics under the later Stuarts in terms of the standards, hopes and fears then current: Sir Keith Feiling's *History of the Tory Party, 1640–1714*, J. P. Kenyon's *Robert Spencer, Earl of Sunderland, 1641–1702* and J. H. Plumb's *Growth of Political Stability in England, 1675–1725*.

Of other short books on the Revolution of 1688, G. M. Trevelyan's *The English Revolution, 1688–1689* (Home University Library, 1938) provides a succinct whig–liberal interpretation in the tradition of his great-uncle Macaulay, while Lucile Pinkham's account in *William III and the Respectable Revolution* centres on personal ambition—especially that of William of Orange. Maurice Ashley's *The Glorious Revolution of 1688* is a useful guide to the chronology and sources. John Carswell in *The Descent upon England* describes the international organization which was the basis of William's activity in England and Europe.

Of contemporary sources the most renowned is Gilbert Burnet's *History of His Own Time* which gives a vivid picture both of Charles II's court and of the Revolution as seen from William's entourage. Burnet was a seventeenth-century Macaulay—able but without finesse. Not only was he partisan but his political sympathies were subject to alteration and he rewrote his history accordingly: the process can be followed in H. C. Foxcroft's *Supplement*. The second Earl of Ailesbury's *Memoirs* are an interesting expression of the outlook of a moderate Jacobite, Sir John Reresby's *Memoirs* well express the attitude of a place-hunting tory while John Evelyn's *Diary*—not least in its notes of sermons—reveals the state of mind of a tory whose main preoccupations were religious. For public as opposed to private expressions of contemporary opinion an interesting source is G. de F. Lord (general editor), *Poems on Affairs of State: Augustan Satirical Verse, 1660–1714* (6 vols. so far, Yale University Press, 1963 onward).

Two recent articles whose place is in this note are M. Ashley, 'King James II and the Revolution of 1688—some Reflections on the Historiography', *Historical Essays 1600–1750 Presented to David Ogg*, ed. H. E. Bell and R. L. Ollard (Black, 1963), pp. 185–202; and S. Baxter, 'Recent Writings on William III', *Journal of Modern History*, vol. xxxviii (1966), pp. 256–66.

Index

Abingdon, 292

Abingdon, James Bertie, 1st earl of, 274, 289

Absolutism, 111

Acts of Parliament, *see under* Parliament

Adda, Ferdinand, Count d', 191 n. 3, 200, 204, 208, 221, 233

Administration: its nature, 1660 to 1688, 87–93

Administrators: character of, 89–93

Admiralty, 89–90

Agriculture, 95

Ailesbury, Robert Bruce, first earl of, 39–40, 41, 98

Ailesbury, Thomas Bruce, second earl of, 1, 42–3, 107–8, 109, 110, 139, 141, 144, 287, 288, 295, 298, 304, 320

Albemarle, Christopher Monck, second duke of 49, 79,

Albemarle, George Monck, first duke of, 89, 92, 124, 127–8, 134, 135

Albeville, Ignatius White, marquis d', 205

Aldworth, Dr, of Magdalen College, 217

Algeria, 388

Algiers: pirates of, 251, 254; as Algerines, 255

Allibone, Sir Richard, judge, 57, 59

Alsop, Vincent, 223, 227

American colonies, *see under* Colonies

Andover, 280, 285

Andros, Sir Edmund, 155 n., 379 n.

Anglo-Dutch treaty (1678), 137, 245, 385

Anne, Princess, 203, 240, 249, 252–3, 269, 270, 274, 280, 283, 285, 303, 305, 315, 318, 319, 374, 397; as queen, 398

Annesley, Samuel, 162 n. 1

Apreece, Robert, 216, 217

Apsley, Sir Peter, 105 n. 1

Archer, Sir John, 56

Argyll, Archibald Campbell, ninth earl of: rebellion of, 148, 247

Arlington, Sir Henry Bennet, earl of, 91, 92, 115, 117, 179, 181, 244

Armed forces: post-1660, 121 ff.

Arms: in private possession, 144–5

Armstrong, Sir Thomas, 346

Army: administration of, 89; post-1660, 124–39, 125 n. 2; abuses in, 125–30; paymaster-general and, 126; training, 130–1; reforms in, 131–2; discipline in, 134–6; regiments of, in foreign service, 136–8, 249–50; catholic officers in, 138–9; under William III, 337–9; *see under* Regiments

Arras, 188

Arrest: crown's powers of, 64–5

Articles, Lords of the, in Scotland, *see under* Parliament, Scottish

Arundel of Wardour, Henry, third baron, 179, 194, 198

Ascham, Anthony, 7, 12; *Confusions and Revolutions of Government*, 322

Ashton, 275

Association: proposed in 1688, 300

Atkyns, Sir Edward, 59

Atkyns, Sir Robert, 56, 144, 178, 310, 335, 346

Atterbury, Francis, 322; *Letter to a Convocation Man* (1697), 374

Aubrey, H., Irish revenue commissioner, 140

Aughrim, battle of (1691), 391

Augsburg, League of (1686), 246, 254

Austen, Col. Robert, 355

Austin, John, 167

Austria, 246, 381, 383, 386, 388, 389, 394; ambassador of, 215, 244

Axminster, 279

Baber, Sir John, 227, 233

Bacon, Francis, 14

405